NCAER

INDIA POLICY FORUM 2013|14

VOLUME 10

EDITED BY

Shekhar Shah

Barry Bosworth

Arvind Panagariya

NATIONAL COUNCIL OF APPLIED ECONOMIC RESEARCH
New Delhi

BROOKINGS INSTITUTION
Washington, D.C.

SAGE www.sagepublications.com
Los Angeles • London • New Delhi • Singapore • Washington DC

First published in 2014 by

SAGE Publications India Pvt Ltd
B1/I-1 Mohan Cooperative Industrial Area
Mathura Road, New Delhi 110 044, India
www.sagepub.in

SAGE Publications Inc
2455 Teller Road
Thousand Oaks, California 91320, USA

SAGE Publications Ltd
1 Oliver's Yard, 55 City Road
London EC1Y 1SP, United Kingdom

SAGE Publications Asia-Pacific Pte Ltd
3 Church Street
#10-04 Samsung Hub
Singapore 049483

Library of Congress Serial Publication Data applied for

ISSN: 0973-4805
ISBN: 978-93-515-0055-1 (PB)

Published by Vivek Mehra for SAGE Publications India Pvt Ltd, typeset in 10.5/13 pt Times by RECTO Graphics, Delhi, and printed at Saurabh Printers Pvt Ltd, New Delhi.

NCAER

INDIA POLICY FORUM 2013|14

VOLUME 10

PURPOSE

This *India Policy Forum 2013–14* comprises papers and highlights of the discussion at the India Policy Forum (IPF) held in New Delhi on July 16–17, 2013. The IPF is a joint venture of NCAER, the National Council of Applied Economic Research in New Delhi, and the Brookings Institution in Washington, D.C. The IPF explores India's rapidly evolving—and sometimes tumultuous—economic transition and the underlying policy frameworks and reforms using policy-relevant, empirical research. This is the IPF's 10th Anniversary Volume.

An international Research Panel of India-based and overseas scholars with an abiding interest in India supports this initiative through advice, active participation at the IPF, and the search for innovative papers that promise fresh insights. An international Advisory Panel of distinguished economists provides overall guidance. Members of the two IPF panels are listed below.

Papers appear in this publication after detailed revisions based on IPF discussants' comments and the guidance provided by the IPF editors. To allow readers to get a sense of the richness of the conversations that happen at the IPF, discussants' comments are also included here, as is an edited summary prepared by the editors of the general discussion on each paper. The papers represent the views of the individual authors and do not imply agreement by the officers and staff of NCAER or Brookings.

Starting in 2011, the IPF began the practice of ending with a Policy Round Table. The 2013 IPF featured a discussion on "'Rights', Cash Transfers, and other Approaches: Is India advancing toward a Modern Safety Net System?" The names of the Round Table panelists are noted at the end of the Editors' Summary.

As in past years, the 2013 IPF featured the annual IPF Lecture, this time on "India: The Way Forward," delivered by Raghuram Rajan, then Chief Economic Adviser to the Government of India and, thereafter, the Governor of the Reserve Bank of India. Video recordings of the IPF Policy Round Table and Lecture are available on www.ncaer.org.

ADVISORY PANEL

PARTNERS

NCAER and Brookings gratefully acknowledge the generous financial support for IPF 2013 from HDFC Ltd, Reliance Industries Ltd, IDFC Foundation, State Bank of India, and Citibank NA.

The support reflects the deep commitment of these organizations and their leadership to rigorous policy research that helps promote informed policy debates and evidence-based policymaking in India. These funders have almost all been with the IPF since its inception. Their support reflects their continuing confidence in the IPF to promote such research and debate in India.

CORRESPONDENCE

Correspondence about papers in this Volume should be addressed directly to the authors (each paper contains the email address of the corresponding author). All author affiliations in the papers are as of the IPF Conference in July 2013. Manuscripts are not accepted for review because the IPF Volume is devoted exclusively to invited contributions. Feedback on the IPF Volume itself may be sent to: The Editor, India Policy Forum, NCAER, 11, Indraprastha Estate, New Delhi 110 002, or to ipf@ncaer.org.

NCAER TEAM

Over the 10 years of the IPF, NCAER has been and continues to be primarily responsible for the planning, organization, author selection, program design, publication, and fund-raising for the India Policy Forum. The editors are deeply grateful to the following NCAER staff for their dedication and hard work on the IPF:

Geetu Makhija	*Team leader and author coordination*
Jagbir Singh Punia	*Publication*
Sudesh Bala	*Invitee & event coordination*
P. P. Joshi	*Hospitality & logistics*
Sangita Chaudhary	*Event coordination*
Praveen Sachdeva	*Production & graphics*

Editors' Summary

The India Policy Forum (IPF) celebrated its 10th anniversary at the 2013 conference in New Delhi on July 16 and 17. This volume of the IPF journal contains the papers presented at the conference, the comments of the formal discussants, and a summary of the floor discussion of each paper. The five IPF papers cover topics that have dominated much of the discussion of the Indian economy in recent years. The first paper is devoted to an evaluation of the impact of laws that govern the operation of India's labor market within the organized industrial sector. The second paper analyzes India's role, or lack thereof, in the rapid development of international production networks. The third paper examines the conduct of monetary policy since the onset of the global financial crisis, with a special focus on the persistence of high rates of inflation in India. The fourth paper provides an overview of both fiscal and monetary policies in the years after the financial crisis. The volume concludes with an assessment of the value of social audits, widely advocated as a tool for improving public accountability, in the specific context of an audit of the rural public employment program in Andhra Pradesh.

State-level Labor Reform and Firm-level Productivity in India

The first paper, by Sean Dougherty, Veronica Frisancho, and Kala Krishna (DFK), examines the effects of labor market reform on the performance of industrial establishments in different Indian states in recent years. Using plant-level data for a period from the late 1990s to the late 2000s, the study provides evidence of the impact of reforms of employment protection legislation (EPL) and related labor market policies on plant-level productivity in India. Identification of the effect of EPL reforms follows from a "difference-in-differences" estimator that takes advantage of the state-level variation in labor regulation and heterogeneous industry characteristics. The fundamental identification assumption is that EPL is more likely to restrict firms operating in industries with higher labor intensity. The results show that labor market reform mattered, and more so in labor intensive industries.

Discussions of labor-market reforms have intensified recently. Impetus for this has partially come from the recent contract labor cases that have split the Supreme Court's bench. In addition, the government has expressed a newfound desire to seize the demographic dividend, increasing the potential to put labor policies as an important issue back on the reform agenda.

The collective experience of Organisation for Economic Co-operation and Development (OECD) countries, summarized in Martin and Scarpetta (2012), suggests that flexible regulation of the labor market is essential to allow employers to react to output growth by taking on labor and increasing employment. Similarly, Dougherty (2009) found that labor market reforms in India boosted manufacturing job creation rates. He further suggests that it was not just the Industrial Disputes Act that was harming labor market outcomes, but rather the wider range of labor legislation. This result is consistent with the views of labor law experts that cite the complexity and uncertainty caused by the manifold overlapping laws and antiquated (often colonial era) provisions, that are in dire need of simplification (Anant et al. 2006; Panagariya 2008; World Bank 2010).

Despite solid gains in overall employment in recent years, net increases in employment have occurred almost exclusively in the least productive, unorganized, and typically informal sectors of the economy, which employ nearly 90 % of the Indian workforce. This is partly due to the uneven protection of employment across formal and informal sectors, with the latter being virtually unregulated. Such a dichotomy forces Indian firms to remain small and informal to avoid regulation, leading to a skewed firm size distribution with a very long tail of smaller, less productive firms (Alfaro and Chari 2012; Dougherty et al. 2009; Hasan and Jandoc 2013; Hsieh and Klenow 2012). Within the formal sector, most of the productivity gains recorded in the last three decades have been driven by large continuing firms (Bollard et al. 2013; Sivadasan 2009), which is explained by existing rigidities in the reallocation of labor inputs across firms and sectors.

DFK study the effects of labor market reform on productivity among registered manufacturing plants. A distinguishing feature of their paper is that the labor reform measure (OECD 2007) used is more comprehensive than the Besley–Burgess index, popular in the EPL literature in India. The OECD Labor Reform Index they use covers 50 specific subjects of possible reform in seven major areas of labor regulation in addition to the Industrial Disputes Act, taking into account both formal and informal amendments at the state level. An additional feature is the use of plant-level information from the Annual Survey of Industries (ASI) to evaluate the direct effect of EPL in India. The authors take advantage of the recently available ASI panel data to obtain plant-level TFP measures that control for simultaneity and selection bias (using the Olley–Pakes approach) in contrast to previous work on the topic that has mostly measured the effects of EPL on labor productivity at the industry level.

DFK find that the modest easing of regulations in Indian states that has taken place in recent years was enough for firms in states with higher levels of pro-employer reform to benefit substantially through gains in total factor productivity (TFP). Their point estimates indicate that, on an average, plants in labor intensive industries and in states that have transited toward more flexible labor markets have TFP residuals 25.4% higher than those registered for their counterparts in states with less EPL reforms. However, no important differences are identified among plants in industries with low labor intensity when comparing states with high and low levels of EPL reform.

The authors also find that the different strategies used by plants to overcome the constraints imposed by labor regulations generate heterogeneous effects of state-level labor reform both by plant size and type of ownership. Given the extensive use of contract labor among large plants which is a way around labor regulations, and voluntary retirement schemes among public plants, which is another way of relaxing restrictions on firing, smaller plants and private plants tend to accrue the largest productivity gains from state-level labor reforms.

Although the authors' EPL reform indicator shows that state-level actions, both de facto and de jure, have already led the way in labor reform, these reforms could be taken much further. Out of the 20 states surveyed, only three had conducted more than half of the potential procedural or administrative changes they were surveyed on, suggesting that there is still much room to ease the burden of labor regulations at the state level. Given the difficulty in carrying out reforms at the central level, states may be in a better position to accelerate their own labor reform processes while prioritizing reforms according to the characteristics of their home industries. However, the central government urgently needs to resolve ambiguities in the Supreme Court's ruling and provide clear general guidelines, particularly in areas such as contract labor and fixed-term contracts.

How India Fits into Global Production Sharing: Experience, Prospects, and Policy Options

The second paper, by Prema-chandra Athukorala, deals with a different aspect of Indian manufacturing—its role in global production sharing, which refers to the breakup of production processes into separate stages, with each country specializing in a particular stage of the production sequence. The phenomenon has been an increasingly important facet of economic globalization over the past three decades. This process of the international division of labor opens up opportunities for countries to specialize in different slices or tasks of the value chain in vertically integrated global industries in line with their relative cost advantages. Trade in parts and components, and final assembly within global production networks, often called network trade, has been growing at a much faster rate compared to trade in traditional labor-intensive products such as apparel, footwear, and sport goods.

The author examines India's role in global production sharing from a comparative East Asian perspective in order to inform the contemporary policy debate on India's export performance, including its failure to specialize in labor-intensive manufacturing despite being a highly labor-abundant economy. Following a stage-setting analytical narrative of global production sharing and an overview of India's export performance during the post-reform period, the paper examines emerging patterns of world network trade and India's performance in relation to China and the other high-performing East Asian economies. An econometric analysis is also undertaken using the standard gravity-model framework to examine the determinants of inter-country differences in the degree of involvement in network trade. The author employs a new data set culled from the United Nations (UN) Comtrade trade database, which systematically delineates trade in parts and components and final assembly from total manufacturing trade.

Although India's overall export performance has improved significantly during the reform era, it still accounts for only 1.8% of world exports compared to China's 12% and its share in total exports from developing countries has remained virtually unchanged at 4% for the past five decades compared with China's 39% currently. At the disaggregated level, no particular commodity category—even the traditional labor intensive products in which India has considerable untapped potential—stands out for its faster growth compared to the major East Asian countries. The comparative analysis in this paper suggests that by far the most important reason for India's lacklustre export performance is its failure to cash in on the rapid expansion of network trade and the dramatic shift in trade within production networks from developed to developing countries. Between 1990–91 and 2010–11 network exports recorded an almost five-fold increase, from US$12.8 trillion to US$59.1 trillion, with the share of developing countries in the total increasing from 11.9% to 45.1%. Network products accounted for nearly 70% of the total increment in manufacturing exports from East Asia between 1990–91 and 2010–11; the comparable figure for India was 22%.

India's comparative export performance has been particularly weak in electronics and electrical goods, which account for the lion's share of total world network exports. A number of large electronics and electrical goods producing multinational enterprises (MNEs) have set up production bases in India, but they are predominantly involved in production for the domestic market. In most East Asian countries Special Economic Zones (SEZs) have proved to be an effective vehicle for integrating domestic manufacturing into production networks in these global industries. However, although SEZs have mushroomed in India following the new SEZ Law that came into force in 2005, electronics and electrical goods account for only a tiny share of exports from these zones (2.3%).

The view widely held in some policy circles that India has already missed the boat for joining global production networks, as a result of the MNEs' long-standing attachment to existing production bases and China's emergence as the premier assembly center within global production networks, is not consistent with the East Asian experience surveyed in this paper. In recent years, production networks have begun to spread in a big way to Vietnam, and also to Cambodia. There has been a contraction in the final assembly of consumer electronics and electrical goods exported from the other East Asian countries as an outcome of competitive pressure from China, but overall a close complementarity between China and these countries within production networks there has evolved, dispelling the crowding out fear. The upshot of this analysis is that the explanation for India's poor performance in network trade lies primarily on the supply side, in India's overall business and investment climate.

The findings of this study give credence to the case made in a number of influential studies for completing India's unfinished reform agenda, encompassing trade, investment policy, and behind-the-border reforms. Further reforms are even more important for linking India to global production networks than for the expansion of standard labor-intensive products and other conventional exports. Vertical integration of manufacturing across national borders naturally increases the country risks associated with supply delays and disruptions in a given location within the production network because it can bring the operation of the entire production network to a halt. In the current business climate in India such disruptions could take many forms, including shipping delays, strikes, power outages, and transportation bottlenecks. In many instances it is impossible for firms to fully offset these risks even by writing complete contracts.

According to Athukorala, there is also a strong case, based on the experiences in East Asia and elsewhere, for combining further reforms with a proactive investment promotion campaign to attract MNEs engaged in global production networks. Over time global production sharing has expanded well beyond the confines of intra-firm activities of MNEs but there is compelling evidence that MNEs are still the leading vehicle for developing countries to enter global production networks. In global industries like electronics and electrical goods, initial success in attracting big players to set up operations in a country breeds more success because in these industries there is a herd mentality in the site selection process of MNEs.

The author argues that effective investment promotion should go beyond simply marketing the country and also focus on facilitating and coordinating the prerequisites for setting up operations and effective functioning when MNEs decide to set up production plants. As part of designing an investment promotion strategy, it is also vital to probe why Indian SEZs have so far not been successful as an effective second-best option for providing investors with a suitable investment climate that is insulated from distortions in the rest of the economy.

Post-Global Crisis Inflation Dynamics in India: What has Changed?

In the third paper, Michael Patra, Jeevan Khundrakpam, and Asish George of the Reserve Bank of India (RBI) focus on an analysis of the post-crisis inflation and the source of its persistence. India rebounded rapidly from the global financial crisis of 2008, outperforming many advanced and emerging market economies. However, 2009 also witnessed a strong acceleration of price inflation. By the time the RBI responded in early 2010, headline inflation had surged above 10% per year and food inflation reached 20%. This inflation persisted at a roughly 9% annual rate into 2013, despite successive increases in the policy rate, and periodic increases in the cash reserve ratio. In other episodes in the not-too-distant past, people's anger at similar rates of inflation led them to vote out the offending government of the day. This time around, the public bought gold, determined not to let stubborn inflation gnaw away at their purchasing power. Gold imports surged beyond 1,000 tonnes, and the current account deficit reached 6.7% of GDP in the third quarter 2012–13.

This episode has been notable for both the persistence of inflation and the extent of the debate over its causes and the appropriate policy responses. At one end of the spectrum is the view that the inflation reflects sector-specific cost-push factors for which orthodox monetary measures would be of little avail. Any policy-induced compression of demand would simply impair future growth. The opposing perspective argues that its persistence is the result of costly policy errors: a misreading of this inflation as being narrowly based, leading to delayed reactions and the growth of a public perception that future policies would be very accommodative.

Patra, Khundrakpam, and George point to a series of supply-shocks as the origin of this inflation, but go on to show that inflation quickly became very general. They construct a Diffusion Index of changes in the components of the Wholesale Price Index (WPI), and show that the dispersion of inflation across major components of the price index actually declined over the period, which they interpret as evidence of a rapid generalization of inflation in the aftermath of supply shocks. They also show that the WPI and the national accounts deflator yield highly correlated measures of price inflation, but that the CPI had episodes of highly divergent rates of change—especially since 2012 Q2. They attribute much of the divergence to the heavy weights assigned to food and fuel in the CPI, but they also point to the divergent movement of some finished goods prices in the CPI compared to the prices of raw and intermediate materials in the WPI.

The large body of work in the literature on modeling price-setting behavior and price stickiness has broadly identified four factors that account for the persistence of inflation: (a) *intrinsic persistence*, the tendency to be backward-looking in the price-setting mechanism; (b) *extrinsic persistence*, a reduced sensitivity to changes in the basic determinants of inflation such as the output gap; (c) *expectations-based persistence* built on the formation of strong inflation expectations; and (d) *policy-driven persistence*, persistence due to restrictions on the speed of monetary policy adjustments, best captured, for instance, in the degree of interest rate smoothing.

The autoregressive properties of headline inflation and its components show that inflation persistence in general has gone up in the post-crisis period for headline inflation, and significantly for the manufactured products category and for food. However, an expanded model that allows for cyclical influences, pass-through effects from exchange rate changes, and expectations of future inflation yields a more complex story. There has been some decline in intrinsic persistence, but also a substantial increase in the contribution of inflation expectations, which the authors interpret as implying some decline in the credibility of monetary policy and its ability to achieve a particular inflation outcome. They also report a flattening of the aggregate supply curve in the post-crisis period and higher costs of disinflation.

They assess RBI's monetary policy response through the sequential estimation of a reaction function that is elaborated beyond the initial emphasis on a hard inflation target and extended to the joint consideration of a multiple-indicator approach, as reflected in inflation and output gaps, the exchange rate, and the short-term interest rate. The inflation and output gaps are both consistent influences on the policy rate. There is a high degree of interest rate smoothing in all cases, suggesting a slow or a so-called calibrated response to inflation shocks.

The RBI explicitly states a numerical threshold of 5% as its inflation tolerance and a target of 3% as its medium-term goal. While inflation is the dominant focus of monetary policy in India, it is accompanied by an emphasis on stabilizing output around its potential to contain inflation spill overs. The authors suggest that the increase in inflation persistence will require a more pre-emptive and aggressive monetary policy reaction to break inflation expectations before they become entrenched. Furthermore, most inflation persistence episodes tend to emanate from food price shocks that quickly become generalized. Consequently, accommodating food inflation on the argument that the Indian economy is more prone to supply shocks than demand shocks is a perilous strategy.

India's Recent Macroeconomic Performance: An Assessment and the Way Forward

In the fourth IPF paper, Muneesh Kapur and Rakesh Mohan assess the potential for India to return to a path of high, sustained growth over the next several decades and beyond. The decade of the 2000s witnessed growing optimism about the success of the Indian economy. Economic growth averaged 7% per annum and accelerated to 9% in the four years preceding the global financial crisis. Initially, India appeared to manage the shock of the global financial crisis with assuredness: maintaining a 7% growth rate in the face of a severe recession in the United States and Europe, and growth again accelerated to nearly 9% in 2009–11. However, the situation has deteriorated dramatically. Growth has slowed to an average of 5–6%, a pattern that is expected to hold for the near future. There has been a substantial deterioration of many of the main economic indicators; the current account and fiscal deficits have widened, while inflation has climbed to an elevated level. With the observed decline in the rates of domestic saving and investment, concerns have also arisen that India's potential growth rate may have fallen. Furthermore, given the large twin deficits, concerns have also been expressed about the possible emergence of some external vulnerability.

Kapur and Mohan examine the role of domestic macroeconomic policies in the growth slowdown and analyze the factors that led to the widening of the current account deficit. They perceive the growth slowdown reflecting a number of factors. First, while the macroeconomic policy response—both monetary and fiscal policy—to the onset of the financial crisis in the United States was admirably rapid, with hindsight there was overshooting of the stimulus. Moreover, the quality of the fiscal stimulus, with its focus on tax cuts and increased revenue expenditure (particularly on subsidies), while keeping capital outlays relatively stagnant, added to demand pressures. These pressures were then mirrored in high inflation. While the fiscal and monetary stimuli were large and rapid, their withdrawal was overly gradual, and incomplete in the case of fiscal measures.

The overshooting of the policy stimulus and its far too gradual withdrawal sowed the seeds of inflation and current account pressures. The use of subsidies to delay the pass-through of higher international oil prices into domestic prices added to the fiscal pressures, while also impeding the domestic expenditure adjustment of both oil and non-oil consumption that would have emanated from higher domestic oil prices. The adjustment in domestic oil consumption, had domestic prices been appropriately increased, would have also contributed to lower oil imports and a smaller current account deficit. The incomplete withdrawal of the fiscal stimulus led to a crowding out of private sector spending, which in conjunction with other policy bottlenecks, has contributed to the decline in private corporate investment.

High inflation and negative real deposit rates led to a switch away from financial savings toward saving in the form of gold, leading to higher gold imports, which further added to current account deficit pressures. The current account was also hit by domestic policy bottlenecks, which, inter alia, have led to higher coal imports and lower iron ore exports. Unlike many other major emerging market economies, India had a deficit on its current account before the financial crisis and the combination of domestic and global factors quickly raised the current account deficit to 4.8% by 2012–13.

Overall, Kapur and Mohan suggest that appropriate policies in regard to domestic oil prices can help contain fiscal subsidies as well as oil imports. They suggest that taking into account the fiscal correction planned in the near term, some by the finance minister in his 2013–14 Budget that preceded the IPF Conference, public sector saving should recover. This could result in the gross domestic saving rate increasing by around 2–3% of GDP and a substantial reduction in the crowding out of spending by the private sector. They argue that fiscal consolidation would also provide the basis for a durable reduction in inflation and low and positive real interest rates for both depositors and borrowers, which in turn should have a moderating impact on gold imports and the current account deficit.

Looking ahead, the authors believe that the economic slowdown has a large cyclical component, reflecting both domestic and global influences. They argue that factors such as poor infrastructure, although they must be addressed, cannot explain the slowdown because those deficiencies existed when India was growing rapidly. The structural drivers of growth—the favorable demographics and the high saving and investment rates—are still present. Based on these assumptions, even a conservative estimate would result in a sustained gross domestic saving rate of about 35%, which could facilitate growth of 8–8.5%, given moderate incremental capital–output ratios. Given growth and inflation expectations, interest rates in India can be expected to remain above those in advanced economies, even with an end to the present aberrations of near-zero interest rates in the major advanced economies. Therefore, they argue that a prudent approach to the opening up of debt flows to foreign investors needs to be pursued.

Kapur and Mohan argue that the key policy priority for restoring Indian growth to sustained rates in excess of 8% is to reestablish macroeconomic stability. They attach the highest importance to a reduction in medium-term inflation to rates achieved in the decade prior to the financial crisis. Reforms in the markets for both labor and land are viewed as essential to make the economy more flexible. Among the Asian emerging market economies, India is notable for its low share of manufacturing in both value added and employment. This has also impeded the growth of non-agricultural employment and the pace of the rural–urban transformation. They argue that a realistic exchange rate policy, combined with policies promoting labor flexibility and skill development, need to be adopted to promote growth in manufacturing. The revival of manufacturing competitiveness is essential to achieve 10% plus growth in this sector, without which it will not be feasible to achieve sustained GDP growth rates of 8% and above.

Despite increasing private investment in infrastructure, they also call for an expansion of public investment on a sustained basis. For this to take place, the use of user charges must be reinforced so that infrastructure investment is remunerative. In addition, with increasing incomes, expenditures on non-merit subsidies must be curtailed and directed toward such infrastructure investment. They point out that the revenue receipts/GDP ratio of the central government is now below the levels prevailing in the late 1980s. Public investment in both physical and social infrastructure will be difficult to achieve without revenue enhancement consistent with income growth.

Social Audits and MGNREGA Delivery: Lessons from Andhra Pradesh

In the fifth IPF paper, Farzana Afridi and Vegard Iversen set out to study the impact of social audits on theft and corruption under the Mahatma Gandhi National Rural Employment Guarantee Act (MGNREGA) in the state of Andhra Pradesh (AP). Citizens' participation and social accountability are increasingly perceived in India as mechanisms that foster transparency and improve public program delivery, in some instances treated even as sufficient conditions for greater accountability that can compensate for the state's governance deficit. For example, in the public works under MGNREGA, mandatory social audits are supposed to empower beneficiaries to effectively scrutinize program expenditures and to monitor and track program delivery to ensure no theft and corruption take place. As with many other areas of policymaking in India over the past decade, despite widespread claims by the government and NGO activists that social audits are low-cost and powerful participatory tools with substantial, positive program impact, there is sadly little rigorous empirical evidence to show that community monitoring has lived up to its promise.

AP is widely seen as a best-practice example of MGNREGA implementation, partly because of an exceptional record of conducting regular and systematic social audits of MGNREGA projects since 2006, as compared to Indian states, where audits have either not been conducted or implemented in an ad-hoc, unsystematic manner. Based largely on the carrying out of audits rather than serious evidence on their effectiveness, the AP model is being scaled up and adopted by other Indian states and other public programs.

AP's social audit machinery comprises state-level, district-level and village-level social auditors. State and district auditors recruit and train village-level auditors in two-day workshops that provide training in MGNREGA rights and regulations, conducting social audits, and obtaining information under India's *Right to Information Act*. In the week following the training, the teams organize social audits in all gram panchayats (GPs) within a *mandal* or a sub-district. In each GP, official labor expenses are supposed to be verified by laborers listed on the muster-rolls. Complaints by individuals or groups of beneficiaries and by the audit team are recorded and attested. For verification of material expenditures, auditors are supposed to undertake worksite inspections. The completion of the audits is followed by a public hearing to discuss audit findings, with all officials implementing MGNREGA projects required to attend. Complaints are read out, testimonies verified, and officials accused of alleged misconduct are given an opportunity to defend themselves. The AP social audits seek to combine a top-down approach with grass-roots participation in order to increase program impact.

The authors propose a model in which successful community monitoring requires three key elements: (a) high stakes for beneficiaries in the outcomes that are audited—for MGNREGA, these include the availability of employment when needed and the timely payment of guaranteed wages; (b) the capacity of beneficiaries to detect irregularities or inefficiencies—employment provided or wages received are easier to track but embezzlement and manipulation of wage records, worksite logs, and material expenditures are harder to detect except for obvious and easy-to-detect irregularities such as ghost or non-existent projects; and (c) credible, timely enforcement of social audit findings with clear accountabilities for how the guilty are to be penalised and by whom.

The authors' model leads them to anticipate a dynamic game-theoretic process in which local auditing can become more effective with repeated audits because the auditors learn. However, it is also possible that violations and theft also become more sophisticated due to learning by corrupt politicians, officials and contractors. Improved monitoring may thus result in the substitution of one type of irregularity for another as the thieves learn how to exploit weaknesses in the new system. Easy-to-detect irregularities can then be expected to decline with repeated audits and hard-to-detect irregularities to rise.

Afridi and Iversen use special AP panel data assembled by extracting and translating official social audit reports during 2006 to 2010 and covering up to three social audit rounds from close to 300 GPs in eight districts in AP. Testing their predictions is made harder because social audits were not rolled out randomly in AP and because information relating only to complaints (rather than malfeasance proactively detected by the auditors) were recorded by the social auditors. The authors test whether performance, measured by irregularities in program implementation, is affected by additional audits within the same mandal during 2006–10. Their analysis accounts for other factors that could impact corruption and the quality of program delivery, including rising beneficiary awareness and confidence in the integrity of the audit process, and improved audit quality as audit teams become better at identifying discrepancies.

Controlling for mandal-level attributes, and overall and district-level time trends, the authors observe a marginal reduction in the real rupee amount per labor complaint, but an insignificant effect of the repeated social audits on reducing the aggregate number of complaints. This is accompanied by an overall increase in the aggregate number of the harder-to-detect materials-related irregularities (e.g., inflated bills and missing official records) over successive audit rounds with no change in the number of labor-related, easier-to-detect irregularities (e.g., non-payment or delayed wage payments) or harder-to-detect irregularities (e.g., ghost workers). The authors' findings suggest that while the top-down and participatory elements of the audit process may have been effective in "detecting" irregularities, the audits were not effective in "deterring" and "reducing" irregularities. The impact of social audits on other program outcomes such as employment generation was insignificant.

Despite beneficiary learning and increase in the capacity of the social auditors to detect theft in later audit rounds, the authors find no overall impact of the social audits on deterring easier-to-detect malpractices. The authors suggest that this failure, together with the rise in the harder-to-detect material theft, indicated a change in the architecture of corruption.

The authors try to explain this failure of social audits by analyzing administrative data on social audits that suggest that weak follow-up and enforcement of punishments are responsible. While this may have been mitigated by the establishment of vigilance cells in AP after 2010, during 2006–10 less than 1% of irregularities in which program functionaries were held responsible led to their termination/removal from service or criminal action. Even more modest penalties, such as suspensions, show-cause notices, or being black-listed for future contractual work, were meted out to less than 3% of these cases. Eighty-seven percent of the money missing during 2006–10 had not been recovered by 2013. It would appear that the very same governance deficits that may have led the government and nongovernmental organization (NGO) activists to put their faith in a proxy process of social audits may have come back to haunt the process.

The Afridi–Iversen work also underlines the need for incorporating far more rigorous program evaluation, whether of the social kind or otherwise, in the roll out of social programs. Post 2008–09 there has been a three-fold increase in Central government funds allocated to rural works projects. In 2011–12, MGNREGA spent some ₹40,000 crores to provide employment to some 40 million households, or ₹10,000 per household. The Afridi–Iversen results should be a wake-up call for proponents of social audits with deeply held but evidence-free beliefs in the efficacy of participatory evaluation, as currently carried out, in reducing theft and improving public program performance.

Annual IPF Lecture and IPF Policy Roundtable

Though not included in this IPF volume, following the tradition set in 2004 when it started, the 2013 IPF also featured the annual IPF Lecture given this year by Raghuram Rajan, then the Chief Economic Adviser to the Government of India and thereafter Governor of the Reserve Bank of India. Rajan spoke on "India: The Way Forward," focusing on the challenges that any Indian government will have to face up to if India is to regain the path of high economic growth with universal opportunity.

Since 2011, the IPF has also featured a concluding Policy Roundtable. The panelists on the 2013 IPF Policy Roundtable took on the topic of "'Rights', Cash Transfers, and other Approaches: Is India advancing toward a modern Safety Net System?" reflecting concerns about how India can build an appropriate, affordable, and effective social protection system as it hopefully transitions to a middle-income country. The topic of the Roundtable seems particularly appropriate now because of the Indian voters near complete rejection in the 2014 Elections of the UPA government's policy of promoting service delivery through a rights-based approach led by its National Advisory Council. The Roundtable was expertly chaired by Montek S. Ahluwalia (Planning Commission) with a distinguished panel comprising Pranab Bardhan (Berkely), T. N. Ninan (*Business Standard)*, Shubhashis Gangopadhyay (IDF), and Abhijit Banerjee (MIT).

Materials on both events are available on NCAER's Web site, www.ncaer.org.

References

Alfaro, Laura and Anusha Chari. 2012. "Deregulation, Misallocation, and Size: Evidence from India," NBER Working Papers 18650.

Anant, T. C. A., R. Hasan, P. Mohapatra, R. Nagraj and S. K. Sasikumar. 2006. "Labour Markets in India: Issues and Perspectives," in *Labour Markets in Asia: Issues and Perspectives,* edited by Jesus Felipe and Rana Hasan, pp. 205–300. London: Asian Development Bank and Palgrave Macmillan.

Bollard, Albert, Peter J. Klenow and Gunjan Sharma. 2013. "India's Mysterious Manufacturing Miracle," *Review of Economic Dynamics*, 16(1): 59–85.

Dougherty Sean. 2009. "Labour Regulation and Employment Dynamics at the State Level in India," *Review of Market Integration*, 1(3): 295–337.

Dougherty, Sean, Richard Herd and Thomas Chalaux. 2009. "What is Holding Back Productivity Growth in India? Recent Microevidence," *OECD Economic Studies*, 45(1): 59–80.

Hasan, Rana and Karl Robert Jandoc. 2013. "Labor Regulations and the Firm Size Distribution in Indian Manufacturing," in *Reforms and Economic Transformation in India*, edited by Jagdish Bhagwati and Arvind Panagariya, pp. 15–48. New York: Oxford University Press.

Hsieh, Chang-Tai and Peter Klenow. 2012. "The Life Cycle of Plants in India and Mexico." NBER Working Papers 18133.

Martin, John P. and Stefano Scarpetta. 2012. "Setting it Right: Employment Protection, Labour Reallocation and Productivity," *De Economist*, 160(2): 89–116.

OECD. 2007. "Improving the Performance of the Labour Market," in *Economic Survey of India*. Paris: OECD.

Panagariya, Arvind. 2008. *India: The Emerging Giant*. New York: Oxford University Press.

Sivadasan, Jagadeesh. 2009. "Barriers to Competition and Productivity: Evidence from India," *The BE Journal of Economic Analysis & Policy*, 9(1): 1–64.

World Bank. 2010. *India's Employment Challenge: Creating Jobs, Helping Workers*. Washington, D.C.: The World Bank and Oxford University Press.

SEAN DOUGHERTY[*]
OECD Economics Department and Paris School of Economics

VERONICA FRISANCHO[†]
Inter-American Development Bank, Research Department

KALA KRISHNA[‡]
The Pennsylvania State University and NBER

State-level Labor Reform and Firm-level Productivity in India[§]

ABSTRACT We examine the effects of labor market reform on establishment performance in different Indian states over a contemporaneous period. Using plant-level data for a period from the late 1990s to the late 2000s, the study provides plant-level cross-state/time-series evidence of the impact of reforms of employment protection legislation and related labor market policies on productivity in India. Identification of the effect of employment protection legislation follows from a difference-in-differences estimator inspired by Rajan and Zingales (1998) that takes advantage of the state-level variation in labor regulation and heterogeneous industry characteristics. The fundamental identification assumption is that employment protection legislation is more likely to restrict firms operating in industries with higher labor intensity and/or higher sales volatility. The results show that firms in labor intensive or more volatile industries benefited the most from labor reforms in their states. Point estimates indicate that, on average, firms in labor intensive industries and in flexible labor markets have total factor productivity residuals 25.4% higher than those registered for their counterparts in states with more stringent labor laws.

[*] *sean.dougherty@oecd.org*
[†] *vfrisancho@iadb.org*
[‡] *kmk4@psu.edu*

[§] We would like to thank T.C.A. Anant (Ministry of Statistics), Alok Sheel (Prime Minister's Economic Advisory Council), and Kaushik Basu (Ministry of Finance, now at the World Bank) for their support of this project, which was partially carried out while Sean Dougherty was visiting the National Institute of Public Finance and Policy (New Delhi) and Veronica Frisancho was an external consultant to the OECD. Useful feedback was received from OECD colleagues and from seminars at the Paris School of Economics and Pennsylvania State University, and, especially, at the 10th India Policy Forum in New Delhi. Especially helpful comments were received from Aditya Bhattacharjea, Matthieu Crozet, Ron Davies, Romain Duval, Lionel Fontagné, Robert Ford, Bishwanath Goldar, Isabelle Joumard, Shekhar Shah, T. N. Srinivasan, and two anonymous referees. The views expressed in this paper are those of the authors and do not necessarily reflect those of the OECD nor its member countries or partners.

However, no important differences are identified among plants in industries with low labor intensity when comparing states with high and low levels of employment protection legislation reform.

Keywords: *Employment Regulation Legislation, Labor Laws, Job Protection, Total Factor Productivity, Firm-Level Volatility*

JEL Classification: *D24, F16, J5, J8, K31*

1. Introduction

It is well-known that India's formal Employment Protection Legislation (EPL) is among the most stringent in the world. Many believe that this is one of the main reasons behind the stagnant share of manufacturing output in India's GDP during the last 40 years (OECD 2007). Although the country has recorded impressive output growth rates since the 1970s, the share of manufactures in total output has remained between 14% and 18%. Though infrastructure and product market regulation have been major challenges, strict labor laws have been blamed in particular for the poor performance of large-scale labor intensive manufactures despite India's labor abundance (Conway and Herd 2009; Dougherty et al. 2009; Panagariya 2008). According to the MCI (2011), the top five goods exported during 2010–11 represented almost 50% of the country's total exports and they were all relatively capital intensive goods such as petroleum products, gems and jewelry, transport equipment, machinery and instruments, and pharmaceutical products. In contrast, ready-made garments, traditionally an unskilled-labor intensive export, has seen its share in total Indian exports decline from 12.5% to 6% between 2000 and 2010. In 2010, India was the fifth largest exporter of apparel with 3.2% of the world's exports, lagging behind China, the European Union, Hong Kong, and Bangladesh (WTO 2011).

Industrial relations in India fall under the joint jurisdiction of central and state governments, an arrangement that has generated a degree of variation in labor regulations across states. Although all states had essentially the same starting point under the License Raj, each state has independently amended labor regulations, rules and practices during the post-Independence period. In the last decade, this "natural experiment" setting has been exploited by several empirical studies that have tried to assess the effects of labor regulation on output, employment, and productivity. However, and despite increasing interest in the topic, the evidence for India is still inconclusive and mostly limited to industry-level analysis.

One of the most influential studies of India is Besley and Burgess (2004), which constructs an index summarizing state-level amendments to the Industrial Disputes Act (IDA) between 1949 and 1992. The index, henceforth referred to as BB, is used along with several control variables to explain state-level outcomes corresponding to the organized manufacturing sector using industry-level panel data for 1958–92. The authors identify a negative impact of pro-worker regulation on output, investment, employment, and labor productivity among registered manufacturing firms. Several papers that also rely on the BB index reach similar conclusions.[1] Nonetheless, the validity of the BB index and the econometric methodology used to identify the effect of excessive pro-worker regulation has been extensively criticized. The main concerns with the use of this index are related to problems in the coding of labor laws and its exclusive focus on formal reforms to the IDA. This study tries to overcome the shortcomings of the previous empirical evidence in the tradition of Besley and Burgess to evaluate the effect of labor regulation on the Indian organized manufacturing sector. We make use of a more comprehensive measure of labor market regulations proposed in OECD (2007) and elaborated in Dougherty (2009). We argue that this index is superior to the BB index as it includes information on formal and informal labor market reforms, not only to the IDA but in seven additional areas: the Factories Act, the State Shops and Commercial Establishments Acts, the Contract Labor Act, the role of inspectors, the maintenance of registers, the filing of returns and union representation.

Using this comprehensive EPL measure and plant-level data from the Annual Survey of Industries (ASI) for all the fiscal years between 1998–99 and 2007–08, we evaluate whether labor market regulation differences across Indian states led to a differential response in industrial performance.[2] However, one must keep in mind that differences across states in terms of labor regulation may be endogenous since a higher number of pro-employer reforms in a given state may be driven by the characteristics of the firms located in that state.

Following Rajan and Zingales (1998), we focus on the details of the theoretical mechanisms at play. As we will show below, unit labor costs increase with more stringent EPL, and more so for firms operating in industries with higher labor intensity. This implies that firms in industries with

1. See Aghion et al. (2008) and Ahsan and Pagés (2009) as examples.

2. In this paper, EPL is used as a shorthand to refer to a customized measure of state-level labor regulation reforms in India (see Dougherty 2009). The official OECD measure is country-specific and has a longstanding standardized definition, as most recently elaborated in Venn (2009).

higher labor shares will suffer the most from the additional costs of hiring and firing workers. In addition, to the extent that such costs act as adjustment costs, they will have more of an effect in more volatile industries so that the productivity of firms in more volatile sectors should be more affected by strict labor laws. Thus, we implement a difference- in-difference estimator that exploits both the variation in EPL by state, as well as the variation in industry-specific characteristics related to labor intensity and volatility. By focusing on a specific mechanism through which EPL reform operates (labor intensity or volatility), this approach provides stronger evidence of causality.

Previous studies have also exploited the variation in state and industry characteristics[3] but their focus was at the industry level. To our knowledge, this is the first study of India to evaluate the direct effect of labor regulation on plant-level productivity using a longitudinal sample,[4] and is one of only a few studies on any country to examine the impact of labor regulation at the plant-level.

The evidence presented here shows that firms in industries with higher labor intensity or higher sales volatility benefited the most from labor market reforms in their states. The positive effect of relaxed EPL on organized manufacturing firms in labor intensive industries is experienced through higher total factor productivity (TFP). Similarly, firms in more volatile industries that experience pro-employer labor reforms tend to have higher levels of TFP. We also identify a heterogeneous effect of EPL in labor intensive industries by plant size and ownership type. In particular, we find that smaller firms and private firms with a high usage of labor inputs tend to benefit the most from relaxation of state labor laws. In general, our results suggest that state-level reforms can help to mitigate the detrimental effects that strict federal labor laws have on industrial outcomes in the organized Indian manufacturing sector.

Our paper contributes to two strands of literature. First, it adds to the literature that focuses on the effect of labor and product regulation on industrial outcomes and economic performance, of which Besley and Burgess (2004) has been one of the most influential studies. It also contributes to some recent studies on the potential links between labor markets and comparative advantage that have received special attention in the trade literature. Within this literature, our study is particularly related to Cuñat and Melitz (2007) and Krishna and Levchenko (2009), who examine how firm-level volatility can determine the pattern of comparative advantage.

3. See Gupta et al. (2008) and Bassanini et al. (2009).

4. Harrison et al. (2013) use a similar dataset also based on the ASI to examine market share reallocations; however they focus on trade, foreign direct investment (FDI) and licensing policy reforms, and control for interactions with labor reforms.

The rest of the paper proceeds as follows. Section 2 sketches out the major findings in the literature. Section 3 describes the data as well as some basic stylized facts. The empirical strategy is described in Section 4. Section 5 displays the results as well as some robustness checks while Section 6 concludes.

2. Previous Literature

Despite increasing interest in the effect of institutions and regulation in industrial performance, the theoretical and empirical evidence to support or negate the beneficial effect of EPL relaxation is still limited. Although labor market equilibrium models such as Garibaldi (1998) and Mortensen and Pissarides (1999) predict a negative effect of stricter EPL on job mobility, its effects on productivity are not that straightforward. There is even a branch of the literature which suggests that the net effects of EPL on productivity may be positive. Workers could be more willing to invest in human capital specific to the firm if their jobs are better protected. Firms may also be willing to invest more to increase labor productivity as an alternative to downsizing. Bassanini et al. (2009) provide an extensive discussion of these theoretical results, suggesting that there might be an "optimal" level of EPL.

Stricter labor regulation increases the costs of hiring and firing workers, making it more difficult for the firm to react to demand or supply shocks that require labor reallocation or staff reduction. The restriction of labor movement even in more productive firms or sectors can thus result in lower productivity levels. Poschke (2009) develops a model that takes into account firm dynamics and where firms receive idiosyncratic productivity shocks. He shows that selection eliminates the active firms with the lowest productivity, and entrants imitate more productive survivors. In this setting, strict EPL ends up reducing firm value, discouraging not only entry but also the exit of less productive firms. Product or technology innovation can also be discouraged if the firm has to face high labor costs and high layoff costs in case of failure (Samaniego 2006). Moreover, growth losses tend to be larger when productivity is more volatile. This latter result is in line with previous findings of worse effects of strict EPL for firms operating in more turbulent sectors (see Bentolila and Bertola 1990).[5]

5. Under a general equilibrium framework, Hopenhayn and Rogerson (1993) show how the distortion induced by firing restrictions pushes firms to use resources less efficiently. EPL is likely to make it more difficult for firms to react quickly to rapid changes in technology or product demand that requires reallocation of staff or downsizing. As a result, employment levels adjust at a slower speed and productivity is reduced.

A paper by Cuñat and Melitz (2007, 2012) studies the link between volatility, labor market flexibility, and international trade. They develop a model and test it using country–industry data and find that countries with more flexible labor markets fare better in more volatile industries, where their ability to adjust to unexpected shocks is more important. This implies that labor market reforms might have differential effects across industries and that their effects might be more beneficial among sectors with a higher dispersion of within-industry shocks.

More broadly, the empirical literature is quite inconclusive and has tried to measure the effects of EPL on industrial outcomes using cross-country studies with industry-level data or industry-state-level data. Among the first group of papers, Micco and Pagés (2007) implement a difference-in-differences estimator in a cross-section of industry-level data for a sample of developed and developing countries. They are able to identify the effect of EPL by arguing that sector differences in the intrinsic volatility of demand and supply shocks can lead to differential responses to labor regulation. Their results show that EPL reduces turnover, employment, and value added in more volatile industries but they only find weak evidence of a negative relationship between labor regulation stringency and labor productivity. Similarly, Bassanini et al. (2009) use aggregate cross-country/time-series data on OECD countries to measure the differential effects of country-level EPL on industry-level productivity. They find that dismissal regulations tend to generate larger TFP growth loses among industries with a high layoff propensity relative to industries where firms rely less on layoffs to adjust labor-inputs' usage.

A recent strand in the empirical literature focuses on India, one of the countries with the strictest labor regulation in the world. Although Indian labor laws were strongly influenced by the British model inherited on independence, it is clear that Indian labor regulation is substantially more protective than the UK's present system, as shown in Figure 1. The gap between these countries broadens after 1979, which is when a conservative government committed to labor market deregulation was elected in the United Kingdom. India fares even worse when compared to the United States. However, the Indian case is particularly interesting and a nice setting for empirical studies given the ability of state governments to introduce formal and informal amendments to the labor laws. Consequently, changes in the application of the law at the state-level have resulted in important variations in the stringency of EPL within the same country.

FIGURE 1. Evolution of Labor Law in India, United Kingdom, and the United States

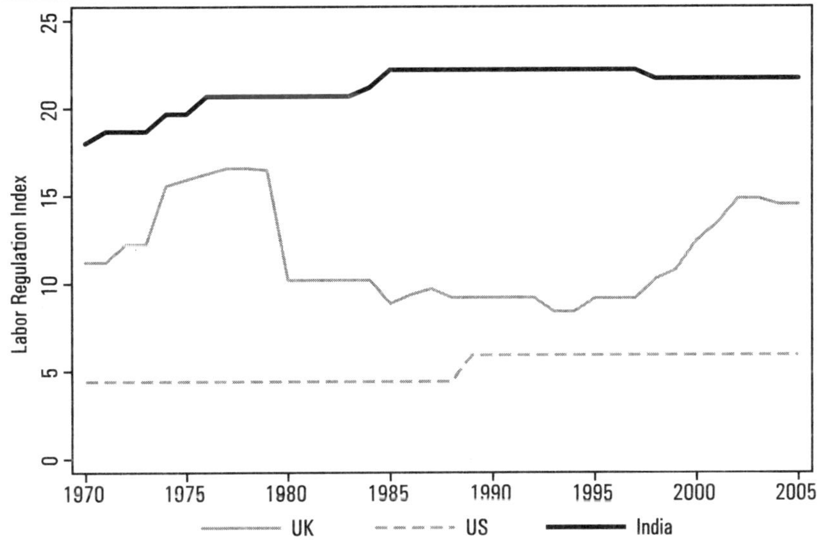

Source: Deakin et al. (2007).

Note: The laws reported for India are mostly federal laws. The authors also report some state-level variations in case law, especially for the most heavily industrialized states. Their Labor Regulation Index is a score obtained out of 40 possible points, where higher values indicate more stringent regulation.

First promoted by Besley and Burgess (2004), most studies focusing on India tend to use cross-state and intertemporal variation in labor legislation as measured by state IDA amendments. These studies find that changes toward more flexible labor regulation are correlated with higher levels of manufacturing output, employment, and labor productivity in the organized industrial sector. For example, Aghion et al. (2008) find that, following delicensing in the 1980s and early 1990s, industries located in states with pro-employer labor regulations grew more quickly than those in pro-worker environments. Ahsan and Pagés (2009) also use the BB index over a similar period, but decompose it into amendments that reduce transaction costs of initiating and sustaining industrial disputes and those that increase job security and reduce labor flexibility. Their results suggest that regulations that increase the cost of settling disputes are more costly for employment than the restrictions directly imposed by the IDA.

Focusing on rural India in the same time period, Adhvaryu et al. (2012) developed a partial equilibrium model where agriculture exists alongside industry. They used rainfall fluctuations to measure exogenous unobserved demand and cost shocks, and analyzed the response of states with different labor regulations as measured by the BB index. Their results show that the change in employment is significantly greater in states with laxer labor laws. However, shocks do not generate a differential response in output or profits. This is explained by a greater adjustment of the use of capital and materials in pro-worker states.

Despite its extended use in the empirical literature, the BB index has been heavily criticized. Bhattacharjea (2006, 2009) claims that the Besley and Burgess (2004) scoring system can erroneously classify a state as pro-employer or pro-worker with just one or two amendments to the IDA in the 50 years covered by the index. Nagaraj (2004) points out that the BB index focuses only on the IDA, abstracting from several other labor laws that affect industrial performance. Another important critique is its exclusive focus on "formal" amendments, which ignores changes in the actual practices and enforcement of the labor laws. In fact, most recent changes in state-level practices have resulted from judicial interpretations of the laws by the Supreme Court. It is thus not surprising that updates of the BB index, including our own, using the most recent edition of Malik (2011), show very few changes in labor regulation after 1992. In addition, Bhattacharjea (2009) emphasizes the fragility of Besley and Burgess (2004) econometric results. In particular, Bhattacharjea criticizes the use of irrelevant state-level control variables and inadequate tests for robustness, as well as the fragility of their results once state-specific time trends are introduced in their model.

A recent study by Gupta et al. (2008) tries to overcome some of the BB index's measurement problems by using a simple majority rule across three EPL measures available in the empirical literature, including the BB index. They argue that this approach has the advantage of weeding out any measurement error, unless there are systematic mistakes in coding the states across different indicators. Using this state-level composite measure of EPL, they exploit industry-level variation in labor usage to test the differential impact of product and labor market regulations. They find that labor intensive industries in states with flexible labor regulation have higher levels of value added.

Bhattacharjea (2009) departs from Besley and Burgess's (2004) work by focusing on the legislative content of the state-level amendments as well as on the judicial interpretations to Chapter V of the IDA.[6] He critiques the earlier studies for various omissions and insufficient attention to judicial

6. This chapter relates to firms' requirements to obtain government permission for layoffs, retrenchments and closures.

interpretations, and shows that the BB index should not be relied upon to capture the variation in labor regimes. He also proposes a series of empirical tests that examine the effect of state-level labor regulation reform on the number of factories, value added, and share of contract labor. The results from these tests are mixed, and mostly inconclusive, and he highlights that his main contribution lies on his critique of the earlier literature.

All in all, the evidence on the effects of EPL on TFP and/or TFP growth in India is still scarce. This gap in the literature is even larger when we focus on the evidence available at the plant or firm level. One exception is the work by Harrison et al. (2013), which is tangentially related to our work. The authors decompose aggregate productivity gains after the trade reforms from the early 1990s between market-share reallocations and average productivity improvements. They find that a very small share of the TFP gains in Indian manufacturing was due to market-share reallocations and test whether this result is explained by labor rigidities due to strict labor laws. In general, they find that labor laws, as measured by the number of close-down or layoff requests granted, do not generate a differential effect of trade reforms on productivity, measured using an index number approach. However, they find that in states where labor regulation is more rigid, foreign direct investment (FDI) reform has a larger impact on TFP. They claim that this is evidence that FDI reform only matters when labor regulation makes it more difficult for firms to optimize their production.

Besides the well-known difficulties involved in TFP estimation at the plant-level, the fact that state-level changes in labor regulation may be endogenously determined requires sources of exogenous variation in the data to identify the effect of EPL on plant-level productivity. In particular, we expect differences in labor regulation to have heterogenous effects on productivity across industries with different levels of labor intensity and volatility. A Cobb–Douglas production function is assumed, specific to each manufacturing industry, $Y = AL^{\alpha} K^{1-\alpha}$, and thus the unit cost function (which is inversely related to A, multifactor productivity) will be given by:

$$c = \frac{R_s^{\alpha}}{A}\left(\frac{w}{\alpha}\right)^{\alpha}\left(\frac{r}{1-\alpha}\right)^{1-\alpha} = \frac{1}{A'}\left(\frac{w}{\alpha}\right)^{\alpha}\left(\frac{r}{1-\alpha}\right)^{1-\alpha} \tag{1}$$

where w and r are the labor and capital input prices and A' is what is measured as TFP.

Employment protection legislation is captured through the constant R_s, which multiplies wages in state s to capture the effective cost of labor, consistent with our view of employment protection in India as being roughly proportional to the number of workers in a firm. Whenever labor legislation imposes additional costs through layoff regulation or hiring restrictions, R_s will be above one. Clearly, A' falls as R_s rises.

The effect of EPL on measured TFP, A', is identified by taking advantage of the state-level variation in labor regulation as well as the industry-level variation in labor intensity as measured by an estimate of α.

3. Data

The data used in this study came from the Indian ASI, conducted by the Indian Ministry of Statistics (MOSPI). Previous studies using the same data source have been unable to build a plant-level panel due to the lack of factory identifiers that have only been made available recently.[7] A notable exception is Harrison et al. (2013), which uses the ASI panel to examine the role of market-share reallocations in aggregate productivity growth in India's organized manufacturing sector over 1985 to 2004.

3.1. Description

We have used ASI data from 1998–99 through 2007–08 fiscal years to obtain an unbalanced panel of registered manufacturing plants. The ASI's sampling frame is constructed by the Chief Inspector of Factories and the Labor Commissioner in each State or territory. It includes all factories employing 10 or more workers using power, or 20 or more workers without using power. In general, the ASI's basic strategy over the years has been to divide the survey frame into census and sample sectors, where the census sector includes larger plants. Although this strategy has remained intact, the definition of census and sample sectors has undergone some changes over the years. Between the 1998–99 and 2007–08 rounds, the size threshold for the census sector fluctuated between 50 and 200 workers, so that only plants employing 200 or more workers were "always" surveyed during the years analyzed.[8] The remaining plants are randomly sampled. For more details about the sampling design changes as well as a detailed description of the

7. We thank India's Central Statistical Organization (CSO) for providing us the data we have used for this study. The confidentiality of the unit level data was maintained and adequate precautions have been taken to avoid disclosing the identity of the units directly or indirectly.

8. All industrial units belonging to the five least industrially developed states (Manipur, Meghalaya, Nagaland, Tripura, and Andaman & Nicobar Islands) were also included in the census sector.

data problems present in ASI see Bollard et al. (2013); Harrison et al. (2013) discuss the new longitudinal sample specifically.

The data provided factory reports on output, value added, fixed capital, investment, materials, fuel, labor, and labor expenditures. It also provides information on the type of ownership, the type of organization, as well as the start-up year of each plant. The ASI reports the book value of fixed capital both at the beginning and at the end of the fiscal year, net of depreciation. Our measure of fixed capital will be the average of the net book value of fixed capital at the beginning and at the end of the fiscal year, while all other variables are measured at the end. The data collected from the ASI are at current prices and must be corrected for price changes over time. Details on the specific deflators used for each variable can be found in the Annex to Dougherty, Frisancho and Krishna (2011).

The raw data consists of about 384,000 observations over 10 years, with an average of about 38,000 plants surveyed each year. We remove observations corresponding to non-operative plants (26,553) and plants with non-positive values of output and negative values of fixed capital stock (499). Table 1 shows that following this, on average, 26% of the observations in each round have missing values for output, value added, materials, fuels, fixed capital, or labor. After removing these observations, we also drop three manufacturing industries (2-digit NIC) with too few observations: other mining and quarrying, recycling, and office, accounting, and communication equipment. Following Aghion et al. (2008) and Gupta et al. (2008), we also drop "other" manufacturing industries. This category groups different activities which are likely to vary across states, making it incomparable across states. Finally, we also drop the states and union territories of Jammu & Kashmir, Chandigarh, Nagaland, Manipur, Tripura, Meghalaya, Daman & Diu, Dadra & Nagar Haveli, Pondicherry, and Andaman & Nicobar Islands due to lack of information on employment legislation. We also exclude Lakshadweep due to lack of data in the ASI and Goa given its economy's dependence on tourism.

The final sample consists of 239,921 plant-year observations with data on 103,478 plants in 20 states. Almost 60% of the observations and 74% of the plants in our data come from the sample sector. Moreover, almost 50% of the plants appear in only one round of the survey. As expected, these are smaller plants, with an average of 48 workers. This is an important limitation of the ASI; since plants in the sample sector are not deliberately followed over time, entry and exit for smaller plants is missed. Due to changes in the census threshold size, exit and entry is only consistently observed for census plants with at least 200 workers. We call this sample the "restricted" census

TABLE 1. Percentage of Missing Observations in Each ASI Round

Year	*Total Obs.*[a]	*Missing Obs.*[b]	*% Missing*
1998–99	23,620	4,290	18.2
1999–2000	24,684	6,944	28.1
2000–01	31,053	8,349	26.9
2001–02	33,387	8,579	25.7
2002–03	33,800	8,625	25.5
2003–04	45,429	12,483	27.5
2004–05	39,714	11,503	29.0
2005–06	43,675	10,039	23.0
2006–07	43,304	12,812	29.6
2007–08	38,439	10,777	28.0
Total	357,105	94,401	26.4

Source: Annual Survey of Industries (ASI) 1998–99 to 2007–08.

Notes: [a] After removal of non-operative plants and plants with non-positive values of output and fixed capital stock. Only 7% of all observations are dropped for these reasons.

[b] Observations are coded as missing when the factory does not have data on output, value added, materials, fuels, fixed capital, labor, or labor expenditures.

sample which contains 49,895 plant-year observations on 11,343 plants. Basic statistics on the final sample are presented in the Annex.

We rely on the restricted census sample to obtain TFP estimates but use information on all the plants surveyed to measure the effect of EPL on productivity. To take into account simultaneity and selection biases, we obtain production function estimates using the Olley–Pakes estimator. Since this approach uses information on plants' exits and lagged values of some variables, we only apply it to the restricted census sample. We then apply estimates of the production function's parameters to the full sample of plants and obtain TFP residuals for all plants in ASI's census and sample sectors.

An additional problem posed by ASI data is the substantial number of outliers. To reduce their influence in our estimates, we "winsorized" the data, following Bollard et al. (2013). This procedure basically implies top-coding and bottom-coding the 1% tails for each plant-level variable. In other words, for each year and each variable we replace outliers in the top 1% tail (bottom 1% tail) with the value of the 99th (1st) percentile of that variable. This procedure was applied separately to each 2-digit industry.[9]

A final issue with the ASI data is that it only provides information at the plant-level. Many may argue that plants are not independent units but that

9. We do not remove these outliers because we would have generated an additional loss of 59,896 observations, about 25% of the complete sample.

instead, most production decisions are made at the firm level.[10] In any case, as Harrison et al. (2013) also point out, the difference between "plant" and "firm" in the ASI data is likely to be negligible since most firms are single-plant. In our final pool of plants, an average of 4.5% of them are under the control of a multiplant firm each year.

Our measure of labor reform comes from the OECD index which summarizes state-level indicators of procedural changes to the implementation of labor laws either through formal amendments or through de facto practices (Dougherty 2009).[11] The OECD, with the support of the All-India Association of Employers (AIOE), surveyed 21 Indian states in 2007. The EPL index reflects the extent to which procedural or administrative changes have reduced transaction costs in relation to labor issues. It is constructed using data from a survey instrument developed to identify areas in which Indian states have experienced specific changes to the implementation and administration of labor laws over the 1990s and 2000s. The survey covered 50 specific subjects of possible reform in seven major areas of labor regulation in addition to the IDA: the Factories Act, the State Shops and Commercial Establishments Acts, the Contract Labor Act, the role of inspectors, the maintenance of registers, the filing of returns and union representation. We use the ordinal EPL count index, rebased and rescaled from zero to one, which is essentially the percentage of areas in which pro-employer labor reform occurred. It is worth emphasizing that, although the OECD index can be separated by its subcomponents, we rely on the aggregate measure of labor reform since the index was designed to capture a state's general stance toward labor regulations, more than the character of specific reforms.

It is important to emphasize that the index only incorporates rules that relate to issues that affect the transaction costs of labor market arrangements, but not those related to worker health or safety. As such, rules that increase the rigidity or reduce the flexibility of mutually beneficial employer–employee agreements, and reduce red tape are coded as pro-employer reforms. Moreover, even in the case of union representation, the

10. Unfortunately, there is no firm-level data source with an adequate sample frame in India. The only alternative would be the Prowess dataset, from the Centre for Monitoring Indian Economy (CMIE). However, this database only covers publicly traded companies, some unlisted public and private limited firms, and a few unregistered companies. Their primary source of data are the Annual Reports of individual firms, which implies that their sample frame is biased toward much larger firms.

11. Unfortunately, while it would have been desirable to separate the de facto from the de jure procedural changes, as Davies and Vadlamannati (2013) do in a different context, it is not possible to do so given the questionnaire design.

issues covered relate to rules that give clear and cohesive representation to unions. More details can be found in Dougherty (2009).

To add state-level controls to our estimates, we gathered time series data on population, telephone availability, installed electric capacity, and paved road length. State population comes from census population data for 1991, 2001, and 2011, and it is linearly interpolated for other years. Time series data on fixed and mobile phones per 100 population comes from the Ministry of Statistics and Programme Implementation's (MOSPI) Web site. Installed electric capacity, measured as kilowatts per million people on the state, is obtained from the Annual Report of the Indian Ministry of Power for the years 1997–98, 2000–01, 2001–02, 2002–03, 2003–04, 2004–05, 2005–06, and 2007–08. State-wise surfaced road length is obtained from two sources: (a) the Basic Road Statistics of India report from the Ministry of Road Transport and Highways for the years 2004–05, 2005–06, 2006–07, and 2007–08, and (b) the Planning Commission's 9th and 10th Five Year Plans. Road density is measured as paved kilometers per thousand people in the state.

We also include an OECD measure of state-level product market regulation as a time- invariant control to take into account the potential role of product regulation as a complement (or substitute) of labor market laws. The product market regulation index is taken from OECD (2007) and it contains information on state intervention and legal or administrative barriers to entrepreneurship (see Conway and Herd 2009).

In our robustness checks, we will also make use of the BB index that we update through 2008 using Malik (2011) as well as Gupta et al.'s (2008) labor market regulation composite index. The latter is based on a simple majority rule across three sources: Besley and Burgess (2004), Bhattacharjea (2006), and Dougherty (2009). States are coded as pro-labor, pro-business, or neutral if the majority of the studies considered classified them as such. Additionally, we check the robustness of our results using industry-level layoff propensity instead of the measure of labor intensity captured by the estimated *as*. Layoff propensities are measured for the United States between 2002 and 2003 with data from the 2004 CPS Displaced Workers Supplement (see Table A.3 in Bassanini et al. 2009).[12] Using these propensities, we construct a dummy variable for above and below the median industry.

We must emphasize that the ASI only provides data on organized manufacturing plants. In a country where the informal sector constitutes a

12. The industry classification in this data (ISIC Rev. 3) does not exactly match the 2-digit industry classification of the ASI, so in some cases we had to merge Indian industries to make them comparable to those in the United States.

majority of the labor force and the unorganized sector produces a third of total manufacturing value added, there is also a need to understand how EPL reforms have affected unorganized plants. A source of data on these plants is the National Sample Survey Organization's (NSSO) survey, but it is only carried out every five years. This lack of data comparable to the ASI forces most researchers to focus exclusively on the registered or organized sector. However, this focus is also appropriate since labor market rigidities in the organized sector constrain the absorption of formal workers, who tend to be more productive, receive higher wages, and face better working conditions than workers in the informal sector (see Gupta et al. 2008). Moreover, Goldar and Aggarwal (2010) provide some evidence on the effects of labor market reforms in the unorganized manufacturing sector. Using the OECD labor market reform index for Indian states, they find a negative and significant relationship between labor laws' flexibility and the probability of being a casual worker both in the formal and informal manufacturing sector, although the effect in the former is far stronger.

3.2. Basic Patterns

Using the OECD index, we classified states as having flexible labor markets when they were above the median state according to the degree of labor regulation reforms carried out. Figure 2 plots the cumulative distribution of output and employment by labor laws' rigidity. Panel (a) suggests that the variation in labor standards across states may have allowed some states to fare better than others; the distribution of output in states with flexible labor laws first-order dominates that of states with more stringent regulation, according to a two-sample Kolmogorov–Smirnov test for equality of distributions. Specifically, the test cannot reject the hypothesis that output for states with stringent labor regulation is smaller than for states with more flexible laws, and the test rejects that output is higher in strict versus flexible states. However, panel (b) of Figure 2 suggests that EPL does not seem to substantially influence formal employment, and this is confirmed by the corresponding Kolmogorov–Smirnov test.

Although these patterns are suggestive, we now control for the states' total population to get a better idea of the general picture. Figure 3 plots output and employment per capita at the state level in 2000 against our EPL reform indicator.[13] Each observation in the scatter plot represents a state. Even after controlling for the state's population, Panel (a) in Figure 3 shows

13. The OECD labor reform index has been re-scaled so that zero corresponds to the lowest level of reform and one indicates the highest level of reform at the state level.

FIGURE 2. Output, Employment, and EPL in 2000

(a)

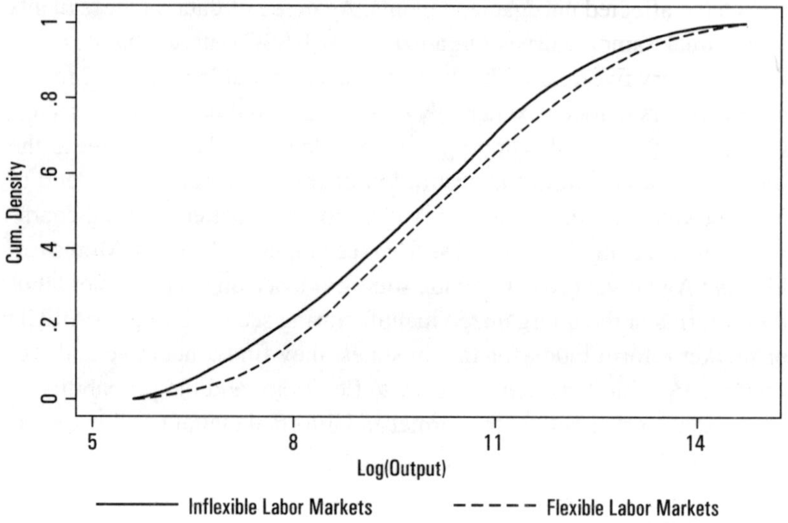

(b)

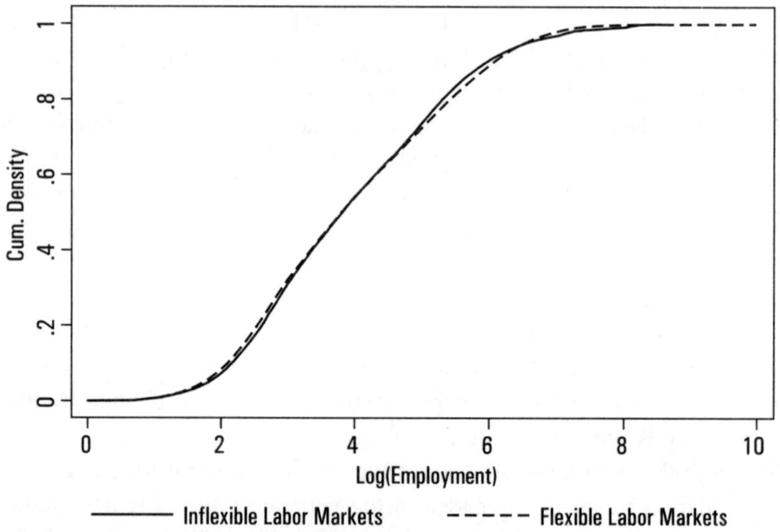

Source: Annual Survey of Industries 1998–99 to 2007–08 rounds.

FIGURE 3. Output and Employment per Capita and EPL in 2000

(a) Output

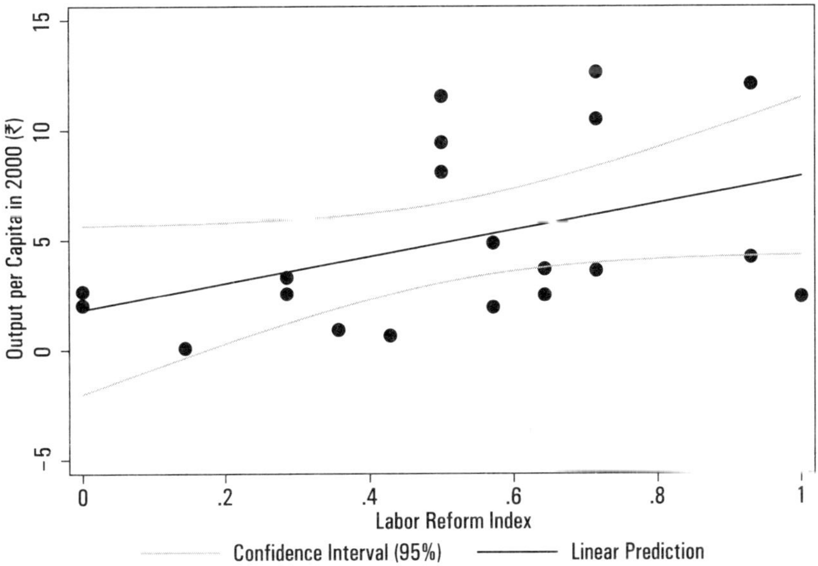

(b) Employment

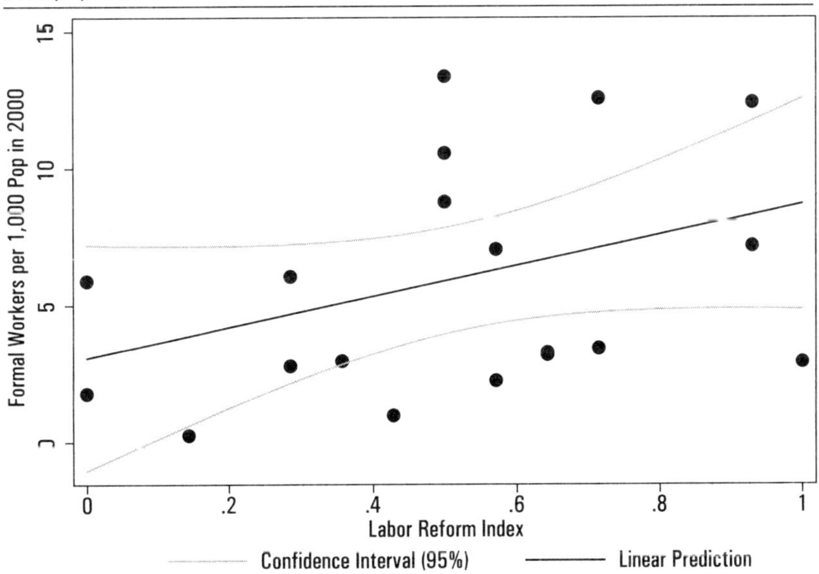

Source: Annual Survey of Industries 1998–99 to 2007–08 rounds.

that there is a modest positive relationship between output per capita and the preponderance of labor law reforms in the state. However, this pattern is much weaker for formal employment per capita, as shown in panel (b).

However, differences in the number of plants in each state may be driving these patterns. To deal with this, Figure 4 decomposes total output and employment by EPL flexibility into their extensive and intensive margins. While the extensive margin is captured by the number of plants (N), the intensive margin is measured by the average output or average employment per plant (Q/N or $/N$). Both in terms of output and employment, states with more flexible regulation fare better than plants operating in more restrictive labor markets. However, most of this "advantage" seems to be explained by the evolution of the extensive margin. On average, intensive margin differences explain about 36% of the output gap and 9% of the employment differences between flexible and inflexible states.[14]

Figure 5 plots the distribution of TFP by EPL and labor intensity. We obtain TFP estimates separately for each industry (so that scaling is not an issue) using the Olley–Pakes approach in the subsample of ongoing plants in ASI's panel. Sub-section 4.1 describes the details of the estimation of TFP residuals, which yields unbiased estimates of the production function coefficients. In particular, we rely on the output elasticity with respect to labor, α, estimated in the panel and identify labor intensive industries as those with an $\hat{\alpha}$ above the median industry. Panels (a) and (b) show that industries with high labor intensity experience a greater improvement in their TFP distribution from the relaxation of labor laws' enforcement when compared to less labor intensive industries. A two-sample Kolmogorov–Smirnov test for equality of distribution shows significant differences of the distribution of TFP across states with different labor regulation in labor-intensive industries. Specifically, we cannot reject that there are lower TFP values—but we can reject that there are higher TFP values—in strict states when compared with laxer ones. The corresponding test performed among

14. Let the subscripts 0 and 1 correspond to outcomes in inflexible and flexible labor markets, respectively.

Output differences can be decomposed in the following way:

$$\left(\frac{Q}{N}\right)_1 N_1 - \left(\frac{Q}{N}\right)_0 N_0 = \left[\left(\frac{Q}{N}\right)_1 - \left(\frac{Q}{N}\right)_0\right] N_1 + \left(\frac{Q}{N}\right)_0 [N_1 - N_0]$$

where the first term in the right hand side captures output differences coming from the intensive margin for a fixed number of plants. The second term fixes output per plant to capture extensive margin differences.

FIGURE 4. Labor Market Regulations and Manufacturing Production and Employment

(a) Total output

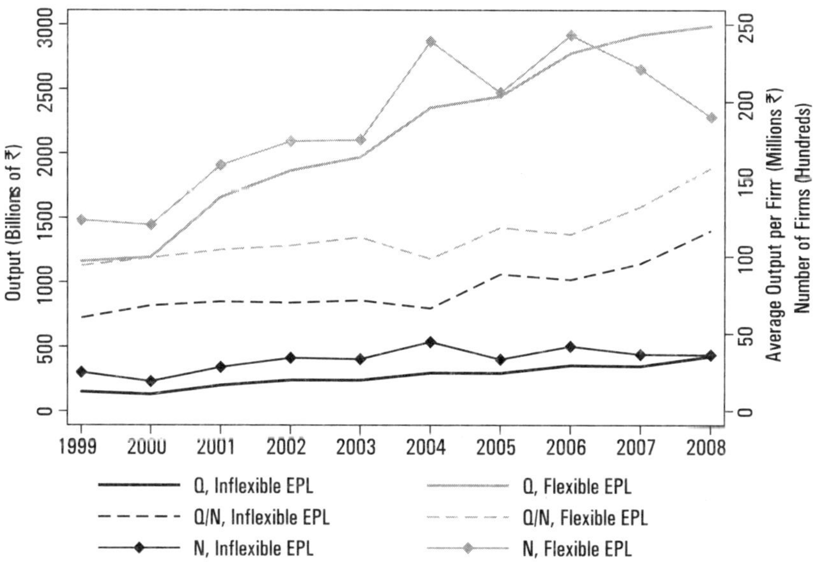

(b) Total employment

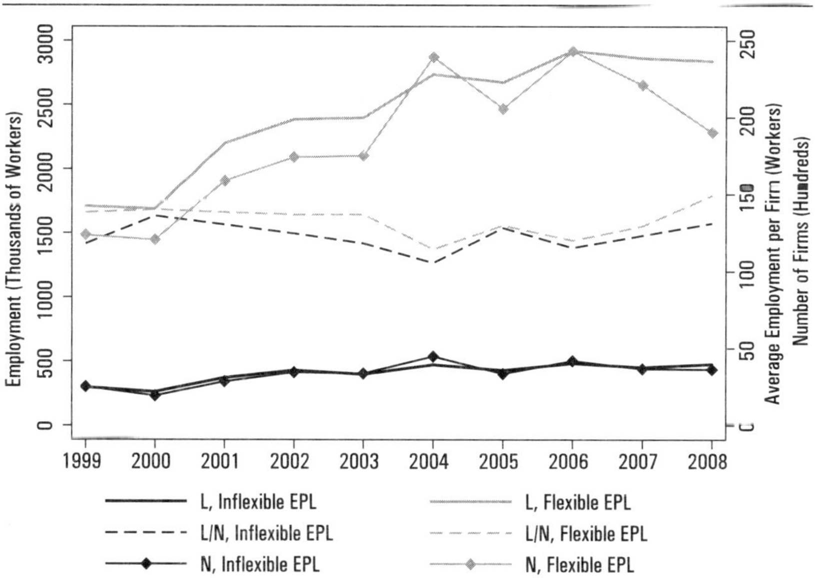

Source: Annual Survey of Industries 1998–99 to 2007–08.

FIGURE 5. Labor Market Regulation, Labor Intensity, and Productivity

(a) TFP: High labor intensity

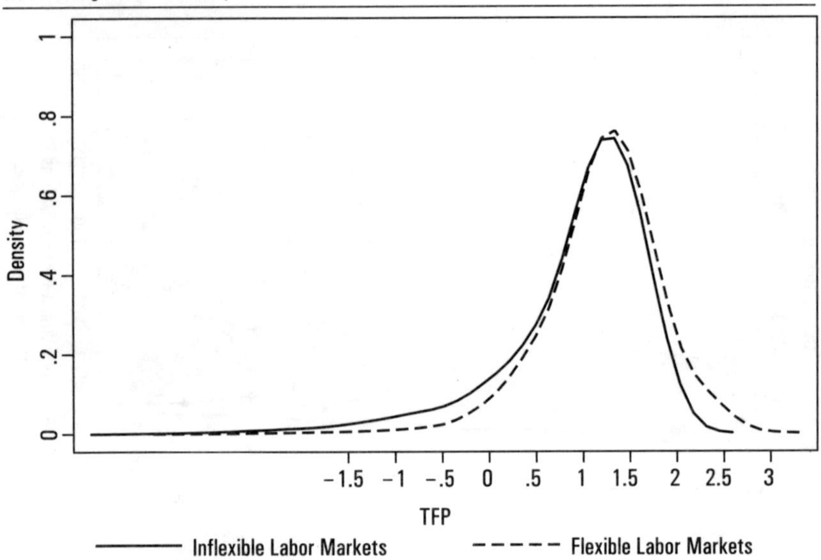

(b) TFP: Low labor intensity

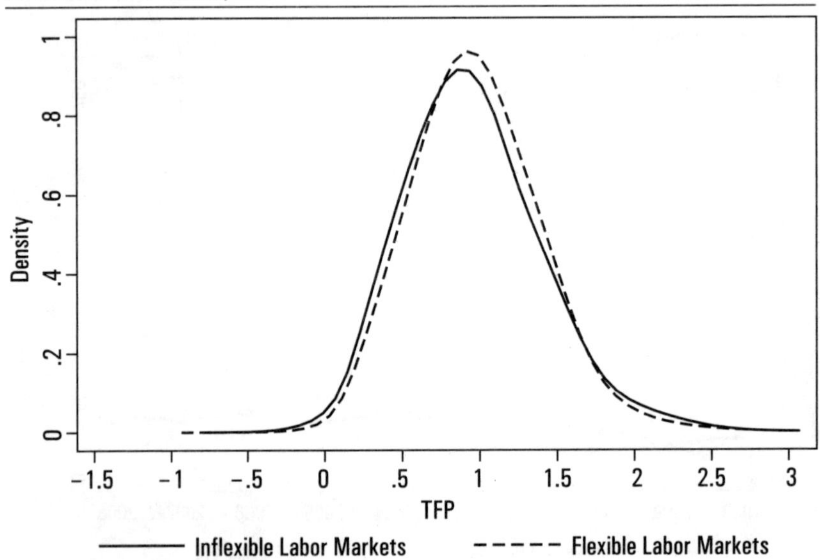

Source: Annual Survey of Industries 1998–99 to 2007–08.

industries with lower labor intensity shows that the distributions are different; however, the test rejects neither lower values of TFP nor higher values of TFP in strict versus flexible states.

So far, this preliminary evidence suggests that labor intensive industries benefit the most from EPL relaxation in Indian states. Section 5 will test if the patterns identified for productivity remain relevant after a more rigorous analysis.

4. Empirical Strategy

The main objective of this study is to assess the effect of employment regulation reform in India on TFP between 1998–99 and 2007–08. The basic specification proposed to evaluate productivity performance is similar to the one used by Aghion et al. (2008), in the sense that we take advantage of state-level variation in labor regulation, but we extend it to incorporate industry-level variation. Our fundamental assumption is that EPL reform is more likely to restrict plants operating in industries with higher labor intensity, or alternatively higher volatility.

Consider the partial equilibrium effect of a change in EPL derived in equation (1). The impact on productivity is expected to be larger in industries where plants rely more on labor than in industries in which this input is relatively less important. We can also think of more volatile industries having a harder time adjusting their labor input usage when strict labor regulations are in place. To capture the effect of labor regulation reform, we use a difference-in-differences estimator inspired by Rajan and Zingales (1998). By comparing cross-industry differences in states with different levels of labor reform we can evaluate the effect of EPL changes toward pro-employer legislation on productivity levels. Labor-intensive industries will be more constrained by labor regulation so the impact of EPL reform is identified using industries with lower output elasticity with respect to output as a control group. Relaxation in labor regulation may also interact with industry-level differences in the dispersion of plant-level shocks to generate larger TFP gains among sectors with a higher dispersion of these shocks.

Further, we briefly describe the TFP estimates used in this study. Next, we proceed to describe the econometric model used to measure the impact of labor reform on manufacturing plants.

4.1. TFP Measures

When trying to estimate a production function using observed plant-level variables, obtaining TFP measures from the residuals encompasses several measurement and econometric problems. One issue is that measurement of outputs and inputs generates an aggregation problem, especially in multi-product plants. Another measurement issue relates to capital usage; since it is very tough to obtain data on capital consumption as an input in the production process, the researcher has to settle for the book value of total capital and machinery involved in the production process.

Although the previous problems are complex enough, there is not much the empirical researcher can do about them but try to collect better quality and more detailed micro data. In addition to these problems, several econometric difficulties arise when estimating production functions at the plant-level. Two of the most prominent and serious problems are simultaneity and selection biases.

Assume a Cobb–Douglas production function like the one described below:

$$Y_{it} = A_{it} L_{it}^{\alpha} K_{it}^{\beta} M_{it}^{\gamma} F_{it}^{\lambda}$$

where Y_{it} are physical units of output and L_{it}, K_{it}, M_{it}, and F_{it} measure labor, fixed capital, materials, and fuels, respectively. Since A_{it} enters the right hand side in a multiplicative way, affecting all the other factors' marginal product simultaneously, it represents the TFP. Taking logarithms allows us to use a linear estimation model described by:

$$Y_{it} = \alpha l_{it} + \beta k_{it} + \gamma m_{it} + \lambda f_{it} + \mu_{it} \tag{2}$$

where small letters are used for logs.

From the estimation of equation (2), we can retrieve the error term u_{it}, which is the log of plant-specific A_{it}, provided that the coefficients on the inputs are consistently estimated. OLS estimation does not yield consistent estimates if plants' choices on exit and on factor demands (when they continue operating) depend on their productivity. This fact generates both a selection and a simultaneity problem in the estimation of production functions.

Olley and Pakes (1996) deal with the simultaneity problem by using the firm's investment decision to proxy for unobserved productivity shocks.[15]

15. See Olley and Pakes (1996). Their approach assumes a strictly monotonic relationship between output and investment so that all observations with zero investment are dropped.

It is assumed that a higher value of the productivity shock observed by the firm (but unobserved by us) will induce higher investment today. The Olley–Pakes approach also offers a correction for selection bias due to exit. In the first stage, a probit of survival is estimated as a function of a polynomial of capital and investment, and the fitted values from this regression are used in the second stage to consistently estimate the production function parameters.[16]

Since this technique requires information on exit and lagged values of some variables, we estimate the parameters in equation (2) using Olley–Pakes in the restricted census sample, for which panel data is available. We estimate the coefficients for capital, labor, materials, and fuels separately for each industry and assume that these estimates are applicable to plants in the census as well as in the sample sector. We can then obtain TFP as a residual for all the plants using the industry-specific coefficient estimates. Estimating TFP using industry-specific regressions allows for differences in the production function's coefficients, including a constant term, which yields unit-free productivity residuals that are comparable across industries. In the end, TFP residuals are obtained as the exponential of the residual in equation (2).[17]

To estimate TFP at the plant-level, we use real gross output instead of value added as the dependent variable. According to Basu and Fernald (1997) and Carlsson, Messina, and Skans (2011), the use of value added

---

An alternative approach to deal with the simultaneity bias is offered by Levinsohn and Petrin (2003), who use intermediate inputs as a proxy for investment to avoid losing observations. However, only 4% of the plant-year observations in the restricted census sample used to estimate TFP have zero investment. Moreover, unlike Olley–Pakes, Levinsohn–Petrin methodology does not offer a correction for selection bias. For more details on the problems faced when estimating productivity as well as available solutions, see Arnold (2005).

16. Recent developments in the literature offer potential avenues of future extensions. For example, Gandhi, Navarro, and Rivers (2013) propose a simple non-parametric estimator for the production function and productivity. They rely on the first order condition of the firm's profit maximization problem and use this information without any parametric assumption on the production function to identify productivity while dealing with the endogeneity of input choices. This is the first paper that we know of that departs from the traditional Cobb–Douglas assumption frequently used in structural methods that try to deal with the transmission and selection biases present in the estimation of TFP. Zhang (2013) also relies on the first order condition to obtain a measure of productivity that accounts for capital and labor-augmenting efficiency, separately. He claims that an advantage of his approach is that the estimation does not impose a Markov process assumption on the productivity evolution process and thus cross-sectional data suffices.

17. Notice that since the error is mean zero, this explains why the mean of the TFP distribution in Figure 5 is so close to one.

is only valid for TFP estimation under perfect competition and constant returns to scale.[18] Labor is measured in number of workers and fixed capital is measured as the average of the net book real value of fixed capital at the beginning and at the end of the fiscal year. The amount of fuels and materials consumed is used to measure the usage of these inputs. Investment is measured by the gross value of additions to fixed capital. All the variables are measured in rupees at the end of the period and in 1993–94 constant prices, unless otherwise noted.

In essence, Olley–Pakes allows for a considerably more general firm-level fixed effect but the latter is nested within it. With 10 years of annual observations we are sure that we have enough intertemporal variation to identify the parameters in the production function; in fact, Olley and Pakes (1996) themselves used 12 years of data while Levinsohn and Petrin (2003) relied on eight years.

4.2. Econometric Model

Our analysis of the impact of labor reform on manufacturing outcomes relies on this basic econometric model:

$$\log(TFP_{fist}) = \theta_0 + \theta_1 LI_i + \theta_2 R_S + \theta_3 (LI_i \times R_S) + \eta_t + \varepsilon_{fist} \quad (3)$$

where TFP_{fist} is the Olley–Pakes residual for plant f, in industry i and state s, at year t. LI_i denotes industry's i labor intensity measure while state labor reform is captured by R_S.

Our indicator of R_S is a dummy variable based on the normalized count of EPL reforms in each state. We label states as having flexible regulation when their labor reform index is at or above the median state in terms of the proportion of state-level reforms (using the count index). We adopt this dummy specification because the OECD measure of labor reform cannot be considered a continuous variable but is closer to an ordinal or categorical variable. However, there are too many categories to use it as such and the dummy specification eases presentation of the results.

18. See Appendix C in Carlsson, Messina, and Skans (2011). They show that a residual measure of TFP that comes from value added is not independent of the use of intermediate inputs and factor input growth when there are increasing or decreasing returns to scale.

To measure LI_i, we construct a dummy variable for above and below the median labor-intensive industry based on the $\hat{\alpha}$s obtained from the estimation of equation (2). We believe that the use of $\hat{\alpha}$ to measure the intrinsic labor intensity in each industry is superior to the use of the share of labor expenditures in total output. The use of the estimated output elasticity with respect to labor overcomes the potential biases that the ratio of labor expenditures to output may have due to the endogeneity of the plant's input choices. Moreover, since our TFP estimation using the Olley–Pakes methodology takes into account year fixed effects, $\hat{\alpha}$ provides a clean estimate of the underlying labor intensity of each industry that is not biased by exogenous demand or supply shocks in the inputs markets.

An alternative specification of equation (3) uses industry volatility measures instead of labor intensity. In that case, we follow Krishna and Levchenko (2009) and measure industry volatility by the standard deviation of the annual growth rate of plants' output. We then construct a dummy variable for above and below the median volatile industry.

Since our measure of EPL reform is time-invariant and measured at the state level, we cannot include state fixed effects. Similarly, our labor intensity indicator is fixed at the industry level, so it restrains us from including industry fixed effects.[19] We control for year fixed effects, denoted by ηt in equation (3), and add a plant-specific trend.[20] We also incorporate additional controls in our estimates to make sure we take into account the effect of state-level characteristics.

As argued by Bertrand et al. (2004), the estimation of difference-in-differences with an outcome variable measured at a lower level of aggregation when compared to the treatment variable—TFP at the establishment level and labor law reforms at the state level—may be subject to a serial correlation problem due to reduced variation within each state-year cell. Although this problem does not create an issue around the estimate of the intervention, it could understate the standard deviation and thus, the significance, of the coefficient in the interaction between the time dummy and the treatment variable, θ_3 in equation (3). To deal with this potential serial correlation problem, all our estimates allow for an arbitrary autocorrelation process when computing the standard errors. In particular, we specify the standard errors to allow for intragroup correlation within each state, relaxing

19. Full collinearity restrains us from including industry-year, state-year, or industry-state fixed effects.

20. Of course, this trend is only relevant for plants present in multiple years and its removal does not quantitatively or qualitatively affect the results.

the usual requirement that the observations are independent both across and within groups.[21]

The coefficient θ_3 on the interaction between LI_i and R_S will capture the heterogeneous effect of EPL reform on industries with different labor intensity. Given that R_S is higher when state labor reforms make EPL more flexible, a positive coefficient on the interaction implies that plants in industries that use labor more intensively fare better in states with pro-employer labor regulation. In the alternative specification, which uses industry volatility in place of labor intensity, the interaction term should also have a positive coefficient since more volatile plants are expected to benefit the most from laxer labor regulations.

Note that equation (3) is in no way related to the model in Sub-Section 4.1. While the latter sought to highlight the difficulties associated with measuring TFP as a residual, relying on a simple model of the firm, this section proposes an empirical strategy to identify the effect of labor regulation on productivity. To do so, we compare average multifactor productivity across states with different levels of regulation and across industries with different levels of labor intensity.

5. Results

The results presented in column (I) in Table 2 provide initial evidence of a beneficial effect of pro-employer labor reform on multifactor for labor intensive industries. The positive and significant interaction of LI_i and R_s shows that manufacturing plants with high labor requirements that operate in states moving toward more flexible regulation exhibit larger TFP gains than plants in less labor intensive industries.

The point estimates from column (I) in Table 2 imply that there are important multifactor productivity gains from conducting more labor reforms, particularly for plants in labor intensive industries. In 2008, the ratio of the geometric mean of TFP for plants in states with flexible labor markets over the same mean of TFP for plants in states with inflexible labor markets is 1.31 in labor intensive industries, but it is close to one in industries with lower $\hat{\alpha}$s.[22] In other words, a plant in a labor intensive industry that moves

21. Bertrand et al. (2004) suggest the use of this strategy as one of the best solutions to the autocorrelation within each cell over time, especially when dealing with large samples.

22. Using our estimates from column (I) in Table 2, the mean values of the trend, and the year dummy corresponding to 2008, we predict log(TFP) for 4 groups: (a) plants in states with high levels of EPL reform and high $\hat{\alpha}$s, (b) plants in states with low levels

TABLE 2. Effect of EPL Reforms on TFP by Labor Intensity

	(I)	*(II)*
Constant	0.907***	1.360***
	(0.032)	(0.328)
High labor intensity	−0.020	−0.034
	(0.074)	(0.081)
Flexible EPL	0.022	−0.027
	(0.036)	(0.044)
High labor intensity x Flexible EPL	0.246***	0.253***
	(0.082)	(0.087)
Time-variant state controls		
Log(Telephones/100 pop)		0.049**
		(0.020)
Log(Installed electricity capacity/million pop)		−0.019
		(0.025)
Log(Paved roads/1000 pop)		0.017
		(0.016)
Time-invariant state controls		
Product Market Regulation		−0.067
		(0.054)
Observations	224,867	224,867
R-squared	0.059	0.065
Firm trend	yes	yes
State-level controls	no	yes
Year FE	yes	yes

Source: Annual Survey of Industries 1998–99 to 2007–08.
Notes: State-level clustered standard errors in parentheses.
***$p < 0.01$, **$p < 0.05$, *$p < 0.1$

from an inflexible to a flexible state would get an average TFP improvement of about 31% while TFP gains are close to zero in industries with lower labor intensity.

To check the robustness of our findings, in column (II) we add a number of control variables to take into account state characteristics. These include both time-variant as well as time-invariant controls at the state level. Among the first group, we use the log of fixed and mobile phones' availability per 100 population, log of the installed electric capacity per million people, and the log of road density. Information on telephones, installed electric capacity, and road density are reasonable proxies for the general conditions of infrastructure, which are expected to be positively related to manufacturing

of EPL reform and high $\hat{\alpha}$s, (c) plants with high levels of EPL reform and low $\hat{\alpha}$s, and (d) plants with low levels of EPL reform and low $\hat{\alpha}$s. To obtain 1.31, for example, we get the difference between the predictions of log(TFP) for group (a) and (b) and exponentiate it to get the ratio of their TFP in levels.

output. We also include the OECD product market regulation index that measures how much regulations restrict competition.

Column (II) in Table 2 shows that the positive effect identified for labor intensive plants in flexible labor markets is still present for TFP once we control for state characteristics. The interaction between EPL reform and high labor intensity is positive and significant. Once state-level controls are introduced, our point estimates indicate that, on average, plants in labor intensive industries and operating in flexible labor markets have a TFP residual that is 25% higher than it is among plants in states with low levels of EPL reform and high $\hat{\alpha}$s. Among plants in industries with low $\hat{\alpha}$s, TFP "losses" from EPL reform are almost negligible, under 3%.

Next, we try to identify differential effects by plant size and type of ownership. Let X_{fist} denote a specific plant characteristic, such as size or ownership type. We extend the model in equation (3) in the following way:

$$\log(W_{fist}) = \theta_0 + \theta_1 LI_i + \theta_2 R_s + \theta_3(LI_i \times R_s) + \theta_4 X_{fist} + \theta_5(LI_i \times X_{fist}) \\ + \theta_6(R_s \times X_{fist}) + \theta_7(LI_i \times R_s \times X_{fist}) + \eta_t + \varepsilon_{fist}$$

Although θ_3 will still give us the average effect of the interaction of labor intensity and labor reform on productivity, the coefficient θ_7 becomes particularly important since it will capture any heterogeneous effects due to differences in X_{fist}.

In the case of plant size, X_{fist} will be a matrix of four size dummies. These are constructed using the number of workers with cutoffs at 50, 100, and 250. The first cutoff corresponds to the presence of a few labor laws that are enforced starting at this establishment size. The second cutoff is consistent with IDA's national threshold set in 1982. The last cutoff is in line with empirical evidence for India, above which plant TFP was observed to be substantially higher (see Dougherty et al. 2009). This check is particularly important since larger plants are subject to stricter labor regulation but are also more likely to subcontract workers to evade labor laws.

Let the share of contract labor in total expenditures for each plant be given by:

$$h^*_{fist} = \delta X_{fist} + \nu_i + \nu_s + \nu_t - \mu_{fist}$$

where ν_i, ν_s, and ν_t denote industry, state and year fixed effects. From this latent variable, we construct a categorical variable, h_{fist}, such that $h_{fist} = 1$ if the plant hires no contract labor, $h_{fist} = 2$ when the plant spends 20% or less of their labor costs on indirect labor, and $h_{fist} = 3$ when the plant spends more than 20% of total labor expenditures on hiring labor through contractors. Let the cutoffs for h^*_{fist} be given by $\xi_0 = -\infty$, $\xi_1 = 0$, $\xi_2 = 0.2$, and $\xi_3 = \infty$. The probability of $h_{fist} = H$ is given by:

$$\Pr(h_{fist} = H \mid X_{fist}) = \Pr(\xi_{H-1} < h_{fist}^* < \xi_H \mid X_{fist}$$
$$= \Phi(\delta X_{fist} + v_i + v_S + v_t - \xi_{H-1}) - \Phi(\delta X_{fist} + v_i + v_S + v_t - \xi_H)$$

where Φ is the normal cumulative distribution with mean zero and variance σ^2.

Table 3 reports δ estimates from an interval regression model like the one above. We find that larger plants are more likely to hire labor indirectly: the share of contracted labor increases by a factor of 0.317 when we compare plants with 250 or more workers to plants with less than 50 workers. Similarly, relative to the smallest plants, medium size plants with 50 to 99 workers and 100 to 249 workers see their share of contract labor expenditures increased by a factor of 0.268 and 0.3, respectively. Clearly, the tendency of larger plants to hire more workers through contractors helps them partially bypass labor legislation. Consequently, we expect them to benefit less from the state-labor reforms.

TABLE 3. Interval Regression Results for the Share of Contract Labor in Total Labor Expenditures

Firm size (base: < 50 workers)	δ	*S.E.*
[50–100[	0.268***	0.004
[100–250[	0.300***	0.003
250 or more	0.317***	0.003
Observations	229693	
Log likelihood	−165507.27	
σ	0.384***	
Year FE	yes	
Industry FE	yes	
State FE	yes	

Source: Annual Survey of Industries 1998–99 to 2007–08.
Note: ***$p < 0.01$, **$p < 0.05$, *$p < 0.1$

Estimates with the size dummies shown in column (I) in Table 4 confirm our initial prediction. The coefficient on the interaction between pro-employer EPL reform and labor intensity is positive and significant. Moreover, the coefficient on the triple interaction between EPL, labor intensity, and plant size (θ_7) is not significant for medium size plants but it is negative and significant for larger plants in both columns. Plants with more than 250 workers in industries with high labor intensity perform much worse than their smaller counterparts from pro-employer labor reforms. This result is consistent with the fact that larger plants face higher restrictions in inflexible labor regulation settings. Since many norms and regulations apply only to them, it looks like they have found a way out by reducing their dependence on a permanent workforce and relying more on temporary labor hired through contractors as suggested by Table 3. It has been well documented that casual or contract labor in India provides unskilled labor at wages below the minimum wage and without benefits, so the substitution of regular labor for casual labor can help larger plants reduce the labor costs imposed by more stringent EPL.

TABLE 4. Effect of EPL Reforms on TFP by Labor Intensity and Firm Characteristics

	(I)	*(III)*
Constant	1.505***	1.432***
	(0.311)	(0.325)
High labor intensity	−0.137	−0.107
	(0.101)	(0.074)
Flexible EPL	−0.043	−0.046
	(0.037)	(0.050)
High labor intensity x Flexible EPL	0.278**	0.331***
	(0.104)	(0.081)
Firm Size (Base: < =50 workers)		
]50–100]	0.117	
	(0.071)	
]100–250]	−0.031	
	(0.057)	
>250	0.039	
	(0.055)	
High labor intensity x]50–100]	0.039	
	(0.109)	
High labor intensity x]100–250]	0.201	
	(0.153)	
High labor intensity x >250	0.408***	
	(0.099)	
Flexible EPL x]50–100]	−0.055	
	(0.071)	
Flexible EPL x]100–250]	0.092	
	(0.062)	
Flexible EPL x >250	0.041	
	(0.060)	

(Table 4 Contd)

(Table 4 Contd)

	(I)	*(III)*
High labor intensity x Flexible EPL x]50–100]	0.051	
	(0.114)	
High labor intensity x Flexible EPL x]100–250]	−0.081	
	(0.162)	
High labor intensity x Flexible EPL x > 250	−0.215*	
	(0.117)	
Public firm		−0.006
		(0.046)
High labor intensity x Public firm		0.291***
		(0.090)
Flexible EPL x Public firm		0.070
		(0.050)
High labor intensity x Flexible EPL x Public firm		−0.311***
		(0.093)
Time-variant state controls		
Log(Telephones/100 pop)	0.051**	0.050**
	(0.020)	(0.020)
Log(Installed electricity cap./million pop)	−0.033	−0.023
	(0.024)	(0.026)
Log(Paved roads/1000 pop)	0.024	0.019
	(0.016)	(0.016)
Time-invariant state controls		
Product Market Regulation	−0.059	−0.074
	(0.050)	(0.054)
Observations	224,867	224,768
R-squared	0.089	0.069
Firm trend	yes	yes
State-level controls	yes	yes
Year FE	yes	yes

Source: Annual Survey of Industries 1998–99 to 2007–08.
Notes: State-level clustered standard errors in parentheses.
$^{***}p < 0.01$, $^{**}p < 0.05$, $^{*}p < 0.1$

We also estimated the effects of pro-employer EPL reform separately for publicly and privately owned plants, where $X_{f\,ist}$ is a dummy that is equal to one when the plant is publicly owned. In the sample periods analyzed, publicly owned plants tend to have lower rates of job destruction and creation than privately owned plants. Although public plants tend to have a lower turnover rate than privately owned plants, their net contribution to employment is highly negative in half of the rounds analyzed. A proposed explanation for this lies in voluntary retirement schemes (VRS), which are used as a mutually agreeable mechanism for downsizing. Since VRS has allowed public plants to bypass labor regulation and adjust their labor usage it may be possible that the effect of EPL within them is smaller than among private plants.

Column (II) in Table 4 presents the results obtained by ownership type. Public plants in labor intensive industries tend to have higher multifactor productivity as shown by the interaction of the ownership dummy and the labor intensity dummy. Moreover, the interaction between pro-worker EPL reform and labor intensity is positive and significant, which shows that the average beneficial effect of labor reform on labor intensive industries is higher. As we expected, the triple interaction for EPL reform, labor intensity, and public ownership is negative and significant. This implies that labor intensive public plants in flexible markets exhibit lower TFP gains from EPL reform, which is in line with the use of VRS among public plants as a strategy to circumvent labor regulation. Through this strategy, constrained public plants have been able to ameliorate the negative effects of inflexible regulation on productivity so that pro-employer labor reforms have smaller relative effects among them.

In general, the results show that there are important TFP gains for labor intensive plants that operate in states with laxer EPL. Moreover, the different strategies used by plants to overcome the constraints imposed by labor regulation generate differential effects of state-level labor reform both by plant size and type of ownership.

5.1. Volatility

We now test if laxer labor regulation benefits volatile industries relatively more as suggested by Poschke (2009) and others. Our measure of volatility is similar to Krishna and Levchenko's (2009): the standard deviation of the annual growth rate of plants' output in a given industry. Notice that we need a plant-level growth measure to quantify volatility, so we will obtain a proxy for each industry from the restricted census sample, average it over all the ASI rounds we use, and apply it to the complete sample of plants. We then construct a dummy variable which classifies industries as highly volatile when they are at or above the median industry in terms of the average standard deviation of annual growth rate of output.

Panels (a) and (b) in Figure 6 present preliminary evidence on the existence of a comparative advantage among more volatile plants in flexible markets. State-level labor reforms seem to shift the TFP distribution to the right only in more turbulent industries, which is in line with Cuñat and Melitz (2007) findings.

FIGURE 6. Labor Market Regulation, Volatility, and Productivity

(a) TFP: High volatility

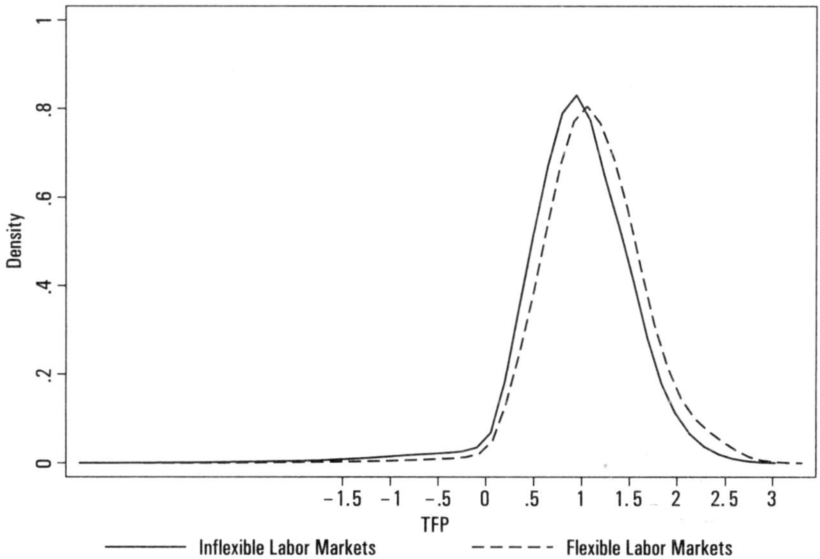

(b) TFP: Low volatility

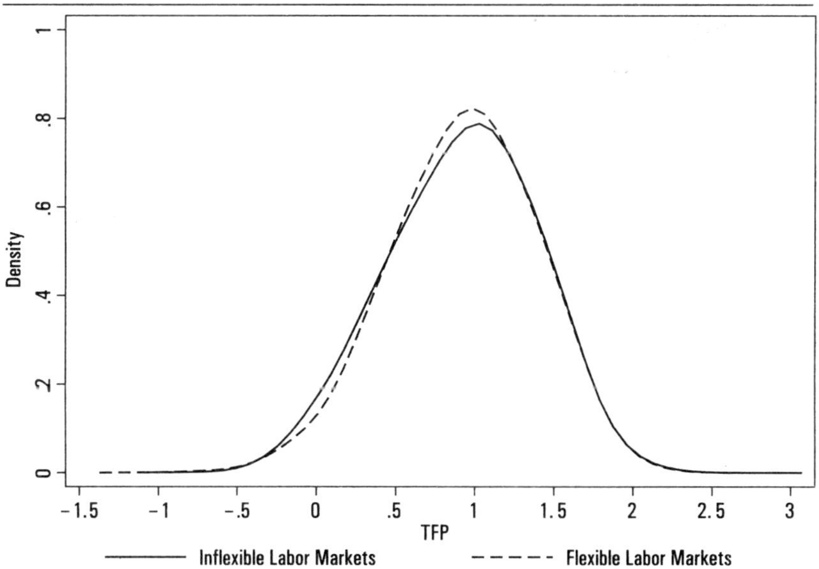

Source: Annual Survey of Industries 1998–99 to 2007–08.

Table 5 confirms these patterns. The interaction between EPL and volatility is positive and significant, which implies that plants in more volatile industries that operate in flexible labor markets have a comparative advantage in terms of multifactor productivity. The larger costs of hiring and firing people imposed by strict EPL seem to be particularly restrictive in sectors with higher volatility, generating an unequal distribution of the productivity gains that come from labor market deregulation.

TABLE 5. Effect of EPL Reforms on TFP by Volatility

Volatility	*(I)*
Constant	1.475***
	(0.386)
High volatility	0.044
	(0.052)
Flexible EPL	-0.057
	(0.043)
High volatility x Flexible EPL	0.147**
	(0.063)
Time-variant state controls	
Log(Telephones/100 pop)	0.053**
	(0.024)
Log(Installed electricity cap./million pop)	-0.016
	(0.028)
Log(Paved roads/1000 pop)	0.017
	(0.018)
Time-invariant state controls	
Product Market Regulation	-0.137*
	(0.066)
Observations	224,867
R-squared	0.048
Firm trend	yes
State-level controls	yes
Year FE	yes

Source: Annual Survey of Industries 1998–99 to 2007–08.
Notes: State-level clustered standard errors in parentheses.
$^{***}p < 0.01$, $^{**}p < 0.05$, $^{*}p < 0.1$

5.2. Robustness Checks

In the previous section, we showed that plants in more labor intensive and/or more volatile industries are the big winners of pro-worker labor reforms in India. The interactions between higher levels of EPL reform and labor intensity as well as between pro-worker EPL reform and volatility were positive and significant even after the introduction of state-level controls.

Moreover, the Appendix shows that our results are not sensitive to a different specification of the labor intensity measure. Including labor intensity in the model either as the value of $\hat{\alpha}$ or the relative ranking of each industry implied by $\hat{\alpha}$ does not affect the results presented (see Table A.2).

This section provides additional robustness tests of the impact of labor regulation on organized manufacturing plants. First, we try out two alternative measures of EPL available in the literature. We use the composite measure proposed by Gupta et al. (2008), which we refer to as EPL-G, as well as the BB index updated by ourselves through 2009 using Malik (2011). Both measures classify states into inflexible, neutral and flexible in terms of their EPL strictness.

We also check if our results hold when we use industry layoff propensity instead of labor intensity. According to Bassanini et al. (2009), the firm's natural propensity to adjust through layoffs will influence the size of the costs imposed by EPL so we would expect that plants that operate in industries that are more likely to adjust through layoffs will benefit the most from more flexible labor laws, especially those pertaining to retrenchment and firing of workers.

Column (I) in Table 6 shows the estimates using Gupta et al.'s (2008) EPL indicator.[23] If we focus on the interaction effect identified for states classified as flexible by EPL-G, the estimates are very much in line with those obtained with our measure of EPL reform.

When the BB index is used, the positive effects of labor regulation previously identified among plants in labor intensive industries go away. Column (II) in Table 6 shows that when the cumulative BB index is used, the interaction effect between EPL reform and labor intensity in states with flexible regulation is negative and significant. These results are not too surprising if we consider that the BB index only captures formal amendments to the IDA, which have been scarce in recent years. In fact, there were only four pro-employer reforms registered in Gujarat (in 2004) and two pro-employer reforms in Madhya Pradesh (in 2003) after 1999. Moreover, the correlation between BB and Dougherty's (2009) proportional index is –0.25, which could be indicating that the lack of reforms to the IDA post-1990 were compensated by formal or informal state-level changes in industrial practices on the ground.

23. Compared to our final sample of states, Gupta et al. (2008) omits two states/union territories, Delhi and Himachal Pradesh, which represent 6.2% of the plant-year observations in our complete sample.

TABLE 6. Robustness Checks: Effect of Alternative EPL Measures on Productivity and by Labor Intensity and Layoff Propensity

	(I)	*(II)*	*(III)*
Constant	1.017**	1.247***	1.261***
	(0.463)	(0.383)	(0.310)
High labor intensity	0.096***	0.246***	
	(0.014)	(0.060)	
High layoff propensity			–0.036
			(0.100)
Neutral EPL-G	0.015		
	(0.031)		
Flexible EPL-G	–0.020		
	(0.027)		
High LI x Neutral EPL-G	0.039		
	(0.053)		
High LI x Flexible EPL-G	0.163***		
	(0.045)		
Neutral EPL-BB		0.020	
		(0.030)	
Flexible EPL-BB		0.025	
		(0.034)	
High labor intensity x Neutral EPL-BB		–0.064	
		(0.066)	
High labor intensity x Flexible EPL-BB		–0.151**	
		(0.061)	
Flexible EPL			–0.029
			(0.043)
High layoff propensity x Flexible EPL			0.364***
			(0.109)
Time-variant state controls			
Log(Telephones/100 pop)	0.037	0.047**	0.052**
	(0.024)	(0.020)	(0.019)
Log(Installed electricity cap./million pop)	0.018	–0.004	–0.012
	(0.036)	(0.035)	(0.022)
Log(Paved roads/1000 pop)	–0.004	0.006	0.012
	(0.022)	(0.021)	(0.015)
Time-invariant state controls			
Product Market Regulation	–0.120*	–0.126**	–0.063
	(0.060)	(0.055)	(0.044)
Observations	215,434	224,867	224,867
R-squared	0.058	0.061	0.101
Firm trend	yes	yes	yes
State-level controls	yes	yes	yes
Year FE	yes	yes	yes

Source: Annual Survey of Industries 1998–99 to 2007–08.

Notes: State-level clustered standard errors in parentheses.

***$p < 0.01$, **$p < 0.05$, *$p < 0.1$

We conclude by testing if plants in industries with a higher layoff propensity benefit the most from labor reforms as suggested by Bassanini et al. (2009).[24] The evidence provided in column (III) in Table 6 shows that, indeed, plants in industries with higher layoff propensity experience the largest TFP improvements from state-level labor reforms. The magnitude of the interaction effect of EPL reforms and layoff propensities implies that, on average, plants in industries with a high layoff propensity are 40% more productive in flexible states than in inflexible states.

6. Conclusions

Labor reform in India has taken a backseat in discussions of structural reforms in recent years, although Supreme Court decisions related to contract labor have forced the issue of contract labor into the recent debate (AIOE 2012). Not long ago, the government expressed a newfound desire to "seiz[e] the demographic dividend", which increased the potential to put labor policies as an important issue back on the reform agenda (see MF 2013).

The collective experience of OECD countries summarized in Martin and Scarpetta (2012) suggests that flexible regulation of the labor market is essential in order to ensure that employers respond to growth of output by taking on labor rather than capital. Similarly, Dougherty (2009) found labor market reforms boosted manufacturing job creation rates in India. That analysis and compilation of state-level labor reforms suggested that it was not just the Industrial Disputes Act that was harming labor market outcomes, but rather the wider range of labor legislation. This result is consistent with the views of labor law experts that cite the complexity and uncertainty caused by the manifold overlapping laws and antiquated (often colonial-era) provisions, that are in dire need of simplification (Anant et al. 2006; Panagariya 2008; World Bank 2010).

Despite solid gains in overall employment in recent years, a dichotomy has emerged, with net increases in employment occurring almost exclusively in the least productive, unorganized and typically informal parts of the economy. This is partly due to uneven protection of employment between the formal and informal sectors, with the latter virtually unregulated, and job turnover rates among smaller—more often informal—firms being far

24. Due to lack of adequate US data, tobacco industries were dropped from our original sample. This generates a loss of 1.35% of the plant-year observations.

higher than in larger firms (Kotwal et al. 2011). Many of the productivity gains that have occurred have taken place within large continuing firms (Bollard et al. 2013; Sivadasan 2009) rather than through new entry, exit, and reallocation, as has been the case in most developing economies. Due to rigidities in the exit and expansion of firms, a very long tail of smaller, less productive firms has skewed firm size distribution in India (Alfaro and Chari 2012; Dougherty et al. 2009; Hasan and Jandoc 2013; Hsieh and Klenow 2012).

This paper studies the extent to which the effects of EPL on productivity among registered manufacturing plants change by labor intensity and sales volatility. To do this, we rely on a difference-in-differences strategy that includes state-level EPL reforms and industry-level labor intensity interactions. Our paper thus offers a likely lower bound of the perverse effects of labor market rigidities on productivity, as it measures the differential effects of labor reform across firms with different levels of labor intensity. We find that the modest easing of regulations in Indian states that has taken place in recent years was enough for firms in the more flexible states to benefit substantially through gains in total factor productivity. Our point estimates indicate that, on average, plants in labor intensive industries and in flexible labor markets have TFP residuals 25.4% higher than those registered for their counterparts in states with more stringent labor laws. A similar, but smaller effect on TFP of plants in more volatile industries and in states that experienced more pro-employer reforms is found.

We also find that the different strategies used by plants to overcome the constraints imposed by labor regulations generate heterogeneous effects of state-level labor reform both by plant size and type of ownership. Given the extensive use of contract labor among large plants and voluntary retirement schemes among public plants, smaller plants and private plants tend to accrue the largest productivity gains from state-level labor reforms.

Our study is important for three reasons. This is the first study that makes use of plant- level information from the ASI to evaluate the direct effect of EPL in India. Second, we take advantage of the recently available ASI panel data to obtain plant-level TFP measures that control for simultaneity and selection bias using the Olley–Pakes approach, whereas previous papers on the topic have only measured the effects of EPL on aggregate measures of TFP at the industry-level. Finally, our measure of labor regulation is much more comprehensive and appropriate for the post-1991 period analyzed than the BB index, popular in the EPL literature in India. Moreover, the "OECD" labor reform index used takes into account both formal and informal amendments to the labor laws at the state level that are relevant to current policy.[25]

Although our labor reform indicator shows that state-level actions, both formal and informal, have already led the way in labor reform, these reforms could be taken much further. Given that the average number of state-level reforms in the EPL index is only 21 out of 50, and the most reform-minded state only has a score of 28, there are many areas in which procedural or rule changes could be made at the state level to ease the burden of these regulations.

Given the difficulty in carrying out reforms at the central level, states may be in a better position to accelerate their own labor reform processes, such as through offering special treatment for Special Economic Zones, which can provide a laboratory for demonstrating the benefits of pro-flexibility reform. While some flexibility exists at present for states to make labor reforms, they can be aided through a constitutional amendment that would shift the jurisdiction of labor regulation from a concurrent central-state to just a state issue. In the absence of such a provision, it is necessary that the central government resolves ambiguities and provides greater clarity on the extent of the independence of the states to implement reform, particularly in areas such as contract labor and fixed-term contracts (see OECD 2007).

25. Although the coverage of our EPL reform indicator is a plus, we acknowledge the important data limitations posed by the OECD index. Our analysis could greatly benefit from a time series version of the labor reform indicator that could allow the evaluation of short versus long-term effects, as well as to include fixed effects at the state level. However, this time series is very hard to obtain, especially since the index goes beyond formal amendments to cover informal changes to labor rules and practices. Many of the latter are not systematically notified in a consolidated publication or circular, and so they are very difficult to track over time especially at the state level.

A. Appendix: Additional Tables

TABLE A.1. Descriptive Statistics: All Years

(a) All plants

Variable	*Obs*	*Mean*	*S.D.*	*Min*	*Max*
Output	240131	191.65	1143.22	0.00	97904.74
Value added	240131	24.04	106.64	–126.19	9533.84
Fixed capital	240131	77.95	507.85	0.00	42049.52
Number of workers	240131	175.75	420.80	0.00	21637.00
Investment	240131	10.29	95.20	0.00	13650.28
Fuel expenditures	240131	3.12	17.90	0.00	1330.33
Intermediate inputs	240131	136.21	878.35	0.00	66449.92
Share of contract labor	239934	0.09	0.20	0.00	1.00
Age of the plant	239298	20.92	19.61	0.00	208.00
Plant size dummies (based on # workers)					
< 50	240131	0.52		0.00	1.00
[50 – 100[	240131	0.13		0.00	1.00
[100 – 250[	240131	0.16		0.00	1.00
≥ 250	240131	0.18		0.00	1.00
Public ownership (dummy)	239995	0.23		0.00	1.00
TFP (Olley–Pakes residuals)	239171	1.04	0.54	–6.96	5.26
Volatility (S.D. of annual growth rate of output)	240131	0.67	0.19	0.31	1.01

(b) Restricted census sample

Variable	*Obs*	*Mean*	*S.D.*	*Min*	*Max*
Output	49939	737.98	2416.86	0.01	97904.74
Value added	49939	96.22	216.01	–126.19	9533.84
Fixed capital	49939	318.84	1066.52	0.00	42049.52
Number of workers	49939	646.60	745.07	200.00	21637.00
Investment	49939	40.40	196.65	0.00	13650.28
Fuel expenditures	49939	12.61	37.31	0.00	1330.33
Intermediate inputs	49939	512.64	1867.88	0.14	66449.92
Share of contract labor	49917	0.10	0.18	0.00	1.00
Age of the plant	49924	28.89	25.35	0.00	208.00
Plant size dummies (based on # workers)					
< 50	49939			0.00	0.00
[50 – 100[	49939			0.00	0.00
[100 – 250[	49939			0.00	1.00
≥ 250	49939			0.00	1.00
Public ownership (dummy)	49908			0.00	1.00
TFP (Olley–Pakes residuals)	49923	1.12	0.55	–6.96	4.06
Volatility (S.D. of annual growth rate of output)	49939	0.69	0.19	0.31	1.01

Source: Annual Survey of Industries (ASI) 1998–99 to 2007–08.

TABLE A.2. Robustness Checks: Effect of EPL Reforms on TFP by Labor Intensity as Measured by $\hat{\alpha}$ and a Relative Ranking Based on $\hat{\alpha}$

	(I)	(III)
Constant	1.578***	1.384***
	(0.410)	(0.342)
High labor intensity ($\hat{\alpha}$)	−3.137***	
	(0.664)	
High labor intensity (ranking)		−0.010
		(0.010)
Flexible EPL	−0.154**	−0.197**
	(0.058)	(0.081)
High labor intensity ($\hat{\alpha}$) x Flexible EPL	3.257***	
	(0.768)	
High labor intensity (ranking) x Flexible EPL		0.030***
		(0.011)
Time-variant state controls		
Log(Telephones/100 pop)	0.068***	0.051**
	(0.018)	(0.018)
Log(Installed electricity cap./million pop)	−0.012	−0.016
	(0.031)	(0.026)
Log(Paved roads/1000 pop)	0.018	0.016
	(0.018)	(0.016)
Time-invariant state controls		
Product Market Regulation	−0.081	−0.056
	(0.069)	(0.056)
Observations	224,0C7	224,0C7
R-squared	0.047	0.062
Firm trend	yes	yes
State-level controls	yes	yes
Year FE	yes	yes

Source: Annual Survey of Industries 1998–99 to 2007–08.
Notes: State-level clustered standard errors in parentheses.
***$p < 0.01$, **$p < 0.05$, *$p < 0.1$

References

Adhvaryu, Achyuta, Amalavoyal Chari and Siddharth Sharma. 2013. "Firing Costs and Flexibility: Evidence from Firms' Employment Responses to Shocks in India," *The Review of Economics and Statistics*, 95(3): 725–40.

Aghion, Philippe, Robin Burgess, Stephen J. Redding and Fabrizio Zilibotti. 2008. "The Unequal Effects of Liberalization: Evidence from Dismantling the License Raj in India," *American Economic Review*, 98(4): 1397–412.

Ahsan, Ahmad and Carmen Pagés. 2009. "Are all Labor Regulations Equal? Evidence from Indian Manufacturing," *Journal of Comparative Economics*, 37(1): 62–75.

AIOE. 2012. "Industrial Relations & Contract Labour in India," Technical Report, All-India Organisation of Employers.

Alfaro, Laura and Anusha Chari. 2012. "Deregulation, Misallocation, and Size: Evidence from India," NBER Working Papers 18650.

Anant, T. C. A., R. Hasan, P. Mohapatra, R. Nagraj and S. K. Sasikumar. 2006. "Labour Markets in India: Issues and Perspectives," in *Labour Markets in Asia: Issues and Perspectives,* edited by Jesus Felipe and Rana Hasan, pp. 205–300. London: Asian Development Bank and Palgrave Macmillan.

Annual Survey of Industries (ASI). 1998–99 to 2007–08 Unit Level Data. Government of India, Ministry of Statistics and Programme Implementation, New Delhi, India.

Arnold, Jens. 2005. "A Short Note on Productivity Estimation at the Firm Level. A Practical Guide," Working Paper, Bocconi University.

Bassanini, Andrea, Luca Nunziata and Danielle Venn. 2009. "Job Protection Legislation and Productivity Growth in OECD Countries," *Economic Policy, CEPR, CES, MSH*, 24: 349–402.

Basu, Susanto and John G. Fernald. 1997. "Returns to Scale in U.S. Production: Estimates and Implications," *Journal of Political Economy*, 105(2): 249–83.

Bentolila, S. and G. Bertola. 1990. "Firing Costs and Labor Demand: How Bad Is Eurosclerosis?" *Review of Economic Studies*, 57: 381–402.

Bertrand, Marianne, Esther Duflo and Sendhil Mullainathan. 2004. "How Much Should We Trust Differences-in-Differences Estimates?" *The Quarterly Journal of Economics*, 119(1): 249–75.

Besley, Timothy and Robin Burgess. 2004. "Can Labor Regulation Hinder Economic Performance? Evidence from India," *The Quarterly Journal of Economics*, 119(1): 91–134.

Bhattacharjea, Aditya. 2006. "Labour Market Regulation and Industrial Performance in India: A Critical Review of the Empirical Evidence," *The Indian Journal of Labour Economics*, 49(2): 211–32.

———. 2009. "The Effects of Employment Protection Legislation on Indian Manufacturing," *Economic and Political Weekly*, 44(2): 55–62.

Bollard, Albert, Peter J. Klenow and Gunjan Sharma. 2013. "India's Mysterious Manufacturing Miracle," *Review of Economic Dynamics*, 16(1): 59–85.

Carlsson, Mikael, Julián Messina, and Oskar Nordström Skans. 2011. "Wage Adjustment and Productivity Shocks." IZA Working Papers 5719.

Conway, Paul and Richard Herd. 2009. "How Competitive is Product Market Regulation in India? An International and Cross-state Comparison," *OECD Economic Studies*, 45(1): 149–74.

Cuñat, Alejandro and Marc Melitz. 2007. "Volatility, Labor Market Flexibility, and the Pattern of Comparative Advantage." NBER Working Papers 13062.

———. 2012. "Volatility, Labor Market Flexibility, and the Pattern of Comparative Advantage," *Journal of the European Economic Association*, 10(2): 225–54.

Davies, Ronald B. and Krishna Chaitanya Vadlamannati. 2013. "A Eace to the Bottom in Labour Standards? An Empirical Investigation," *Journal of Development Economics*, forthcoming.

Deakin, Simon, Priya Lele and Mathias Siems. 2007. "The Evolution of Labor Law: Calibrating and Comparing Regulatory Regimes," *International Labor Review*, 146(3–4): 133–62.

Dougherty, Sean. 2009. "Labour Regulation and Employment Dynamics at the State Level in India," *Review of Market Integration*, 1(3): 295–337.

Dougherty, Sean, Richard Herd and Thomas Chalaux. 2009. "What is Holding Back Productivity Growth in India? Recent Microevidence," *OECD Economic Studies*, 45(1): 59–80.

Dougherty, Sean, Veronica Frisancho and Kala Krishna. 2011. "Employment Protection Legislation and Plant-Level Productivity in India." NBER Working Papers 17693, December.

Gandhi, Amit, Salvador Navarro and David Rivers. 2013. "On the Identification of Production Functions: How Heterogeneous Is Productivity?" Working Paper.

Garibaldi, Pietro. 1998. "Job Flow Dynamics and Firing Restrictions," *European Economic Review*, 42(2): 245–75.

Goldar, Bishwanath and Suresh Chand Aggarwal. 2010. "Informalization of Industrial Labour in India: Are Labour Market Rigidities and Growing Import Competition to Blame?" Institute for Economic Growth, New Delhi, Manuscript.

Gupta, Poonam, Rana Hasan and Utsav Kumar. 2008. "Big Reforms but Small Payoffs: Explaining the Weak Record of Growth in Indian Manufacturing," *India Policy Forum*, 5(1), 59–123.

Harrison, Ann, Leslie Martin and Shanthi Nataraj. 2013. "Learning Versus Stealing: How Important are Market-share Reallocations to India's Productivity Growth?" *World Bank Economic Review*, 27(2): 202–28.

Hasan, Rana and Karl Robert Jandoc. 2013. "Labor Regulations and the Firm Size Distribution in Indian Manufacturing," In *Reforms and Economic Transformation in India*, edited by Jagdish Bhagwati and Arvind Panagariya, pp. 15–48. New York: Oxford University Press.

Hopenhayn, Hugo and Richard Rogerson. 1993. "Job Turnover and Policy Evaluation: A General Equilibrium Analysis," *Journal of Political Economy*, 101(5): 915–38.

Hsieh, Chang-Tai and Peter Klenow. 2012. "The Life Cycle of Plants in India and Mexico." NBER Working Papers 18133.

Kotwal, Ashok, Bharat Ramaswami and Wilima Wadhwa. 2011. "Economic Liberalization and Indian Economic Growth: What's the Evidence?" *Journal of Economic Literature*, 49(4): 1152–99.

Krishna, Pravin and Andrei Levchenko. 2009. "Comparative Advantage, Complexity, and Volatility." NBER Working Papers 14965.

Levinsohn, J. and A. Petrin. 2003. "Estimating Production Functions Using Inputs to Control for Unobservables." *Review of Economic Studies*, 70(2): 317–41.

Malik, P. L. 2011. *Industrial Law: A Manual of Central Labour and Industrial Laws Incorporating State Amendments with Rules, Regulations and Select Notifications.* Lucknow: Eastern Book Company.

Martin, John P. and Stefano Scarpetta. 2012. "Setting it Right: Employment Protection, Labour Reallocation and Productivity," *De Economist*, 160(2): 89–116.

MCI. 2011. *Annual Report 2010–2011*. New Delhi: Ministry of Commerce and Industry.

MF. 2013. "Seizing the Demographic Dividend," in *Union Budget & Economic Survey 2012–13*. New Delhi: Ministry of Finance.

Micco, Alejandro and Carmen Pagés. 2007. "The Economic Effects of Employment Protection: Evidence from International Industry-Level Data." IDB Research Network Working Papers 592, Inter-American Development Bank 592.

Mortensen, D. T. and C. A. Pissarides. 1999. "Unemployment Responses to 'Skill Biased' Shocks: The Role of Labor Market Policy," *The Economic Journal*, 109: 242–65.

Nagaraj, R. 2004. "Fall in Organised Manufacturing Employment: A Brief Note," *Economic and Political Weekly*, 39(30): 3387–90.

OECD. 2007. "Improving the Performance of the Labour Market," in *Economic Survey of India*. Paris: OECD.

Olley, S. and A. Pakes. 1996. "The Dynamics of Productivity in the Telecommunications Equipment Industry," *Econometrica*, 64(6): 1263–97.

Panagariya, Arvind. 2008. *India: The Emerging Giant*. New York: Oxford University Press.

Poschke, M. 2009. "Employment Protection, Firm Selection, and Growth," *Journal of Monetary Economics*, 56(8): 1074–85.

Rajan, Raghuram and Luigi Zingales. 1998. "Financial Dependence and Growth," *American Economic Review*, 88(3): 559–86.

Samaniego, Roberto M. 2006. "Employment Protection and High-tech Aversion," *Review of Economic Dynamics*, 9(2): 224–41.

Sivadasan, Jagadeesh. 2009. "Barriers to Competition and Productivity: Evidence from India," *The BE Journal of Economic Analysis & Policy*, 9(1): 1–64.

Venn, D. 2009. "Legislation, Collective Bargaining and Enforcement: Updating the OECD Employment Protection Indicators." OECD Social, Employment and Migration Working Papers 89.

World Bank. 2010. *India's Employment Challenge: Creating Jobs, Helping Workers*. Washington, D.C.: The World Bank and Oxford University Press.

WTO. 2011. *International Trade Statistics*. Geneva: World Trade Organization.

Zhang, Hongsong. 2013. "Biased Technology and Contribution of Technological Change to Economic Growth: Firm-Level Evidence." Working Paper 150225.

Comments and Discussion

Professor T. N. Srinivasan
Yale University

It is a pleasure to be back at the IPF and it was a pleasure to read the Dougherty et. al. paper on an very important issue, namely the consequences of the labor laws and the productivity gains that may accrue, were they to be relaxed or repealed. Let me start with some introduction. The draconian laws enacted by the Union Parliament during the Indira Gandhi regime in 1970s consisting of an alphabet soup—MRTP, FERA, COFEPOSA, amendments to Industrial Disputes Act (IDA) and other policies including nationalization of commercial banks, left a major impact on the functioning of the economy, mainly in the direction of poor efficiency and poor distributional consequences. A comprehensive set of controls enforced through a non-rule based discretionary system that came to be known as the Licence Permit Raj (LPR) was another feature of that legacy. The administrative and political corruption this Licence Permit Raj engendered became a cancer in the body politic. The cancer is still not in remission as one can see from reading the newspaper every day.

Reforms since mid-1980s, particularly those of 1991 and beyond, have relaxed or repealed many of the elements of the LPR. However, labor laws from amendments to the notorious IDA relating to hiring and firing of workers by enterprises employing more than a specified number of workers have not been repealed. The attempt of the later BJP Finance Minister Mr Yashwant Sinha when he was in the coalition government of Chandrasekhar to raise this specified number of workers for which the employment protection legislations apply from 100 to 1000 failed. I am not sure whether he made the attempt while he was in the Chandrasekhar government or he made the attempt while he was in the BJP government. But in either case it failed and did not go very much further. That is the background from which we should look at the work of Dougherty et al.

Now, labor is in the Concurrent List of the Seventh Schedule of the Constitution so that both States and the Center can legislate on labor. Interestingly enough, when the export processing zones were expanded in the recent decades, the States were given the opportunity to follow China and exclude the firms in the zones from the applicability of labor laws in the rest of China. But if I remember right except for Gujarat or one other state, none of the states have exploited that opportunity to relax their labor constraints even in labor export processing zones. Anyway, inter-state variation in labor laws has been exploited by several authors to identify the productivity effects of labor laws using the Diffs in Diffs technique. Dougherty et al. go further than others in many respects, in particular using a more comprehensive index for the aggregate effect of several laws in each state. Mr Bhattacharjea in his 2009 paper discusses the problems in constructing and using indexes for labor laws, and I am not going to say anything more on the index and I will leave it to him to go into them.

Now, my comments on the paper will be on three dimensions. One is on the economic theory, second is on the data used and the third is on the econometrics. The paper uses a simple microeconomic theory and econometrics to assess the impact of the theory on labor laws on total factor productivity and, in the original conference paper, on value added per worker. As Sean in his presentation did not mention anything about the results relating to value added per worker, I think it was sensible. I do not understand why one would want to use value added per worker at all: it is average labor productivity only, and does not take into account the other factors that are being used in generating labor productivity. I would ignore completely this value added per worker from the empirical analysis as, indeed, the authors have now done in this revised version.

The data used in the analysis consist of panel of plants from the census component of ASI as well as a cross section of plants from the sample component of ASI. Two important elements need to be recognized. The first element is that ASI's sample frame is dubious. There is no meaningful sample frame from which the ASI sample sector or even the census sector has been drawn. The attempt to use the enterprise census to put together a meaningful sample frame has not yet borne fruit. So, the data that are being utilized should not be viewed as being drawn from a properly drawn random sample from a universe of plants that could have been in the sample. This is a major constraint.

The second is even more important than the first for this paper. ASI data are at the plant, and not at the firm level. There are no firm level data. If you want firm level data you have to go to CMIE and that data base also has no proper sample frame. So, if you are thinking in terms of firm level analysis and that is what is relevant, there is no firm level data in India that you could use.

The theory that Sean talked about is about the behavior of firms, not about the behavior of plants. A firm could own several plants, produce different products across plants and has several options to respond to shocks.

The theory of firm behavior cannot be used to analyze what happens at the plant level without substantial modification and I do not think the paper makes any such modification.

Now, a multiplant firm has the option to respond to shocks to production or to EPLs or to output or to prices of outputs or inputs for example by closing altogether or scaling down one or more of its plants, possibly in different states and opening new plants or scaling up of existing plants in other states. That adjustment option is completely left out as far as I can see by focusing on plant level data. By the same token, a new firm entering an industrial sector could establish several plants, each possibly producing more than one product and different products across plants operating in different states. Also, a single or multiplant firm when faced with bankruptcy could seek the help of Bureau of Industrial and Financial Restructuring, the famous BIFR. There is no mention in the paper and it has been suggested that deliberately the entrepreneurs have used this mechanism for bleeding the plants, bleeding the firms, driving them to bankruptcy, and throwing the responsibility of restructuring them on the public sector in the BIFR. None of that features in the analysis.

A model of entry or exit of plants is mentioned in the paper but is not laid out explicitly. While exit option applies only to existing firms, and some firms which have not exited survive, the entry option is open to the universe of firms in India and abroad who have not yet entered. The data would be available only for firms that entered at the time of their entry but we don't have data on those who have not entered and chose not to enter. I have no idea how to deal with this issue since one doesn't have any information of the potential firms that could have entered but did not and how it is handled in the paper. I am not convinced that the Olley–Pakes (OP) method will take care of this problem. A plant level Cobb–Douglas Production Function with factor and non-factor inputs is estimated using the OP Method with the panel of plants in the census component. The same production function is assumed to apply to sample component plants as well. This is a very strong assumption. The TFP estimates calculated as a difference between actual output and the predicted output from inputs used based on the estimated production function for the entire set of plants in the dataset form the basic data for the econometric analysis. All the TFP data are from this procedure. I suspect the TFP estimates for non-census plants may not only be subject to significant measurement error but possibly be biased as well because of the possibility that the estimated production function may not apply to them.

I view the environmental protection laws as restricting the labor input choices in response to shocks. As such, to what extent choices of other inputs can mitigate or exacerbate the impact of EPL will depend on how substitutable they are to labor. I would have estimated a CES production function instead of a Cobb–Douglas production function which is also in the CES class. I would have compared the impact of environmental protection laws as a function of the elasticity of substitution and with the presumption that the impact will be a decreasing function of the elasticity. They are more elastic if you can substitute other factors for labor. The restriction on the adjustment through labor will have less of an impact but that is not what is done in the paper. The authors find that plants with higher labor intensity and more volatile output benefit from moving to states with more flexible EPLs. Labor intensity is measured mostly by the estimated elasticity of output, the Cobb–Douglas coefficient with respect to labor. Now, with labor intensity usually measured as the labor capital ratio at a given wage-rental ratio, this measure is inversely proportional to the wage-rental ratio. The elasticity of output is a constant in the Cobb–Douglas function. The wage-rental ratio and the labor capital ratio are proportional to each other and the proportionalities are increasing functions of the elasticity of output. So, instead of using labor elasticity of output as a measure of labor intensity had they used labor capital ratio it would have been better but that raises the endogeneity problem because the input choice is endogenous. But the elasticity in the production function is an exogenous measure.

Now, the econometric model of equation (3), strictly speaking, is not based on any specific economic theory. The economic theory is all about production function set up, and the Cobb–Douglas Production Function based theory is a specific one but equation (3) is a general specification and it has no specific economic theory behind it. The only sense in which theory comes in is in the measurement of TFP using Cobb–Douglas Production Function. So, this is a bit of a disappointment for me because most of the estimates being used come from the estimated parameters in equation (3), but there is no economic theory behind it other than the presumption that the coefficient should go this way or that way, it is not derived from any theory.

Now, the econometric tests are impressive. In the section on basic patterns, the cumulative density functions are, as I had recommended in my original remarks, now formally compared using the Kolmogorov–Smirnov Test for comparing distribution functions. The other thing is the errors in measurement all over the place in many variables. Now, if there was only one variable in the right hand side, which has errors of measurement we know the estimate of its coefficient would be biased downward but when more than one variable on the right hand side is measured with an error even that presumption is not true. It depends upon correlation of measurement errors across variables.

The third econometric point I would like to make is that the Olley–Pakes method yields consistent estimates of coefficients. But the consistency property of an estimate is a large sample property. As far as I can see the only relevant sample size *n* is not the number of plants observed but the number of the time periods observed. The OP method uses the investment at each time point but there are only 10 annual observations. I do not know how much you buy by using consistency property of OP estimates for a sample of 10 observations.

By and large I find that the authors have addressed all my concerns. I could quibble about whether they have satisfactorily done so in all instances; for example, the concern about the consistency property of the Olley–Pakes method that they draw upon. But quibbles apart, I am satisfied. Thank you.

Aditya Bhattacharjea
Delhi School of Economics

First, let me say there is much to admire in this paper, in particular its attempts to estimate productivity at the plant level, and its creative use of the difference-in-difference technique. Most of my reservations concern the authors' attempts to measure the restrictiveness of labor laws. But before I go down that road, let me take up a few technical points. Prof. Srinivasan and I did not consult each other on our comments, but it so happens that many of these issues have already been raised by him. Let me just mention a couple of additional areas of concern in the construction of variables other than labor regulation. The paper appears to interpolate inter-census population figures with a linear interpolation. Population of course grows exponentially, so that is not the right way of doing it. A more serious issue is that the authors take the book value of capital stock from the ASI and say that, well there is nothing much that we can do about it. But, there is quite a lot you can do about it: the standard approach is to use the perpetual inventory method with a revaluation factor to construct a capital stock series at replacement value.

So, let me come to what Prof. Srinivasan left entirely to me: the measurement of labor market flexibility. The authors start out by referring to the famous paper by Besley and Burgess. There have been many in that tradition inspired by Besley and Burgess. They all claim to be measuring the strength of EPL or the inflexibility of labor markets, using variation in state-level amendments of the IDA. A recent paper by Adhvaryu et al., cited in this paper, actually uses the term "firing costs" in the title. But when we talk of employment protection legislation or labor market inflexibility or firing costs, strictly speaking, it is only Chapter V of the Industrial Disputes Act that is relevant. In fact Sean's own OECD Survey (2007), applying a standard methodology which they use for many countries, showed that India is an outlier in terms of the stringency of EPL only on account of Chapter V(B); otherwise it is at about the average for all OECD countries. So, if we are going to talk about EPL we should focus only on Chapter V of the IDA. But the actual indices that all these authors use—whether it is the Besley–Burgess Index, or its subsequent modifications, or the OECD Index used by Sean and his co-authors—actually measure something much bigger, as I shall now show.

The Besley–Burgess index tries to quantify state-level amendments to the entire IDA, but as already pointed out by Ahsan and Pages in their 2009 paper, only some of those amendments actually involved EPL. Ahsan and Pages distinguished a distinct category of amendments which dealt with the ability of either workers or employers to initiate or sustain industrial disputes. These industrial disputes can arise out of conflicts which have little or nothing to do with employment flexibility as it is normally understood, while some of the amendments do concern the layoffs, retrenchments, and closures which are at the core of the EPL discussion. Ahsan and Pages constructed separate indices for these two distinct types of state-level amendments using Besley and Burgess' own coding which itself has problems, but they were faithful to it. Ahsan and Pages showed that there is very little correlation between these two indices, which means that the two types of amendments are really capturing two different aspects of labor regulation in the Industrial Disputes Act. I recently went through the Besley and Burgess tabulation again, and found that only 31 out of the 113 state-level amendments coded by them affected Chapter V. That is, I included not just amendments to V(B), but also V(A), which imposes somewhat less stringent restrictions on smaller firms employing between 50 and 100 workers. They do not require permission to layoff or close down, but they do have to give notice and compensation which is standard even in developed countries, except maybe the United States. I take it even further and include the relevant definition clauses of Section 2 of the IDA. So, even taking a more generous view of EPL than just Chapter V(B), less than a third of the state-level amendments coded by Besley and Burgess are relevant.

In my 2006 paper I pointed out illustratively a few gross errors made by Besley and Burgess in encoding particular amendments. Other people have constructed a "corrected" index out of these, and Dougherty et al. use one of these "corrected" indices for their robustness test. But my observations were just illustrative, and in my later paper in 2009 I pointed out several more coding errors. When I looked at the BB paper again for the purpose of this workshop I found even more, in fact, every time I look at that Act and compare it with the Besley and Burgess coding I find that they were completely wrong. It is not just a question of different interpretation of amendments. They (or probably their research assistants) made gross errors in transcribing these amendments from Malik's compendium and they constructed an index. So, that index deserves to be buried, and I think Sean has helped to bury it saying it just does not work for the more recent period.

But then people will say measurement errors in an explanatory variable cause attenuation bias; doesn't that make the BB results stronger? In fact I acknowledged that possibility in my 2006 paper, but as Prof. Srinivasan has pointed out, you can't really say that attenuation bias saves them. In fact I would go further. Attenuation bias occurs when there are random errors in the measurement of an explanatory variable, but in fact almost all the errors in the Besley–Burgess coding are in the same direction. Instead of being coded one they should have been coded zero. That would result in much less variation in the Index, and thus presumably higher standard errors. Of course one could check that by running regressions, but I would not do that, because I am on record in my 2009 paper saying that various state High Courts throughout the 1980s and 1990s struck down various sections of chapter V(B) as unconstitutional; these judgments were much later reversed with retrospective effect on appeal to the Supreme Court, or by curative amendments of the IDA. So throughout this period of uncertainty it is impossible to say whether a particular section was operative or not in a particular state.

Now, what about the index used by Sean and his co-authors? It is a definite advancement over Besley and Burgess in that it covers a wider range of laws than just the IDA. It also covers some rules that do not require legislative approval. It also tries to measure actual implementation, which is crucial because as we all know in India there is a huge gap between what is in the laws and what actually happens on the ground. And also it is an advance—as Sean pointed out—in that it covers the first few years of the current century whereas Besley and Burgess stopped their coding in 1992. But as a result of this widening of coverage, this OECD index is even less focused on the kind of restrictions which one would call EPL. I have gone through the summary of the questionnaire given in Dougherty (2009), and only six out of the 50 topics on which questions were asked concerned the IDA, and of these only three concerned EPL as normally defined.

If we take a more generous view of EPL, the Contract Workers Act is also relevant. That is the act which allows the use of contract labor in certain types of activities in certain industries, and that is left to the discretion of the state governments. Nine topics in Sean's index pertain to the Contract Labor

Act. But most of those questions do not relate to organized manufacturing which is the subject of the econometric analysis in his paper, but rather the services sector, the BPO units, and perhaps a few manufacturing units in the export processing zones. The index was compiled before the setting up of most of the new SEZs, where perhaps more generous exemptions will be given.

The other topics on which the OECD survey questions were asked concerned many other Acts and rules, as well as purely bureaucratic administrative requirements like maintenance of registers, inspections and so on: of course all very important to anyone running a business, but are these really EPL-type restrictions? In fact at one point in the paper Sean and his co-authors say, "The index was designed to capture a state's general stance toward labor regulations, more than the character of specific reforms." That is an accurate characterization of what their index actually does, but unfortunately that stray comment is going to be occluded by the many references to flexibility, inflexibility, employment protection, and job security, which are scattered throughout the paper.[26]

The measurement errors I exposed in the Besley–Burgess index are not directly relevant for the more broad-based index used in this paper, but it does suffer from a problem of indeterminacy for a different reason. As Sean has pointed out, very often their coding was not done on the basis of documented rules, but rather the respondent officials' subjective assessment of the direction of change in labor regulation. It is very possible that without formal legal backing, within a state different firms were subject to different rules, depending on their nexus with the particular official they were dealing with. So even for this index there is a strong element of uncertainty about the actual situation prevailing in a state.

So, what do these indices really measure, if not EPL? They measure what we would more generally call regulatory compliance costs and transactions costs in the labor markets, of which EPL forms a part—and an important part—but there is a lot else besides. So, all this hammering away at rigidity, inflexibility, job security, firing costs, etc., really amounts to what in literature is called synecdoche: substituting the part for the whole. Economists sometimes use figures of speech effectively, but is this kind of substitution legitimate?

26. I have already critiqued the authors' results on the interaction of EPL, labor intensity and public ownership, as reported in an earlier OECD study by Dougherty, in my 2009 *Economic and Political Weekly* article.

General Discussion

Pranab Bardhan raised two questions and made one observation. First, what do we mean by extending the analysis to labor laws other than Chapter V(B) of the Industrial Disputes Act (IDA), 1947. For example, since the reform of the latter is taken to mean the removal of Chapter V(B), are we saying that we should get rid of worker safety regulations in the Factories Act? Second, regarding the authors' claim that they are the first to use plant-level data to this type of analysis, there is a recent paper, in the World Bank Economic Review by Harisson, Martin and Nataraj who used the same ASI plant-level data. Barshan went on to observe that when he looked at the scatter of ASI data on plant size, he did not find a break in the series at 100 workers. This suggests that Chapter V(B) of IDA has not had a binding effect.

Sean Dougherty responded that he and his co-authors had found bunching of firms in the ASI data at a couple of threshold sizes when he examined the data for a couple of years. They saw it happen at around 10–20 workers and then again around 50 and again around just under 100 but the observation may be sensitive to the year of analysis and the ASI dataset. Dougherty further noted that he had seen the working paper version of the Harisson et al. paper but did not see the labor market results to which Bardhan had referred. In terms of going to labor laws beyond Chapter V(B), Dougherty said he did not think Bardhan's comment was a fair one. The paper was trying to stay clear of anything related to protection of workers' safety, so that at least it is not intended to be included in any of the measures. Instead, the paper was focusing purely on the sort of administrative, what potentially could be unnecessary administrative burdens. The focus was on regulations that don't allow for sufficient flexibility from a kind of normative perspective and the paper had tried to stay completely clear of anything that would be related to say workers' safety or basic protections and when it came to union rules, the focus was on those union rules that would obstruct making clear decisions. So, the scope of EPL and the reason the paper used it liberally was broader.

In response to the discussants' comments, Dougherty said that the ASI sample frame was indeed not ideal, so additional caution may be warranted. In terms of the firm versus plant level dimension, the paper did skirt over it a little bit. The paper is at the level of the plant although at least according to the Chief Statistician of Ministry of Statistics at the state level, plants are aggregated within state when there are multiplant firms. But Dougherty agreed that most of T. N. Srinivasan's criticisms on this aspect were warranted.

In terms of applying the production coefficients of the larger firms to small firms, Dougherty stated that this maybe a source of bias but he and his co-authors did judge that it would be better to use the Olley–Pakes method and apply to small firms rather than just using OLS method that is biased. He said that there was a suggestion that the authors could use different production function approach and he would think about that.

Returning to the size issue, Arvind Panagriya said that Rana Hassan shows that in apparel industry in 2004–05, about 93% of the work force in India is employed in firms that are less than 49 workers with 85% in firms with 7 workers or less; 5% are in large firms with 200 or more workers per firm, and in the middle you got another 2%. That is India. China is exactly the opposite. A little over 50% of workers are in the firms that are large, another 33% are in medium-size firms and the rest in small. So, in China, there are hardly any small firms and in India hardly any large firms. The question arises is, why? One can speculate. Panagariya went on to add that a reasonable hypothesis is the following. The stringency of Indian labor laws progressively rises. You go from 7 to 8, the Trade Unions Act kicks in, go from 9 to 10 when using power, the Factories Act kicks in, 19 to 20, other things kick in, if you go from 49 to 50, some additional provisions of the IDA kick in, and then you go from 99 to 100 and Chapter V(B) of IDA kicks in. In the labor-intensive sector such as apparel, where the labor costs are something like 85–90% of the per unit cost of production, only a few firms seem to bite the bullet and say that we will take advantage of the economies of scale. We will become export oriented, hit the large markets, but only those who bite the bullet are the ones which choose to operate maybe at something like 400–500 workers or even larger. There are very few such forms. Most choose to remain tiny: seven workers or less. Bunching at 100 may not be observed because you either choose to stay small or become very large to overcome the fixed costs of satisfying restrictive labor laws.

Panagariya further noted that large firms do exist in manufacturing in India but they are in the capital-intensive sectors such as automobiles. That is where labor costs are just 7 or 8% of the total costs. With high margins per-worker, these firms are able to given golden handshakes to lay off the workers. Apparel firms, in contrast, have very low margins per worker and are unable to afford such handshakes.

Panagariya then specifically asked Bardhan if it was his view that India must first sort out exactly what proportion of the productivity impact is coming from what, only then it should worry about labor law reforms, or he is saying that, well, you simply want to know the quantitative importance of different factors at work but recommend moving ahead with the labor law reforms?

Bardhan answered that the Chinese firms were large partially because historically they were owned by the state and state-owned firms tended to be large. He also argued that while the Chinese labor laws were flexible, of late, they were becoming more stringent though not as stringent as in India. He added that China also has a much better infrastructure. He asked what prevented the eight employees to become 80 employees, because the labor law does not kick in.

To the question of labor reforms, Bardhan said that yes, he wanted the reforms. But he did not think that labor reforms alone would suffice and that labor reform had to be a package deal: while making labor law more flexible, sufficient unemployment compensation must be introduced.

Another speaker from the floor said that the strongest evidence of the benefits of labor market flexibility in terms of generating employment existed in our own backyard. Just compare employment growth in manufacturing versus employment growth in services which are not bound by the IDA and therefore the binding constraint of the inflexibility or the barriers to firing and you have evidence that labor market flexibility does work. But the analytical foundation I think requires little bit of tightening because the direct link in labor market reform and productivity growth is subject to many complexities along the way; for example, the states that have flexible labor markets also have better provision of other factors such as infrastructure, coastline giving better access to the world markets and so on. So, there may be a sort of a correlation coming out of that overall reform strategy which is contributing to productivity growth, not necessarily what has just happened in the labor front.

The speaker added that the proximate outcomes of labor market reform which are the most important policy objectives are those that will bring more workers into the formal or the organized sector which then gives them all of the protections and the rights that you would like them to have. Such movement will also mean greater role for larger firms where productivity is higher. So, the prediction is if you have labor reforms, you have (a) a larger share of organized sector employment in manufacturing and (b) a larger share of workers in large establishments. Productivity is an outcome. This is sufficient policy justification for labor reforms. It is not necessary to go as far as saying that we have to have evidence on productivity growth.

Shekhar Shah suggested whether there was need to undertake an exercise for developing a comprehensive labor-law regime that would replace all existing labor laws. The motivation for this exercise comes from a similar exercise undertaken for financial sector in India, which was sponsored by the Ministry of Finance. Shah said that he was pointing to the Financial Sector Legislative Reform Commission that had just issued its report and had come up with an Indian Financial Code that would comprehensively look at consumer protection, systemic risk and micro-prudential measures. Much in the same way one could think of a similar exercise in labor market.

Rajnish Mehra suggested that an experiment could be run using the plant-level data to verify if labor laws had a bite. You have firms with plants in many different states. Firms can be assumed to allocate capital optimally across plants. One could then look at capital-labor ratios across states and verify if these differ significantly. If not, then we have some prima facie evidence that these laws are actually not binding and maybe there is subcontracting and other things that allow the firms to get around the stringency.

Sean Dougherty responded that his paper certainly did not argue that labor reform was the only issue involved. Infrastructure was clearly a major burden. The paper did try to include some simple-minded measures of infrastructure in the equations and they were not that significant or in any case they did not affect the results. So there did seem to be an independent role that labor market rigidities were playing. So, the paper's working hypothesis was that there was an overall difficult climate for labor and the transaction costs were quite high and a very broad clean up and clarification of labor market regime was probably necessary.

Dougherty suggested that uncertainty was a much bigger burden than clear rigidity. If you knew that the regime was rigid and clear at least you knew what you were going to have to pay to layoff some workers but frequently employers didn't know and they couldn't even get approval when they were willing to pay large costs, so, sometimes they just abandoned firms.

On the issue of moving workers into the formal sector, Dougherty said that his study had focused on mid-sized to larger firms within the ASI. It did not focus on the transition from informal to formal sector, which is a subject needing further research. This would require a careful integration of the NSS data with the ASI data because that is exactly where the divergence lies.

Dougherty concluded with a final comment on multiplant-firm issue. He said he was not aware of a straightforward strategy using existing Indian data to look at the multiplant aspect. T. N. Srinivasan had mentioned about work done by others, you could get a little bit there but there seemed no straight forward way to tie multiplant firms to specific plants. There is some limited data on this area in the CMIE data but that is for very large firms and it only has limited information at the plant level. Within the ASI data, there is no way to actually tie the plants across states to the firm identity.

PREMA-CHANDRA ATHUKORALA*
Arndt-Corden Department of Economics, Crawford School of Public Policy, Australian National University

How India Fits into Global Production Sharing: Experience, Prospects, and Policy Options

ABSTRACT Global production sharing—the breakup of the production processes into separate stages, with each country specializing in a particular stage of the production sequence—is a phenomenon of major significance that is increasingly manifesting itself in patterns of global production and trade. This paper examines India's role in global production sharing from a comparative East Asian perspective in order to contribute to the contemporary policy debate in India on the link between export performance and "jobless growth" in domestic manufacturing in India. The analysis reveals that India has so far failed fitting into global production networks in electronics and electrical goods, which have been the prime movers of export dynamism in China and the other high-performing East Asian countries. Further reforms to improve the overall investment climate is even more important for reaping gains from this new form of international exchange compared to the standard labor-intensive exports. There is also a strong case, based on the experiences in East Asia and elsewhere, for combining further reforms with a proactive investment promotion campaign to attract multinational enterprises engaged in global production networks.

Keywords: *Global Production Sharing, Production Fragmentation, Foreign Direct Investment, Export Performance*

JEL Classification: *F21, F23, F53, O33*

1. Introduction

Global production sharing—the breakup of the production processes into separate stages, with each country specializing in a particular stage of the production sequence—has been an increasingly important facet

* *Prema-chandra.athukorala@anu.edu.au*

I am grateful to the two discussants, Mihir Desai and Rajesh Chadha, and participants at the IPF, including T.N. Srinivasan, Rajnish Mehra, and Rohini Somanathan for excellent comments and suggestions. I also thank Shekhar Shah and Vijay Joshi for encouraging me to write the paper and Arvind Panagariya for his guidance in finalizing it for publication. Omer Majeed and Shahbaz Nasir provided excellent research assistance.

of economic globalization over the past four decades.[1] This process of international division of labor opens up opportunities for countries to specialize in different slices (tasks) of the production process in line with their relative cost advantages. Global production sharing is heavily concentrated within industries which are commonly classified as high-tech and capital-intensive, such as electronic, electrical goods, and transport equipment. However, economic theory postulates, and the East Asian experience illustrates, that in a labor abundant economy, tasks undertaken within global production networks tend to be relatively more labor-intensive (and hence "pro–poor"). Moreover, trade based on global production sharing, that is parts and components and final assembly traded within global production networks, has been growing at a much faster rate compared to traditional labor-intensive products such as apparel, footwear and sport goods.

The purpose of this paper is to examine India's role in global production sharing from a comparative East Asian perspective, with a view to broaden our understanding of why India is lagging behind China and other emerging East Asian economies in benefitting from this new form of international exchange. The paper is motivated by the growing emphasis in the contemporary policy debate in India on the link between emerging export patterns and "jobless growth" of domestic manufacturing (Bhagwati and Panagariya 2013; Joshi 2008; Panagariya 2008, 2013; Panagariya and Sundaram 2013). Although the rate of export growth has been much faster during the past two decades, India still remains a small player in world manufacturing trade, and the composition of manufacturing exports has continued to exhibit a bias on capital- and skill-intensive products (Veeramani 2012). Recent studies of India's export performance, and the failure of emerging export patterns to reflect the country's comparative advantage in labor-intensive production, have largely focused on the country's relative performance in the standard labor-intensive manufactured goods such as clothing and footwear. The implications of the ongoing process of global production sharing for effective integration of the Indian economy into global manufacturing networks and the related policy issues have not been systematically explored. This paper aims to fill this gap, focusing specifically on merchandise exports.[2]

The paper is structured as follows: Section 2 provides a stage-setting analytical overview of the process of global production sharing, patterns, and determinants of network trade, and emerging opportunities for countries

1. In the recent international trade literature an array of alternative terms have been used to describe this phenomenon, including international production fragmentation, intra-process trade, vertical specialization, slicing the value chain, and offshoring.

2. India's role in production sharing in the global software services industry has been extensively studied. See Arora (2008) and the works cited therein.

to specialize in line with their relative cost advantage. Section 3 surveys India's export performance during the reform period in order to provide the context for the ensuing analysis. Section 4 examines emerging patterns of world network trade and India's comparative performance, paying particular attention to complementarities in production sharing between India and the East Asian countries. An econometric analysis is undertaken in Section 5 using the standing gravity modeling framework to examine the determinants of inter-country differences in the degree of involvement in network trade. Section 6 summarizes the key findings, followed by a discussion on policy options for India to effectively link domestic manufacturing into global production networks. The analysis in Sections 4 and 5 is based on a systematic separation of trade in parts and components and final assembly ("network trade") from total manufacturing trade flows using data set extracted from the United Nations (UN) trade database. The procedure followed in data compilation is discussed in the Appendix.

2. Global Production Sharing

Global production sharing is not entirely a new phenomenon.[3] What is new about the contemporary process of global production sharing is its wider and ever increasing product coverage, and its rapid spread from mature industrial countries to developing countries.[4] With a modest start in the electronics industry in the late 1960s, international production networks have gradually evolved encompassing many developing countries and spreading to many industries such as sport footwear, automobile, televisions and radio receivers, sewing machines, office equipment, electrical machinery, machine tools, cameras, watches, light emitting diodes, solar panel, and surgical and medical devices. In general, industries that have the potential to break up the production process to minimize the transport cost involved are more likely to move to peripheral countries than other heavy industries.

3. By the late 1950s, when the national trade data reporting systems of mature industrial countries had begun to produce disaggregated data to warrant some tentative estimation, components of machinery accounted for nearly 15% of manufacturing exports of these countries (calculation based on the data appendix in Maizels 1963).

4. Production sharing can occur both within a given country and across national border. The sole focus of this paper is on the latter, the international dimension of production sharing, which is directly relevant for understanding the patterns and determinants of India's comparative export performance. Of course, for a systematic analysis of the growth impact of the export performance it is important to probe both aspects of global production sharing, because activities of domestic firms that undertake subcontracting for exporting firms are not captured in the standard trade data.

The expansion of global production sharing has been driven by three mutually reinforcing developments (Helpman 2011; Jones 2000; Jones and Kierzkowski 2001, 2004; Yi 2003). First, rapid advancements in production technology have enabled the industry to slice up the value chain into finer, "portable" components. As an outcome of advances in modular production technology, some fragments of the production process in certain industries have become "standard fragments" which can be effectively used in a number of products.[5] Second, technological innovations in communication and transportation have shrunk the distance that once separated the world's nations, and improved speed, efficiency, and economy of coordinating geographically dispersed production process. This has facilitated, and reduced the cost of, establishing "service links" needed to combine various fragments of the production process across countries in a timely and cost efficient manner.[6] Third, liberalization policy reforms across the world over the past four decades have considerably removed barriers to trade and foreign direct investment (FDI).

At the early phase of development (in the 1960s and 1970s), production sharing was basically a two-way exchange between the home and host countries undertaken by multinational enterprise (MNEs); parts and components were exported to the low-cost, host country for assembly and the assembled components were re-imported to the home country to be incorporated in the final product (Brown and Linden 2005; Grunwald and Flamm 1985; Helleiner 1973). As production operations in the host countries became firmly established, MNE subsidiaries began to subcontract some activities to local (host country) firms, providing the latter with detailed specifications and even fragments of their own technology. Over time, many firms which were not part of original MNE networks have begun to undertake final assembly by procuring components globally through arm's-length trade, benefitting from the ongoing process of standardization of parts and components. These developments suggest that an increase in production-sharing based trade may or may not be accompanied by an increase in the

5. Examples include long-lasting cellular batteries originally developed by computer producers and now widely used in cellular phones and electronic organizers; transmitters which are now used not only in radios (as originally designed) but also in computers; and electronic chips which have spread beyond the computer industry into consumer electronics, motor vehicle production and many other product sectors.

6. There is an important two-way link between improvement in communication technology and the expansion of production sharing within global industries. The latter results in lowering the cost of production and rapid market penetration of the final products through enhanced price competitiveness. Scale economies resulting from market expansion in turn encourage new technological efforts, enabling further fragmentation of production processes (Jones and Kierzkowski 2004).

host country's FDI and focusing on MNEs as the sole agent of global production sharing leads to an underestimation of the importance of the phenomenon (Brown et al. 2004; Jones 2000). However, there is clear evidence that MNEs are still the leading vehicle for developing countries to enter global production networks. The presence of key players in a particular country is vital, both as an "investment-stalk" or signalling effect to other foreign firms less familiar with that country, and an agglomeration magnet by which firms benefit from being part of a geographical network or cluster-related activities and specialized support services (Dunning 2009; Lall 2002; Ruwane and Gorg 2001; Wells and Wint 2000).[7]

As supply networks of parts and components became firmly established, producers in advanced countries have begun to move final assembly of an increasing range of products (for example, computers, mobile phones, and other hand-held devices, TV sets and motor cars) to developing country locations (Krugman 2008). Many of the MNEs in electronics and related industries now undertake final assembly in developing country locations, retaining only design and coordination functions at home. A major development in the institutional setting for global production sharing which facilitated this process is the emergence of a new breed of MNCs, contract manufacturers, which undertake final assembly for original manufacturing MNEs using parts and components procured from various producers (Sturgeon 2002).[8] Many original manufacturing MNEs in electronics and related industries have begun to rely increasingly on contract manufacturers (CMs) as their "virtual assembly plant," while increasingly focusing on competencies such as product design and sales promotion.

There is evidence that trade in parts and components, and final assembly traded within global production networks (henceforth referred to as

7. However, the experiences of South Korea and Taiwan have some unique features. Firms in these two countries entered global production network from the early 1990s without direct involvement of MNEs through FDI. Korean companies relied on imports of capital equipment, plans and core components, mainly from Japan with the Japanese trading companies playing a vital intermediary role. In Taiwan, Taiwanese and Chinese American entrepreneurs who had a strong presence among Silicon Valley firms started assembly firms drawing on their connections with US MNEs (Feenstra and Hamilton 2006). In both countries some of these firms have grown to become major MNEs in their own right within global production networks. In the early 1970s, at the initial stage of global production sharing, MNEs set up production bases in Southeast Asian countries bypassing Korea and Taiwan, because of the highly selective FDI approval policy that did not permit full foreign ownership (Grunwald and Flamm 1985), and also presumably because of political risk considerations, "the upheaval caused by the Cultural Revolution in the mid- and late 1960s" (Goh 1993: 253).

8. The best example is Foxconn, a Taiwanese contract manufacturer that assembles all products of Apple Corporation from its production bases located in China.

"network trade") has grown at a much faster rate than total world manufacturing trade over the past four decades. In a pioneering analysis of trade data for the OECD countries, Yeats (2001) found that parts and components accounted for 30% of total trade in machinery and transport equipment[9] of these countries in 1996, compared to around 15% in the middle of 1980s. According to estimates by Ng and Yeats (2003), exports of parts and components from Asian countries increased more than fivefold over the period 1984–96, compared to an approximately three-fold increase in total merchandise exports. Following Yeats's approach, but with broader commodity coverage, Athukorala (2011) estimated the share of parts and components in total world manufacturing trade in 2007 at 32.1%, up from 23.6% in 1992. According to his estimates, total network trade (parts and components, and final assembly) accounted for over a half of total manufacturing trade in 2007. A number of studies have used the input–output technique to measure the degree of dependence of manufacturing production and trade of selected countries on global production sharing (Dean et al. 2011; Hummels et al. 2001; Johnson and Noguera 2012; Koopman et al. 2008). Hanson et al. (2001 and 2005) have measured the extent of production sharing using trade flows between US multinational enterprises and their foreign affiliates. All these studies, regardless of the yardstick used, point to the growing importance of production sharing in world trade and increasing cross-border interdependencies in the world economy.[10]

In recent years the popular press has begun to pay attention to the phenomenon of "reshoring" (also termed "reverse offshoring" or "onshoring"), shifting by MNEs of manufacturing facilities from overseas locations to the home country (Gray et al. 2013). There have been a number of highly published cases of US MNEs reshoring (or planning to restore) assembly processes from China to plants in the United States. However, whether this is a new structural (lasting) phenomenon, or simply a case of some isolated instances of shifting production bases receiving media attention against the backdrop of the political rhetoric of "bringing manufacturing back home" and the erosion of the size of the United States–China wage differentials, is yet to be seen. As Gray et al. (2013: 31) argue: "….as emerging economies grow and thus demand increases in these locations while levelling in the

9. These are the products belonging to Section 7 of the Standard International Trade Classification (SITC 7). They roughly account for more than one-half of all trade in manufacturing.

10. In addition to these direct quantifications, there are a large number of case studies and media commentaries of the nature and growing importance of production sharing (Krugman 2008 provides a summary).

United States and other developed countries, firm might want to reconsider their location decisions....to be close in proximity to demand." Also, as we have already discussed, global production sharing has already expanded well beyond the domain of the MNEs headquartered in the United States and the other developed countries.

Global production sharing opens up opportunities for developing countries to participate in a finer international division of labor. The nature of factor intensity of the given segments and the relative prices of factor inputs in comparison with their productivity jointly determine which country produces what components. It may be that workers in a given country tend to have different skills from those in other countries, and the skills required in each production block differ so that a dispersion of activity could lower marginal production cost (as in the Ricardian model). Alternatively, it may be that the production blocks differ from each other in the proportion of different factors required, enabling firms to locate labor-intensive production blocks in countries where productivity adjusted labor cost is relatively low (as in the Heckscher–Ohlin model). However, several preconditions need to be satisfied for a country to effectively participate in international production networks.

First, assembly processes within production networks require much more middle-level supervisory manpower (in addition to the availability of trainable low-cost unskilled labor) than the traditional labor-intensive manufacturing.[11] Under global production sharing, developed countries normally shift low skill-intensive parts of the value chain to developing countries. But, the least skill-intensive activities in the developed country can be more skill-intensive than the most skill-intensive activities in the developing country (Feenstra and Hanson 2003). Second, successful participation in global production sharing will not occur if the extra costs of service links associated with production sharing—cost involved in arrangements for connecting/coordinating activities into a smooth sequence resulting in the production of the final good—outweigh the gain from the lower costs of the activity abroad. These extra costs relate to transportation, communication, and other related tasks involved in coordinating the activity in a given country with what is done in other countries within the production network. Third, the policy regime and the domestic investment climate need to be conducive for involvement in production sharing. The decision of a firm

11. See also Steve Jobs' discussion with President Obama on Apple's assembly operations in China in Isaacson (2011: 546). "At that time, Apple had 700,000 factory worker employed in China, and that was because it needed 30,000 engineers on-site to supervise those workers. If you could educate these engineers, he said, we could move more manufacturing plants here."

to outsource production processes to another country—either by setting up an affiliated company or establishing an arm's length relationship with a local firm—entails "country risks". This is because supply disruptions in a given overseas location could disrupt the entire production chain. Such disruptions could be the product of shipping delays, political disturbances, or labor disputes (in addition, of course, to natural disasters). In many instances it is impossible to fully offset these risks by writing "complete contracts" (Helpman 2006; Spencer 2005).

Finally, why should governments in developing countries pay specific attention to global production sharing as part of outward oriented development strategy? There is no hard empirical evidence to address this issue. But the available evidence on the emerging patterns of global production sharing, when combined with the standard literature on gains from export oriented development (e.g., Dornbusch 1992; Grossman and Helpman 1992; Srinivasan 1999), suggests that growth prospects would be greatly enhanced through engaging in this form of international exchange. As discussed, network trade accounts for a large and increasing share of world manufacturing trade compared to the traditional manufactured goods such as apparel and footwear. Thus there can be considerable gains from improved resource allocation in line with social marginal cost and benefits, and from economies of scale and scope that arise in wider markets. Participation in global production sharing also has the potential to yield growth externalities (spillover effects) through transfer of technology and managerial know-how, skill development, and "atmosphere creation" effect. Engaging in global production sharing is an effective way of linking domestic manufacturing to dynamic global industries of electronics, electrical goods, medical devices, and transport equipment, which are the incubators of new technology and managerial skills. Labor training in a given stage/segment of a production process not only helps in moving up the value ladder within the given industry but also helps attract new investors in related industries by creating a pool of skilled labor.[12] Finally, participation in global production sharing is likely to have a favorable atmospheric effect: the creation of a Schumpeterian environment conducive to growth. The very nature of the process of global production is the continuous shaking up of industry through the emergence of new products and production processes in place of old

12. For instance the trained labor pool created by semiconductor assembly was a key pull factor for the subsequent expansion of hard disk drive industry in Singapore and Malaysia. More recently Penang (Malaysia) has become a preferred location for the major MNEs in the medical devices industry because of the availability of a sizeable skilled labor pool created by the electronics industry over the past two decades (Athukorala 2014; Wong 2007).

ones. Engagement in a manufacturing process involving a variety of goods and inputs could contribute more to growth than perpetual specialization in a narrow range of products.

3. India's Export Performance: An Overview

During the first four decades of the postindependence era India continued to remain an underperformer in world export markets, relative to both her own potential and the performance of many other developing countries. The overriding aim of the Indian development policy from the inception was across-the-board import substitution in the context of a foreign trade regime, which relied extensively on quantitative restrictions (QRs). Until about the mid-1970s the overall policy trend was towards tightening controls on both foreign trade and domestic industry. The pull of resources into import substitution industries by the high level of protection, plus overvaluation of the real exchange rate resulting from upwards shift in demand for imports and a rate of domestic inflation above that of trading partners, discouraged production for export. Also, the inflexibilities created by the pervasive controls on domestic manufacturing handicapped the ability of firms to penetrate export markets (Panagariya 2004, 2008; Singh 1964; Srinivasan 1998).

India's share of world non-oil exports fell continuously from 2.3% in the 1950s to 0.6% in the 1970s as shown in Figure 1. Notwithstanding some selective measures introduced to ameliorate the anti-export bias, India's world market share fell further to an average level of 0.5% by the middle of the 1980s. The degree of export orientation of the economy, measured by exports to GDP ratio, remained virtually unchanged around 6% throughout the 1970s and 1980s. The fall in India's share in total exports from developing countries during this period was much sharper, from 3.2% in the 1960s to 1.5% during the 1980s. Moreover, India's failure to keep up with overall export performance of other developing countries[13] was much more clearly visible in manufacturing trade: India accounted for 2.6% of manufacturing exports from developing countries in the late 1980s, compared to 10.2% in the early 1960s. In 1962 (the earliest year for which comparable country-level data are available), India was the second largest exporter of manufactured goods in the developing world (accounting for 14.2% of exports from

13. In this paper the standard United Nations country classification is used to identify developing countries. According to this classification "developing countries" encompasses developing Asia (the member countries of the Asian Development Bank), Latin America, Africa, and the Middle East.

developing countries after Hong Kong (19.8%). By the time the liberalization reforms began in the early 1990, India was the 10th largest exporter (2.6%), after the Philippines (2.9%), and China's share (25.6%) was over 10 times larger than that of India.[14]

FIGURE 1. India's Share in Total World Exports and Exports from Developing Countries, 1962–2011[1]

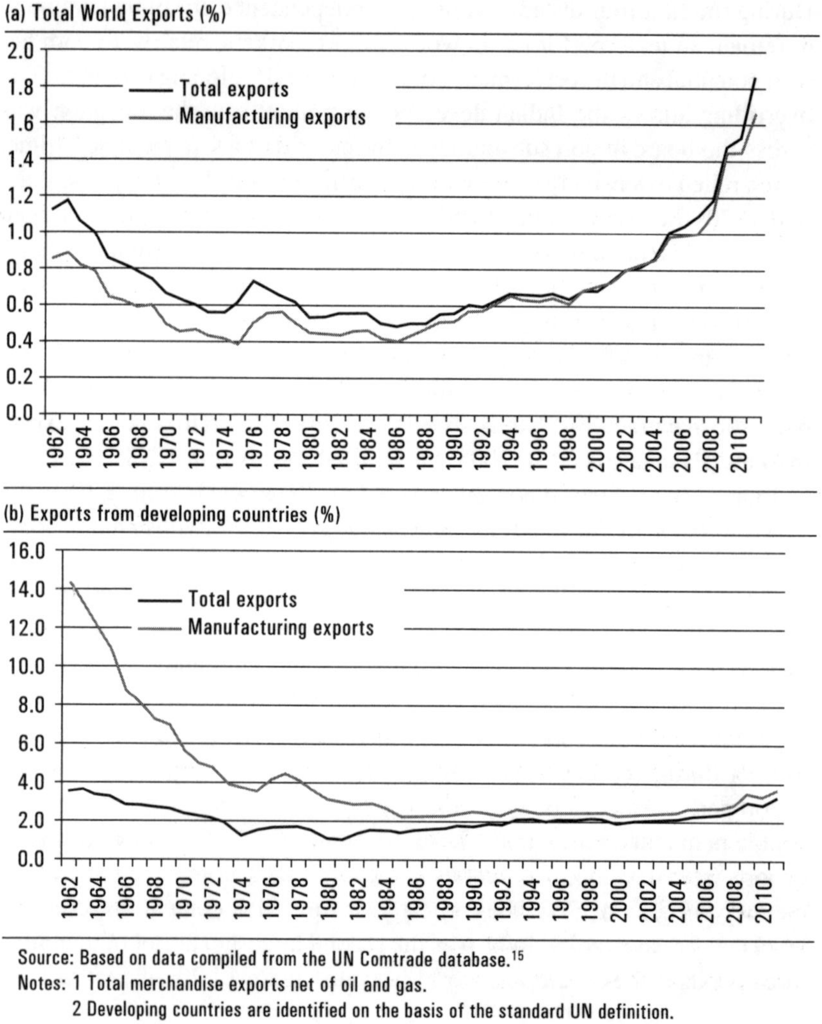

Source: Based on data compiled from the UN Comtrade database.[15]

Notes: 1 Total merchandise exports net of oil and gas.

2 Developing countries are identified on the basis of the standard UN definition.

14. The data reported in this paper, unless otherwise stated, are based on the UN *Comtrade* database (http://comtrade.un.org/db/ accessed in January–March 2013).

15. http://comtrade.un.org/db/ (accessed in January–March 2013)

India's overall export performance has improved significantly following the liberalization reforms. Its share in total world non-oil exports recovered to the level of the early 1960s (about 1.2%) by 2002 and increased further to 1.8% in 2011. However, as yet there has not been any noticeable improvement in India's relative export performance among developing countries. Its share in total exports from developing countries has not yet surpassed the levels of the early 1960s (about 3.8%). India has so far failed to cash in on the "the great transformation of world trade" (Krugman 2008: 103), the dramatic shift in manufacturing exports from developed to developing countries that has occurred over the past four decades.

In Tables 1 and 2 India's export performance is compared with the East Asian developing countries by broad commodity categories.[16] India's share in world manufacturing exports increased from 0.6% in 1990–91 to 1.6% in 2010–11. Over the same period, China's share jumped from 2.5% to 15.3%. By 2010–11, China was accounting for 38.5% of total manufacturing exports from developing countries compared to India's share of 4.2%. The share of manufactured goods in total non-oil exports has continued to remain low (around 80%) in India compared to China and most other countries in East Asia.

India's world market shares in all commodity categories have increased over the past three decades, but no particular commodity category stands out for markedly rapid world market penetration in a comparison with the East Asian countries. During this period, Indian export expansion has been heavily concentrated in two product categories: resource-based products (products classified by material, Standard International Trade Classification, SITC 6),[17] and miscellaneous product (SITC 8, clothing, footwear, and other standard labor-intensive products).[18] A startling difference in India's export patterns compared to China and the other East Asian countries is the rather small share accounted for by the product group of machinery and transport

16. In order to minimize the effect of possible random shocks and measurement errors, henceforth two-year averages are used in inter-temporal comparison throughout this paper. All data are calendar year based.

17. Gems and jewelry, which constitute over 15% of Indian exports, are included in this category.

18. It is important to note that even in miscellaneous manufactured goods, a product group in which India has considerable untapped potential, India's performance has been lacklustre in international comparisons. For instance, between 2005 and 2012, India's share in world apparel exports remained virtually unchanged around 5.3% whereas Bangladesh's share surged from 4.5% to 8.1% (data compiled from the UN Comrade database). India's export performance in apparel and other labor intensive manufactured goods has been extensively documented and analyzed by Panagariya (2008).

TABLE 1. Shares in World Manufacturing Exports: India and Developing East Asian (DEA) Countries, 1990–91, 2000–2001, and 2010–11 (%)[1]

				Manufacturing (SITC 5 to 8–68)				
		Total exports[2]	*Primary products (1 to 4 + 68)*	*Total*	*Chemicals and related products (5)*	*Products classified by material (6 – 68)*	*Machinery and transport equipment (7)*	*Miscellaneous manufacturing (8)*
India	1990–91			0.6	0.5	1.4	0.1	2.2
	2000–01	0.8	1.1	0.7	0.8	2.0	0.1	2.9
	2010–11	1.6	2.0	1.6	1.6	3.4	0.7	3.2
East Asia countries	1990–91	15.2	12.1	16.3	7.3	15.7	17.3	69.3
	2000–01	20.2	12.2	22.4	11.9	20.0	29.5	47.6
	2010–11	29.1	15.0	33.1	17.5	27.2	45.5	57.0
China	1990–91	2.5	2.7	2.5	1.4	3.6	1.3	13.0
	2000–01	4.6	3.4	5.0	2.2	5.3	4.5	18.6
	2010–11	12.8	3.4	15.3	5.9	13.9	19.5	37.9
Hong Kong	1990–91	3.6	1.3	4.1	2.1	4.6	3.5	15.6
	2000–01	3.6	0.9	4.1	1.7	3.4	4.3	12.2
	2010–11	3.2	0.5	3.7	1.1	2.2	6.4	6.5
Korea, Rp	1990–91	2.5	0.8	2.9	1.0	3.2	2.7	10.0
	2000–01	2.8	0.7	3.2	2.3	3.5	3.9	2.4
	2010–11	3.5	0.7	4.2	3.2	3.3	4.5	0.5
Taiwan	1990–91	2.2	0.7	2.8	0.8	2.8	2.8	18.6
	2000–01	2.6	0.5	3.3	1.9	3.8	4.7	6.0
	2010–11	2.5	0.5	3.2	1.9	3.1	5.0	3.9
Indonesia	1990–91	0.6	1.3	0.5	0.3	1.3	0.0	2.6
	2000–01	0.8	1.8	0.7	0.5	1.4	0.5	2.4
	2010–11	1.1	3.9	0.6	0.6	1.2	0.4	2.0

(Table 1 Contd)

(Table 1 Contd)

Malaysia	1990–91	1.0	1.9	0.8	0.2	0.5	1.5	1.9
	2000–01	1.5	1.3	1.6	0.7	0.8	3.2	1.1
	2010–11	1.3	1.8	1.3	0.8	0.9	2.2	1.1
Philippines	1990–91	0.2	0.3	0.1	0.1	0.1	0.2	1.2
	2000–01	0.6	0.4	0.7	0.1	0.2	1.5	1.3
	2010–11	0.4	0.3	0.3	0.1	0.2	0.7	0.4
Singapore	1990–91	1.7	1.1	1.8	1.3	0.8	3.6	2.2
	2000–01	2.2	0.6	2.4	1.7	0.6	4.7	0.9
	2010–11	2.3	0.5	2.5	2.6	0.7	4.5	0.3
Thailand	1990–91	0.9	2.1	0.7	0.2	0.7	0.8	4.2
	2000–01	1.2	2.0	1.1	0.7	1.0	1.5	1.9
	2010–11	1.5	2.2	1.4	1.2	1.3	1.7	1.2
Vietnam	1990–91	–	–	–	–	–	–	–
	2000–01	0.2	0.7	0.1	0.0	0.1	0.1	0.9
	2010–11	0.6	1.1	0.5	0.1	0.5	0.4	3.1
Developing countries	1990–91	19.0	21.2	19.2	9.8	21.5	18.6	81.7
	2000–01	26.7	23.7	28.4	15.6	28.4	34.4	63.6
	2010–11	36.9	30.7	39.7	22.1	37.2	50.4	68.0
World, $ billion	1990–91	2,708.6	407.5	2,241.9	274.7	472.4	749.1	76.4
	2000–01	5,469.8	615.2	4,602.5	567.0	820.2	1,764.7	195.2
	2010–11	13,400.4	1,914.8	10,756.6	1,724.1	2,051.3	3,808.1	373.9

Source: Compiled from UN Comtrade database.[19]

Notes: 1. Standard International Trade Classification (SITC) codes are given in brackets.
2. Excluding oil and gas.
– Data not available.

19. http://comtrade.un.org/db/ (accessed in January–March 2013).

TABLE 2. Composition of Exports: India and Developing East Asian (DEA) Countries, 1990–91, 2000–2001, and 2010–11 (%)

		Primary products (1 to 4 less 68)	Manufacturing (5 to 8–68)					Total US$ billion
			Total	Chemicals and related products (5)	Products classified by material (6–68)	Machinery and transport equipment	Miscellaneous manufacturing (8)	
India	1990–91	24.9	73.3	8.1	36.6	7.6	20.9	17.5
	2000–01	17.1	80.4	11.0	39.7	8.3	21.4	41.4
	2010–11	17.6	78.0	12.8	32.3	17.2	15.6	214.1
East Asia	1990–91	12.0	88.9	4.9	18.0	34.9	28.8	411.2
	2000–01	6.8	93.0	6.1	14.9	50.8	21.3	1,106.1
	2010–11	7.4	91.2	7.7	14.3	50.9	17.8	3,905.1
China	1990–91	16.4	83.6	5.5	25.1	16.8	36.2	67.5
	2000–01	8.2	91.6	5.0	17.1	35.2	34.3	252.5
	2010–11	3.8	96.1	5.9	16.6	49.2	24.4	1,712.5
Hong Kong	1990–91	5.3	94.3	5.8	22.2	28.5	37.8	98.6
	2000–01	2.9	96.5	5.0	14.4	39.2	37.9	196.4
	2010–11	2.3	93.3	4.5	10.6	57.5	20.7	427.3
Korea, Rp	1990–91	4.8	95.0	4.2	22.6	41.2	26.9	67.3
	2000–01	2.8	96.3	8.6	18.7	61.3	7.8	152.7
	2010–11	2.7	96.7	11.7	14.7	60.3	10.1	468.0
Taiwan	1990–91	4.6	95.4	3.7	22.0	48	30.9	71.7
	2000–01	2.0	98.0	7.5	21.5	65.3	11.5	139.1
	2010–11	3.1	96.9	9.9	18.6	59.5	7.7	291.5
Indonesia	1990–91	33.1	66.0	4.5	36.9	3.2	21.5	16.4
	2000–01	24.0	75.1	6.6	25.8	21.7	21	45.7
	2010–11	51.0	47.8	6.8	16.3	14.2	10.5	145.7

(Table 2 Contd)

(Table 2 Contd)

Malaysia	1990–91	28.9	70.5	2.0	9.5	46.4	12.6	26.5
	2000–01	9.2	89.8	4.5	7.8	68.2	9.3	84.1
	2010–11	19.6	79.6	7.8	11.0	49.6	11.3	177.1
Philippines	1990–91	25.5	74.5	3.6	8.9	29.1	33	4.3
	2000–01	6.5	93.2	1.0	3.8	76.1	12.3	34.7
	2010–11	12.6	76.1	3.5	8.1	57.4	7	48.7
Singapore	1990–91	9.8	88.4	7.8	8.6	61.1	10.9	46.0
	2000–01	3.2	92.7	8.1	4.1	71.3	9	120.1
	2010–11	3.3	86.7	14.6	4.7	58.9	8.5	311.8
Thailand	1990–91	33.3	65.5	2.4	13.0	23.3	26.8	25.5
	2000–01	19.3	77.5	6.0	12.0	44.2	15.3	64.9
	2010–11	21.2	75.7	9.9	13.1	41.9	10.8	200.8
Vietnam	1990–91	–	–	–	–	–	–	–
	2000–01	38.3	58.0	1.6	7.7	11.4	37.4	11.2
	2010–11	28.0	71.3	3.1	12.5	19.8	35.9	76.7
Developing countries	1990–91	16.8	83.8	5.2	19.7	31.2	25.8	514.8
	2000–01	10.0	89.5	6.0	15.9	47.6	20	1,462.4
	2010–11	11.9	86.3	7.7	15.4	46.6	16.1	4,945.1
						0	0	
World	1990–91	15.0	82.8	10.1	17.4	42.7	12.5	2,708.6
	2000–01	11.2	84.1	10.4	15.0	45.1	13.8	5,469.8
	2010–11	14.3	80.3	12.9	15.3	39.5	12.6	13,400.4

Source: Compiled from UN Comtrade database.[20]

Notes: 1 Standard International Trade Classification (SITC) codes are given in brackets

– Data not available.

20. http://comtrade.un.org/db/ (accessed in January–March 2013).

equipment (SITC 7), which accounts for nearly a third of world merchandise trade and over 40% of total manufacturing trade. In 2010–11, machinery and transport equipment accounted for only 17.2% of total merchandise exports of India, compared to 59.2% in that of China and even larger shares in Korea, Taiwan, Malaysia, and Singapore. As we will see in the next section, the ongoing process of global production sharing is heavily concentrated within this product group.

An obvious caveat relating to the comparison of India's export performance in the Asian context using standard trade data (which records trade in "gross" terms), as we have done here, is that this could understate India's relative export performance. This is because export composition of China and the other East Asian countries, unlike that of India, is dominated by network trade which is characterized by a high degree of import intensity arising from two sources—multiple-border crossing of parts and components before they get finally embodied in final products, and the liberalization of each country in a given slice of the production process.[21] In order to understand this possible bias we compiled data on manufacturing exports both in gross (Customs-record based) and value-added terms from a new database put together by the Organization for Economic Cooperation and Development (OECD). The data are reported in Table 3 for those Asian countries for which both data series are available.

Per unit value added (that is value-added exports as a percentage of gross exports) is much bigger in India compared to China and the other East Asian countries except Indonesia (Table 3, last column). However, the use of the standard (gross) or the value-added export value series does not make a significant difference to India's relative export performance. In gross terms, India ranks sixth among the 11 countries, after China, Korea, Taiwan, Malaysia, Singapore, and Thailand. When value added data are used, India is evaluated to be at the fourth position, slightly above Thailand, Malaysia and Singapore. However, the big difference between China and India remains virtually unchanged: in gross terms Indian exports in 2009 amounted to only 10% of China's export and in value added terms this figure only increases marginally to 11%.

21. In recent years there has been a lively debate on the appropriateness of official trade statistics for the purpose of studying trends and patterns of manufacturing trade in the presence of global production sharing and how to modify and integrate the System of National Accounts (SNA) and Customs data reporting systems for the measurement of trade data in value-added terms. On this debate see various contributions in Mattoo et al. (2013).

TABLE 3. Comparison of Gross and Value-added Exports from Selected Asian Countries,[1] 2009

	Gross exports US$ billion	Country rank	Value added exports[2] US$ billion	Country rank	Value added share of gross export (%)
China	1042.0	1	666.0	1	63.9
Korea	328.7	2	178.8	2	54.4
Chinese Taipei	201.8	3	103.7	3	51.4
Singapore	116.6	4	53.4	7	45.8
Thailand	114.4	5	62.0	5	54.2
India	103.9	6	75.3	4	72.4
Malaysia	92.6	7	57.1	6	61.7
Indonesia	65.9	8	51.5	8	78.2
Philippines	37.8	9	19.8	9	52.3
Vietnam	20.6	10	8.3	10	40.3
Hong Kong, China	9.5	11	5.0	11	52.8

Source: Compiled from OECD StatExtracts.[22]

Notes: 1. Domestic value added in gross (Customs record based) exports calculated using national input-output tables.
2. Domestic value-added embodied in gross exports.

4. India in Network Trade

Between 1990–91 and 2010–11, world exports taking place within global production networks (network exports)[23] recorded an almost five-fold increase, from US$12803 billion to US$59070, with the share of developing countries in the total increasing from 11.9% to 45.1%, as given in Figure 2. This has contributed disproportionally to the shift in the geographic profile of manufacturing trade from developed to developing countries. The share of network products in exports from developing countries increased from 41.4% in 1990–91 to 60.1% in 2010–11. These exports accounted for over 60% of the total increment in manufacturing exports from developing countries over these two decades.[24]

22. OECD-WTO Trade in Value Added (TiVA) database available at stats.oecd.org/Index.aspx?queryid=47807 (accessed on November 23, 2013).

23. The procedure followed in delineating network exports (parts and components, and final assembly) from the standard trade data reported on the basis of the SITC is explained in Appendix (a).

24. The data on the share of network products, in particular electronics and electrical goods, in total manufacturing reported here (which are based on nominal manufacturing value added) presumably understate the relative importance of this form of trade because during this period the prices of these products grew at a much slower rate compared to those of most other manufactured products (Krugman 2008).

FIGURE 2. Manufacturing Exports from Developing Countries, 1990–2011

(a) Export Value, US$ billion

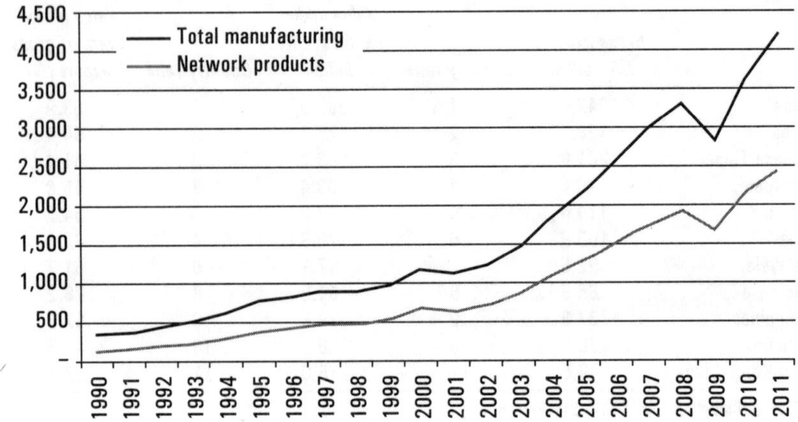

(b) Developing Countries' Share in World Exports (%)

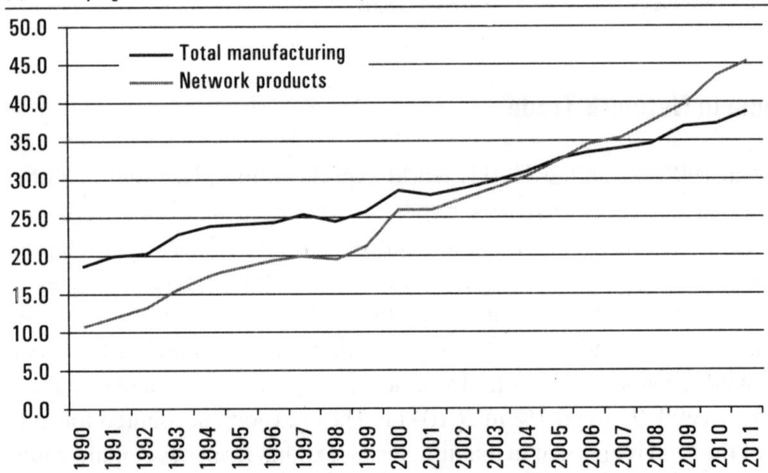

Source: Based on data compiled from the UN Comtrade database.[25]

Data on the contribution of global production sharing to the expansion of manufacturing exports from India and East Asian countries are summarized in Table 4. On average network products have accounted for over a half of total manufacturing exports from all East Asian countries (except Indonesia)[26] over the past two decades, with this share recording a notable

25. http://comtrade.un.org/db/ (accessed in January-March 2013).

26. The "outlier" status of Indonesia within East Asia in relation to its role in global production sharing is discussed too.

TABLE 4. Global Production Sharing and Manufacturing Exports: India and Developing East Asian Countries

Share in total manufacturing exports (%)

	Parts and component			*Final assembly*			*Network products*			*Contribution to export increment between 1990–91 and 2010–11*
	1990–91	*2000–01*	*2010–11*	*1990–91*	*2000–01*	*2010–11*	*1990–91*	*2000–01*	*2010–11*	
India	7.0	8.3	11.0	4.9	4.1	12.3	11.9	12.4	23.4	23.4
East Asia	23.9	42.0	39.3	20.0	18.1	23.2	43.9	60.0	62.5	68.9
China	11.4	25.0	30.7	12.7	17.2	25.1	24.1	42.3	55.8	63.5
Hong Kong	18.6	31.8	52.4	18.9	17.0	15.6	37.5	48.8	68.0	59.7
Korea, Rp	22.2	39.0	34.9	23.3	26.8	36.5	45.6	65.8	71.4	81.3
Taiwan	23.5	49.0	53.5	26.9	23.7	23.0	50.4	72.6	76.5	88.1
Indonesia	3.0	22.1	18.2	3.0	8.7	13.1	6.0	30.8	31.3	42.3
Malaysia	47.3	62.5	50.6	21.6	16.7	16.5	68.9	79.2	67.1	82.6
Philippines	37.3	77.8	66.8	8.5	5.8	11.3	45.7	83.6	78.1	87.7
Singapore	49.3	71.9	63.1	24.5	10.9	10.7	73.8	82.8	73.8	88.0
Thailand	26.6	42.3	35.9	12.3	17.5	23.1	38.9	59.8	59.0	70.2
Vietnam	–	16.8	20.1		4.6	10.3		21.4	30.5	21.4
Developing countries	22.3	38.6	36.4	19.1	19.6	23.6	41.4	58.3	60.1	66.6
World	27.4	33.1	29.7	29.7	26.2	25.2	57.1	59.3	54.9	61.4

Source: Compiled from UN Comtrade database.[27]

Note: – Data not available.

27. http://comtrade.un.org/db/ (accessed in January–March 2013).

increase in the past decade. Network product exports from India, too, have increased during this period, but these products accounted for only 23.4% of total Indian manufacturing exports in 2010–11. Network products accounted for nearly 70% of the total increment in manufacturing exports from East Asia between 1990–91 and 2010–11; the comparable figure for India was 22%.

As regards to the composition of network products, a striking common feature of East Asian countries' engagement in global production sharing is the heavy concentration of production within the broader commodity group of machinery and transport equipment (SITC 7). Within this product group telecommunication and sound recording equipment, semiconductors and other electrical machinery and equipment account for the lion's share of total network exports as seen in Tables 5 and 6. By contrast, these dynamic products still account for a much smaller share (26%) of network product exports from India.

A notable difference in the commodity composition of network exports from India compared to that of the East Asian countries is the relatively larger share accounted for by transport equipment. Table 5 shows road vehicles and other transport equipment accounted for 28% of total Indian network exports in 2010–11, compared to an East Asian regional average of 13.2%. Interestingly, the total volume of transport equipment exports from India is rapidly approaching the level of Thailand, which is the most successful second-tier automotive exporting country (after Japan and Korea) in Asia. India's total transport equipment exports increased from US$1.3 billion in the early 1990s to nearly US$19 billion in 2010–11. Thailand's transport equipment exports in 2010–11 were US$21.0 billion.

A number of leading automakers and auto part suppliers have established assembly plants in India and some of them have already begun to use India as an export platform within their global production networks (Humphrey 2003; Sen and Srivastava 2012). For example, Toyota Kirloskar Auto Parts, a joint venture between Toyota and a local manufacturer is exporting gearboxes from India to assembly plants in various countries including Thailand, South Africa and Argentina. Toyota Indonesia, which specializes in multipurpose vehicles has integrated its production system with its operations in India, importing engine components from Indonesia and exporting gearboxes and auto parts. Suzuki India has developed a two way sourcing network encompassing its plants in China, India and Indonesia. Almost all companies now export assembled cars (completely built units) to both regional and extra-regional markets. Until about the early 2000, parts and components accounted for the bulk of automotive exports from India.

TABLE 5. Composition of Networks Exports, 2010–11 (%)

	Office machines and automatic data processing machines (75)	*Telecom and sound recording equipment (76)*	*Electrical machinery excluding semi-conductors (77)*	*Semi-conductors²*	*Road vehicles (78)*	*Other transport equipment (79)*	*Professional and scientific equipment (87)*	*Photographic apparatus and optical goods, watches and clocks (88)*	*Other²*	*Total US$ billion*
India	1.9	10.9	14.1	1.9	26.3	22.0	3.0	1.0	18.8	34.6
East Asia	19.1	18.8	14.4	17.3	7.8	6.2	5.5	2.1	8.8	1,841.2
China	24.9	22.9	16.2	7.8	6.1	5.4	5.3	1.5	9.9	851.1
Hong Kong	17.7	25.8	17.4	25.1	0.6	0.2	3.4	5.0	4.9	264.2
Korea, Rp	4.5	12.9	9.9	14.9	20.1	17.5	10.8	1.5	7.8	297.9
Indonesia	11.3	22.7	24.3	4.7	15.2	6.6	1.2	1.0	13.0	20.5
Malaysia	23.0	14.6	11.9	36.2	1.8	1.5	5.3	1.2	4.5	90.4
Philippines	25.7	3.0	14.3	42.7	7.1	2.3	0.9	2.2	1.8	28.7
Singapore	15.1	6.2	8.7	44.6	2.3	4.7	4.3	1.6	12.5	190.6
Thailand	21.4	10.5	15.1	11.4	22.4	2.8	2.1	3.2	11.2	81.6
Vietnam	15.6	33.4	19.6	4.0	5.3	4.2	2.1	4.0	11.8	16.0
Developing countries	17.2	18.3	14.5	15.0	11.8	6.1	5.4	1.9	9.8	2,150.4
World	10.9	12.1	13.8	9.2	21.8	6.6	6.5	2.2	16.9	5,236.6

Source: Compiled from UN Comtrade database.[28]

Notes: 1. Standard International Trade Classification (SITC) codes are given in brackets.

2. These two categories contain parts and components only.

28. http://comtrade.un.org/db/ (accessed in January–March 2013).

TABLE 6. Shares of Parts and Components in Total Networks Exports, 2010–11 (%)[1]

	Office machines and automatic data processing machines (75)	*Telecom-munication and sound recording equipment (76)*	*Electrical machinery excluding semiconductors (77)*	*Road vehicles (78)*	*Other transport equipment (79)*	*Professional and scientific equipment (87)*	*Photographic apparatus and optical goods, watches and clocks (88)*	*Total*
India	87.3	45.2	79.3	31.8	24.3	28.3	14.4	53.2
East Asia	75.9	60.1	64.7	40.1	9.0	12.1	25.3	66.1
China	64.4	55.4	55.8	45.4	3.8	10.3	22.6	59.3
Hong Kong	97.6	62.9	77.3	25.9	61.7	22.1	23.2	79.1
Korea, Rp	96.8	85.2	74.0	33.1	2.5	3.1	11.4	53.0
Indonesia	95.9	33.0	69.2	50.2	8.5	19.3	24.4	61.5
Malaysia	71.5	56.1	75.7	75.6	51.3	32.8	53.8	78.8
Philippines	86.4	79.9	66.2	93.6	20.8	22.7	8.9	86.1
Singapore	97.5	79.2	79.1	77.6	52.8	27.6	27.5	89.4
Thailand	99.6	39.0	57.9	27.8	54.3	40.7	48.1	66.8
Vietnam	99.6	35.8	89.0	78.6	3.1	19.5	84.5	68.9
Developing countries	76.3	57.5	65.4	34.2	10.4	12.6	24.6	63.8
World	82.1	60.7	68.5	30.1	18.1	14.5	17.6	61.0

Source: Compiled from UN Comtrade database.[29]

Note: 1. Standard International Trade Classification (SITC) codes are given in brackets.

29. http://comtrade.un.org/db/ (accessed in January–March 2013).

Since then exports of completely built units (CBUs) have increased at a much faster rate. Figure 3 shows that in 2010–11 CBUs accounted for nearly three quarters of total automotive exports of over US$19 billion.

FIGURE 3. Exports of Transport Equipment from India, 1988–2011

(a) Value (US$ million)

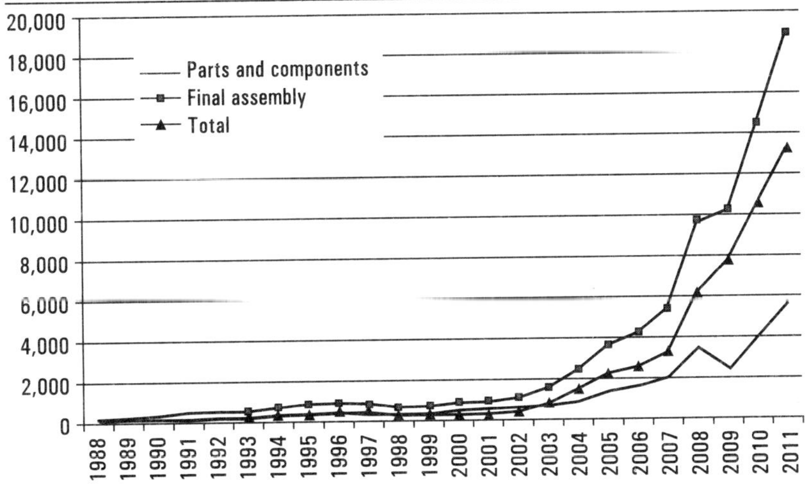

(b) Share in Total Manufacturing Export (%)

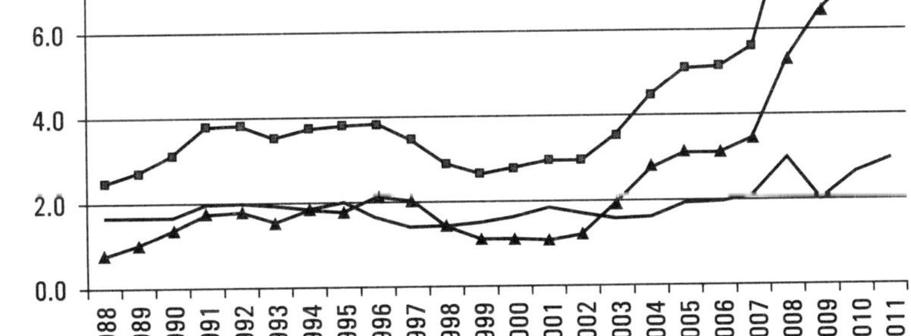

Source: Based on data compiled from the UN Comtrade database.[30]

30. http://comtrade.un.org/db/ (accessed in January–March 2013).

In a sharp contrast to automobile, as yet there are no signs of Indian manufacturing linking to production networks in electronics, electrical goods and other related products. A number of large electronics and electrical goods producing MNEs (e.g., Nokia, Samsung, LG) have set up production bases in India, but they are predominantly involved in production for the domestic market.

In most East Asian countries Special Economic Zones (SEZs) (until recently known as free trade zones or export processing zones have proved to be an effective vehicle for integrating domestic manufacturing into global production networks in these global industries (Sachs and Warner 1995). In these countries, SEZs provided an investment climate characterized by free trade conditions, a liberal regulatory framework and high-quality infrastructure. In India the first SEZ (in Kandla, Gujarat) was set up in 1965. A second SEZ was set up in Santacruz (Mumbai) in 1973, with a specific focus on attracting electronics firms. During the 1980s, five more zones were set up. By 2005 there were 17 SEZs in operation (Aggrawal 2012). But these SEZs never took off because of several reasons, such as their relatively limited scale; the government's general ambivalence about attracting FDI, and unclear and changing incentive packages attached to the zones (Bajpai and Sachs 2000; Kumar 1989). Moreover, unlike in the East Asian countries, where SEZs were an integral part of an overall export-led industrialization strategy, in India SEZs had to operate in the context of a highly restrictive trade and investment policy regime. It was difficult to insulate the zones from this unfavorable external investment climate (Aggarwal 2013).

Inspired by the notable success of SEZs in China, the Indian government announced a revamped approach to SEZs as part of the Foreign Trade Policy of 2000–01 (Panagariya 2008). This was followed by the enactment of the SEZ Act of 2005 to provide the overall legal framework within which the SEZs operate. The Act, which became operational in February 2010, provides for the setting up of SEZs by the private sector, in addition to state governments and the central government, and gives the Indian states some flexibility for the relaxation of labor laws and the offer of specific incentives to investors.

The past five years have seen a rapid proliferation of SEZs in India: by early 2011, 580 SEZs had been formally approved and, of them, 122 had begun operations (Aggarwal 2013). Table 7 illustrates the share of exports by SEZ enterprises in total exports from the country increasing from 9.1% in 2007–08 to 27.4% in 2009–10. However, so far there has not been a significant presence of foreign firms in electronics and other vertically integrated global industries. Electronics and electrical goods account for only a tiny share of exports (2.3% in 2009–10). It could be that despite significant recent reforms, in the eyes of foreign investors India's foreign investment regime still reflects the tension between the traditional aversion to foreign investment and the current recognition of its importance to economic development. The smooth functioning of SEZs has also been constrained by the controversial issue of land acquisition and unresolved issues relating to the relaxation of labor laws for the SEZ firms (Panagariya 2008: 271–73).

TABLE 7. India: Exports from Special Economic Zones, 2007–10[1] (%)

Product	*2007/08*	*2008/09*	*2009/10*
Biotech	0.3	0.9	0.2
Computer/electronic software	6.0	16.3	20.7
Computer hardware[2]	16.7	13.1	7.9
Electronics	0.8	0.4	0.4
Engineering	2.5	3.1	1.9
Gems and jewelry	34.5	33.5	19.9
Chemical and pharmaceuticals	2.2	6.4	33.5
Handicraft	0.1	0.0	0.0
Plastic and rubber	1.0	0.4	0.3
Leather, footwear, and sport goods	0.9	0.3	0.2
Food and agricultural products	0.9	0.3	0.2
Nonconventional energy	0.2	0.2	0.6
Textiles and garments	2.0	3.0	1.5
Trading and services	31.4	18.9	11.3
Miscellaneous	1.4	3.4	1.3
Total (%)	100	100	100
US$ billion	14.8	22.2	49.1
Memo item			
Percentage of India's total exports	9.1	12.0	27.4

Source: Compiled from WTO (2013), Table 111.19.
Notes: 1. Data are based on Indian financial year.
2. Assembly of computers and printers.

What explains the rapid growth of automotive exports compared to electronics and other machinery exports? The human capital base developed during over a half-a-century of import-substitution industrialization and the removal of restrictions on the entry of foreign automotive producers as part of the liberalization reforms provided the setting for the expansion of the Indian automobile industry (Humphrey 2003). But it is necessary to look into the peculiarities of automobile production in order to understand its unique export performance record.

Unlike electronics and electrical goods, automotives are bulky and "low-value-to weight" goods, and hence transport cost is a key determinant of market price. There is also a need to design the product to suit the taste and affordability of the consumer. Therefore, there is a natural tendency for final assembly plants to be located in countries with large domestic markets. Once auto makers choose to set up assembly plants in a given country, parts and component producers follow them because of two reasons. First, and perhaps more importantly, most auto parts also have low value-to-weight ratios, which makes its too costly to use air transport for the timely delivery required for just-in-time production schedules of the final assembler (Hummels 2007).[31]

Second, there is an asymmetrical market-power relationship between component makers and auto makers within the global automobile industry; the products of many auto part manufacturers are used in vehicles made by a handful of car makers. This is different from electronics parts, like integrated circuits and semiconductors, that are used in many industries. Thus, there is an incentive for the part makers to set up factories next to the assemblers in order to secure their position in the market (Klier and Rubenstein 2008: Chapter 3; Kohpaiboon and Jongwanich 2013).

Once a complete production base (involving both final assembly and component assembly/production) is established in a given (large) country, exporting to third countries becomes a viable option for automakers. Scale economies gained from domestic expansion makes exporting of both parts and components and assembled vehicles profitable as part of their global profit maximization strategy. Adaptation of products to suit domestic demand conditions and lower transportation cost compared to exporting from the home base also become important drivers of exporting to regional markets from the new production base.

An important aspect of the performance of Indian auto industry is the coexistence of high tariff protection (which implies an anti-export bias) and rapid export growth. In spite of some reductions in recent years, tariffs on completely built automotives continued to remain much higher (60% on average) than tariffs on other imports (average tariff of 8.5%) (WTO 2011). Moreover, given the cascading nature of the tariff structure (parts and components tariffs of about 21%), the rate of effective protection for domestic automotive assembly is presumably even higher than the average applied nominal rate. Viewed from the mainstream policy advocacy for designing export promotion policy, an interesting issue here is why continuing the

31. Air shipping is the mode of transport for over two-thirds of electronics exports from Singapore, the Philippines, Thailand, and Malaysia to the USA (estimate based on US Trade Commission data on trade by mode of transport between 2000 and 2005).

anti-export bias has not been a deterrent to rapid export growth. A possible explanation is that export expansion has been predominantly driven by MNEs, which have set up production plants in India to produce for the global market, not just for the Indian market. The conventional advocacy for removing anti-export bias as a precondition for export expansion is based on the implicit assumption that exporting is an act of domestically owned firms whose marketing decision is driven by the relative profitability of exporting compared to selling in the domestic market. Relative profitability in selling in the domestic market is probably not a binding consideration for the MNEs involved in sourcing and marketing within a global production network.

For the poor export performance record in electronics, the only major East Asian country whose experience resembles that of India is Indonesia. An understanding of why Indonesia, notwithstanding the obvious advantageous position in terms of its location and relative wages, has continued to remain a small player in regional production networks seems to hold lessons for India. Indonesia's engagement has so far been limited only to some low-end assembly activities undertaken mostly by Singaporean subcontracting companies in the Batam economic zone. In the early 1970s, two major electronic MNEs, which had already established production bases in Singapore, did set up assembly plants in Indonesia (Fairchild and National Semiconductor, established in 1973 and 1974 respectively), but both plants were closed down in 1986. At that time there was a worldwide slump in the semiconductor business. However, it is not clear whether external demand factors played an important role in their departure from Indonesia. Both these MNEs continued their operation in both Singapore and Malaysia with some restructuring and labor shedding in response to demand contraction. The unfavorable business environment in Indonesia, in particular labor market rigidities, that hindered restructuring operations in line with global changes in the semiconductor industry, appears to be the major reason. According to press accounts at the time, in 1985 Fairchild announced a plan to introduce a new technology that would have involved some reduction in their workforce, but the Ministry of Manpower opposed any retrenching that would have resulted from automation (Thee and Pangestu 1998).

Recently the issue of why Indonesia has been left behind in global production networks was brought into sharp relief when the Canadian firm, Research in Motion (RIM), the Blackberry producer, decided (in September 2011) to set up an assembly plant in Penang, Malaysia bypassing Indonesia (Manning and Purnagunawan 2011). Indonesia is the largest market for the Blackberry in Southeast Asia, accounting for some 75% of its total annual sales in the region, and almost ten times the annual sales of 400,000 in

Malaysia. Therefore, when RIM announced its plan to set up a production base in Southeast Asia, there were high hopes in Indonesian policy circles that Indonesia would be its preferred location. Indonesian authorities were, therefore, perplexed by RIM's decisions to go to Penang and the industry minister even announced the possible introduction of punitive import tariffs on luxury goods such as the BlackBerrys. However, it is not hard to understand the reason behind RIM's decisions in favor of Penang. For nearly three decades, Penang has been a world center for electronics (Athukorala 2011), whereas Indonesia has had a chequered record in attracting multinational enterprises involved in global production sharing. There has not been any notable improvement in the investment climate in the country compared to the situation in the 1980s when Fairchild and National Semiconductor closed down their operations (Wells and Ahmed 2007).

It is widely held in some policy circles that India (and Indonesia, for that matter) has "missed the boat" to join the electronics production network given the MNEs' long-standing attachment to the existing production bases and China's emergence as the premier assembly center in the world. This view is, however, not consistent with the ongoing developments in global production networks in East Asia. For instance, in recent years, the East Asia production networks have begun to spread to Vietnam and Cambodia.

Following the market-oriented policy reforms started in the late 1980s, a number of Korean, Taiwanese and Japanese firms set up assembly plants in Vietnam, but these ventures were predominantly of the conventional import-substitution variety with little links to the global production networks of the parent companies. From about the late 1990s part and component assemblies within regional production networks began to emerge, mostly with the involvement of small- and medium-scale investors from Taiwan and Korea, with only one major global player, Hitachi from Japan. A major breakthrough occurred with the decision made in February 2006 by Intel Corporation, the world's largest semiconductor producer, to set up a $300 million testing and assembly plant (subsequently revised to $1 billion) in Ho Chi Minh City. The Intel plant started commercial operation in early 2011 and is expected to eventually employ over 3,000 workers. The early experience in Singapore, Malaysia, Thailand and the Philippines indicates that there is something of a herd mentality in the site selection process of MNEs in the global electronics industry, particularly if the first entrant is a major player in the industry.

It seems that following Intel's entry, this process has already begun to replay in Vietnam (Athukorala and Tien 2012). A number of other major players in the electronics industry have already come to Vietnam following the footsteps of Intel. These include the Taiwanese-based Hon Hai Precision Industry and Compact Electronics (the world's largest and second-largest electronics contract manufacturers) and Nidec Corporation (a Japanese manufacturer of hard disk drive motors and electrical and optical components). In 2009, Samsung Electronics set up a large plant in Hanoi for assembling hand held products (HHPs) (smart phones and tablets). Over the past four years, Samsung has been gradually shifting HHP assembly from its plant in China to the Vietnam plant as part of a strategic production diversification strategy in response to increasing wages and rental cost in China. In 2009, 65% of Samsung's global HHP supply came from China, with Vietnam contributing to a mere 3%; by the end of 2012 these figures had changed to 45% and 33%, respectively. In 2012, Samsung Vietnam's production capacity reached 150 million units, and its total exports (about US$11 billion) amounted to 11% of Vietnam's total merchandise export earnings.[32]

There are also early signs of regional production networks expanding to Cambodia. In 2011, Minebea, a large Japanese MNE which produces a wide range of parts and components for the automotive and electronics industries, set up a plant (Minebea Cambodia) in the Phnom Penh Special Economic Zone to assemble parts for cellular phones using components imported from its factories in Thailand, Malaysia, and China. Minebea Cambodia currently employs 1,300 workers and it has plans to expand to a total workforce of 5,000 within two years. The other MNEs which have set up assembly plant in Cambodia include Sumitomo Corporation, Japan (wiring harnesses for cars); Denso, Japan (motorcycle ignition components); Pactics, Belgium (sleeves for sunglasses made by premier eyewear companies); and Tiffany & Company, USA (diamond polishing). There is anecdotal evidence that a number of other Japanese companies which have production bases in China and Thailand are planning to relocate some segments of their production process to Cambodia. Rising wages and rental costs in China and the neighboring Thailand, and production disruption caused by recent floods in Thailand are considered the drivers working to Cambodia's advantage (*Business Day* 2013).

When China began to emerge as a major trading nation in late 1980s, there was a growing concern in policy circles in Southeast Asia, and in other Asian countries, that competition from China could crowd out their export

32. The discussion here on Samsung's operation in Vietnam is based on a conference presentation made by Seokmin Park, Vice President and Head, Corporate Supply Chain Management of Samsung (Park 2013).

opportunities (Athukorala 2009). Initially, the "China fear" in the region was mainly related to export competition in the standard light manufactured good (clothing, footwear, sport goods, etc.), but soon it turned out to be pervasive as China begun to rapidly integrate into global production networks in electrical and electronics products through an unprecedented increase in foreign direct investment in these industries. The rapid increase in China's share in world exports markets in these product lines, coupled with some anecdotal evidence of MNEs operating in Southeast Asian countries relocating to China, led to serious concern about possible erosion of the role of Southeast Asian countries in global production networks. These concerns gained added impetus from China's subsequent accession to the WTO, which not only provided China with most-favored nation (MFN) status in major markets, but also enhanced China's attractiveness to export-oriented investment by reducing the country risk of investment.

As can been seen in the data reported in Table 4, there has been a significant contraction in final assembly of consumer electronics and electrical goods exported from some countries in Southeast Asia as an outcome of competitive pressure from China for final assembly.[33] However, this structural shift has not resulted in a "hollowing out" of production bases in Southeast Asia. On the contrary, the past two decades have seen a close complementarity between China and Southeast Asian countries within global production networks, for two reasons. First, expansion in final assembly in China has created new demand for parts and components assembled in Southeast Asia. Benefitting from this, electronics firms involved in component design, assembly and testing restructured their operations by moving into high-value tasks in the value chain. This process has been greatly aided by the deep-rooted nature of their production bases and the pool of skilled workers developed over the past three decades (Athukorala 2009). Second, a number of large electronics MNEs have shifted regional/global headquarter functions to Singapore and Penang. Manufacturing is only part of their operations. Their activities now encompass corporate and financial planning, R&D, product design and tooling, sales and marketing. Most MNEs which have shifted final assembly of consumer electronics and electrical goods to China perform global headquarter functions of their China operations from Singapore and Penang. Some of them now use their Penang affiliates as an integral part of their global training and skill enhancement programs (Athukorala 2014).

33. Final assembly is generally more labor intensive than component assembly, production and testing.

5. Determinants of Exports

This section reports the results of an econometric exercise undertaken to examine the determinants of inter-country differences in export performance, with emphasis on engagement in network trade. The analytical tool used here is the gravity model, which has become the workhorse for modelling bilateral trade flows.[34] After augmenting the basic gravity model by adding a number of explanatory variables which have been found in previous studies to improve explanatory power, the estimation equation is specified as,

$$
\begin{aligned}
Ln\ TRE_{ijt} = {} & \alpha + \beta_1 lnGDP_{it} + \beta_2 lnGDP_{jt} + \beta_3 lnPGDP_{it} + \beta_4 lnPGDP_{jt.} \\
& + \beta_5 lnDST_{ij} + \beta_6 lnRER_{ijt} + \beta_7 INS_{it} + \beta_8 lnLPI_{it} + \beta_9 FTA_{ijt} \\
& + \beta_{10} ADJ_{ijt} + \beta_{11} COML_{ijt} + \beta_{12} lnCLNK_{i,jt} + \beta_{13} AFC + \beta_{14} GFC \\
& + \beta_{15} DIND + \beta_{16} DODV + \gamma T + \varepsilon_{ij}
\end{aligned}
$$

where the subscripts *i* and *j* refer to the reporting (exporting) and the partner (importing) country, and *ln* denotes natural logarithms. The explanatory variables are listed and defined below, with the postulated sign of the regression coefficient in brackets.

TRE	Bilateral exports
GDP	Real gross domestic product (+)
PGDP	Real per capita gross domestic product (+)
DST	The distance between the economic centers of *i* and *j* (–)
RER	Real bilateral exchange rate (+)
INS	Institutional quality
LPI	Logistic performance index (+)
FTA	A binary dummy which is unity if both *i* and *j* belong to the same regional trade agreements (*RTA*) and 0 otherwise (+)
ADJ	A binary dummy variable which takes the value one if *i* and *j* share a common land border and zero otherwise (+)
COML	A dummy variable which takes the value one if *i* and *j* have a common language (a measure of cultural affinity) and zero otherwise (+)
CLNK	Colonial economic link dummy which takes the value one for country pairs with colonial links and zero otherwise (+)

34. The gravity model originated in Tinbergen (1962), purely as an attempt to capture empirical regularities in trade patterns. For recent attempt to provide a theoretical justification for its formulation and applications to trade flow modeling, see various contributions in Bergeijk and Brakman (2010).

AFC	A dummy (1 for 1997, 1998 and 1999 and zero otherwise) included to capture trade disruption caused by the Asian financial crisis (+).
GFC	A dummy (1 for 2008 and 2009 and zero otherwise) included to capture trade disruption caused by the global financial crisis (+).
DIND	A dummy variable for India (which takes the value one for India and zero for the other countries
DODV	A dummy variable for non-East Asian developing countries other than India (which takes the value one for non-East Asian developing countries other than India and zero for the other countries)
α	Constant term
T	A set of time dummy variables to capture year-specific "fixed" effects
ε	Stochastic error term, representing omitted influences on bilateral trade

The three variables, *GDP* of the reporting country and the partner countries and the distance *DST* between them, are the standard gravity model arguments. The common reasoning for the use of GDP as an explanatory variable is that larger countries have more variety to offer in international trade than smaller countries (Tinbergen 1962). The use of this variable in our trade equation is also consistent with the theory of international production fragmentation, which predicts that the optimal degree of fragmentation depends on the size of the market, because the scale of production would determine the extent to which such division of labor can proceed. In other words, the size of GDP can be treated as a proxy for market thickness (the economic depth of trading nations) which positively impacts on the location of outsourcing activity (Grossman and Helpman 2005; Jones and Kierzkowski 2001). There are also reasons to believe that GDP per capita has a positive effect on network trade over and above the effect of GDP. As countries grow richer, the scale and composition of industrial output could become more conducive to production sharing. In addition, more developed countries have better ports and communication systems that facilitate production sharing by reducing the cost of maintaining the services links involved in vertical liberalization (Golub et al. 2007).

It is important to note that per capita GDP is also widely used in the empirical trade and growth literature as a good surrogate for the capital–labor ratio. Thus, at first blush, one could interpret a statistically significant positive coefficient in our estimated equation to imply that capital-labor endowment is an important determinant of a country's successful integration within global production networks. However such an inference is not consistent with the theory of global production sharing; production sharing opens up opportunities for labor abundant and capital poor countries to specialize in labor-intensive slices of the value chain of high-tech (capital and skill-intensive) global industries (Jones 2000: Chapter 7; Jones and Kierzkowski 2001). Nor is it consistent with the experiences of the East Asian economies. For instance Singapore and Penang (Malaysia) specifically focused on electronics assembly at the very early stages of their development (Singapore in the mid-1960s and Malaysia in the early 1970s) particularly because of its suitability in creating a vent for their surplus labor pool, and capital almost entirely came from MNEs (Athukorala 2014; Goh 1993; Yew 2000). As discussed, production networks have begun to expand to Vietnam and Cambodia. Korea and Taiwan joined production networks in the early 1990s following almost two decades of rapid export growth based on liberalization in traditional labor-intensive products, but this sequence had much to do with the nature of the foreign investment regimes of the two countries and perhaps also international political conditions during the early post-war period (see Note 7).

Geographic distance is a proxy measure of transport (shipping) costs and other costs associated with time lags in transportation such as spoilage. Technological advances during the post-war era have contributed to the "death of distance" when it comes to international communication costs. However, there is evidence that geographical distance is still a key factor in determining international transport costs, in particular shipping costs (Evans and Harrigan 2005; Hummels 2007). Transport cost could be a much more important influence on vertical trade than on final trade, because of multiple border-crossings involved in the value-added chain.

The real exchange rate (*RER*) is included to capture the impact of the overall macroeconomic climate on international competitiveness of tradable goods production. *LPI* and *INS* are included to captures the cost of "service links" involved in connecting production blocks within global production networks: *LPI* measures the quality of trade-related logistic provisions, and *INS* captures various aspects of governance that directly affect property rights, political instability, policy continuity and other factors which have a bearing on the ability to carry out business transactions. Adjacency (*ADJ*) and common business language can facilitate trade by reducing transaction cost and through better understanding of each other's culture and legal systems.

The free trade agreement dummy variable (*FTA*) is included in the model to capture the impact of tariff concessions offered under these agreements. All countries covered in our data set are members of one or more FTAs. In theory, network trade is considered to be relatively more sensitive to tariff changes (under an FTA or otherwise) compared to conventional horizontal trade (Yi 2003). Normally a tariff is incurred each time a good in process crosses a border. Consequently, with a one percentage point reduction in tariff, the cost of production of vertically-integrated goods declines by a multiple of this initial reduction. Moreover, a tariff reduction may make it more profitable for goods previously produced in their entirety in one country to now become vertically fragmented. Consequently, the trade-stimulating effect of an FTA would be higher for network trade than for normal trade, other things remaining unchanged. However, in reality, the trade effect of any FTA would depend very much on the nature of the rules of origin (ROOs) built into it. The trade-distorting effects of ROOs are presumably more detrimental to network trade than to conventional final goods trade, because of the inherent difficulties involved in delineating the product for duty exemption and because of the transaction costs associated with the bureaucratic supervision of the amount of value-added in production coming from various sources (Krishna 2006). Formulating ROOs for network related trade is a rather complicated business. The conventional value-added criterion is virtually not applicable to this trade because the products involved are low-value-added by their very nature. The only viable option is to pursue the so called change-in-tariff-lines-based ROOs, but this leads to insurmountable administrative problems because trade in electrical and electronics goods, and their related components, belong to the same tariff codes at the HS-6 digit level, which is the normal base for designing these type of ROOs. Moreover, the process of global production sharing is characterized by the continuous emergence of new products. Given the obvious administrative problems involved in revising ROOs in tandem, the emergence of new products naturally opens up room for unnecessary administrative delays and the tweaking of rules as a means of disguised protection.

Among the other variables, the two country dummy variables, *DIND* and *DODV*, are included (by treating the East Asian countries as the base dummy) to capture the impact of various other factors not captured by the other explanatory variables on export performance of India and the other developing countries, respectively. Finally, *DAFC* and *DGFC* are included to control for trade disruptions during the East Asian financial crisis and the recent global financial crisis.

The export equation is estimated using annual data compiled from exporter records in the UN trade data system[35] during the period 1996–2009. Even though the prime focus of our analysis is on network trade, disaggregated into parts and components and final assembly, we estimate the model for total manufacturing trade as well for the purpose of comparison. Our data set covers the export trade of 20 developing countries with 45 partner countries (including the 20 countries). All countries that accounted for 0.01% or more of total world manufacturing exports in 2004–05 are included in the country list. The trade data in nominal US$ are converted into real terms using US trade price indices extracted from the US Bureau of Labor Statistics database. Data on real *GDP* and per capita *GDP* are extracted from the World Bank *World Development Indicators* database. Data on *LPI* is taken from the *Logistics Performance Index* database of the World Bank (Arvis et al. 2007). This index is based on a worldwide survey of global freight forwarders and express carriers complemented by a number of qualitative and quantitative indicators of the domestic logistics environment, institutions, and performance of supply chains. Logistic quality of the individual countries covered are assessed on a "1-to-5 scale" (1 for the worst performance and 5 for the best) focusing on seven areas of performance: (a) efficiency of the clearance process by customs and other border agencies; (b) quality of transport and information technology infrastructure; (c) ease and affordability of arranging international shipments; (d) competence of the local logistics industry; (e) ability to track and trace international their shipments; (f) domestic logistic costs; and (g) timeliness of shipments in reaching their destination.

Institutional quality (*INS*) is measured by the International Country Risk Guide (ICRG) index compiled by the Political Risk Services Group, which is the most widely used variable to measure the quality of governance in the empirical growth and trade literature. It measures the ability of governments to carry out their declared programs and legislative strength.[36] The indicator runs on a seven point scale from 0–6, with higher values representing less corruption (or a higher control over corruption). The data on bilateral distance comes from the trade patterns database of the French Institute for Research on the International Economy (CEPII). The CEPII distance measure is a composite measure of the bilateral great-circle distance between

35. United Nations Statistical Office, Commodity Trade Statistics (Comtrade) Database. http://comtrade.un.org/db/ (accessed in January–March 2013).

36. In experimental runs we used three other alternative indicators of institutional quality (governance), (rule of law, government effectiveness, control of corruption) from the World Bank's World Governance Indicators database. The results were comparable in the standard OLS estimation. However, we were not able to use these indicators in FE and HT estimations because of data gaps.

major cities of each economy compiled by taking into account the trading significance of each city in each economy. For a complete listing of variables and data sources see Appendix B.

Of the three standard panel data estimation methods (pooled OLS, random-effects, and fixed-effects estimators), the fixed effect estimator is not appropriate in this case because the model contains a number of time-invariant explanatory variables which are central to our analysis. In experimental runs, we used both pooled OLS and random-effects (RE) estimators. The Breusch Pagan Lagrange multiplier test favored the use of the random effects estimator (REE) over the OLS counterpart. However the simple RE estimators can yield biased and inconsistent coefficient estimates if one or more explanatory variables are endogenous (that is, if they are jointly determined with the dependent variable). In our case, there are reasons to suspect that FTA and reporting country GDP are potentially endogenous for a number of reasons (Baier and Bergstrand 2007; Brun et al. 2005). The endogeneity problem is particularly important in estimating the impact of FTA on bilateral trade flows because the trade agreements are normally signed between countries that already have achieved certain levels of bilateral trade. Unobserved characteristics of some country pairs that may facilitate FTAs, such as political links and security concerns, can also result in the correlation of FTA dummies with the error term. There can also be reverse causation running from trade to GDP, even though the potential endogeneity problem may not be as important as in the case of the FTA variable in the context of a cross-country gravity model. Given these concerns, we reestimated the model by the instrumental variable estimator proposed by Hausman and Tayler (1981) (henceforth HTE estimator). The HTE addresses the endogeneity problem in cross-section gravity models by using instruments derived exclusively from inside the model to capture various dimensions of the data. Its superiority over REE in generating consistent coefficient estimates of the gravity model has been demonstrated by a number of recent studies.[37]

The preferred HTE estimates for exports of network products and total manufacturing are reported in Table 8. Note that we have deleted the dummy variables for common language (COML), common land border (ADJ) and colonial links (CLK) for the final estimates because these three variables turned out to be statistically insignificant in experimental runs in all cases. In order to examine whether there are differences between parts and components (P&C) and final assembly in relation to the postulated impact of the

37. See Egger (2005) and Serlenga and Shin (2007), and the works cited therein.

explanatory variables, we estimated the equation for total network products with an intercept dummy variable for P&C and its interaction with all other determinants (slope dummies). This approach is equivalent to estimating two separate regressions for the two categories but has the added advantage of providing a direct test of the statistical significance of the differences between the estimated coefficients. In all regression runs, the logistic performance index (LPI) variable turned out to be statistically insignificant in the full models, for both network products and total manufacturing, because of its high correlation with the exporter's per capita GDP (PGDP-exporter). We have therefore reported two equations, with and without PGDP-exporter, given the importance of LPI for our analysis.

In the final equation for network products we have retained only the statistically significant dummy interaction terms of P&C.[38] Only three interaction variables (*P&C*logPGDPimporter*, *P&C*logRER* and *P&C*FTA*) turned out to be statistically significant, and the magnitude of the regression coefficients are very small. The results therefore suggest that there is no notable difference between exports of P&C and final assembly in terms of the relevant determinants.

The coefficients of the two standard gravity variables (GDP and DST) in all equations, and those of most of the other variables statistically significant with the expected signs. The magnitude of the coefficient of the distance variables (about 1.5) is consistent with results of previous gravity model applications to modeling trade flows (Bergeijk and Brakman 2010).

To comment specifically on the evidence directly relevant for this paper, the hypothesis that the level of development, measured by per capita GDP relevant for explaining network trade is strongly supported by the results. The elasticity of network exports to per capita GDP of the exporter and the partner is 0.39 and 0.36, respectively (Equation 1.1). The comparable figures for total manufacturing exports (0.21 and 0.17) are much smaller in magnitude and the differences are statistically significant.[39] Interestingly, the coefficient of LPI is statistically insignificant (albeit with the expected positive sign) in both cases, supporting our hypothesis that the stage of development (measured by per capita GDP) is a good surrogate variable for the quality of trade related logistics. The coefficient of LPI becomes highly significant for network products when the equation is estimated after

38. The deletion of the other dummy variables was supported by the standard F test for joint significance.

39. In this section we simply infer statistical significance of the difference between two coefficients by testing whether the difference is within ("insignificant") or beyond ("significant") two standard-error bands from each coefficient.

TABLE 8. Determinants of Bilateral Trade Flows (1996–2009)

Variable	*Network products*		*Total manufacturing*	
	Equation 1.1	*Equation 1.2*	*Equation 2.1*	*Equation 2.2*
	(3)	*(4)*	*(1)*	*(2)*
Log GDP exporter	1.25***	1.56***	1.31***	1.41***
	(7.80)	(19.87)	(13.08)	(22.05)
Log GDP importer	1.14***	1.72***	1.50***	1.70***
	(5.70)	(16.96)	(13.49)	(24.29)
Log PGDP exporter	0.39***		0.21***	
	(4.21)		(2.78)	
Log PGDP importer	0.36*	0.33***	0.17*	0.14*
	(5.71)	(5.32)	(1.95)	(1.87)
Log DST	−1.55***	−1.42***	−1.57***	−1.54***
	(−6.02)	(−10.68)	(−11.90)	(−15.67)
Log RER	0.40***	0.38***	0.28***	0.27***
	(10.29)	(9.66)	(10.21)	(9.83)
Log INS	0.36***	0.40***	0.33***	0.35***
	(5.71)	(6.27)	(7.88)	(8.38)
FTA	0.16***	0.18***	0.11***	0.11***
	(2.88)	(2.84)	(2.80)	(2.84)
LPI	0.11	0.40***	0.03	0.19*
	(0.36)	(2.89)	(0.26)	(1.86)
AFC	−0.06	−0.27**	0.18**	0.10*
	(0.68)	(3.74)	(3.23)	(21.98)
GFC	−0.26***	−0.34***	−0.23***	−0.25***
	(−5.93)	(−7.59)	(−7.13)	(−7.58)
IND	−1.76***	−3.34***	−1.37***	−1.87***
	(−2.82)	(−8.11)	(−2.82)	(−5.83)
ODV	−1.54***	−2.96***	−1.34***	−1.65***
	(−3.78)	(−7.42)	(−3.78)	(−7.42)
P&C* log PGDP-importer		0.02***		
		(7.85)		
P&C* log RER	−0.05***	−0.05***		
	(−4.97)	(−4.56)		
P&C *FTA	−0.06***	−0.06***		
	(3.86)	(3.66)		
Constant	−23.05***	−23.05***	−43.93***	−30.65***
	(−7.45)	(−7.45)	(−13.00)	(−16.45)
F statistic	38.62	38.62	73.24	49.31
Observations	10417	10417	11862	11881
Number of pairs	911	911	922	911

Source: Own estimations based on data sources detailed in the text.

Notes: T-ratios are given in brackets with statistical significance of regression coefficients denoted as *** 1%, ** 5%, and *10%. The t-ratios are based on standard errors computed from the robust covariance matrix that allows for clustering as well as heteroskedasticity. Time dummies are included in all regressions but are not reported here.

deleting the exporting country per capita GDP variable (Equation 1.2). The result suggests that a one notch upward movement in the LPI quality ladder is associated with 0.4% increase in total network exports. The coefficient of LPI in the equation for total manufacturing exports is much smaller (0.19) and is significant only at the 10% level. Thus the results point to the importance of the quality of service link cost in determining a country's attraction as a location within global production network.

The results for the real exchange rate RER variable suggest that network trade is relatively more sensitive to the international competitiveness of traded goods production in a given country: RER elasticity of network exports is 0.40 compared to 0.28 for total manufacturing and the difference is statistically significant. The coefficient of the FTA variable is statistically significant in all four equations but larger in magnitude for network products (0.16 compared to 0.12 for total manufacturing). This result is consistent with the fact that tariffs on final electrical and transport equipment still remain high in most countries (WTO 2011). The coefficient of the FTA variable for parts and components is smaller (0.12) compared to that for final assembly (0.18). This is consistent with the fact that almost all Asian countries permit duty-free entry of parts and components as part of their export promotion policy package. Also most countries covered in our dataset have significantly liberalized trade in information technology products as part of their commitments under the WTO Information Technology Agreement which came into effect in 1996 (Menon 2013).

Finally, the coefficient of the India dummy variable (DIND) is highly significant with a negative sign in all equations. The estimated coefficient for network exports suggests that after controlling for the other explanatory variables, the level of network exports from India is only one-fifth of the average level of the East Asian countries. There is, however, no notable difference between India and the other developing countries relative to the East Asian countries.

There can be many country-specific idiosyncratic effects that lie behind the India–East Asia difference. But one particularly important difference is that as first comers in this area of international specialization, East Asian countries offer considerable agglomeration advantages for companies that are already located there. The site selection decisions of MNEs operating in assembly activities are strongly influenced by the presence of other key market players in a given country or neighboring countries. Against the backdrop of a long period of successful operation in the region, many MNEs, particularly the US-based ones, have significantly upgraded the technical activities of their regional production networks in Southeast Asia and assigned global production responsibilities to affiliates located in Singapore and more recently also to those located in Malaysia and Thailand. All in all, the results seems to support the view that MNE affiliates have a tendency to become increasingly embedded in host countries the longer they are present there and the more conducive the overall investment climate of the host country becomes over time (Rangan and Lawrence 1999).

6. Conclusions and Policy Implications

Global production sharing has become an integral part of the global economic landscape. Trade within global production networks has been expanding more rapidly than conventional final-goods trade. The degree of dependence on this new form of international specialization is proportionately larger in the high-performing East Asian countries compared to the other developing countries. India still remains a minor player in global production sharing, notwithstanding its geographical proximity to the dynamic East Asian economies. India's export performance during the reform era has been dominated by resource-intensive products (SITC 6) and the standard labor-intensive products (SITC 8). So far there are no clear signs of India entering into global and regional production networks in electronics and electrical goods, which have been the prime mover of export dynamism in the successful export-oriented economies in East Asia. Of course, India still has a vast untapped potential for expanding traditional labor-intensive manufactured goods, but these goods account for a much smaller and diminishing share in world manufacturing trade compared to trade in parts and components and final assembly within global production networks.

The findings of this study give credence to the case made in a number of influential studies for further reforms to improve India's export performance (e.g., Bhagwati and Panagariya 2013; Joshi 2008; Krueger 2010; Panagariya 2004, 2008, 2013; Srinivasan 2012). Relative to the first four decades following independence, India's policy reforms since 1991 have certainly achieved a great deal in unshackling the economy and integrated it into the world economy. However, as extensively discussed in this literature there are still many unresolved problems relating to the overall investment climate, in general and the anti-export bias in the policy regime, in particular. There is also a significant unfinished agenda of behind-the-border reforms. Regulations impacting on private sector activities have become less onerous since the start of the reforms, but there are various sector-specific regulations in abundance. While the the License Raj (the infamous industrial licensing policy) has been largely eliminated at the center, it still survives at the state level along with a pervasive Inspector Raj. Despite recent reforms, India's foreign investment regime still reflects the tension between the traditional aversion to foreign investment and the current recognition of its importance to economic development. Private investors, both foreign and local, require a large number of permissions (for example, electricity and water supply connections, water supply clearance and so on) from state governments to start business and they also have to interact with the state bureaucracy in the course of day-to-day business. Stringent labor laws and restrictive labor market practices are among other prominent issues. These issues are reflected in India's poor ranking among the countries in the region, in particular the dynamic export-oriented economies in East Asia, in terms of various indicators of ease of doing business.[40] Moreover, so far India has not been successful in using SEZs as an effective vehicle for providing foreign investors with a suitable investment climate that is insulated from the remaining distortions in the rest of the economy. Smooth functioning of the India SEZs has also been constrained by the controversial issue of land acquisition and unresolved issues relating to the relaxation of labor laws for the SEZ firms.

As discussed in Section 2 and supported by the findings of the empirical analysis in the rest of the paper, completing this unfinished reform agenda is even more important for linking India into global production networks than for the expansion of the standard labor-intensive products and other conventional exports. The relative importance attached by firms to service-link costs compared to labor cost is much more important in this new form of international exchange. This means that the economic base of the host country is the ultimate draw for investors in this area: just offering incentives for investors cannot compensate for the lack of such a base. International vertical integration of manufacturing naturally increases the risks associated with supply delays and disruptions in a given location within the production network, because it can bring the operation of the entire production network to a halt. In the current business climate in India such disruptions could take many forms, including shipping delays, strikes, power outage or political disturbances.

40. India's global ranking on various indicators has been extensively documented. For a recent comparison, including comprehensive coverage of the relevant studies, see Hoda and Rai (2013).

Is there a case for proactive policies to attract FDI, in addition to improving the economic base through further reforms in order to effectively link Indian manufacturing to global production networks? As discussed (Section 2), over time global production sharing has expanded well beyond the confines of intra-firm activities of MNEs, but there is compelling evidence that MNEs are still the leading vehicle for developing countries to enter global production networks. There are also compelling economic reasons which support the argument that countries may not be able to attract the volume of FDI that their economic base merits without active investment promotion (Wells and Wint 2000). Despite their size and global reach, MNEs do not always have perfect information on potential sites: "Most companies consider only a small range of potential investment locations [and] many other countries are not even on their map" (Wells and Wint 2000). Given this "market failure in information," the decision making process relating to site selection can be subjective and biased. Moreover, as an increased number of countries embrace liberalization reforms, there is tense competition in the market for investment sites: many potential host countries compete for attracting big players in global industries to their countries. Therefore, it may be worthwhile for a country to invest in altering the perceptions of potential investors by improving its image, and not taking economic fundamentals as given.

It is important to emphasize that investment promotion is not the same as giving subsidies or financial incentives, although incentives can play a role at the margin when investors choose among alternative locations with similar economic fundamentals required for the long term viability of their operations. The focus of the investment promotion campaign can be general (aimed at home countries with potential investors), industry specific (investors in industries in which the host country has an actual or potential competitive edge), or investor specific. Effective investment promotion should go beyond simply marketing the country and also focus on facilitating and coordinating the perquisites for setting up operations and effective functioning when the MNEs decide to set up production plants. This involves addressing potential failures in markets and institutions for skills, technical services or infrastructure in relation to the specific needs of targeted investors.

The experiences of Ireland (Ruwane and Gorg 2001), Singapore (Wong 2007), Costa Rica (MIGA 2006; Rodriguez-Clare 2001), Penang (Athukorala 2014), and more recently of Vietnam (Altman 2007; Athukorala and Tien 2012) suggest that well-focused investment promotion can be very effective in attracting FDI in line with the country's development priorities. Investment promotion in Ireland, Singapore, and Penang was primarily industry specific, targeting electronics and the related supporting industries. Costa Rica provides an example of targeting a specific MNE (Intel). Vietnam's approach is much more broad-based, but in recent years it has been successful in attracting two large players in the electronics industry (Intel and Samsung) through targeted promotion. In all these countries, investment promotion has gone well beyond the initial marketing stage, to facilitating the operation of the newly established foreign ventures. For instance, in Costa Rica and Vietnam the governments' commitment to invest in training to meet the future skill needs of its local operations was a major factor considered by Intel in its site selection decision. In Singapore, the government went even further and involved MNE managers in designing training and infrastructure programs. The state government of Penang joined hands with MNEs in setting up the Penang Skill Development Centre to train middle-level technicians, which is now hailed the world over as a successful case of public sector MNE collaboration in human capital development. The state government of Penang also adopted an innovative approach of involving managers of MNE affiliates, operating in the state, in its investment promotion campaigns in the respective home countries. The experiences of these countries also show that, in global industries like electronics and electrical goods, initial success in attracting a big player/players to set up operations in a country breeds success because in these industries there is something akin to herd mentality in the site selection process of MNEs.

The remarkable success of the Indian software industry, a highly visible symbol of India's emergence in the world economy, is perhaps illustrative of India's growth potential through production sharing spurred by reforms (Desai 2002; Krueger 2010). The software industry is unique in India in that restrictions on MNE entry have been virtually abolished. Now virtually every major global company in the software industry has a base in India and the entry of MNEs has opened up opportunities for Indian companies to thrive through functional specialization, and to develop niche products and services for large clients abroad. Liberalization of FDI has also been accompanied by the removal of quantitative restrictions on imports of computers and peripherals, and drastic cuts in import tariffs on these products and significant telecommunication reforms. In addition to these reforms, which laid the foundations that made the domestic software industry internationally competitive, there are other product-specific features which make the software industry immune to the trade-retarding effects of the investment climate. For instance, the fact that IT was not heavily dependent on Indian infrastructure (being able to transmit services via satellites) certainly gave

IT firms an advantage over manufacturers who might otherwise have had to depend on roads and ports to export their goods. Regulations surrounding the employment of labor were largely not binding because the labor needs of the IT sector consisted largely of skilled workers. As it was a start-up industry, most of the behind-the-border controls and regulations affecting firms in other industries were not a binding constraint for IT firms (Krueger 2010). Finally, the powerful Indian diaspora in the global software Industry (the so-called IIT mafia) played a vital role in "selling the country… [by]… leveraging its own strength with India's comparative advantage" (Kapur 2010: 262).[41]

Appendix

(A) Trade Data Compilation

The data used in this section for all countries other than Taiwan are compiled from the United Nation's Comtrade Database[42], based on Revision 3 of the Standard International Trade Classification (SITC Rev. 3). Data for Taiwan are obtained from the trade database (based on the same classification system) of the Council for Economic Planning and Development, Taipei. (the UN trade data reporting system, Comtrade database).

Parts and components are delineated from the reported trade data using a list compiled by mapping parts and components in the UN Broad Economic Classification (BEC) with the Harmonized System (HS) of trade classification at the 6-digit level. The product list of the WTO Information Technology Agreement Information, gathered from firm-level surveys conducted in Thailand and Malaysia were used to fill gaps in the BEC list of parts and components. Data compiled at the HS 6-digit level were converted to the SITC (based on the SITC Revision 3) for the final analysis using the UN HS-SITC concordance.[43] It is important to note that parts and components, as defined here, are only a subset of the "intermediate goods", even though the two terms have been widely used interchangeably in the recent literature on global production sharing. Parts and components, are

41. The "diaspora effect" has not materialized in other industries perhaps because of the absence of favorable domestic policies: "The well-known infrastructural and policy weaknesses in manufacturing have steered the diaspora's role in IT more towards the software side, rather than developing the hardware sector" (Kapur 2010: 262).

42. http://comtrade.un.org/db/ (accessed in January–March 2013).

43. For details on the method of classification and the list of parts and components see Athukorala (2010).

inputs further along the production chain. Parts and components, unlike the standard intermediate inputs, such as iron and steel, industrial chemicals and coal, are "relationship-specific" intermediate inputs; in most cases they do not have reference prices, and are not sold on exchanges, and are more demanding on the contractual environment (Nunn 2007). Most (if not all) parts and components do not have a "commercial life" their own, unless they get embodied in a final product.

There is no hard and fast rule applicable to distinguishing between parts/components and assembled products in international trade data. The only practical way of doing this is to focus on the specific product categories in which network trade is heavily concentrated (Krugman 2008). Once these product categories have been identified, assembly trade can be approximately estimated as the difference between parts and components—directly identified based on our list—and recorded trade in these product categories.

Guided by the available literature on production sharing, we identified seven product categories: office machines and automatic data processing machines (SITC 75), telecommunication and sound recording equipment (SITC 76), electrical machinery (SITC 77), road vehicles (SITC 78), professional and scientific equipment (SITC 87), and photographic apparatus (SITC 88). It is quite reasonable to assume that these product categories contain virtually no products produced from start to finish in a given country. However, admittedly the estimates based on this list do not provide full coverage of final assembly in world trade. For instance, the outsourcing of final assembly does take place in various miscellaneous product categories such as clothing, furniture, sporting goods, and leather products. It is not possible to meaningfully delineate parts and components and assembled goods in reported trade in these product categories because they contain a significant (yet unknown) share of horizontal trade. Likewise, assembly activities in software trade have recorded impressive expansion in recent years, but these are lumped together in the UN data system with "special transactions" under SITC 9. However, the magnitude of the bias resulting from the failure to cover these items is unlikely to be substantial because network trade in final assembly is heavily concentrated in the product categories covered in our decomposition (Yeats 2001; Krugman 2008).

Although SITC Rev 3 was introduced in the mid-1980s, a closer examination of country-level data shows that data recording systems in many countries have considerable gaps in the coverage of parts and component trade until about 1990. Therefore, we use 1992 as the starting year of data disaggregation for the inter-country comparison of trade based on global production sharing.

(B) Variables Used in Estimating the Export Equation: Definitions and Data Sources

Label	*Definition*	*Data Source/variable construction*
TRD	Value of bilateral trade (imports and exports) in US$ measured at constant (2000) price.	Exports (at CIF price, US$): compiled from importer records of UN-COMTRADE, online database (http://comtrade.un.org/db/ (accessed in January-March 2013) Exports and import values are deflated by US import and export price indices extracted from the US Bureau of labor Statistics database (http://www.bls.gov/ppi/home.htm).
GDP	Real GDP (at 2000 price)	World Development Indicator, The World Bank
DST	Weighted distance measure of the French Institute for Research on the International Economy (CEPII), which measures the bilateral great-circle distance between major cities of each country	French Institute for Research on the International Economy (CEPII) database
RER	Real exchange rate: $$RER_{ij} = NER_{ij} * \frac{P_j^D}{P_i^W}$$ where, NER is the nominal bilateral exchange rate index (value of country *j*'s currency in terms of country *i*'s currency) currency), PW in price level of country *j* measured by the producer price index and PD is the domestic price index of country *i* measured by the GDP deflator. An increase (decrease) in RER_{ij} indicates improvement (a deterioration) in country's international competitiveness relative to country *j*.	Constructed using data from World Bank, World development Indicators database. The mean-adjusted RER is used in the model. This variable specification assumes that countries are in exchange rate equilibrium at the mean.
LPI	World Bank logistic performance index The original index (1: worst to 6: best scale) converted "1 to 100".	LPI database, World Bank (Arvis et al. 2007)
INS	Institutional (governance) quality ("1:worst to 100: best" scale)	International country risk index RPS Group (http://www.prsgroup.com)
RTA	A binary dummy variable which is unity if both country *i* and country *j* are signatories to a given regional trading agreement (RTA)	CEPII database
COML	A dummy variable which is unity if country *i* and country *j* have a common language and zero otherwise.	CEPII database
ADJ	A binary dummy variable which is unity if country *i* and country *j* share a common land border and zero otherwise	CEPII database

References

Aggarwal, Aradhna. 2012. *Social and Economic Impact of SEZs in India*. New Delhi: Oxford University Press.

———. 2013. "SEZ-led Growth in Taiwan, Korea, and India," *Asian Survey*, 52 (5): 872–99.

Altman, D. 2007. *Connected 24 Hours in the Global Economy*. New York: Farrar, Straus and Goroux.

Arora, Ashish. 2008. "The Indian Software Industry and Its Prospects," in Jagdish N. Bhagwati and Charles W. Calomiris (eds), *Sustaining India's Growth Miracle*, pp. 166–211. New York: Columbia University Press.

Arvis, Jean Francois, M.A. Mustra, J. Panzer, L. Ojala, and T. Naula. 2007. *Connecting to Compete: Trade Logistics in the Global Economy: The Logistic Performance Index and its Indicators*. Washington, D.C.: World Bank.

Athukorala, Prema-chandra. 2009. "The Rise of China and East Asian Export Performance: Is the Crowding-Out Fear Warranted?" *The World Economy*, 32 (2): 234–66.

———. 2010. "'Production Networks and Trade Patterns in East Asia': Regionalization or Globalisation?" Working Paper Series on Regional Economic Integration, No. 56, Asian Development Bank, Manila.

———. 2011. "'Production Networks and Trade Patterns in East Asia': Regionalization or Globalisation?" *Asian Economic Papers*, 10 (1): 65–95.

———. 2014. "Growing with Global Production Sharing: The Tale of Penang Export Hub," *Competition and Change*, 18 (3): 221–45.

Athukorala, Prema-chandra and Tran Quang Tien. 2012. "Foreign Direct Investment in Industrial Transition in Vietnam," *Journal of the Asia-Pacific Economy*, 17 (3): 446–63.

Baier, Scott L., and Jeffrey H. Bergstrand. 2007. "Do Free Trade Agreements Actually Increase Members' International Trade?" *Journal of International Economics*, 71 (1): 72–95.

Bergeijk, Van Peter, and Steven Brakman. 2010. *The Gravity Model in International Trade: Advances and Applications*. Cambridge: Cambridge University Press.

Bhagwati, Jagdish and Arvind Panagariya. 2013. *Why Growth Matters: How Economic Growth in India Reduced Poverty and the Lessons for Other Developing Countries*. New York: Public Affairs.

Brown, Clair, and Greg Linden. 2005. "Offshoring in the Semiconductor Industry: A Historical Perspective," in Lael Brainard and Susan M. Collins (eds), *The Brookings Trade Forum 2005: Offshoring White-Collar Work: The Issues and Implications*, pp. 270–333. Washington, D.C.: Brooking Institution Press.

Brown, Drusilla K., Alan V. Deardorff, and Robert M. Stern. 2004. "The Effects of Multinational Production on Wages and Working Conditions in Developing Countries," in Robert E. Baldwin and L. Allan Winters (eds), *Challenges to*

Globalization: Analysing the Economics, pp. 279–332. Chicago: Chicago University Press.

Brun, Jean-Francois, C. Carrère, P. Guillaumont, and J. de Melo. 2005. "Has Distance Died? Evidence from a Panel Gravity Model," *The World Bank Economic Review*, 19 (1): 99–120.

Business Day. 2013. "Manufacturers Jump Ship from China to Cambodia", *Business Day*, April 10. Available online at http://www.businessday.com.au/business/world-business/manufacturers-jump-ship-from-china-to-cambodia-20130410-2hk3u.html (accessed on April 24, 2013)

Dean, Judith, Kwok Chiu Fung, and Zhi Wang. 2011. "Measuring Vertical Specialization: The Case of China," *Review of International Economics*, 19 (4): 609–25.

Desai, Ashok. 2002. "Comments (on 'Bangalore: The Silicon Valley of Asia?' by Annale Saxanian)" in Anne O. Krueger (ed.), *Economic Policy Reforms and the Indian Economy*, pp. 167–96. Oxford: Oxford University Press.

Dornbusch, Rudigar. 1992. "The Case for Trade Liberalization in Developing Countries," *Journal of Economic Perspective*, 6 (1): 69–85.

Dunning, John H. (2009). "Location and the Multinational Enterprise: A Neglected Factor?" *Journal of International Business Studies*, 40 (1): 5–19.

Egger, Peter. 2005. "Alternative Techniques for Estimation of Cross-Section Gravity Models," *Review of International Economics*, 13 (5): 881–91.

Evans, Carolyn L., and James Harrigan. 2005. "Distance, Time, and Specialization: Lean Retailing in General Equilibrium," *American Economic Review*, 95 (1): 292–313.

Feenstra, Robert C., and Gary Hamilton. 2006. *Emerging Economics, Divergent Paths: Economic Organization and International Trade in South Korea and Taiwan*. Cambridge: Cambridge University Press.

Feenstra, Robert and Gordon Hanson. 2003. "Global Production Sharing and Rising Inequality: A Survey of Trade and Wages," in Eun Kwan Choi and James Harrigan (eds), *Handbook of International Trade*, pp. 146–85. Oxford: Blackwell.

Gray, John, Keith Skowrosky, Gokce Esenduran and M. Johnny Rungtusanatham. 2013. "The Reshoring Phenomenon: What Supply Chain Academic Ought to Know and Should Do," *Journal of Supply Chain Management*, 49 (2): 27–33.

Goh Keng Swee. 1993. "What Causes Fast Economic Growth?" Forth K.T. Li Lecture, Harvard University reproduced in L. Low (ed.), *Wealth of East Asian Nations, Speeches and Writings by Goh Keng Swee*, 1995, pp. 243–58. Singapore: Federation Publication.

Golub, Stephen S., Ronald W. Jones and Henrik Kierzkwski. 2007. "Globalization and Country Specific Service Links," *Journal of Economic Policy Reforms*, 10 (2): 63–88.

Grunwald, Joseph, and Kenneth Flamm. 1985. *The Global Factory: Foreign Assembly in International Trade*. Washington, D.C.: Brookings Institution Press.

Grossman, Gene M. and Elhanan Helpman. 1992. *Innovation and Growth in the Global Environment*. Cambridge, MAS: MIT Press.

Grossman, Gene M., and Elhanan Helpman. 2005. "Outsourcing in a Global Economy," *Review of Economic Studies*, 72 (1): 135–59.

Hanson, Gordon H., Raymond J. Mataloni Jr, and Matthew J. Slaughter. 2001. "The Expansion Strategies of U.S. Multinational Firms," in Dani Rodrik and Susan Collins (eds), *Brookings Trade Forum 2001*, pp. 245–82. Washington, D.C.: Brookings Institution.

Hanson, Gordon H., Raymond J. Mataloni Jr, and Matthew J. Slaughter. 2005. "Vertical Production Networks in Multinational Firms," *Review of Economics and Statistics*, 87 (4): 664–78.

Hausman, Jerry A., and William E. Taylor. 1981. "Panel Data and Unobservable Individual Effects," *Econometrica*, 49 (6): 1377–98.

Helleiner, Gerald K. 1973. "Manufactured Exports from Less-Developed Countries and Multinational Firms," *Economic Journal*, 83 (329): 21–47.

Helpman, Elhanan. 2006. "Trade, FDI, and the Organization of Firms," *Journal of Economic Literature*, 44 (3): 589–630.

———. 2011. *Understanding Global Trade*. Cambridge, Mass: Harvard University Press.

Hoda, Anwarul and Durgesh Kumar Rai. 2013. "Production Networks and Barriers to Trade and Investment in India," New Delhi: Indian Council for Research on International Economic Relations (draft paper).

Hummels, David. 2007. "Transport Costs and International Trade in the Second Era of Globalization," *Journal of Economic Perspectives*, 21 (2): 131–54.

Hummels, David, J. Ishii and Kei-Mu Yi. 2001. "The Nature and Growth of Vertical Specialization in World Trade," *Journal of International Economics*, 54 (1): 75–96.

Humphrey, John. 2003. "Globalization and Supply Chain Networks: The Auto Industry in Brazil and India," *Global Networks*, 3 (2): 121–41.

Isaacson, Walter. 2011. *Steve Jobs*. New York: Simon & Schuster.

Johnson, Robert C., and Guillermo Noguera. 2012. "Accounting for Intermediates: Production Sharing and Trade in Value Added," *Journal of International Economics*, 86 (2): 224–36.

Jones, Ronald W. (2000). *Globalization and the Theory of Input Trade*. Cambridge, Mass.: MIT Press.

Jones, Ronald W. and Henryk Kierzkowski. 2001. "A Framework for Fragmentation," in Seven Arndt and Henryk Kierzkowski (eds), *Fragmentation: New Production Patterns in the World Economy*, pp. 17–34. Oxford: Oxford University Press.

———. 2004. "Globalization and the Consequences of International Fragmentation," in R. Dornbusch, G. Calvo & M. Obstfeld (eds), *Money, Factor Mobility and Trade: Essays in in Honor of Robert A. Mundell*, pp. 365–81. Cambridge, Mass.: MIT Press.

Joshi, Vijay. 2008. "Economic Resurgence, Lopsided Reforms and Jobless Growth," in Heath, A. F. and R. F. Jeffery (eds), *Diversity and Change in Modern India: Economic, Social and Political Approaches*, pp. 73–106. Oxford: Oxford University Press.

Kapur, Devesh. 2010. *Diaspora, Development, and Democracy: The Domestic Impact of International Migration from India*. Princeton, NJ: Princeton University Press.

Klier, Thomas, and James Rubenstein. 2008. *Who Really Made Your Car? Restructuring and Geographic Change in the Auto Industry*. Michigan: W.E. Upjohn Institute for Employment.

Kohpaiboon, Archanun and Juthatip Jongwanich. 2013. "International Production Networks, Clusters, and Industrial Upgrading: Evidence from Automotive and Hard Disk Drive Industries in Thailand," *Review of Policy Research*, 30 (2): 211–39.

Koopman, Robert, Zhi Wang, and Shang-Jin Wei. 2008. "How much of Chinese Exports is Really Made in China? Assessing Domestic Value-added when Processing Trade is Pervasive," *National Bureau of Economic Research Working Paper 14109*. Cambridge, MAS: NBER.

Krishna, Kala. 2006. "Understanding Rules Origin," in O. Cadot, A. Estevadeordal, A. Suwa-Eisenmann, and T. Verdier (eds), *The Origin of Goods: Rules of Origin in Regional Trading Agreements*, pp. 19–34. Oxford: Oxford University Press.

Krueger, Anne O. 2010. "India's Trade with the World: Retrospect and Prospect," in Shankar Acharya and R. Mohan (eds), *India's Economy: Performance and Challenges*, pp. 399–429. New Delhi: Oxford University Press.

Krugman, Paul R. 2008. "Trade and Wages, Reconsidered," *Brookings Papers on Economic* Activity 1: Macroeconomics, pp. 103–38.

Lall, Sanjaya. 2002. "FDI and Development: Research Issues in the Emerging Context," in Bijit Bora (ed.), *Foreign Direct Investment: Research Issues*, pp. 325–45. London: Routledge.

Maizels, Alfred. 1963. *Industrial Growth and World Trade: An Empirical Study of Trends in Production*. Cambridge: Cambridge University Press.

Manning, Chris, and Raden M. Purnagunawan. 2011. "Survey of Recent Developments," *Bulletin of Indonesian Economic Studies*, 47 (3): 303–32.

Menon, Jayant. 2013. "Can FTAs Support Growth or Spread of International Production Networks in Asia?," *Working Papers in Trade and Development 2013/06*, Arndt-Corden Department of Economics, Australian National University.

MIGA (Multilateral Investment Guarantee Agency). 2006. *The Impact of Intel in Costa Rica. Nine Years after the Decision to Invest*. Washington, D.C.: MIGA/ World Bank.

Mattoo, Aditya, Zhi Wang and Shang-Jin Wei (eds), 2013. *Trade in Value Added: Developing New Measures of Cross-Border Trade*. Washington, D.C: World Bank.

Ng, Francis and Alexander Yeats. 2003. "Major Trade Trends in Asia: What are the Implications for Regional Cooperation and Growth?" *Policy Research Working Paper 3084*. Washington, D.C: World Bank.

Nunn, Nathan. 2007. "Relationship-Specificity, Incomplete Contracts, and the Patterns of Trade," *Quarterly Journal of Economics*, 122 (2): 569–600.

Panagariya, Arvind. 2004. "India's Trade Reform," in Suman Bery, Barry Bosworth, and Arvind Panagariya (eds), *India Policy Forum* 1, pp. 1–57. New Delhi: SAGE Publications.

———. 2008. *India: Emerging Giant*. New York: Oxford University Press.

———. 2013. "India and China: Trade and Foreign Investment," in Nicholas C. Hope, Anjini Kochar, Roger Noll, and T.N. Srinivasan (eds), *Economic Reform in India: Challenges, Prospects and Lessons*, pp. 96–138. Cambridge: Cambridge University Press.

Panagariya, Arvind, and Asha Sundaram. 2013. "External Liberalization by India and China: Recent Experience and Future Challenges," *Indian Growth and Development Review*, 6 (1): 8–34.

Park, Seokmin. 2013. "Samsung Electronics 2013," Power-Point Presentation at the Conference on *Plugging into Global Value Chain: A Strategy for Growth*, Seoul National University, 305 June 2013.

Rangan, Subramanian, and Robert Lawrence. 1999. *A Prism on Globalization*. Washington, D.C.: Brookings Institution Press.

Rodriguez-Clare, Andres. 2001. "Cost Rica's Development Strategy Based on Human Capital and Technology: How it got there, the Impact of Intel, and Lessons for Other Countries," *Journal of Human Development*, 2 (2): 311–24.

Ruwane, Frances, and Holger Gorg. 2001. "Globalization and Fragmentation: Evidence for the Electronics Industry in Ireland," in Seven Arndt and Henryk Kierzkowksi (eds), *Fragmentation: New Production Patterns in the World Economy*, pp. 17–34. Oxford: Oxford University Press.

Sachs, Jeffry, and Andrew Warner. 1995. "Economic Reforms and the Process of Global Integration," *Brookings Papers on Economic Activity*, 25 Anniversary Issue, 1–95.

Sen, Rahul, and Sadhana Srivastava. 2012. "Asia's International Production Networks: Will India be the Next Assembly Centre?," *ARTNeT Working Paper Series, No. 118*, Bangkok: Economic Commission for Asia and the Pacific.

Serlenga, Laura, and Yongcheol Shin. 2007. "Gravity Models of Intra-EU Trade: Application of the CCEP-HT Estimation in Heterogeneous Panels with Unobserved Common Time-Specific Factors," *Journal of Applied Econometrics*, 22 (3): 361–81.

Singh, Manmohan. 1964. *India's Export Trends*. Oxford: Clarendon Press.

Spencer, Barbara J. 2005. "International Outsourcing and Incomplete Contracts," *Canadian Journal of Economics*, 38 (4): 1107–35.

Srinivasan, T.N. 1998. "India's Export Performance: A Comparative Analysis," in Isher J. Ahluwalia and I.M.D Little (eds), *India's Economic Reforms and Development: Essays for Manmohan Singh*, pp. 197–228. New Delhi: Oxford University Press.

———. 1999. "Trade Orientation, Trade Liberalization, and Economic Growth," in Garry Saxonhouse and T.N. Srinivasan (eds), *Development, Duality and International Economic Regime: Essay in Honor of Gustav Ranis*, pp. 155–96. Ann Arbor: University of Michigan Press.

Srinivasan, T.N. 2012. *Growth, Sustainability and India's Reforms*. New Delhi: Oxford University Press.

Sturgeon, Timothy J. 2002. "Modular Production Networks: A New American Model of Industrial Organization," *Industrial and Corporate Change*, 11 (3): 451–96.

Thee, Kien Wie, and Mary Pangestu. 1998. "Technological Capabilities and Indonesia's Manufactured Exports," in D. Ernst, T. Ganiatsos, and L. Mytelka (eds), *Technological Capabilities and Export Success in Asia*, pp. 211–65. London: Routledge.

Tinbergen, Jan. 1962. "Appendix VI: An Analysis of World Trade Flows," in Jan Tinbergen, *Shaping the World Economy: Suggestions for International Economic Policy*, pp. 262–93. New York: Twentieth Century Fund.

Veeramani, C. 2012. "Anatomy of India's Merchandise Export Growth: 1993–94 to 2010–11," *Economic and Political Weekly*, 66 (91): 94–104.

Wells, Louis T., and Rafiq Ahmed. 2007. *Making Foreign Investment Safe: Property Rights and National Sovereignty*. Oxford: Oxford University Press.

Wells, Louis T., and Alvin G. Wint. 2000. *Marketing a Country: Promotion as a Tool for Attracting Foreign Investment*. Washington, D.C.: World Bank/International Finance Corporation.

Wong, Poh Kam. 2007. "The Remaking of Singapore's High-Tech Enterprise System," in Henry S. Rowen, Marguerite G. Hancock, and Lilliam F. Miller (eds), *Making IT: The Rise of Asian in High Tech*, pp. 123–74. Stanford, California: Stanford University Press.

World Bank. 2010. *Investing Across Borders: Indicators of Foreign Direct Regulations in 87 Economies*. Washington, D.C.: World Bank.

———. 2012. *Doing Business 2013*. Washington, D.C.: World Bank.

WTO (World Trade Organisation). 2011. *India Trave Policy Review—2011*. Geneva: WTO.

Yeats, Alexander. 2001. "Just How Big is Global Production Sharing?" in S. Arndt and H. Kierzkowski (eds), *Fragmentation: New Production Patterns in the World Economy*, pp. 108–43. New York: Oxford University Press.

Yew, Lee Kuan. 2000. *From Third World to First: The Singapore Story: 1965–2000 Memoirs of Lee Kuan Yew*, vol. 2. Singapore: Singapore Press Holding.

Yi, Kei-Mu. 2003. "Can Vertical Specialization Explain the Growth of World Trade," *Journal of Political Economy*, 111 (1): 52–102.

Comments and Discussion

Mihir Desai
Harvard Business School, Harvard University

Professor Prema-chandra's paper offers a mix of analytical approaches including historical, anecdotal, and descriptive accounts, along with regression based evidence to examine India's experience with global production networks.

The foundation of his argument is that India's export performance has been fairly disappointing, particularly in "network industries" where "global production sharing" is important. While road vehicles have been an exception to India's disappointing export performance, this likely reflects the large domestic market rather than particular strength in this industry. The paper concludes that logistics and institutions appear to matter particularly for network productions. Second, India's poor performance is not fully explained by the variables examined in the paper. Finally, the idea that managerial talent and a middle class workforce are particularly important in these network industries is also suggested. Because India has a reputation for being rich in talent, specifically in engineering and middle level managerial talent, this is a somewhat incongruous result.

For the regression based evidence, I would have liked to pool the samples and constrain some coefficients to be equal providing for a simpler comparison of coefficients. Similarly, I would have liked a much greater discussion on the standard errors given the panel nature of the data with no significant time variation. Finally, I'm not entirely sure that the politics variable from International Country Risk Guide (ICRG) is well suited to this purpose. It is a well-known variable, but it is not clear why it is used here. Variables for intra-firm trade and issues in intellectual property protection would be interesting to use given the emphasis on contractibility.

The paper places a great deal of emphasis on certain manufacturing sectors. In fact, this is really a paper about a few Standard International Trade Classification (SITC) codes, but it remains unclear why these specific codes were chosen over others. Similarly, the distinction between parts and assembly was ambiguous. Assemblies appear to be residuals, meaning they are the sum of parts and components subtracted from the total, however the way in which assemblies are calculated was not clear. At the heart of the paper lies the issue of what "global production sharing" actually refers to. There are several possibilities. The narrowest way to read this paper is that it is about a subset of manufacturing trade. It is about what is going on with these four SITC codes. If this is the correct reading, the reason for choosing these codes should be elaborated further. Alternatively, this paper could be about trade in intermediate goods, in which case a different data source would be more convincing. Finally, this paper may also be about off-shoring and intra-firm trade. Multinationals, in the language of this argument, are the sine qua non for network trade. In this case the paper is really about multinationals, and more attention needs to be paid to intra-firm trade. In particular, there are databases on intra-firm trade for the United States, for Germany, that are very good for this type of issue, and might be more interesting than bilateral trade data.

Another possible focus could be foreign direct investment. Exploring the distinction between horizontal and vertical arrangements and between offshoring and outsourcing would be critical. As one example, Apple's manufacturing is happening at arm's length, or quasi arm's length, through Foxconn. The paper should be clear about the differences between these types of FDI arrangements, and which one it is really focused on. The paper's policy discussion might also expand toward, for example, ownership restrictions. If one is considering FDI decisions and breaking up the production process, then being forced to share ownership is quite important.

Finally, the process of global fragmentation has taken on new levels of sophistication which creates new imperatives for India's policy-makers. Specifically, firms have become adept at splintering their headquarters, which used to be immutable and stationary in one country. Corporations are dividing their financial home, legal home and home for managerial talent across jurisdictions. As one example, one might think of Samsonite as an American company. But, it is listed in Hong Kong. Its legal home is in the Caribbean, and its managerial talent sits in Massachusetts. This shift has taken place in a number of different companies. This is the new domain of competition for jurisdictions. Additionally, these production and headquarter decisions cannot be understood without paying attention to tax incentives. The policy debate in developed countries is largely about tax incentives for mobile income associated with R&D and patents. The location of intellectual property gives rise to significant production locational decisions as well. In Apple's case, a large part of Apple's IP is located in Ireland for tax reasons and this complicates the possibility of locating production facilities in America. In short, tax incentives are altering intellectual property decisions that in turn dictate production decisions.

Rajesh Chadha

NCAER

The paper makes an important contribution to the understanding of India's participation in global production sharing in the manufacturing sectors. While India has played a significant role in sharing global software services, its performance has been unimpressive with regards to manufactured products.

Many input–output technique-based studies measure the degree of dependence of manufacturing production and trade of selected countries on global production sharing using trade flows between MNEs and their foreign affiliates. These studies point to the growing importance of production sharing in world trade and the increasing cross-border interdependencies in the world economy.

The paper provides rich information on network trade. It points out that India lags significantly behind as far as processing and assembly activities are concerned. India's composition of network exports is biased heavily in favor of road vehicles and other transport equipment, accounting for more than 48 % of its total network exports. The corresponding number is 14 % for East Asia and only 11.5 % for China. In contrast, the shares of India's network exports are extremely low for office machines and automatic data processing machines, telecommunication and sound recording equipment and semiconductors. The corresponding values are much higher for China and East Asia on the whole.

The author has argued that the concentration of India's network exports in favor of road vehicles and auto components may be due to very high customs duty on passenger cars as compared with auto parts, thus giving exceedingly high effective protection to road vehicles. This phenomenon has possibly driven automotive MNEs to set up production plants in India to produce for the global market, not just for the Indian market.

On the contrary, India's global production networking is abysmally insignificant in electronics, electrical goods and related products. While a number of large MNEs, including Nokia, Samsung and LG, have set up production bases in India, these are predominantly involved in production for the domestic market and not for exports. The Special Economic Zones, which had played an important role in East Asia's network exports, have not been helpful for India despite the enactment of the SEZ Act of 2005. The only East Asian country which compares with India's failure of developing its network trade in electronics is Indonesia. The labor market rigidities in Indonesia have been cited to be the major cause of the presence of failing MNEs there.

One of my major comments relates to the author's observation on the rapidly growing intermediate or parts and components trade versus the overall manufacturing trade of the finished goods. This is somewhat puzzling because when we talk of parts and components, I do understand that they switch between countries multiple number of times. So when we say that the trade in parts and components has grown by say, 30 % versus the final goods trade growing by 10 %, I do not know how to discount the multiple crisscrossing through countries' borders. So the growth pattern of final assembly or final goods versus the multiple entry of intermediates raises question of data classification of intermediate versus final goods. A good may be "final" for a manufacturing firm in an "exporting country" but the same may be "intermediate" for a manufacturing firm in the "importing country".

Further, comparing export data of, say Hong Kong, with that of, say Malaysia or India, is likely to have some oddity. The distinction between the shares of entrepot trade of a country vis-à-vis its network trade may not be easy.

The issue of network trade is not something new. It has always been there, albeit in smaller proportion. This phenomenon is based mainly on shifting/dynamic forces of Ricardian comparative advantage. A Japanese economist Akamatsu had written about this issue way back in the 1930s and had named it as the "flying geese investment". It is inverted, "V" shaped formation. When a particular sector becomes "sunset" in one country it may be "sunrise" in another country. The relative wage rate advantage in a developing country attracts assembly operations to it from a developed economy. The developed economy may continue to provide the specialized parts and components from its own production facilities or set up such production facilities in some other developing countries.

The share of network trade in India's exports has been low because of the absence of enthusiastic MNEs and FDI which have shied away because of the issues of labor law rigidities, land acquisition, inspector-raj, availability of infrastructure, governance, etc. In fact, these factors have not only discouraged FDI and investment by MNEs but have had equally debilitating effect on domestic investment in manufacturing sectors particularly the unskilled/semi-skilled labor-intensive sectors. The share of manufacturing has been stagnant around 17 % ever since economic reforms were initiated in 1991.

Finally, I would like to draw the author's attention to the new *Made in the World* initiative taken by WTO (http://www.wto.org/english/res_e/statis_e/miwi_e/miwi_e.htm).

> Today, companies divide their operations across the world, from the design of the product and manufacturing of components to assembly and marketing, creating international production chains. More and more products are "Made in the World" rather than "Made in the UK" or "Made in France". The statistical bias created by attributing the full commercial value to the last country of origin can pervert the political debate on the origin of the imbalances and lead to misguided, and hence counter-productive, decisions. The challenge is to find the right statistical bridges between the different statistical frameworks and national accounting systems to ensure that international interactions resulting from globalization are properly reflected and to facilitate cross border dialogue between national decision makers.

New databases are required to undertake more sophisticated studies on global production sharing, network and processing trade. One such initiative has been taken by the European Commission by preparing the *World Input–Output Database* (http://www.wiod.org/new_site/home.htm).

> Production processes increasingly fragment across borders. This fundamentally alters the nature of international trade with deep consequences for the location of production. The World Input–Output Database (WIOD) is the first public database that contains new information on these trends and provides the opportunity to analyse the consequences of fragmentation, for example for shifting patterns in demand for skills in labor markets, or for local emissions of air pollutants. WIOD provides time-series of world input–output tables for forty countries worldwide and a model for the rest-of-the-world, covering the period from 1995 to 2011. These tables have been constructed in a clear conceptual framework on the basis of officially published input–output tables in conjunction with national accounts and international trade statistics. In addition, WIOD provides data on labor and capital inputs and pollution indicators at the industry level that can be used in conjunction enlarging the scope of possible applications.

A very useful paper that may also be referred to is: http://www.wiod.org/publications/papers/wiod10.pdf.

General Discussion

Rohini Somanathan expressed surprise at India being more successful in high value-added products such as automobiles. She enquired about the importance of the price of land as well as the domestic market. It is said that there is a big domestic market for automobiles and that also helps exports. But it seems that when Ford initially set up its plant in Chennai, it exported more than it sold in the Indian market.

Following up on the comments by Mihir Desai, T.N. Srinivasan said that it was not clear why there is focus on a particular component of trade—in this case what is being termed network trade—unless it is associated with some externalities that otherwise would not be realized. If we view the policy problem as creating an environment in which the decisions taken by all who are participating in the production, consumption and trade enable their transactions costs to be minimized that is one thing. There you do not focus on any one set of products but on creating a broad favorable environment for trade.

Srinivasan further said that if the intra-firm trade is at the heart of this trade, the aggregate country level data which the paper is using for the analysis is not the right one and firm level data is what would be required.

Rajnish Mehra said that taxation may be crucial to this trade, especially the intra-firm component. So if you look at R&D, which is expensed rather than depreciated, you find these being concentrated where you have the highest marginal tax rates. So a lot of these decisions are tax-based decisions. Luxembourg has almost zero manufacturing but has the headquarters of so many firms, and that is just a tax arbitrage within the EU. Supposing you brought goods into Germany you would pay the VAT, export the goods, and collect the VAT back. In contrast, Luxembourg has tax free zones near the airport where essentially you park your goods, you pay no VAT and you ship them out. These are things of first order importance, especially for US firms, which want to make sure that tax liability is kept as low as possible.

In his response, Prema-chandra Athukorala opened by stating that he would pick up points that are more interesting and relevant. The flying geese phenomenon to which Rajesh Chadha pointed is entirely different from production sharing. In the former, you start with labor-intensive products and, when the wages increase, you move on to more capital-intensive production. Here we are talking about specialization within a product. Perhaps the paper needs to provide a little bit historical material.

Turning to Mihir's comments, Athukorala said that he would address them when revising the paper. Regarding Srinivasan's comment on intra-firm trade, he opined that it was only part of the full story as most of the fragmentation trade initially occurred within multinationals. Then, there are these new firms called contract manufacturers like Foxconn, which emerged because most of the components eventually become modular products. They can be used in many products. Also, companies like Foxconn assemble for many other firms. Therefore, if you simply focus on intra-firm trade you are going to miss a huge chunk of the story.

Athukorala agreed that firm level data is ideal but said that their access is largely limited. There are a number of papers on intra-firm trade within production networks, including one by Slot and others in the *Review of Economics and Statistics*.

Athukorala also said that the distinction between standard intermediate goods and parts and components is very important. Parts and components trade is relation-specific, unlike other intermediate goods. Therefore, even though people use both terms interchangeably, the former are a particular type of intermediate goods. Ronald Jones terms this intra-process trade which is different from trade in standard intermediate goods.

Regarding the externality point raised by Srinivasan , Athukorala argued that there are lot of sources of externalities from trade in network products. This has been the most rapidly growing segment of manufacturing trade and once you are there, you have many more opportunities. Ten years ago, we did not know a product called iPod. They have been the outcome of global production sharing. Therefore, this area is much more different from standard specialization. New products are emerging. If you are in this area you benefit more out of it. Penang (Malaysia) offers the case of the best known electronic hub. Firms in this region began with simple electronic assembly with Intel, AMD and others coming in the intial phase. That base has allowed the country to move on to many new product areas. Now Penang has got the hub for medical devices.

Finally, responding to the point by Somanathan, Athukorala said that he did not have data on land prices but that rental cost is a very important determinant of production locations. One of the reasons why Motorola started shifting from Singapore to other countries was the high rental cost. In India, it is not the cost but the bureaucratic hurdles involved in accessing land that remain a matter of concern. This needs to be studied as part of the special economic zone idea. The Chennai story is interesting, but the advent of these companies was facilitated through the large size of the market. Therefore, the component base developed and companies started exporting. Perhaps a few companies export more than what they sell domestically. This is exactly what happened in Thailand. Initially, as you know, the Hilux was basically designed by these companies in Thailand, in order to meet the requirements of farmers (due to the latter's requirement of a multiple-use vehicle that could be used for transporting, traveling and other uses). Then, these companies started developing products for exports due to a good investment environment. Now Thailand is the biggest Hilux vehicle exporter in the world, bigger than the United States. Unlike in electronics, there is a very important relationship between the domestic production base, the size of the market and exporting. Again, if you look at Brazil and Mexico the unfolding story here is exactly similar to what is happening in these countries.

Srinivasan rejoined pointing out that Athukorala had distinguished the particular products on which he was focusing from the general intermediate products category by appeal to the relationships between firms or within firm. But then without firm level information it is difficult to pursue the relation specific component. Regarding externalities, Srinivasan said that Athukorala seemed to say that they flowed from participation in this type of trade. Now, the exact nature of this is not very clear. Think of innovation. For innovating new products using some of the components and others that are being produced elsewhere, do you have to have a manufacturing location in your country? You can be anywhere, the products might be produced anywhere. You can think of a new product which could combine the components and parts from everywhere and locate yourself through a tax advantage to some other place and so on. None of this is crucially dependent on being a participant in this particular trade. So, the nature of externalities is not clear at all.

MICHAEL DEBABRATA PATRA*
Reserve Bank of India

JEEVAN KUMAR KHUNDRAKPAM†
Reserve Bank of India

ASISH THOMAS GEORGE‡
Reserve Bank of India

Post-Global Crisis Inflation Dynamics in India: What has Changed?§

ABSTRACT This paper explores the sources of inflation persistence in India in recent years. The cross-sectional distribution of inflation shows that supply side shocks in the form of relative price increases, particularly for food, and reflected in mainly positive skew, influenced aggregate prices lastingly. A diffusion index captures the quick generalization of price increases in this high inflation episode. Inflation persistence, based on univariate analysis, increased in the post global crisis period. Multivariate analysis by estimation of a new Keynesian Phillips curve points to expectations as the main source of the increase in persistence, suggesting some discounting of monetary policy credibility. Shocks to inflation will require forceful, more than proportionate policy responses. Estimates of reaction functions indicate that the central bank places the highest weight on inflation stabilization, while emphasizing output stabilization, and reaping inflation control properties therefrom. High degree of interest rate smoothing—"baby steps"—could be imparting persistence to the inflation process. The debate on the appropriate monetary policy framework for India is being overtaken by impending legislative changes. A flexible inflation targeting framework of constrained discretion appears to be the overwhelming choice.

* *mdpatra@rbi.org.in*

† *jeevankh@rbi.org.in*

‡ *ageorge@rbi.org.in*

§ The authors are deeply grateful to Dr Barry Bosworth for inviting them to write this paper and for constant encouragement and guidance at various stages of its preparation. They also express sincere thanks to Dr Urjit R. Patel who has been the motivation for this effort. Valuable support and comments from Harendra Behera, Joyce John, S. Gangadharan, and Jessica M. Anthony are gratefully acknowledged. Sitikantha Pattanaik, who agreed to edit the paper at short notice, deserves special mention. The views expressed in this paper and all errors, whether of omission or commission, are to be attributed to the authors only. All the usual disclaimers apply.

Keywords: *Inflation Rate, Relative Prices, Inflation Persistence, Monetary Policy, Phillips Curve, Taylor Rule*

JEL Classification: E31, E52, E58, C22, C26, C54

1. Introduction

India rebounded from the global financial crisis of 2008 robustly and ahead of advanced economies as well as several comparators among large emerging economies. By the first quarter of 2009, real gross domestic product (GDP) growth was close to 8% and climbing, reviving aspirations of double-digit growth. Every silver lining has a cloud though. The weather gods summoned a familiar but dreaded scourge—inflation. Sinisterly on the heels of this bounce back, it crept in under the radar of the Reserve Bank of India (RBI) in middle of 2009 in the form of food inflation that crossed 10% following a weak monsoon and subsequent flooding. This was a virulent strain relative to recent history, becoming generalized by October 2009 when headline inflation crossed the tolerance threshold of 5% of the RBI. By the time the RBI responded with a 75 basis points (bps) raising of cash reserve requirements in January 2010 followed by a 25 bps increase in the policy repo rate in March, headline inflation had surged above 10% and food inflation to 20%.

Looking back in the middle of 2013–14 (April–March: India's financial year) when inflation dipped below 5% for the first time in 40 months, this visitation of high inflation has also turned out to be drug (read policy)-resistant until the time of writing. Its most notable feature has been its stubborn persistence around 9% through January 2010 to January 2013, despite successive increases in the policy rate of up to 375 bps supported by intermittent cash reserve ratio (CRR) increases, cumulating to 100 bps, right up to October 2011. In other episodes in the not too distant past, people's emotive resentment against pernicious inflation of this order led them to vote out the offending government of the day. This time around, they had moved on, but only more diabolically. Withdrawing their trust from perceived irresponsibility in policy governance, they reposed it where time had been tested and withstood—they bought gold, determined not to let stubborn inflation gnaw away at their purchasing power. By 2010–11, an average annual level of 700–800 tonnes of gold imports, already the highest by any country in the world, surged beyond 1000 tonnes and stayed above that level. The current account deficit (CAD), which on an average was near zero as a proportion to GDP over the period 2003–09, burgeoned to above 4% of GDP in 2011–12 and kept rising unrelentingly, reaching 6.7% in Q3 of 2012–13. This unique, textbook-defying co-existence of high inflation and a high CAD was no less a vote of no-confidence.

Perhaps eclipsing all other inflation events in India's independent history, this one will be remembered as much for its tenacity as for the heat and dust it has stirred in its indolent passage. Several strands of opinion intertwine and uncoil in the full spectrum of this animated debate, but in the interest of brevity rather than generalization, it is perhaps useful to sketch out the end-points while recognizing that a rich diversity populates the space in between. At one end is the coagulation of opinion drawing from institutional and structural characteristics of the economy that this inflation was due to sector-specific cost-push factors—fuel and other commodity prices (Bhanumurthy et al. 2012; Hatekar et al. 2011; Rakshit 2011); adverse supply shocks to agricultural output (Balakrishnan 2011; Rakshit 2011; Sen and Himanshu 2011); clear evidence against a wage-price spiral in operation (Bose 2012)—all of which argues that orthodox monetary measures would be of little avail in an economy operating in the horizontal range of the aggregate supply curve (Mundle 2011). Many of these views were expressed at a seminar organized by the National Institute of Public Finance and Policy, New Delhi and have been encapsulated in Bose (2012). Any policy-induced compression of demand will cause output to fall and inflation to be pushed up. The RBI's anti-inflation actions spread over January 2010–October 2011, it is lamented, have been driven by the fever of a false sense of independence that make it pursue a monetarist policy into a morass of depression while ignoring the broader developmental objectives (Shetty 2013). Instead, the onus rests with the government to alter the agricultural supply side (Chand 2012; Sen and Himanshu 2011) through raising productivity and investment in agriculture and extension services, and more effective intervention through parastatals (Balakrishnan 2011; Chand 2011). In the articulation of this polarity, it has been argued that given the irrelevance of purely macroeconomic factors or overall excess demand, orthodox monetary (or fiscal) measures would be of little avail as anti inflationary devices. Not only are their limitations specific to the conditions prevailing during the inflation episode, but given the nature and structure of the Indian macroeconomy, the case for orthodox measures appears extremely weak when inflation is the consequence of supply side shocks (Rakshit 2011). It has also been argued that excess demand for credit generated by financial inclusion, for instance, can cause the velocity of circulation of money to rise and put pressure on prices. In these conditions, monetary tightening through raising interest rates will have no effect on inflation and that there could be a price to pay for this tightening without the attendant benefit of reduced inflation (Basu 2011), including in terms of unemployment and impairment to future growth (GOI 2011). At the other pole is the view that inflation persistence is essentially a result of costly policy errors in terms of misreading it as "narrowly based" and therefore misjudging the speed of its generalization, compounded by delayed reactions—"policymakers deliberately chose to fall behind the curve"—and by public communication of accommodation—"hand wringing"—all of which could have been avoided had inflation data per se been allowed "to do the talking" (Darbha and Patel 2012). Leaning towards this position is the view that, whether measured by real interest rates or by Taylor-rule type benchmarks, monetary policy was accommodative (IMF 2011).

Did the RBI succumb to time inconsistency? Or did it over-react to supply shocks and sectoral prices? The RBI's view has been that the high inflation that set in since the second half of 2009/10 has been due to a combination of global and domestic supply and demand factors—crude oil and other global commodity prices and pass through to domestic raw material prices; depreciation of the rupee; increased demand for food and especially proteins; increase in rural wages; crisis driven fiscal and monetary stimulus and consequent abundance of liquidity. In the context of the last factor, it has been explained as to why it was difficult to exit the "excessively accommodative monetary policy"—headline inflation had barely turned positive and was entirely driven by food inflation; industrial production had started to pick up but exports were still declining; and globally, most central banks favored continuing stimulus. Consequently, the view was that any aggressive monetary tightening at that point would have affected the recovery, though it was recognized that even after the subsequent tightening, the real policy rate was negative and monetary policy was still accommodative (Mohanty 2013). The preference for "a much more calibrated approach" to the emergence of inflationary pressures over the sharp and quick actions in response to the global crisis was seen as justified by the enormous amount of liquidity in the system—rendering transmission sluggish—amidst high uncertainty surrounding domestic and global scenarios. A frequent series of small rate hikes was regarded as "the best way to balance potentially conflicting objectives" i.e., between minimizing the sacrifice of growth and not letting expectations run out of control (Gokarn 2011). An abiding theme in the RBI's communication on monetary policy has been the concern about elevated food inflation and its persistence with the structural dimensions of proteins at its kernel, and its disappointment with the lack of an adequate supply response, given that the direct role of monetary policy in combating food price pressures is limited (Gokarn 2011; Subbarao 2011). In a non-trivial way, this came to be associated with the persuasive argument for acquiescing to a new normal for inflation (Reddy 2012) that had started making rounds in the global circuit (Blanchard et al. 2010; Krugman 2012). Eventually, the case for a new normal for inflation had to be comprehensively rejected in the public domain by the Governor of the RBI (Subbarao 2013).

Following this debate can indeed be an absorbing intellectual pursuit, even if only for the worthwhile exercise of recording and evaluating the strength of conviction and the backing of evidence in these exchanges surrounding a definitive moment in recent history and accumulating the wisdom of hindsight for future use. Yet, perhaps, enough has gone into this discussion. Rather than being overwhelmed by it, this paper uses it as a motivation. Drilling into the granularities of this debate to explore India's inflation experience of the post-global crisis period, the paper asks: (a) have the underlying dynamics of inflation changed? and, (b) is a reassessment of the monetary policy framework warranted? The next section explores the characteristics of inflation to ascertain what has changed in relation to the pre-crisis years. Section 3 undertakes an analytical investigation of inflation persistence and its drivers, extending and refining previous contributions to the subject. Section 4 employs the findings thrown up in Sections 2 and 3 to critically evaluate the case for or against moving to an explicit inflation targeting framework in India, as in other emerging economies that have seen virtue in the predominantly Anglo-Saxon approach that started out in the late 1980s, alternatively lauded and vilified by the experience of the ensuing years including through the global crisis. The final section brings it all together and concludes the paper.

2. Anatomy of Postcrisis Inflation Persistence

Neither fish nor fowl, what then was this infliction? In this section, we probe the phenomenon of postcrisis inflation persistence by examining the inflation generating process to see if this time was different. *En passant*, we begin by addressing some stylized facts on situating this recent inflation experience in geography and time.

2.1. Made in India or Global?

An issue that has vexed one pole of the debate outlined in the preceding section is the embarrassment that India has had the dubious distinction of having the highest inflation in the world, or at least among major comparators (Darbha and Patel 2012; Srinivasan 2011). The RBI too, has regarded India as an "outlier" among emerging market economies in inflation performance (RBI 2010a, 2012). The other end of the debate is more sanguine, asserting that India was nowhere near hyperinflation, that this current bout has not taken inflation to its highest level by India's own history—that occurred in 1974 when inflation reached 33%—or by the history of any other country of the world—the record is held by Hungary in 1945 when prices rose 3.8×10^{27} times and led to the replacement of its currency (Basu 2011).

Does height matter? The answer to this question appears to be country-specific and contextual. Prima facie, the stylized facts appear to respond in the negative. This is evident, for instance, in the wide variations in levels of inflation targets adopted around the world; the range is between 1 and 10% as shown in Table 1. Moreover, the widely accepted 2% positive inflation target among advanced economies is also state and time contingent—New Zealand, the first country to adopt inflation targeting, started out with a target of 0–2% in 1989. If Germany, arguably the most fiercely anti-inflation country, would have chosen an inflation target during the 1980s it would have had to be closer to 3% to be credible; in the 1970s, it would have been 5%! Several emerging and developing countries adopting inflation targeting have begun with targets higher than the golden mean of 2% prevalent among their advanced peers. Some countries, including Turkey and Russia, have had to revise their inflation targets within short periods of time. Perhaps it is better to evaluate a country's inflation performance in terms of its own context. In terms of inflation gaps i.e., actual inflation minus inflation targets/threshold for each specific country, it may be seen in Table 1 that in the postcrisis period, there has been reason to mind the gap—several countries experienced positive inflation gaps. In fact, the majority in our sample, which includes all inflation targeting countries as well as the USA and India, experienced persistent positive deviations. In the United Kingdom, Turkey, Iceland, Russia and Brazil, for instance, the deviations exceeded defined tolerance levels. Inflation deviations depicted on an annual basis may underplay the duration of inflation persistence. To illustrate, the Governor of the Bank of England wrote 10 open letters during the period March 2009–February 2012 to the Chancellor of the Exchequer to state that the inflation target had been missed, the reasons why and what was intended to bring inflation back to target. Other countries that wrote open letters in this period include the Philippines and Turkey. Importantly, although India's inflation gap was in the higher reaches of the country range, several countries did experience inflation gaps larger than that of India in the postcrisis period.

TABLE 1. Inflation Heat Map

Country	*Inflation Target (%) (implicit/explicit)*	*Inflation Gap (percentage points)*						
		2006	*2007*	*2008*	*2009*	*2010*	*2011*	*2012*
Armenia	4.0+/–1.5	–1.0	0.6	5.0	–0.5	3.3	3.7	–1.5
Australia	2.0–3.0	0.6	–0.7	1.4	–1.2	–0.1	0.3	–1.2
Brazil*	4.5+/–2.0	–0.3	–0.9	1.2	0.4	0.5	2.1	0.9
Canada	1.0–3.0	–1.0	–0.9	–0.6	–2.7	–1.2	–0.1	–1.5
Chile	3.0 +/–1.0	0.4	1.4	5.7	–1.5	–1.6	0.3	0.0
China**	3.5**	–2.0	1.3	2.4	–4.2	–0.2	1.9	–0.9
Colombia	2.0–4.0	0.3	1.6	3.0	0.2	–1.7	–0.6	–0.8
Czech Republic	2.0+/–1.0	0.5	0.9	4.3	–1.0	–0.5	–0.1	1.3
Euro area	<2.0	0.2	0.1	1.3	–1.7	–0.4	0.7	0.5
Georgia	6.0	3.2	3.2	4.0	–4.3	1.1	2.5	-6.9
Ghana	8.7+/–2.0	1.5	2.0	7.8	10.6	2.0	0.0	0.5
Guatemala	4.5+/–1.0	2.1	2.3	6.9	2.6	–0.6	1.7	–0.7
Hungary	3.0	0.9	4.9	3.1	1.2	1.9	0.9	2.7
Iceland	2.5	4.2	2.6	10.2	9.5	2.9	1.5	2.7
Indonesia	4.5 +/–1.0	8.6	2.2	5.3	0.3	0.6	0.9	–0.2
Israel	1.0–3.0	–0.9	–2.5	1.6	0.3	–0.3	0.5	–1.3
Korea	3.0 +/–1.0	–0.8	–0.5	1.7	–0.2	–0.1	1.0	–0.8
Mexico	3.0 +/–1.0	0.6	1.0	2.1	2.3	1.2	0.4	1.1
New Zealand	1.0–3.0	0.4	–0.6	1.0	–0.9	–0.7	1.0	–1.9
Nigeria	10.0	–1.8	–4.6	1.6	2.5	3.7	0.8	2.2
Peru	2.0 +/–1.0	0.0	–0.2	3.8	0.9	–0.5	1.4	1.7
Philippines	4.0 +/–1.0	1.5	–1.1	4.2	0.2	–0.2	0.7	–0.9
Poland	2.5/+–1.0	–1.5	0.0	1.7	0.9	0.1	1.8	1.2
Romania	3.0 +/–1.0	3.6	1.8	4.8	2.6	3.1	2.8	0.3
Russia	5.0–6.0	3.7	3.0	8.1	5.7	0.9	2.4	–0.9
Serbia	4.0 +/–1.5	6.7	2.9	8.4	4.1	2.2	7.1	3.3
South Africa#	3.0–6.0	–1.3	1.1	5.5	1.1	–1.7	–1.0	–0.3
Sweden	2.0	–0.6	0.2	1.4	–2.5	–0.8	1.0	–1.1
Switzerland	0–2.0	–0.9	–1.3	0.4	–2.5	–1.3	–1.8	–2.7
Thailand	3+/–1.5	1.6	–0.8	2.5	–3.9	0.3	0.8	0.0
Turkey	5.0+/–2.0	9.5	8.7	10.4	6.2	8.5	6.4	8.9
Uganda	7.0	0.2	–0.9	5.0	6.1	–3.0	11.7	7.1
United Kingdom	2.0	0.3	0.3	1.6	0.1	1.3	2.5	0.8
USA	2.0	1.2	0.9	1.8	–2.3	–0.4	1.1	0.1
Uruguay	4.0–6.0	0.4	2.1	1.9	1.1	0.7	2.1	2.1
India^	5.0	1.0	–0.1	3.7	–2.6	4.6	4.5	2.5

Inflation Gap ≥ 3 ▇ Inflation Gap ≥ 1.5 ▇ Inflation Gap > 0 ▇

Sources: www.centralbanknews.info, www.inflation.eu, IMF's World Economic Outlook (WEO) database and from "State of the Art of Inflation Targeting" by Gill Hammond, 2011, Centre for Central Banking Studies Handbook, No. 29, Bank of England.

Notes: *Official website of Central Bank of Brazil; **China has lowered inflation target recently for 2013.
Target announced since Feb 2009.
##Thailand proposed target at the start of 2012.
^ WPI data.

Turning inwards from the vertical to the horizontal, a sift through the history of independent India reveals 10 episodes of inflation persistence—parsimoniously measured as inflation above 5% and sticky for a period of 12 months and above as seen in Table 2.

TABLE 2. Episodes of Inflation Persistence

Period	*No. of Months*
Mar 56–Aug 57	18
Dec 59–Mar 61	16
Dec 63–Jan 68	50
Jan 72–May 75	41
Apr 79–Jan 82	34
Nov 82–May 85	31
July 86–Dec 95	114
Mar 2000–Aug 01	18
Feb 08–Jan 09	12
Dec 09–March 13	40

Source: Authors' estimates.
Note: The table above depicts the period in months where inflation remained above an implicit target of 5%.

These visitations were relatively frequent right up to the middle of 1990s, including the one that lasted 114 months between July 1986 and December 1995, and was actually two episodes that collided. Whereas in the 1950s and 1960s, they were mainly associated with droughts and wars, the most infamous and widely cited is the one that occurred in the oil shock of the early 1970s when inflation stayed above 20%, and even above 30% for four consecutive months (Basu 2011 provides a panoramic overview). From the late 1980s, factors such as large and persistent fiscal deficits and exchange rate depreciations added their weight to the supply shocks and to inflation persistence. The balance of payments crisis of 1991 was a watershed, for in its aftermath came the correction, supported by an IMF stabilization program. Inflation fell below 7% briefly in early 1993 but was only biding its time in the shadow of deep-seated structural reforms, including trade and industrial sector liberalization. The institution of a market-based exchange rate regime in 1993 and opening up to foreign investment brought surges of capital inflows well above the economy's absorptive and sterilization capacity. Inflation returned in its full fury, averaging 12% over the period January 1994 to May 1995. The RBI, stung by public censure, embarked on a harsh disinflation strategy that broke the back of inflation persistence but posted the economy into a long slowdown.

Occurrences of inflation persistence became infrequent in the 2000s, attesting to a degree of weather-proofing of the economy as well as to its progressive integration in a favorable global environment. This would soon prove to be a double-edged sword. In the latter part of this benign period, the seeds of the brief episode of inflation persistence during February 2008–January 2009 were being sown in the bed of capital flows driven monetary expansion. The episode itself was triggered by a surge of global commodity prices, partly demand-driven and partly by the proliferation of commodities as an independent investment asset class. Importantly, the usual suspects—fiscal deficits; weather adversities—were dormant. It was the global crisis that squelched this episode and pulled inflation into negative territory in June 2009.

Coming back to the present. What were the forces at work in the current episode that has lasted 40 months? In short, all of the above—drought albeit relatively short-lived; oil and commodity price shocks; large stimulus-driven fiscal deficits; depreciation; capital flows in 2010–11; monetary accommodation; and, supply capacity retardation (Annexure 2; Table 1).

Measured inflation is subject to transitory elements as well as general tendencies. Typically, monetary policy is expected to react to the "general" or generalized components of inflation which are induced by the changes in aggregate demand and expectations (Woodford 2003), given aggregate supply. Transitory components are associated with movements in relative prices and since they are typically supply driven, they should be ignored by forward looking monetary policy setting. Yet, it has been shown that relative price movements or changes in transitory components can become generalized and cause inflation persistence, and not only when it is a monetary phenomenon (*à la* Friedman and Schwartz 1963). Influential work has demonstrated that in the presence of nominal rigidities and frictions, there are menu costs in responding to all price changes. Large supply shocks warrant large responses to them and thus shifts in relative prices can affect the aggregate price level (Ball and Mankiw 1995). The influence of particularly volatile prices, such as those of petroleum and food, and prices set by government regulation—administered prices in the Indian context—have been cited as cases of relative price movements distorting the aggregate inflation rate (Roger 2000). Accordingly, a careful analysis of the cross-sectional distribution of inflation is important for the conduct of monetary policy, especially since it is found not to conform to the Gaussian or Normal distribution (Kottaridi et al. 2009).[1]

1. Roger (2000) reviewed work on this theme that dates back to Jevons in 1863.

2.2. The Moments of Inflation

Investigating the moments of the inflation process assumes importance for understanding the dynamics of the inflation process. These moments provide a useful summary of the cross-sectional distribution of its components, and thereby, insights into its formation and persistence. In view of the time span availability of disaggregate component-wise information on the wholesale price index or WPI (which has been used by the RBI as the measure of headline inflation in its communication) in the public domain on a comparable basis, this analysis is restricted to the period 1981–2013 using annual data. This brings into the ambit of our analysis the most persistent inflation experience spanning 1986–95 referred to in Table 2.

2.2.1. The Mean

In the 1986–95 high inflation episode, the crossing of the threshold of 5% by the first moment, the mean rate of inflation, was driven by a pick-up in food inflation, followed after a year by a rise in non-food manufactured products inflation, both in monotonic elevation over the period of persistence right up to the peak in 1994–95. By contrast, in the next episode—March 2000 to August 2001—the mean was almost entirely associated with fuel price inflation and turned out to be relatively short-lived. In the third and fourth episodes in 2008 and in 2010–13, inflation was generalized across constituent categories, but starting from food inflation and followed by non-food manufactured products inflation (Annexure 2: Table 2). This suggests that since the late 1980s, fuel prices impacted the mean in the form of short-lasting shocks. On the other hand, high inflation episodes triggered by food inflation typically spread to non-food manufactured products inflation with varying lags and became generalized and persistent. This is corroborated by analyses of inflation dynamics in India in a new Keynesian Phillips curve framework (IMF 2011). This suggests that food inflation in India is rarely transitory and is most likely to be followed by rising non-food manufactured products inflation.

2.2.2. Higher Order Moments

It is observed that the mean has a "zero breakdown point" i.e., even one large outlying observation is enough to drag it away from the true "centre" of the data distribution (Catik and Onder 2010). Headline inflation should, therefore, be seen in conjunction with higher order moments—standard deviation (SD) or the second moment, which provides a measure of the dispersion of the data around the mean; the third moment, skewness, which provides a summary of the shape of the distribution in terms of the distance of the tails from the mean; and kurtosis, the fourth moment, indicates the extent to which the distribution has fat or thin tails relative to a normal distribution (Kearns 1998).

The relationship between the mean and dispersion is observed in the literature to be one of two way causality—inflation may affect the variance of relative price changes and the variance of relative price changes may affect inflation (Assarsson 2003). In India, over the period 1981–2013, the standard deviation has been high with occasional spikes, with some evidence of high levels of cross sectional volatility corresponding to periods of upside shocks to mean or headline inflation. In the postcrisis period, on the other hand, the rising mean of inflation has, in fact, been associated with declining dispersion. This has been regarded as evidence of generalization of inflation—concentration of commodity prices around the higher mean (RBI 2010b). In our view, however, this inference cannot be drawn without considering skewness.

Analysis of the movements of second, third and fourth moments of the distribution of headline inflation in India provides interesting insights which could miss the naked eye. Skewness has a positive relationship with the mean of the distribution. Variance tends to magnify the asymmetry in the tails—a larger variance is inflationary when the distribution is skewed to the right and deflationary when it is skewed to the left. The cross-sectional distribution of inflation in India since 1980 is positively or right skewed throughout with an average coefficient of 1.4, other than in 1985–86, 1988–89, 1996–97 and 2007–08 when instances of negative skewness were evident. The preponderance of the positive skew is on account of sharp relative price changes coming out of supply side shocks which are not counter-balanced by equally large price decreases in other sectors. Such relative price movements can be interpreted as shifts in the Philips curve. The micro-foundations of this relationship draws from menu costs associated with pricing decisions of firms which create a range of inaction in response to shocks (Ball and Mankiw 1995)[2]—as mentioned earlier, firms are inclined to reset prices only in the face of large shocks. Darbha and Patel (2012) find high right skewness coinciding with high inflation only in the recent bout of inflation persistence and not in the episode of the mid-1990s. This is presumably because their sample period begins in 1994–95 when the

2. Bryan and Cecchetti (1999) argued that this is a small sample bias problem. Balke and Wynne (2000) on the other hand, attributed it to productivity shocks. Bils and Klenow (1998) provides an explanation for the positive relationship by combining the business cycle model with the nominal rigidity/skewness model of Ball and Mankiw (1995).

episode was ending; its origins were, however, earlier, as set out in Table 2 and Annexure 2: Table 3. Following Dopke and Pierdzioch (2001), the kernel density estimates of the WPI's cross-sectional inflation rates show high right skews in the early 1990s too (Annexure 2: Figure 1).

Thus, supply side price shocks have always impacted the Indian economy in the form of relative price increases which have influenced the aggregate level of prices in a lasting manner. The coefficient of the fourth moment or kurtosis has always been greater than 3 (other than for a brief period between 1989–90 and 1991–92), implying that the distribution of price changes has been leptokurtic or fat tailed—a large portion of the price index (WPI) experienced price changes significantly different from the mean or headline inflation rate (Figure 1).

FIGURE 1. WPI (YoY) Inflation Moments

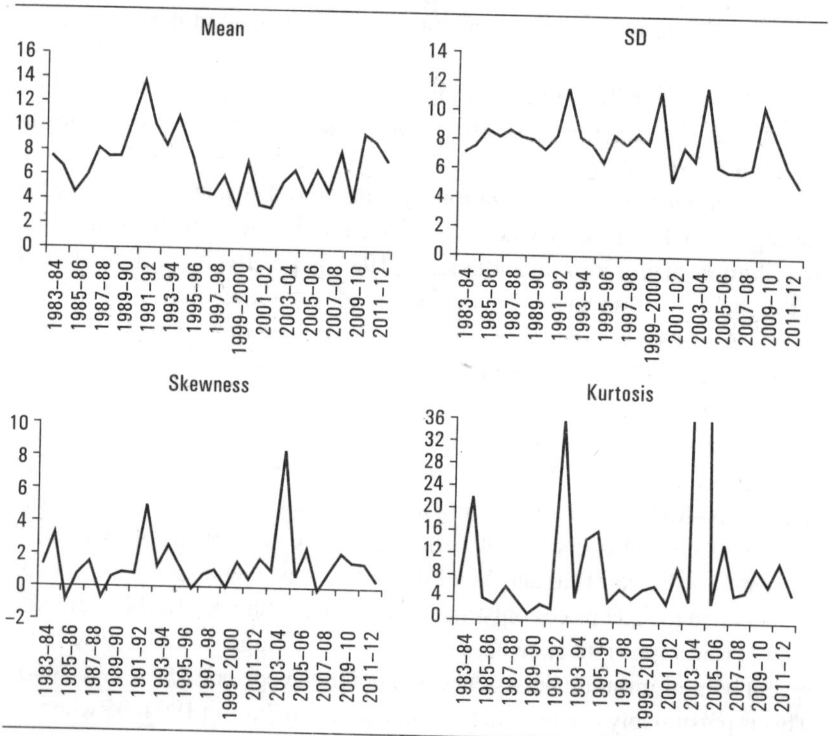

Source: Authors' estimates.

Following Kearns (1998), we move underneath the analysis of trends in moments to their interplay. The positive correlation between inflation (mean) and skewness in India is in line with the priors set in the vast theoretical and empirical literature (see Assarsson, 2003, for an overview). The high correlation between kurtosis and skewness indicates that a sizable number of constituent items of WPI contributed to the overall asymmetry observed in the distribution as well as to the positive skewness observed, especially in the postcrisis period (Table 3).

TABLE 3. Correlation Coefficient of Moments

	Mean	*Standard Deviation*	*Skewness*	*Kurtosis*
Mean	1.00			
Standard Deviation	0.28	1.00		
Skewness	0.24	0.55	1.00	
Kurtosis	0.07	0.55	0.91	1.00

Source: Authors' estimates.

In the tradition of Ball and Mankiw (1995), we formally estimate the effects of variance and skewness on the mean of inflation using quarterly data for the period 1983 to 2013 (first quarter). Mean inflation is regressed on its skewness (SK) and standard deviation (SD), an interaction term between standard deviation and skewness (SD*SK) in order to capture the magnifying impact of variance on skewness, and lagged inflation in order to explain other effects (Equation 1 of Table 4). The results indicate that both skewness and standard deviation contribute positively and significantly to the observed inflation mean. However, the interaction terms SD*SK, though significant, is negatively signed, contrary to Ball and Mankiw (1995); but this negative sign has also been noted by studies conducted on Canada (Amano and Macklem 1997) and India (Tripathi and Goyal 2011). This is explained by the fact that the SD*SK interaction is susceptible to outliers and there is the need for an alternative measure which is robust to outlier effects (Amano and Macklem 1997).

Hence, in Equation 2, as suggested in Ball and Mankiw (1995) and Amano and Macklem (1997), we develop an alternative parsimonious measure to capture asymmetry due to the direct effect of skewness and the magnifying effect of variance with a single variable. Such a measure was also constructed for India by Tripathi and Goyal (2011). For any cut-off level X, the variable is defined as:

$$ASYMX = \Sigma_{i=1}^{N} r_i D_i^- + \Sigma_{i=1}^{P} r_i D_i^+$$

Where r_i is the ith industry relative price change (i.e., an industry inflation rate minus the mean of industry inflation rates) weighted for industry size.

TABLE 4. Inflation and Distribution of Price Changes

	Dependent Variable: Inflation (yoy)	
	Equation 1	*Equation 2*
Constant	–0.81	1.19
	(–1.01)	(3.57)
Lagged Inflation	0.76	0.77
	(18.32)	(17.00)
Standard Deviation (SD)	0.23	
	(3.15)	
Skewness (SK)	0.73	
	(1.84)	
SD* SK	– 0.06	
	(–1.89)	
ASYMX		0.37
		(3.72)
Dummy Variable (2009Q1, 2009Q2)	–2.75	–2.55
	(–7.03)	(–5.79)
Dummy Variable (1991Q3)	4.50	4.42
	(22.82)	(23.36)
$\bar{R}^2$	0.83	0.83
L. M	0.97	0.87
	(0.62)	(0.65)
Breusch-Pagan-Godfrey	8.08	2.76
	(0.23)	(0.74)

Source: Authors' estimates.

Notes: 1. Figures in parenthesis are t-statistics based on HAC standard errors & covariance (Bartlett kernel, Newey-West fixed bandwidth = 5.0000).

2. Breusch-Pagan-Godfrey results gives the computed test statistic of Obs*R-squared and p-value of the null of homoskedasticity.

3. L.M reports Lagrange Multiplier Test statistic and p-value for the null of no autocorrelation for a lag of 2.

4. Estimation is by OLS for the sample period 1983:Q2 to 2013:Q1.

The variables D_i^- and D_i^+ are binary variables: the former takes the value one when the ith industry's relative price change falls in the lower 10% of the distribution and zero otherwise, whereas the latter variable is one when the ith industry's relative price change falls in the upper 10% of the distribution and zero otherwise (Tripathi and Goyal 2011). In other words, *ASYMX* accumulates the relative price increases in the upper tail of the distribution and subtracts them from the absolute value of the accumulated relative price declines in the lower tail. Hence, *ASYMX* is zero for a symmetric distribution of relative price changes, positive when the right tail is larger than the left tail, and negative when the left tail is larger. Moreover, for any given skewness, *ASYMX* rises in absolute value when a larger variance magnifies the tails (Amano and Macklem 1997; Ball and Mankiw 1995).

The results presented in Equation 2 of Table 4 show that ASYMX is statistically significant and positively contributes to explaining the mean inflation rate. The goodness of fit of Equation 2 is unchanged in relation to that of Equation 1 where skewness, standard deviation, and their interaction were considered separately, implying that re-specification does not result in any loss of explanatory power.

Thus, relative price changes emanating from supply shocks have had a significant role in explaining the origin and nature of inflation persistence episodes; ignoring them as outside the realm of policy scrutiny and action risks a credibility question, with inflation becoming inertial and expectations unhinged.

2.3. A Diffusion Index for Policy Monitoring

Having established that relative prices matter, it is important to monitor the pace at which they generalize into high aggregate inflation episodes. This is accomplished through a summary measure that captures the momentum of price increases across items constituting the WPI. The inflation diffusion index or IDEX categorizes constituent items in the WPI basket according to whether their prices are rising, stagnant or falling over the previous month and aggregates them to show whether the month-over-month (m-o-m) momentum of price changes overall has been expansionary or contractionary. A reading above 50 signals a broad expansion or inflation across the WPI basket and a reading below 50 signals a broad based deflation. In the context of business cycles, diffusion indices are employed to determine turning points, and are also observed to have lead indicator characteristics (Gets and Ulmer 1990). Our IDEX is defined as follows:

$$IDEX_t = \left(\frac{\sum_{i=1}^{N} wgt_i \times WPI_{it}}{N} \right) * 100$$

$$where\, WPI_{it} = 1\, if\ \Delta WPI_{it} \geq 0.05\%,$$

$$WPI_{it} = 0.5\, if\ -0.05\% \leq \Delta WPI_{it} < 0.05\%$$

$$WPI_{it} = 0\, if\ \Delta WPI_{it} < -0.05\%$$

where *wgt* is the weight of item *i* in the WPI index and *N* is the total number of items in the WPI index.

For our computation, each item of the WPI is classified into the categories based on the Conference Board's[3] methodology of defining m-o-m

3. The Conference Board methodology for constructing diffusion indices as part of its Composite Index of Leading Indicators for the United States is utilized for determining the

price increases base on a threshold level of 0.05%. All items are seasonally adjusted. As we have combined WPI indices with three different base years, the number of items in the IDEX, its composition and sensitivity in terms of number of quotations would vary over time, but it would still give a reasonably accurate overview of the broad long-term trends in generalization of price increases (Figure 2 and Annexure 2: Table 4).

FIGURE 2. Diffusion Index of WPI Items

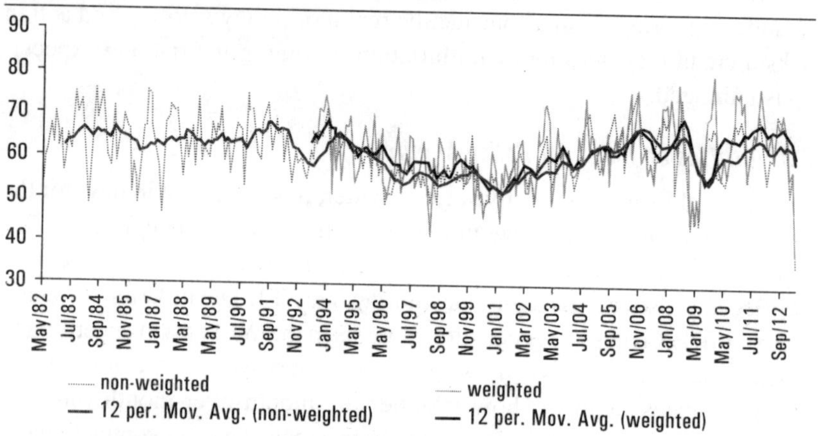

12 per. Mov. Avg. implies 12 month moving average of m-o-m IDEX

Source: Authors' estimates.

Though m-o-m movements tend to be noisy, the 12 month moving average of the IDEX indicates that episodes of high inflation in the 1980s, the 1990s and the recent post-global crisis experience indubitably showed a rapid spread or build-up of momentum of price increases. Moreover, prices increase over a large number of items persisted during these episodes. In the post-global crisis inflation episode, the IDEX showed a sharp reversal from a broad based deflationary situation in the second half of 2008–09 to one of quick increases in the diffusion of price increases during 2010–13. Thus, the IDEX provides a visual validation of the hypothesis that, in India, inflation formation starts from sharp relative price shocks, often in food prices, which quickly translate into broad based prices increases that are sustained for a considerable period of time.

threshold levels. Details on the methodology are available at http://www.conference-board.org/data/bci/index.cfm?id=2180

2.4. Is the Observed Prices Behavior Unique to WPI?

It will be remiss to close this section without addressing an issue in inflation measurement that has featured in the recent debate—which index to use, the WPI or the Consumer Price Index (CPI), with the former akin to a producer price index and the latter measuring prices at the retail level?[4] It has been pointed out that there are considerable differences in inflation measurement between these matrices in magnitude, dispersion and phasing, especially in the post-global crisis period, and the use of the WPI as an inflation measure has been criticized (Rakshit 2011). The opposing view is that it does not matter which index is used, since inflation measured by all these indices tend to converge over time. In a country with high disparity in incomes and living standards, it is difficult to think of a representative consumer meaningfully. Moreover, the CPI for industrial workers reveals a small but systematic upward bias (Basu 2011). Then there is the agnostic view that inflation measured by the WPI is used by the RBI, that it is the most comprehensive index in terms of disaggregation and that it is important to understand inflation dynamics, irrespective of the price data series (Darbha and Patel 2012). Adding to this debate has been the advocacy for the use of GDP deflator on the basis of its comprehensiveness in terms of fuller coverage of service sector prices, to understand inflation behavior. The counter argument is that GDP deflator by itself contains little additional information on prices than what is provided by WPI and CPIs (Shah et al. 2011). Moreover, there are considerable lags involved in obtaining GDP deflator data, currently two months, which reduces its usefulness as a real time indicator of price behavior.

The trends in inflation based on CPI, WPI and the GDP deflator reveals that WPI and GDP deflator based inflation show close co-movement during most of the period considered, but CPIs show considerable divergence, especially since 2012 Q2, as shown in Figure 3.

The co-movement between WPI and the GDP deflator has been attributed to the use of WPI by the Central Statistics Office of the Government of India in estimating the GDP deflator (Shah et al. 2011). The sharp divergence in recent period between CPIs and WPI, on the other hand, has been attributed to the considerable difference in weights and composition (Annexure 2: Table 5). However, it is often difficult to disentangle the effects of different weights and baskets in explaining the price movements between CPI and

4. Until recently, CPIs in India have been compiled for different classes of consumers—industrial workers, agricultural laborers and rural laborers, with the CPI for industrial workers being widely used as CPI measure for India. Since January 2011, a new national CPI, named as CPI-Combined (CPI-C), is being released by the Central Statistics Office (CSO).

FIGURE 3. YoY Inflation Based on Various Price Indices

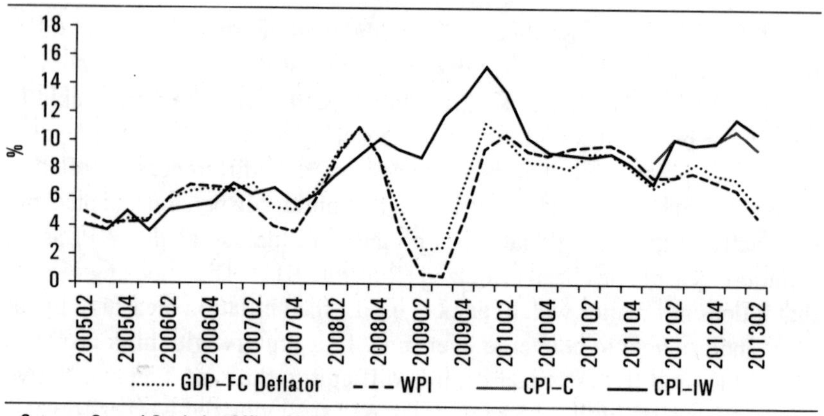

Sources: Central Statistics Office, Ministry of Statistics and Programme Implementation, Labour Bureau, Government of India; Office of the Economic Adviser to the Government of India, Ministry of Commerce and Industry and Authors' Estimates.

WPI, as item level data and weights for CPIs are not available. In the absence of item level data, one way of ascertaining the impact of a divergent basket of commodities in the movements between CPI and WPI groups would be to construct commodity groups in WPI based on the consumer durable and non-durable goods in WPI which are reflected in the CPI basket. While WPI excluding food and fuel groups constitutes 61% of the WPI basket, a WPI group constructed based on items in CPI excluding food and fuel groups would translate only to 20% of WPI basket.[5] This could result in episodes of divergence between the CPIs and the WPI. Trends in services price, which are captured directly in CPIs but not in WPI, would also add to the divergence in price trends. As seen in the bottom right panel in Annexure 2: Figure 2, WPI based on items in CPI excluding food group and fuel group, also exhibits elevated inflation in the recent period. In case of food items, a CPI basket based WPI inflation and WPI food inflation were almost same, implying the close similarity between CPI and WPI food baskets. Moreover, actual food inflation in WPI and CPIs were also broadly similar. Hence, information on food price trends captured by the CPIs and WPI could be more or less similar, largely due to the similarity of food items in CPIs and the WPI baskets. However, in case of inflation excluding food and fuel groups, episodes of divergence between the CPIs and WPI can arise, primarily due to composition differences. The impact of food and non-food items on overall inflation would also depend on the commodity weighting patterns in the CPIs and WPI.

5. The remaining items in WPI excluding food and fuel consist mainly of industry basic, intermediate and capital goods.

3. Analytics of Inflation Persistence: Methodological Issues and Results

Informed by these abstemious insights, we turn now from the relative to the absolute. No analogy is perfect, but in order to start out with a reasonable intuitive fix, persistence can perhaps be likened to inertia in physics—the resistance of a body to changing its velocity unless acted upon by an external force (Fuhrer 2009). The Inflation Persistence Network (IPN), a collaboration between the European Central Bank and the national central banks of the Eurosystem, provides a formal definition of inflation persistence: "the tendency of inflation to converge slowly to its long-run value following a shock" (Altissimo et al. 2006). Understanding the speed and manner in which inflation adjusts to shocks of varying nature, and measuring the patterns and determinants of inflation persistence is critical for fashioning the monetary policy response to upsurges in inflation—reacting heavy-handedly to short-lived episodes can lead to overkills of economic activity; by contrast, too delayed or too feeble a response to long-lasting inflation occurrences runs the risk of hardening inflation expectations and entrenching them at elevated levels with harmful effects that can even impair potential growth (IMF 2011). While the size and timing of monetary policy reactions are eventually judgment calls, empirical measurement of inflation persistence can shine light on the judgment process. Furthermore, this has to be country-specific since the characteristics of the economy in question play a determining role in the dynamics of inflation.

3.1. The Sources of Inflation Persistence

In the post-global crisis episode in India, inflation has stayed above its threshold for a prolonged period, despite the output gap falling and even turning negative, which highlights the importance of understanding the nature of shocks. Was there a series of shocks? Was the initial response to inflation too inertial by economic agents—firms, households and policy makers? Or was there an error in estimation of the "true" domestic potential growth or of global economic conditions, especially as green shoots of recovery from an unprecedented crisis were being seen? Quite clearly, the circumstances in which inflation forms matter.

The large body of work on modeling inflation persistence and price stickiness has broadly identified four factors on the sources of inflation persistence: (a) backward-lookingness in the price-setting mechanism or "intrinsic" persistence; (b) inheritance from the mark-up over costs as reflected in marginal costs or the output gap—"extrinsic" persistence; (c) the formation of inflation expectations or "expectations-based" persistence; and (d) persistence due to monetary policy regime shifts or "policy-driven" persistence which are best captured, for instance, in the degree of interest rate smoothing in policy reaction functions (Angeloni et al. 2006).

3.2. Modeling Inflation Persistence

A common approach in the "early" efforts to model inflation persistence is to estimate univariate autoregressive (AR) time series models and to measure persistence as the sum of the estimated AR coefficients (Fuhrer and Moore 1995; Nelson and Plosser 1982; Pivetta and Reis 2007). The advantage of this approach is that it needs to rely on time series on inflation only. Moreover, its relative simplicity reduces specification errors. This model can be written as follows:

$$\pi_t = C + \sum_{j=1}^{k} \alpha_j \pi_{t-j} + \varepsilon_t \tag{1}$$

where π is the rate of inflation, α is the autoregressive coefficient and ε is a serially uncorrelated, but possibly heteroskedastic random error term. The measure of persistence is the sum of the AR coefficients, $\rho \equiv \Sigma\alpha_j$ (Andrew and Chen 1994), which can be obtained by rewriting equation (1) as,

$$\pi_t = C + \rho\pi_{t-1} \sum_{j=1}^{k-1} \beta_j^{\Delta} \pi_{t-j} + \varepsilon_t \tag{2}$$

where ρ is the persistence parameter, while β parameters are transformations of AR coefficients in equation (1), $\beta_{k-1} = -\alpha_{k.}$ It has been shown, however, that the AR coefficients will be exaggerated if structural breaks in the mean are not considered (Perron 1989). Allowing for a mean break, the persistence parameter can be estimated as,

$$\pi = c_0 + c_1 D_t + \rho\pi_{t-1} \sum_{j=1}^{k-1} \beta_j^{\Delta} \pi_{t-j} + \varepsilon_t \tag{3}$$

D_t equals zero for $t < T$ and 1 for $t \geq T$.

The measure of inflation persistence derives from this autoregressive function—the inflation series will be regarded as persistent if its correlation with its own past decays slowly. Typically, the model is estimated through rolling regressions to allow for shifts in the mean of inflation over different sub-samples. Moreover, by lowering the sub-sample size, the number of structural breaks that occur gets reduced.

Time series estimates of inflation persistence are essentially measures of unconditional persistence. They assume a stable mean and do not take into account the various factors driving the inflation data generating process, alluded to earlier, each of which exhibits its own level of persistence. This could impart a bias to measured persistence (Levin and Piger 2004). Moreover, rolling regressions do not entirely rule out the possibility of shifts in a specific sub-sample, especially when shifts are frequent, and they impose limits on the degrees of freedom. It follows, therefore, that each of these factors—intrinsic, extrinsic, expectations, and policy-driven—must be explicitly taken into account when modeling the inflation process and its persistence. In particular, for an economy like India, the persistence in macroeconomic shocks hitting inflation should be accounted for so that accurate estimates of inflation persistence are obtained. Accordingly, "newer generation" approaches to estimation of inflation persistence rely on small structural models of inflation dynamics which relate the evolution of inflation to its past as well as to its expected future path and the deviation of the economy's price mark-up over desired levels that is linked to some measure of economic activity. For emerging market economies, exchange rate movements display significant short-term volatility and are amongst the important determinants of short-term inflation (Batini et al. 2006; Ho and McCauley 2003; Ito and Sato 2006). Essentially, these approaches boil down to estimating a reduced form hybrid new Keynesian type Phillips curve, as given below:

$$\pi_t = c + \gamma\pi_{t-1} + (1-\gamma)E_t\,\pi_{t+1} + \beta y_t + e_t + \varepsilon_t \qquad (4)$$

where π is inflation, y is the output gap, e is the exchange rate, E denotes the expectation operator and ε is a cost-push shock. In the above representation, γ measures the degree of dependence of inflation on its own past—intrinsic persistence, $(1-\gamma)$ the degree of persistence due to formation of inflation expectations—expectations-based persistence, and β the persistence due to fluctuations in determinants of inflation such as the output gap—extrinsic persistence.

For India, these models have been estimated with reasonably robust results, indicating that the new Keynesian type Phillips curve is alive and well here (Kapur and Patra 2003; Patra and Kapur 2012a, 2012b; Patra and Ray 2010; RBI 2002). This is found to hold after accounting for supply shocks and even without accounting for them (Mazumder 2011), thereby overturning the orthodoxy that ruled in the 1980s and the early 1990s which posited that the Phillips curve does not exist in India (Bhattacharya and Lodh 1990; Dholakia 1990; Rangarajan 1983; Rangarajan and Arif 1990).

3.3. Period of Study and Time Series Properties

For analyzing the autoregressive properties of headline inflation and its components, we use both monthly and quarterly data spanning from April 1982 to March 2013. Monthly data are used for updating Khundrakpam (2008) which analyzed the period from April 1982 to March 2008. Univariate analysis using quarterly data is employed to validate the results from monthly data and also to enable a comparison with the results obtaining from the multivariate Phillips curve estimation that follows. Analyses based on quarterly data cover the period April 1996 to March 2013, the choice of period being determined by the availability of quarterly data on real GDP for India. Since monthly and quarterly estimates corroborate each other, the latter are reported here for the sake of continuity into the multivariate analysis while monthly estimates are reported in Annexure 3. All the variables are seasonally adjusted using the X-12 algorithm of the US Department of Commerce and transformed into percentage changes, except for the policy rate, the Fed funds rate and the OECD growth rate (used to proxy external demand). The output gap and the gross fiscal deficit (GFD/GDP) gap are measured as the difference between actual and trend obtained by the Hodrick–Prescott (HP) filter.

As regards the policy interest rate, we follow Patra and Kapur (2012a, 2012b) in using the effective policy rate i.e., the interest rate through which the RBI engages in its liquidity operations with market participants, depending on prevailing liquidity conditions.[6]

3.3.1. Times Series Properties

At a basic level, the unit root test is the first gauge of inflation persistence. If inflation contains a unit root, its persistence is unquestionably large and its variance is unbounded. Prior to the 1990s, most studies attest to the presence of a unit root in inflation (Barsky 1986; Ball and Cecchetti 1990); however, more recent work is unable to reject stationarity, ascribing this change to the more vigorous attention to inflation on the part of central banks (Fuhrer 2009). As shown in Table 5, two types of tests, i.e., the Augmented Dickey Fuller (ADF) and Phillips–Perron (PP) statistics reject the null of the presence of a unit root in inflation and its components (all measured in terms of rates of change which is the manner in which they enter the estimated equations). As for other variables, CRR, nominal policy rate (I) and the federal fund rate (FED), FOODG, M3G, NFCG and RNFCG are found to be nonstationary, while the rest are stationary at 5% level of significance by at least one of the tests.

6. Data sources are provided at Annexure 5.

TABLE 5. Unit Root Tests

Variable	*ADF*		*PP*	
	Monthly	*Quarterly*	*Monthly*	*Quarterly*
Rate of Change in WPI and Components				
DCHE	−14.7*	-6.8*	−15.0*	-6.8*
DFOOD	−14.9*	-9.5*	−16.4*	-9.5*
DFUEL	−15.8*	-7.3*	−15.8*	-7.0*
DMAC	−7.4*(t)	-6.3*(t)	−16.4*(t)	-6.3*(t)
DMANU	−7.2*(t)	-6.2*(t)	−14.1*	-6.1*(t)
DMET	−7.0*	-5.9*	−15.7*	-5.5*
DMFOOD	−17.1*	-8.5*(t)	−17.2*	-8.5*(t)
DNFOOD	−14.1*	-7.3*	−14.2*	-7.0*
DPRI	−15.9*	-7.7*	−15.9*	-7.7*
DTEX	−7.0*	-4.7*	−11.8*	-5.9*
DWPI	−14.1*	-6.9*	−14.3*	-7.0*
Other Variables				
Ag_gap	-5.2*		-4.3*	
CRR	-2.6		-2.8	
Ex_rain	-8.4*		-8.4*	
Exrate	-5.3*		-6.4*	
FED	-1.4		-1.4	
FOODG	-2.6		-2.8	
GFD_gap	-3.7*		-14.6*	
I	-2.6		-2.5	
I^r	-4.5*		-2.4	
INV_gap	-3.3**		-3.4**	
M_3G	-2.5		-2.4	
NEERG	-2.9		-3.4**	
NFCG	-1.4		-2.5	
OECD_GR	-4.0*		-3.4**	
OGAP	-3.6*		-3.7*	
OILG	-4.5*		-3.5**	
REERG	-3.6*		-3.8*	
RNFCG	-2.3		-2.4	
WPIG	-6.8*		-2.4	
π_GAP	-7.0*		-2.43	

Source: Authors' estimates.

Notes: * and ** denote significance at 1% and 5% level, respectively. The lag length in the ADF tests was chosen based on Schwarz Bayesian Criterion (SBC). "t" in the parentheses indicate inclusion of a trend component in the estimates, which was based on its statistical significance in the equation.

3.4. Estimation Results

We first extend Khundrakpam (2008) to obtain univariate estimates of inflation persistence incorporating the period following the global crisis i.e., 2009–13. This is followed by a multivariate approach to account for the critique of the time series approach and allow an independent verification of the univariate estimates.

3.4.1. Univariate Estimates

The optimal lag length based on the Akaike Information Criterion (AIC) and the Schwarz–Bayesian Criterion (SBC) together suggest a lag length of order 1 for aggregate inflation as well as for most of the disaggregated components for the quarterly series, while for the monthly series, the AIC, in general, selects higher lags (Table 6; monthly estimates are given in Annexure 3: Table 6).

TABLE 6. Break Estimates in Mean of Inflation—Quarterly

			Lag length	
Variable	*Andrew–Quandt*	*Bai–Perron*	*SBC*	*AIC*
All Commodities (DWPI)	1995:2	1995:2	1	1
I. Primary (DPRI)	No Break	No Break	1	1
Food (DFOOD)	No Break	No Break	1	1
Non-food (DNFOOD)	No Break	No Break	1	4
II. Fuel (DFUEL)	No Break	No Break	1	1
III. Manufacturing (DMANU)	1995:2	1995:2	1	1
Food (DMFOOD)	1998:3	1998:3	1	3
Textiles (DTEX)	1995:2	1995:2	4	4
Chemicals (DCHE)	1995:2	1995:2	1	1
Metals (DMET)	No Break	No Break	1	1
Machinery (DMAC)	1992:4	1992:4	1	1

Source: Authors' estimates.

Structural break in the mean was identified using the Quandt–Andrews unknown break point test and the Bai–Perron break point test. Both the tests indicate a break in the mean of headline inflation in the second quarter of 1995 and more specifically in May 1995. This is also evident in the manufactured products component of the headline. The break coincides with the great disinflation undertaken by the RBI to counter the long inflation persistence that characterized the preceding 106 months. On the other hand, the primary articles and fuel components show no structural breaks in their means.

In view of the statistically significant evidence of a break, equation (2) has been estimated for the full sample period as well as two sub-sample periods—pre-break and post-break. Equation (3) is estimated only for the full sample period since it specifically accounts for the break in mean inflation. These results indicate that inflation persistence has gone up in the post-break period for headline inflation, bearing out Khundrakpam (2008), but with one big difference—inflation persistence in the manufactured products category has gone up significantly, whereas in Khundrakpam (2008), it had declined. There are also non-trivial differences in the size of persistence of inflation in sub-categories of manufactures (Table 7; monthly estimates are given in Annexure 3: Table 7). The only plausible reason for these differences is the inclusion of the data for the post-global crisis period, necessitating a closer investigation.

TABLE 7. Estimates of Persistence During Sub-Samples—Quarterly (1982:2 to 2013:1)

Variable	*First Sample (Pre-Break)*	*Second Sample (Post-Break)*	*Full Sample*	
			No Break	*With Break*
All Commodities(DWPI)	0.283***	0.428*	0.436*	0.369*
I. Primary (DPRI)	–	–	0.340*	–
Food (DFOOD)	–	–	0.146	–
Non-food (DNFOOD)	–	–	0.300*	–
II. Fuel (DFUEL)	–	–	0.254*	–
III. Manufacturing (DMANU)	0.294**	0.499*	0.556*	0.396*
Food (DMFOOD)	0.079	0.403*	0.274*	0.192*
Textile (DTEX)	0.446*	0.417*	0.545*	0.435*
Chemicals (DCHE)	0.490*	0.237**	0.441*	0.395
Metal (DMET)	–	–	0.543*	–
Machinery (DMAC)	0.419*	0.516*	0.585*	0.455*

Source: Authors' estimates.
Note: *, ** and *** denote significance at 1%, 5%, and 10% level, respectively.

Rolling regressions show a steady rise in persistence in headline inflation, fuel inflation and elevated levels of persistence in manufactured products inflation from around the second half of 2008 after having fallen through the period 2004–08. Interestingly, food inflation also shows a sharp increase in persistence, particularly with quarterly data, from around the same time. These are major differences from Khundrakpam (2008) in which lowering of inflation persistence was interrupted only towards the end of the sample period, barring for manufactured products inflation. More importantly, the shift in inflation dynamics and in persistence is located in the second half of 2008 (Figure 4; figures for sub-components and on monthly rolling regressions are given in Annexure 3: Figures 3, 4 and 5). This is interesting because it suggests that the origins of post-global crisis inflation persistence may perhaps be in the expansionary phase of capital flows during 2005–08, ignited by the commodity price-driven inflation episode of February 2008–January 2009.

FIGURE 4. Rolling Regressions of Major Components of WPI–Quarterly

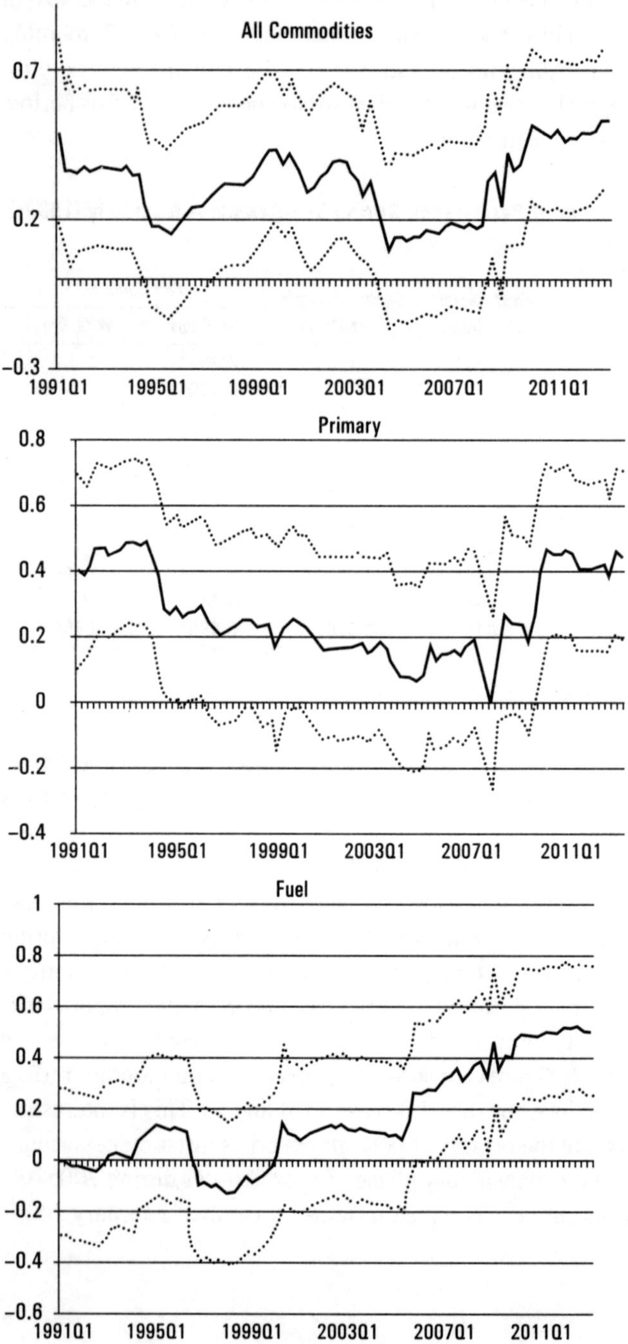

(Figure 4 Contd)

(Figure 4 Contd)

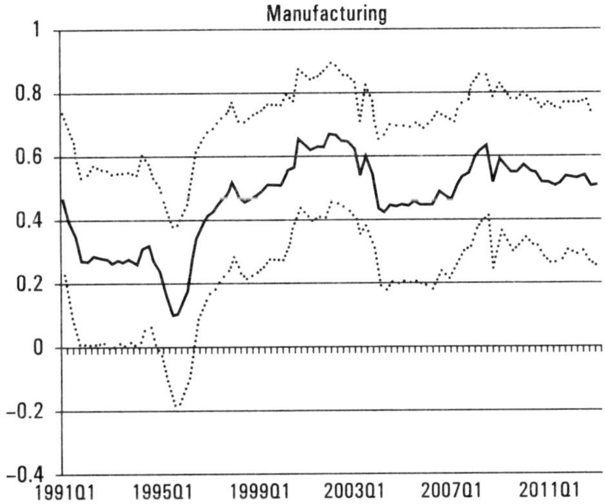

Source: Authors' estimates.

3.4.2. Multivariate Analysis: Structural Model Estimates

Following Clarida et al. (1998, 2000) and Goodhart and Hofmann (2005), we estimate the new Keynesian Phillips curve (NKPC) using the Generalized Method of Moments (GMM) in view of leads/lags of the explanatory variables being used and potential endogeneity of the variables. Estimation of various alternative specifications shows statistical support for the backward-looking Phillips curve which corroborates previous studies mentioned earlier. We also conduct robustness tests by estimating it across two specifications—augmented with quarter-on-quarter exchange rate changes and without them—and over two sample periods—including and excluding the post-global crisis period.

Hansen's J-statistic indicates that the instruments satisfy the orthogonality condition and are, therefore, valid instruments. There is also no evidence of residual auto-correlation, as evidenced by the Q statistic. The Kleibergen–Paap rk Wald F-statistic, which tests the strength of instruments, appears reasonable, though no critical values are available. Accordingly, weak-identification-robust inference statistics for relevance of endogenous regressors such as the Anderson–Rubin (AR) Wald Test are preferred in the literature (for a discussion, see Patra and Kapur 2012a). This test strongly rejects the joint null in all the four specifications and, therefore, indicates that the endogenous regressors are relevant. Thus, the Phillips curve or aggregate supply function appears to be reasonably well identified.

The results turn out to be revealing. Intrinsic persistence, measured from the coefficient on lagged inflation, actually declines from the pre-global crisis period range of 0.58 and 0.74, with and without the exchange rate term, respectively, to the full sample period (including the post-global crisis period) coefficient range of 0.49 to 0.54, again with and without the exchange rate term. Thus, exclusion of the exchange rate term produces a sharper decline in intrinsic persistence than otherwise, suggesting misspecification and validating the need for incorporating exchange rate effects in the NKPC estimation for India. These results also show the exchange rate pass-through to inflation declining i.e., a 10% change in the exchange rate resulted in a 2.8% change in inflation before the global crisis and 0.09% change in inflation when the post-global crisis period is included (Table 8). Cross-country comparisons suggest that intrinsic inflation inertia in India, though declining, is still high.[7]

Turning to extrinsic persistence, its statistical significance is indicative of the presence of both real and nominal rigidities implied by Calvo-type staggered price setting behavior. This could also be reflecting both the substantial share of administered prices in the WPI and the inertia in the adjustment of output to its potential. Extrinsic persistence appears to have slightly increased when the post-global crisis period is included to 0.22 from 0.19 in the pre-global crisis period when the NKPC including the exchange rate term is considered; but, it is only about two-fifth of the intrinsic persistence. The estimated sacrifice ratio with the postcrisis period included is close to 2.3, slightly higher than 2.2 for the pre-global crisis period and also higher than the range of 1–2 in earlier studies for the pre-crisis period (Kapur and Patra 2003; RBI 2002). This suggests that monetary policy induced disinflation of one percentage point from its trend/long-run average is associated with a reduction of 2.3% in output, indicating a flattening of the aggregate supply curve post-global crisis.

Surprisingly, the contribution of expectations to inflation persistence in India, measured by the coefficient on one-period lead inflation, appears to have risen sharply in the post-crisis period to 0.60 from 0.46 in the pre-crisis period (again, only the exchange rate augmented NKPC is considered). This suggests that people lacked information on the nature of shocks impacting inflation, especially on the duration of the food price shock that started the inflation spiral in 2009, and the policy response thereto, and were perhaps confused when vegetable price spikes, which are typically seasonal, became

7. For the United States, it is estimated to be in the range of 0.73 to 0.80 and for the Euro Zone in the range of 0.42 to 0.45 (Dosschey and Everaertz 2007) or generally less than 0.5 (Altissimo et al. 2006). For Brazil, intrinsic inflation persistence has been estimated to be in range of 0.47 to 0.62 (Machado and Portugal 2012).

TABLE 8. Estimates of Inflation Persistence Using Hybrid Augmented Philips Curve

	(Dependent variable inflation-π_t)			
	Pre-crisis period		*Including post-crisis period*	
Constant	−0.014	−0.003	−0.01	−0.007
	(−5.85)	(−0.62)	(−4.43)	(−2.07)
$\pi_{(t-1)}$	0.74	0.58	0.54	0.49
	(22.00)	(11.72)	(17.99)	(13.2)
π^e	0.49	0.46	0.59	0.60
	(19.73)	(10.4)	(21.13)	(13.7)
Y_{gap}	0.16	0.19	0.19	0.22
	(1.88)	(2.68)	(2.28)	(2.20)
Ex_Rain	−0.13	−0.10	−0.08	−0.05
	(−5.06)	(−4.11)	(−3.70)	(−1.88)
X_t		0.12		0.05
		(5.41)		(3.21)
Sacrifice Ratio	1.57	2.17	2.45	2.32
Exchange Rate Pass-through (long-run)		0.28		0.09
$\bar{R}^2$	0.83	0.87	0.87	0.87
J-Statistic	9.75	10.41	12.93	12.12
	(0.83)	(0.58)	(0.61)	(0.52)
LB-Q Statistics	16.1	15.1	20.9	24.9
	(0.71)	(0.77)	(0.41)	(0.20)
Wald Test (χ^2)	29.6	0.21	12.7	2.17
($\pi_{(t-1)} + \pi^e = 1$)	(0.00)	(0.64)	(0.00)	(0.14)
Weak Instruments Tests				
KP Wald Tests	1.58	2.83	3.27	2.36
AR Wald F-Test	15.1	12.4	20.8	32.3
(p-value)	(0.00)	(0.00)	(0.00)	(0.00)

Source: Authors' estimates.

Notes: 1. Figures in parentheses are t-statistics based on HAC standard errors corrected with Newey West/Bartlett window and one-step iteration.

2. LB-Q is the Box-Pierce-Ljung Q-statistic (p-values in parentheses) for the null of no residual autocorrelation for 20 lags.

3. Hansen's J-Statistic test for over-identifying restrictions for GMM estimates; p-values are in parentheses.

4. Estimation is by GMM methodology for the sample period 1997:2 to 2012:4. Instrument variables: Ygap(−2 to −3); GFD_gap(−1); FED(−1 to −3), NEERG(−1), OILG(−1), FOODG(0 to −4); OECDG, (0) and (0 to −1) for equations with and without NEERG, respectively; NFCG(−1), INV_gap(−1); and CRR, (0) and (0 to −1) for equations with and without NEERG, respectively.

5. The null hypothesis in Kleibergen–Paap rk (KP) Wald F-statistic is that the equation is weakly identified. The null hypothesis in the Andersen–Rubin (AR) Wald Test is joint significance of endogenous regressors being zero in the main equation and orthogonality conditions being valid.

longer lasting. The sharp increase in expectations driven inflation persistence also suggests that people discounted the credibility of monetary policy in its ability to lower inflation or in its commitment to the announced policy threshold.

3.5. Assessing the Policy Response

Our results indicate that inflation dynamics have undergone a change in the wake of the global crisis. How monetary policy responded to these changes is the subject of this sub-section. Drawing on the rich literature on the subject, the response of the monetary authority to different shocks impacting the economy can be conceptualized in the form of a quadratic utility-based welfare function that minimizes the squared deviations of output and inflation from potential and target, respectively (Woodford 1997). While the validity of this approach has been questioned (Bernanke and Mishkin 1997; Blinder 1997; Clarida and Gertler 1997; DeLong 1997), our paper is mainly driven by its interest in a policy rule that sets a time path for the policy interest rate which optimizes the objective function subject to linear behaviorial constraints. Following Taylor (1993), this so-called "optimal policy rule" is incorporated in a simple optimizing interest rate specification that allows the central bank to vary its instrument—the interest rate—linearly to movements in inflation and output (Woodford 2001). A forward looking specification is recommended in theory in which the interest rate is adjusted to future inflation and output deviations from target/potential. It is also useful to incorporate interest rate smoothing to represent inertia in policy response (Clarida et al. 2000; Paez-Farrell 2009). Some studies have found that exchange rate smoothing is an important consideration in the policy reaction function of most emerging economies, including India (as in Mohanty and Klau 2004). We also follow the literature in augmenting the policy reaction function with the influence of key international interest rates on domestic monetary policy in the context of the growing degree of trade and financial integration, large capital flows and potential business cycle synchronization. Accordingly, our specification of the policy reaction function takes the form:

$$I_t = c_0 + c_1{*}\, E_{t\text{-}j}\, \pi gap_{t+k} + c_2{*}E_{t\text{-}j}y_{t+m} + c_3{*}I_{t\text{-}1} + c_4{*}\Delta X_t + C_5{*}i^*_t + \varepsilon_t \quad (6)$$

where I is the nominal policy/short-term interest rate, y is the output gap, πgap is the inflation gap (in terms of deviation from the objective level set by the central bank for monetary policy purposes or the threshold level of 5% in India), i^* is the Federal Funds rate, ΔX is the variation (quarter-on-quarter) in the nominal exchange rate of the rupee against the US dollar and "j" represents the possible information lag to which the central bank is subject. If k and m are both positive, we get a forward-looking version of the Taylor rule; the outcome is a backward-looking version if k and m are negative.

The results of estimating the policy reaction function are given in Table 9. Following Mishra and Mishra (2012a), we adopt a sequential approach to the estimation, beginning with the "pure inflation targeting" situation in which the RBI changes its policy rate to movements in the inflation gap alone. This is followed up with the introduction of the output gap, exchange rate changes measured in percent of appreciation/depreciation and the Federal funds rate in that order so as to progressively approximate the multiple indicator approach currently adopted by the RBI. Furthermore, we estimate this family of policy reaction functions for the pre-global crisis period and for the full sample period that includes the post-global crisis experience. Instruments satisfy the orthogonality condition as per the J-statistic and the Q statistic shows no evidence of residual auto-correlation. The Kleibergen–Paap rk Wald F-statistics are reasonably high, particularly in specifications excluding the exchange rate. The AR statistic indicates that the endogenous regressors are relevant.

In the hard inflation targeting case where the policy interest rate responds to future—one period ahead—movements in the inflation gap alone, the coefficient on the inflation gap slightly falls from 1.6 in the pre-crisis period to close to 1.4 in the full sample that includes the postcrisis years. This satisfies an important pre-condition for stability of the policy reaction function emphasized by Kerr and King (1996), Bernanke and Woodford (1997) and Clarida et al. (1998)—the coefficient on the inflation gap is expected to be at or above unity, failing which the policy rule can itself become a source of instability in the model leading to indeterminacy of the equilibrium. With this coefficient below unity, a rise in inflation leads to a decline in the real interest rate which stimulates a rise in aggregate demand which, in turn, induces a rise in inflation, thus confirming self-fulfilling revisions in expectations. When the coefficient is above unity, short-term real interest rates do not adjust to accommodate sunspot shifts in inflationary expectations.

Next, we introduce the output gap as an argument in the policy reaction function. The coefficient on the inflation gap rises to about 1.9 during the pre-global crisis period and to about 1.5 during the full sample period. The output gap coefficient, however, remains more or less unchanged at about 1.1. Third, we introduce the exchange rate into the reaction function. The exchange rate term is statistically insignificant, validating the point that the RBI does not react to exchange rate movements with interest rate changes but instead with foreign exchange interventions and capital controls (Mohan and Kapur 2009). The introduction of the exchange rate term, however, reduces the inflation gap coefficient and raises the output gap coefficient, and pre-global crisis period and full sample period coefficients are the same.

TABLE 9. Estimates of Policy Reaction Function (Dependent Variable Policy Rate: I_t)

	(1)		(2)		(3)		(4)		(5)		(6)	
	Pre	*Post*	*Pre*	*Post*	*Pre*	*Post*	*Pre*	*Post*	*Pre*	*Post*	*Pre*	*Post*
Constant	0.004	0.005	0.004	0.005	0.004	0.005	0.004	0.006	0.007	0.006	0.006	0.005
	(5.05)	(2.37)	(3.06)	(3.28)	(2.00)	(2.54)	(3.48)	(3.80)	(5.50)	(3.88)	(4.10)	(4.30)
π^e_{gap}	0.12	0.15	0.12	0.13	0.10	0.13	0.06	0.15	0.09	0.15	0.10	0.15
	(11.5)	(6.06)	(13.2)	(6.81)	(6.48)	(6.93)	(5.58)	(6.52)	(4.89)	(6.92)	(6.64)	(6.64)
$Y_{gap(t+1)}$			0.07	0.09	0.08	0.11	0.05	0.12	0.06	0.12	0.09	0.13
			(2.31)	(2.89)	(2.53)	(2.97)	(1.63)	(2.11)	(1.66)	(2.42)	(2.48)	(2.99)
ΔX_{t+1}					0.00	–0.00	0.01	0.00	0.00	0.00	–0.00	0.00
					(0.6)	(–0.4)	(1.7)	(0.4)	(0.3)	(0.5)	(–0.2)	(0.4)
$FED_{(t-1)}$									0.07	0.04		
									(3.5)	(1.3)		
$FED_{(t)}$							0.08	0.04				
							(5.93)	(1.53)				
$FED_{(t+1)}$											0.03	0.03
											(1.87)	(1.39)
$I_{(t-1)}$	0.92	0.90	0.94	0.91	0.93	0.91	0.89	0.88	0.84	0.88	0.88	0.89
	(74.8)	(35.9)	(53.7)	(40.1)	(32.6)	(29.5)	(43.6)	(25.8)	(37.6)	(24.6)	(39.1)	(31.4)
Long-run Coefficients												
Inflation	1.58	1.41	1.94	1.51	1.46	1.46	0.58	1.22	0.41	1.26	0.84	1.29
Output			1.09	1.05	1.25	1.24	0.41	0.99	0.55	0.99	0.74	1.16
Fed							0.69	0.35	0.44	0.28	0.24	0.30
Exchange					0.04	–0.03	0.08	0.02	0.01	0.02	–0.01	0.02
$\bar{R}^2$	0.91	0.85	0.89	0.85	0.89	0.84	0.89	0.85	0.91	0.85	0.91	0.85

(Table 9 Contd)

(Table 9 Contd)

J-Statistic	10.85	12.01	11.2	10.43	10.4	9.28	7.97	10.18	8.48	10.3	9.39	9.80
	(0.97)	(0.94)	(0.92)	(0.94)	(0.79)	(0.86)	(0.92)	(0.81)	(0.97)	(0.85)	(0.95)	(0.88)
LB-Q Statistics	23.0	23.5	26.6	20.7	29.0	21.0	29.6	21.5	25.8	21.5	26.5	22.1
	(0.29)	(0.27)	(0.15)	(0.41)	(0.09)	(0.40)	(0.08)	(0.37)	(0.17)	(0.37)	(0.15)	(0.33)
Weak Instruments Tests												
KP Wald Tests	31.0	22.7	17.5	16.4	2.6	1.8	9.5	2.8	9.7	3.7	12.1	4.6
AR Wald	322	72	485	75	135	26	142	29	456	34	456	34
F- Test (p-value)	(0.00)	(0.00)	(0.00)	(0.00)	(0.00)	(0.00)	(0.00)	(0.00)	(0.00)	(0.00)	(0.00)	(0.00)

Source: Authors' estimates.

Notes: 1. Figures in parentheses are t-statistics based on HAC standard errors corrected with Newey-West/Bartlett window and one-step iteration.

2. LB-Q is the Box-Pierce-Ljung Q-statistic (p-value in parentheses) for the null of no residual autocorrelation for 10 lags.

3. Hansen's J-Statistic (p-value in parentheses) for over-identifying restrictions for GMM estimates.

4. Estimation is by GMM methodology for the sample period 1997:2 to 2012:4. Instrument variables: ogap(−1 to −4); π^{e}_{gap} (−1 to −3), except for column 1 which is −1 to −4; I(−2 to −4); EFD_gap, (0 to −1) for column 1 and 2 and (0) for the rest, M3G (0 to −2) for column 1 and 2 and (0 to −3) for the rest ; NFCG; OILG(0 to −2) for column 1 and 2 and (0) for the rest; XRATE(−1); CRR(−1); FED(−1).

5. The null hypothesis in Kleibergen-Paap rk (KP) Wald F-statistic is that the equation is weakly identified. The null hypothesis in the Andersen-Rubin (AR) Wald Test is joint significance of endogenous regressors being zero in the main equation and orthogonality conditions being valid.

The addition of the Fed Funds rate renders the reaction function unstable in the pre-crisis period; in the full sample period, it is not significant.

Overall, there is a high degree of interest rate smoothing in all cases. This suggests a slow or so-called "calibrated" response to shocks to inflation which, in some sense, could be imparting persistence to the inflation process, especially when large and unanticipated changes are warranted to unanchor inflation expectations from elevated levels (Poddar 2012). The preferred specification of the policy reaction function turns out to be the one with the inflation gap and the output gap, given the insignificance of exchange rate term and the federal funds rate.

Finally, in order to evaluate the performance of our estimates equations in an economy-wide framework, we nest the estimated expectations augmented hybrid NKPC in a fully specified New Keynesian macroeconomic model that includes our preferred specification of the policy reaction function and an aggregate demand function which relates the output gap to the real interest rate (derived from the effective policy rate minus inflation), its own lag, world output to reflect external demand effects, lag of excess rain and lag of real bank credit. The full estimated model is given below. In-sample deterministic dynamic simulations show that the model performs reasonably well in terms of the fit of the estimated path, including the turning points as seen in Table 10.

1. Aggregate demand

$$\begin{aligned} y_t = & \underset{(-4.38)}{-0.0048} + \underset{(-2.30)}{-0.036} * I^r_{(t-2)} + \underset{(27.0)}{0.817} * y_{t-1} + \underset{(9.73)}{0.007} * OECD\_gr \\ & + \underset{(9.42)}{0.088} * Ex\_Rain_{(t-1)} + \underset{(2.19)}{0.015} * RNFCG_{(t-3)} - \underset{(-6.60)}{0.03} * Dum2004Q1 \\ & + \underset{(13.5)}{0.017} * Dum2001Q4 \end{aligned}$$

R-bar Square = 0.74; J-statistic = 14.0 (0.93)

2. Aggregate Supply

$$\begin{aligned} \pi_t = & \underset{(-2.07)}{-0.007} + \underset{(13.2)}{0.489} * \pi_{(t-1)} + \underset{(2.20)}{0.22} * y_{t-1} + \underset{(5.11)}{0.511} * \pi^e_{(t+1)} \\ & + \underset{(3.21)}{0.046} * \Delta X_t - \underset{(-1.88)}{0.048} * Ex\_Rain \end{aligned}$$

R-bar Square = 0.87; J-statistic = 12.12 (0.52)

3. Policy Reaction function

$$I_t = \underset{(3.28)}{0.005} + \underset{(6.81)}{0.133} * \pi^e_{gap(t+1)} + \underset{(2.90)}{0.093} * y_{t+1} + \underset{(40.1)}{0.91} * I_{(t-1)}$$

R-bar Square = 0.85; J-statistic = 10.4 (0.94)

Note: Figures in parentheses are t-statistics.

TABLE 10. In-Sample Dynamic Forecasting Performance

Sl. No.	Statistic	Policy rate (I)	Inflation (π)	Output gap (y_t)
1.	Mean Error	–0.0001	0.0008	0.0015
2.	Mean Absolute Error	0.009	0.0067	0.0071
3.	Root Mean Square Error (MSE)	0.012	0.0092	0.0092
4.	Theil's U	0.082	0.074	0.40

Source: Authors' estimates.

4. Appraisal of the Monetary Policy Framework

In the aftermath of the global financial crisis and especially the bout of high inflation persistence, a debate is beginning to brew in India around the need or otherwise for a change in the monetary policy framework to make it relevant, effective and, above all, credible. It is in this context that the case for adoption of inflation targeting (IT) is under scrutiny. This discussion, by itself, is not new in India. On the one hand, it has been argued that the preconditions for inflation targeting are in place and the move to IT is apposite (Khatkhate 2006; Singh 2006), also because multiple objectives are sometimes in conflict (O'Neill and Poddar 2008; Poddar 2012). Others have pointed out that the liberalization of financial markets is far from complete, that the banking system has strong monopoly elements, that fiscal overhang still exists, and that there is a rather weak relationship between short-term interest rates and inflation measures in the Granger causation sense (Jha 2008). An influential view has also been expressed that in India, it is neither desirable nor practical for the central bank to focus exclusively on inflation oblivious of the larger development context in which more often than not, the drivers of inflation in India emanate from the supply side. There is also the formidable challenge of getting a single representative inflation rate for a large economy with 1.2 billion people, fragmented markets and diverse geography. Moreover, the monetary transmission mechanism is impeded by administered interest rates, asymmetric contractual relationships between banks and their depositors, illiquid bond markets and large government borrowings. Also managing large and volatile capital flows is not compatible with IT. At best, flexible IT—if inflation is way off target, a central bank's first call is to bring it within acceptable range, and if inflation is within the range, the central bank should focus on other objectives—is preferable to pure IT (Subbarao 2010). The lack of complete formation of pre-conditions has also been proferred as an argument for establishing flexible inflation targeting despite its theorized suitability to Indian conditions (Mishra and Mishra 2012b).

To date, 28 countries have adopted IT since New Zealand pioneered it in 1989. With the ECB and the US Federal Reserve seen as implicit inflation targeters (Warburton et al. 2012), there are 30 countries that currently keep the faith. The country experience provides insights into what works, where and why (Annexure 4: Table 8).[8] There is no unanimity of opinion in the economics profession on IT. The global crisis itself has brought with a radical re-appraisal of IT. The loss of macro-prudential discipline even while inflation targets were observed is seen as undermining the validity of the IT framework in terms of fostering complacency. It has also been argued that IT is a communications strategy—a means of breaking inflationary psychology. It is an implicit contract with the public—the longer the inflation target is achieved, the greater the credibility of the central banker and of monetary policy. However, as the global crisis showed in 2008, circumstances may arise in which the central bank may want to break this contract. The massive quantitative easing engaged in by systemic central banks go well beyond abrogation of the implicit contract. Unconventional monetary policies have left the public uncertain whether the inflation target will be observed in future. Doubts have arisen about the durability and flexibility of IT to withstand severe financial shocks—a child of its time that cannot mature (Warburton et al. 2012). In fact, the case for a new normal for inflation at 4% (Blanchard et al. 2010) has been regarded as challenge to IT in its present form. The need to combine financial stability with price stability, dealing with asset prices and life at the zero interest rate bound is seen as the new challenges confronting IT in the future.

India's monetary policy framework can be described as de facto flexible IT with feedback. Our results show that the weight assigned to inflation is high by international standards, even in the presence of multiple objectives, and this ensures a stable reaction function. Furthermore, the coefficient on the inflation gap has increased when the post-global crisis period is incorporated into the policy reaction function. A deep-seated inflation aversion in the public's expectations strengthens the perception of inflation at 5% as a threshold beyond which it is harmful for growth itself. The coefficient on the output gap is above unity in all specifications, indicating a strong commitment to output stabilization relative to advanced economy central banks

8. The Bank of England's "State of the Art of Inflation targeting" CCBS Handbook No. 29 provides a rich and comprehensive overview.

(Blattner and Margaritov 2010) and several emerging economies (Mohanty and Klau 2004). Thus inflation is the dominant focus of monetary policy in India but it is accompanied by an emphasis on stabilizing output around its potential. It has been argued that this is indicative of the fact that the RBI regards deviation of output from trend as carrying the seeds of future inflation. What needs to be fixed, then? In our view, the critical issue is that of obtaining an accurate gauge of the nature of underlying inflation dynamics or more specifically of the degree of inflation persistence and its sources. If inflation persistence has increased as our results show, this requires a preemptive and aggressive monetary policy reaction to break inflation expectations before they become entrenched. This suggests a closer scrutiny of the inertia emanating from monetary policy itself as evident in the high degree of policy smoothing. Furthermore, most inflation persistence episodes tend to emanate from food price shocks which become generalized. Consequently, accommodating food inflation on the argument that the Indian economy is more prone to supply shocks than demand shocks (Balakrishnan 1992) is a perilous strategy. The monetary policy framework will also be strengthened by some changes in its institutional apparatus. The new national level CPI must progressively be employed as the official measure of inflation in the RBI's communication, as in all 28 IT countries. This has practical and operational benefits since it is available on a monthly basis, reflects retail inflation, and should be conveyed as a headline measure rather than in its core form—excluding food which comprises 48% would lack credibility. At present, the new CPI is only three years old and lacks sufficient inflation data points to test for its stability and comprehensiveness. Another institutional innovation could be the mainstreaming of inflation expectations into the monetary policy framework. In this context, the RBI's surveys of urban households and professional forecasters hold promise.[9]

The debate on IT for India is, in a sense, being overtaken by the momentum gathering around impending legislative changes to the proposed monetary policy framework. The Report of the Financial Sector Legislative Reforms Commission (GoI 2013) envisages price stability as the prime

9. The Reserve Bank has been conducting the inflation expectations survey of households since September 2005 to obtain the perception of urban households on price and inflation movements for three months ahead and one year ahead. The survey responses are both quantitative and qualitative in nature. At present, the survey covers 250 households from 16 cities. The Reserve Bank has been conducting the Survey of Professional Forecasters on a quarterly basis from the quarter ended September 2007. Point forecasts on inflation are also among the responses elicited from professional forecasters. The forecasts are collected for the entire financial year, various quarters as well for longer periods like 5 and 10 years ahead.

determinant of the conduct of monetary policy, but stops short of specifying such a requirement in its draft Code. Instead, it recommends that the Central Government determine the predominant medium-term objective of monetary policy as well as other secondary but prioritized objectives, each quantified numerically, through a formal process of articulation in a statement released in the public domain. It seeks independence for the central bank through the establishment of a monetary policy committee, with two external members appointed by the Central Government in consultation with the Governor, and the remaining three external members without consultation with the Governor. A formal voting structure, with attribution and public release of the voting record and rationale is also envisaged. The Central Government is also required to establish what constitutes a substantial failure to achieve policy objectives, requiring the central bank head to write a document explaining the failure, propose remedial action and specify a time horizon over which the return to target is to be achieved.

The recommendations of the Commission will inevitably be subjected to a national debate before the preparation of the formal legislation for parliamentary discourse and sanction. It is therefore timely to take note of some caveats to these recommendations in their present form. They essentially draws from the Anglo-Saxon approach of goal dependent, instrument independent monetary policy which was found wanting in the context of the global crisis. It is necessary to carefully evaluate the more pragmatic and resilient alternative of the US Federal Reserve/ECB approach of goal-independent, instrument-independent monetary policy. The latter provides flexibility which is critical to the conduct of monetary policy. It makes the central bank more accountable since it has to report to Parliament.[10] Most importantly, it strictly precludes fiscal dominance in monetary policy, which is particularly crucial in a country like India in which a significant portion of inflation is determined by the Central Government through administered prices (and wages), and monetary transmission is mainly impeded by Government's administered interest rates, directed credit, statutory preemptions and ownership in banking.

If, however, the UK model is preferred in the national debate, the objectives of monetary policy (both predominant and secondary) must be specified

10. In the United Kingdom, for instance, the view at the time of institution of IT was that the Bank of England "would not be able to account for its monetary stewardship on the Floor of the House of Commons. In a parliamentary system of democracy, it is Ministers who are accountable" (Tucker 2007). Similar arguments are raised in the Indian context, but may not hold if the central bank is given statutory independence. Moreover, breaking away from the British model may bring a refreshing improvement in accountability.

clearly in an Act of Parliament, restricting the flexibility of the Central Government in terms of scope for changing the objectives from time to time, unless and until the Act is amended. If the FSLRC Act, hypothetically, mandates the RBI with an "inflation targeting" framework focused on price stability as the predominant objective, then the new Act must also recognize necessary preconditions for such a framework to work—fiscal discipline; better capacity to manage supply constraints and augment supply capacity to contain supply side persistent pressures on inflation (so that trade-off costs of inflation targeting are minimized); and improved monetary policy transmission through more complete and integrated financial markets. The FSLRC also mimics the approach of the Bank of England in its accountability mechanism. Over the period December 2009 to March 2013, the Bank of England has missed its target in several months and communicated its failure through monthly open letters to the Chancellor of the Exchequer (when inflation exceeded the target by 100 basis points). This process, while based on strong institutional foundations, does not at all appear to enhance the credibility of either the monetary policy or the Government. Identification of substantial failure and correctional strategies can only follow the establishment of strong credibility by the MPC in delivering on the target(s) set.

The conduct of monetary policy and the relative weights assigned to objectives is inevitably an informed judgment based on careful analysis of macroeconomic and financial developments. Specifying a medium term hierarchy of objectives with the expectation that they "would be modified only occasionally" (GOI 2013) severely strait-jackets this judgment and could result in sub-optimal monetary policy. As an instrument of public policy, monetary policy is expected to be nimble and forward looking in response to fast changing macroeconomic dynamics relative to other instruments. Furthermore, all objectives may be difficult to quantify numerically as, for instance, financial stability.

5. Conclusion

Writing this paper has been like driving by watching the rear-view mirror—hindsight confers 20/20 vision, but also the sobering reality that objects in the mirror are closer than they appear. What began as an exploration of a recent inflation episode has turned out to be a voyage of introspective discovery, providing valuable insights not just into understanding inflation persistence but also into managing it from a policy perspective.

Policy makers are destined to live a life of self-annihilation, rising from the depths into moments of public discontent (usually), only to repose back into the anonymity of their unresting lives. Theirs cannot be the luxury of theism or intellectual edifices. It is ordained that they shall be judged only by the razor's edge of outcomes, never how, always how much. So they have to be clinical, dispassionate and opportunistic in delivering on assigned objectives. Low and stable inflation is a contract between central banks and the public, an article of faith without escape clauses. Reneging on this commitment never goes unpunished, as the recent experience in India has shown. After forty excruciating months, inflation has begun to reluctantly recede, but the beast is not beaten, far from it. We suspect it lurks, waiting to rear its ugly head, not just in India but across the world, overtly in emerging economies and subliminally in advanced economies in the slosh of abundant liquidity. Consequently, pre-emptive strikes to the unraveling of its dynamics are critical, no driver off the radar, no response off the table. This paper proposes an empirical framework to empower this monetary policy stance.

Our journey has yielded several lessons. First, overestimation of potential output growth has deleterious consequences. Misperceptions of supply capacities lead to emergence of demand pressures and inflation inevitably rises above conscionable levels. If the initial burst of inflation gets entrenched in expectations, the greater persistence in inflation will require prolonged monetary policy tightening which could produce lasting impairment to potential growth itself. To be fair, estimating potential growth is always difficult, and even more so in the aftershock of a global crisis. At the very least, however, there should be a preparedness to revise potential growth regularly and allow these revisions to inform the setting of monetary policy. Secondly, the large variance of inflation associated with a right skew is inflationary and persistent, a characteristic of inflation episodes in India right from the 1980s. A large portion of the components of inflation experience price movements significantly different from the headline or even core. Scrutinizing the cross-sectional distribution of inflation is, therefore, important for monetary policy. The IDEX constructed in this paper tracks well the broad-basing of price increases/decreases across the constituents of the price index.

Our results suggest that inflation persistence has increased in the post-global crisis period. Though the influence of past inflation and that of inheritance from the macroeconomic environment has been declining, both are still high. Shocks to inflation will require forceful, more than proportionate policy responses. Output stabilization has important inflation spillovers and is a legitimate argument in the monetary policy reaction function. Extrinsic persistence works in the same direction as intrinsic persistence, amplifying it through rigidities in the economic structure that impede elastic supply responses and result in high output costs of bringing down inflation. The "surprise" in our estimations and, perhaps, a contribution to the understanding of recent inflation behavior in India, is the role of inflation expectations. Expectations have played a much larger role than before in inflation inertia in the post global crisis period. Did communication and action get decoupled, at least in the period of the incubation of inflation in 2009–10? In fact, only 10.5 to 12.3% of respondents polled in the RBI's household inflation expectations survey believed that the RBI's actions would lower inflation and this proportion was actually lower than in earlier rounds. Also, the high degree of interest rate smoothing in the policy reaction function could have been a source of persistence if agents viewed the "measured" policy responses as inadequate in relation to the magnitude of the increase in inflation.

What does this imply for the monetary policy framework? By itself, it does not suggest a radical change. The RBI explicitly states a numerical threshold of 5% as its inflation tolerance and 3% as its medium-term goal. Transparency instruments include quarterly publications of its inflation report titled "Monetary and Macroeconomic Developments", publication of the minutes of its purely advisory monetary policy committee without attribution, publication of inflation forecasts with fan charts (forecasts of GDP growth as well as the rates of money supply, deposit and credit growth are also provided), speeches by the Governor and Deputy Governors and their testimonies before the Parliamentary Committee on Finance. On the other hand, the fiscal authority is still viewed as profligate and fiscal dominance as large. Monetary policy transmission is fragmented and incomplete, the financial sector is weakening, and the quality of macroeconomic data leaves much to be desired.

The monetary policy regime in India is currently the subject of tectonic change and significant institutional reform is being contemplated that would bring India closer to an inflation targeting regimen than ever before. By all considerations, a flexible inflation targeting framework of constrained discretion appears to be the consensus choice. Inflation is a developmental objective; it is most unjust to the unindexed poor. To end this paper, we can do no better than to back the RBI's resolve in its annual monetary policy statement for the year 2013–14: "*the Reserve Bank will endeavour to condition the evolution of inflation to a level of 5.0 per cent by March 2014, using all instruments at its command.*"

References

Altissimo, Filippo, Michael Ehrmann, and Frank Smets. 2006. "Inflation Persistence and Price-Setting Behaviour in the Euro Area: A Summary of the IPN Evidence", *ECB Occasional Paper Series, No. 46*, June.

Amano, Robert A. and R. Tiff Macklem. 1997. "Menu Costs, Relative Prices, and Inflation: Evidence for Canada," *Working Paper 97–14*, June.

Andrews, D. and W. Chen. 1994. "Approximately Median Unbiased Estimation of Auto-Regressive Models", *Journal of Business and Economic Statistics,* 12: 187–204.

Angeloni, Ignazio, Luc Aucremanne, Michael Ehrmann, Jordi Galí, Andrew Levin, and Frank Smets. 2006. "New Evidence on Inflation Persistence and Price Stickiness in the Euro Area: Implications for Macro Modeling," *Journal of the European Economic Association*, 4 (2–3): 562–74.

Assarsson, Bengt. 2003. "Inflation and Higher Moments of Relative Price Changes," *BIS Papers 19*, Bank for International Settlement, Basel, Switzerland.

Balakrishna, P. 1992. "Industrial Price Behaviour in India: An Error-Correction Model," *Journal of Development Economics*, 37 (3): 309–26.

Balakrishnan, Pulapre. 2011. "Monetary policy not the answer to inflation," *Business Line*, October 2. Available at http://www.thehindubusinessline.com/opinion/monetary-policy-not-the-answer-to-inflation/article2506744.ece (accessed on May 22, 2014).

Balke, N.S. and M.A. Wynne. 2000. "An Equilibrium Analysis of Relative Price Changes and Aggregate Inflation," *Journal of Monetary Economics*, 45: 269–92.

Ball, Laurence and Stephen G. Cecchetti. 1990. "Inflation and uncertainty at short and long horizons," *Brookings Papers on Economic Activity*, 21(1): 215–245.

Ball, Laurence and N. Gregory Mankiw. 1995. "Relative-price Changes as Aggregate Supply Shocks," *Quarterly Journal of Economics*, 110 (1): 161–93.

Barsky, Robert B. 1986. "The Fisher Hypothesis and the Forecastability and Persistence of Inflation," *NBER Working Papers 1927*, National Bureau of Economic Research, Inc.

Basu, Kaushik. 2011. "Understanding Inflation and Controlling it," *Economic and Political Weekly*, 46 (41): 50–64.

Batini, Nicoletta, Peter Breuer, Kalpana Kochhar, and Skott Roger. 2006. "Inflation Targeting and the IMF," *IMF Staff Paper*, Washington, D.C., March.

Bernanke, B., and F. Mishkin. 1997. "Inflation Targeting: A New Framework for Monetary Policy?" *Journal of Economic Perspectives*, 11 (2): 97–116.

Bernanke, Ben S. and Michael Woodford. 1997. "Inflation Forecasts and Monetary Policy," *NBER Working Papers 6157*, National Bureau of Economic Research, Inc.

Bernanke, Ben S., Thomas Laubach, Frederic S. Mishkin, and Adam S. Posen. 1999. *Inflation Targeting: Lessons from the International Experience*. Princeton: Princeton University Press.

Bhanumurthy, N.R., Surajit Das and Sukanya Bose. 2012. "Oil Price Shock, Pass-through Policy and its Impact on India," *Working Papers 12/99*, National Institute of Public Finance and Policy.

Bhattacharya, B.B., and Lodh, M. 1990. "Inflation in India: An Analytical Survey," *Artha Vijnana*, 32 (1): 22–68.

Bils, M., and P.J. Klenow. 1998. "Using Consumer Theory to Test Competing Business Cycle Models," *Journal of Political Economy*, 106: 233–61.

Blanchard, Olivier, Giovanni Dell' Ariccia, and Paolo Mauro. 2010. "Rethinking Macroeconomic Policy," *IMF Staff Position Note*, February 12, 2010.

Blattner, Tobias S., and Emil Margaritov. 2010. Towards a Robust Monetary Policy Rule for the Euro Area, *ECB Working Paper No. 1210*, European Central Bank, Frankfurt, Germany.

Bryan, M.F., and S.G. Cecchetti. 1999. "Inflation and the Distribution of Price Changes," *Review of Economics and Statistics*, 81: 188–96.

Blinder, Alan S. 1997. "What Central Bankers Can Learn from Academics—and Vice-Versa?" *Journal of Economic Perspectives*, 11 (2): 3–19.

Bose, Sukanya. 2012. "Inflation: Sources, Challenges and Policy Options," *Economic and Political Weekly*, 47 (3): 27–30.

Catik, Nazif and Ozlem Onder. 2010. "The Distribution of the Inflation in Turkey," *Ege Academic Review*, 10 (2): 613–25.

Chand Ramesh. 2011. "Understanding the Nature and Causes of Food Inflation," *Economic and Political Weekly*, 45 (9): 10–13.

Chand, Ramesh. 2012. "Development Policies and Agricultural Markets," *Economic and Political Weekly*, 47 (52): 53–63.

Clarida, Richard and Mark Gertler. 1997. "How the Bundesbank Conducts Monetary Policy" in Christina Romer and David Romer (eds), *Reducing Inflation: Motivation and Strategy*, pp. 363–412, Chicago: NBER.

Clarida, Richard, Jordi Gali and Mark Gertler. 1998. "Monetary Policy Rules in Practice: Some International Evidence," *European Economic Review*, 42: 1033–67.

———. 2000. "Monetary Policy Rules and Macroeconomic Stability: Evidence and Some Theory," *Quarterly Journal of Economics*, February: 147–80.

Darbha, Gangadhar, and Patel, Urjit R. 2012. "Dynamics of Inflation 'Herding': Decoding India's Inflationary Process," Working Paper 48, Global Economy and Development, Brookings.

DeLong, J. Bradford. 1997. "America's Peacetime Inflation: The 1970s," in Christina Romer and David Romer (eds), *Reducing Inflation: Motivation and Strategy*, pp. 247–80, Chicago: NBER.

Dholakia, R. 1990. "Extended Phillips Curve for the Indian economy," *Indian Economic Journal*, 38 (1): 69–78.

Dopke, Jorg and Christian Pierdzioch. 2001. "Inflation and the Skewness of the Distribution of Relative Price Changes: Empirical Evidence for Germany," *Kiel Working Paper No. 1059*, July.

Dosschey, Maarten and Gerdie Everaertz. 2007. "Disentangling the Sources of Inflation Persistence," December. Available at http://www.feb.ugent.be/soceco/sherppa/members/maarten/documents/paper1.pdf (accessed on May 23, 2014).

Friedman, Milton and Anna Jacobson Schwartz. 1963. *A Monetary History of the United States, 1867–1960*. Princeton: Princeton University Press for NBER.

Fuhrer, Jeff and George Moore. 1995. "Inflation Persistence," *Quarterly Journal of Economics*, 110: 127–59.

Fuhrer, Jeffrey C. 2009. "Inflation Persistence", *FRB of Boston Working Paper No. 09–14*, November 30, Federal Reserve Bank of Boston, USA.

Gets, Patricia M., and Mark, G. Ulmer. 1990. "Diffusion Indexes: A Barometer of the Economy," *Monthly Labor Review*, Bureau of Labor Statistics, April.

Goodhart, Charles and Boris Hofmann. 2005. "The Phillips Curve, the IS Curve and Monetary Transmission: Evidence for the US and the Euro Area," *CESifo Economic Studies*, 51 (4): 757–75.

Gokarn, Subir. 2011. "Striking the Balance between Growth and Inflation in India," Presentation at the US India Economic and Financial Partnership, CII and Brookings Institution, Washington, D.C., June 27.

Government of India. 2011. "Micro-Foundations of Macroeconomic Development," Economic Survey 2010–11, February.

———. 2013. "The Report of the Financial Sector Legislative Reforms Commission," Vol. I and II, New Delhi, March.

Hatekar, Neeraj, Ashutosh Sharma, and Savita Kulkarni. 2011. "What Drives Inflation in India: Overheating or Input Costs?" *Economic and Political Weekly*, 46 (34): 46–51.

Ho, Corrinne and Robert N. McCauley. 2003. "Living with Flexible Exchange Rates: Issues and Recent Experience in Inflation Targeting Emerging Market Economies," *BIS Working Papers 130*, Bank for International Settlements.

International Monetary Fund. 2011. "Annex 1. Inflation Dynamics in India," *India: 2010 Article IV Consultation-Staff Report*, February: 30–34.

Ito, Takatoshi and Kiyotaka Sato. 2006. "Exchange Rate Changes and Inflation in Post-Crisis Asian Economies: VAR Analysis of the Exchange Rate Pass-Through," *Discussion Papers 06018*, Research Institute of Economy, Trade and Industry. RIETI.

Jha, Raghbendra. 2008. "Inflation Targeting in India: Issues and Prospects," *International Review of Applied Economics*, 22 (2): 259–70.

Kapur, Muneesh and Michael Patra. 2003. "The Price of Low Inflation," *RBI Occasional Papers*, 21 (2 and 3): 191–233.

Kearns, Jonathan. 1998. "The Distribution and Measurement of Inflation," *Research Discussion Paper 9810*, Economic Analysis Department, Reserve Bank of Australia, September.

Kerr, William and Robert G. King. 1996. "Limits on Interest Rate Rules in the IS Model," *Economic Quarterly*, Federal Reserve Bank of Richmond, 82/2 (Spring): 47–75.

Khatkhate, D. 2006. "Inflation Targeting: Much Ado about Something," *Economic and Political Weekly*, 41 (49): 5031–33.

Khundrakpam J.K. 2008. "How Persistent is Indian Inflationary Process, Has it Changed?" *RBI Occasional Papers*, 29 (2): 23–45.

Kottaridi, Constantina, Mendez-Carbajo Diego, and D. Thomakos Dimitrios. 2009. "Inflation Dynamics and the Cross-Sectional Distribution of Prices in the E.U. Periphery," in Takashi Kamihigashi and Laixun Zhao (eds), *International Trade and Economic Dynamics*, pp. 449–75.

Krugman. 2012. "Two Percent Is Not Enough," *The Conscience of a Liberal, The Opinion Pages, New York Times*, January 26. Available at: http://krugman.blogs.nytimes.com/2012/01/26/two-percent-is-not-enough/?_r=0

Levin, Andrew T. and Jeremy M. Piger. 2004. "Is Inflation Persistence Intrinsic in Industrial Economies?" *European Central Bank Working Paper No. 334*, April.

Machado, Vicente da Gama, and Marcelo Savino Portugal. 2012. "Measuring Inflation Persistence in Brazil using a Multivariate Model," available at: http://www.ufrgs.br/PPGE/pcientifica/2012_09.pdf

Mazumder, S. 2011. "The Stability of the Phillips Curve in India: Does the Lucas Critique Apply?" *Journal of Asian Economics*, 22 (6): 528–39.

Mohan, Rakesh and Muneesh Kapur. 2009. "Managing the Impossible Trinity: Volatile Capital Flows and Indian Monetary Policy," *Working Paper No. 401*, Stanford Center for International Development, November.

Mishra, Ankita and Vinod Mishra. 2012a. "Inflation Targeting in India: A Comparison with the Multiple Indicator Approach," *Journal of Asian Economics*, 23 (1): 86–98.

———. 2012b. "Evaluating Inflation Targeting as a Monetary Policy Objective for India," *Economic Modelling, Elsevier*, 29 (4): 1053–63.

Mohanty, M. and M. Klau. 2004. "Monetary Policy Rules in Emerging Economies: Issues and Evidence," *BIS Working Paper, No. 149*, Bank for International Settlement, Basel, Switzerland.

Mohanty, Deepak. 2013. "Indian Inflation Puzzle," *Speech in the Function of Late Dr. Ramchandra Parnerkar,* Outstanding Economist Award 2013, January 31st.

Mundle, Sudipto. 2011. "Millenium Development Goals: How is India Doing?" *Working Papers 11/93*, National Institute of Public Finance and Policy.

Nelson, C. and C. Plosser. 1982. "Trends and Random Walks in Macroeconomic Time Series: Some Evidence and Implications," *Journal of Monetary Economics*, 10: 129–62.

O'Neill, Jim and Tushar Poddar. 2008. "Ten Things for India to Achieve its 2050 Potential," *Global Economics Paper No. 169*, Goldman Sachs, June.

Paez-Farrell, Juan. 2009. "Monetary Policy Rules in Theory and in Practice: Evidence from the UK and the US," *Applied Economics, Taylor and Francis Journals*, 41(16): 2037–46.

Patra, Michael and Partha Ray. 2010. "Inflation Expectations and Monetary Policy in India: An Empirical Exploration," *IMF Working Paper WP/10/84*, International Monetary Fund, Washington.

Patra, M.D. and Muneesh Kapur. 2012a. "A Monetary Policy Model for India," *Macroeconomics and Finance in Emerging Market Economies*, 5(1): 16–39.

———. 2012b. "Alternative Monetary Policy Rules for India," *IMF Working Paper WP/12/118*, International Monetary Fund, Washington.

Paksha, Paul Biru. 2009. "In Search of the Phillips Curve for India," *Journal of Asian Economics*, 20: 479–88.

Perron, P. 1989. "The Great Crash, the Oil-Price Shock, and the Unit-Root Hypothesis," *Econometrica*, 57: 1361–1401.

Pivetta, Frederic and Ricardo Reis. 2007. "The Persistence of Inflation in the United States," *Journal of Economic Dynamics and Control, Elsevier*, 31 (4): 1326–58.

Poddar, Tushar. 2012. "A Formal Inflation Target & a Return to Fiscal Rules are a Must for India," Comments and Analysis, *Economic Times*, November 1. Available at http://articles.economictimes.indiatimes.com/2012-11-01/news/34857886_1_inflation-expectations-policy-rates-formal-inflation-target (accessed on May 23, 2014).

Rakshit, Mihir. 2011. "Inflation and Relative Prices in India 2006–10: Some Analytics and Policy Issues," *Economic and Political Weekly*, 46 (16): 41–54.

Rangarajan, C. 1983. "Conflict Between Employment and Inflation," in A. Robinson, ed., *Employment Policy in a Developing Country—A Case Study of India*, pp. 114–130, London: Macmillan.

Rangarajan, C. and Arif, R.R. 1990. "Money, Output and Prices: A Macroeconometric Model," *Economic and Political Weekly*, 21 (16): 837–52, April.

Reddy, S. 2012. "India's Economic Prospects," Panel Discussion at IGIDR Silver Jubilee International Conference on Development: Successes and Challenges Achieving Economic, Social and Sustainable Progress, December. Available at https://www.youtube.com/watch?v=ipIntkHvhgo.

Reserve Bank of India. 2002. *Report on Currency and Finance 2000–01*, Mumbai, India.

———. 2010a. "Annual Policy Statement for the Year 2010–11," April 20.

———. 2010b. "Supply Shocks, Relative Price Changes and the Role of Monetary Policy," Box II.5, Annual Report 2009–10, August.

———. 2012. "First Quarter Review of Monetary Policy 2012–13," July 31.

Roger, S. 2000. "Inflation Targeting at 20: Achievements and Challenges," *IMF Working Paper WP/09/235*, International Monetary Fund, Washington, DC.

Sen, Abhijit and Himanshu. 2011. "Why Not a Universal Food Security Legislation," *Economic and Political Weekly*, 46 (12): 38–47.

Shah, Ajay, Giovanni Veronese, and Ila Patnaik. 2011. "How Should Inflation Be Measured in India?" *Economic and Political Weekly*, XLVI (16): 55–64.

Shetty S.L. 2013. "Growth Versus Inflation: How RBI Has Missed the Bus," *Economic and Political Weekly*, 48 (8): 70–72.

Singh, Kanhaiya. 2006. "Inflation Targeting: International Experience and Prospects for India," *Economic and Political Weekly*, 41(27–28), (July 8–15): 2958–61.

Srinivasan T.N. 2011. "Trends in Wholesale Prices in India," unpublished draft.

Subbarao, D. 2010. "Challenges for Central Banks in the Context of the Crisis," *Inaugural Address at the International Research Conference* on "Challenges for Central Banks in the Context of the Crisis," Mumbai, February 12. Available at http://rbi.org.in/scripts/BS_SpeechesView.aspx?Id=471 (accessed on May 23, 2014).

———. 2011. "Monetary Policy Dilemmas: Some RBI Perspectives," Comments of Dr D. Subbarao, Governor, Reserve Bank of India, at the Stern School of Business, New York University, New York, September 26, 2011. Available at http://www.rbi.org.in/scripts/BS_SpeechesView.aspx?Id=602 (accessed on May 23, 2014).

———. 2013. "Is There a New Normal for Inflation?" *Speech Delivered at the Bankers' Club*, New Delhi, March 8.

Taylor, J. 1993. "Discretion versus Policy Rules in Practice," *Carnegie–Rochester Conference Series on Public Policy no. 39*.

Tripathi, Shruti, and Ashima Goyal. 2011. "Relative Prices, the Price Level and Inflation: Effects of Asymmetric and Sticky Adjustment," Indira Gandhi Institute of Development Research, *WP-2011-026*, October.

Tucker, P. M. W. 2007. "Central banking and political economy: the example of the United Kingdom's Monetary Policy Committee," speech given at the Inflation Targeting, Central Bank Independence and Transparency Conference, University of Cambridge on 15 June 2007, published in *Bank of England Quarterly Bulletin*, 2007 (Q3): 445–452.

Warburton, Peter, and Joanna Davies. 2012. "Inflation Targeting: A Child of our Time?" Feature, *Central Banking Journal*, February 21. Available at http://www.centralbanking.com/central-banking-journal/feature/2153972/inflation-targeting-child (accessed on May 23, 2014).

Woodford, Michael. 1997. "Doing Without Money: Controlling Inflation in a Post-Monetary World," *NBER Working Paper 6188*, National Bureau of Economic Research, Inc., September.

Woodford, Michael. 2001. "The Taylor Rule and Optimal Monetary Policy," *American Economic Review*, 91 (2): 232–37.

———. 2003. *Interest and Prices: Foundations of a Theory of Monetary Policy*. Princeton: Princeton University Press.

Annexure

Annexure 1: List of Variables

Ag_gap = Agricultural output gap measured as seasonally adjusted real agricultural GDP less trend obtained through HP filter.

ASYMX = Alternative measure of asymmetry for cutoff X percent.

CRR = Cash reserve ratio required to be maintained by banks.

DCHE = Month-on-month/quarter-on-quarter percentage change in manufacture chemicals component of WPI

DFOOD = Month-on-month/quarter-on-quarter percentage change in primary food component of WPI

DFUEL = Month-on-month/quarter-on-quarter percentage change in fuel component of WPI

DWPI = Month-on-month/quarter-on-quarter percentage change in aggregate WPI

DMAC = Month-on-month/quarter-on-quarter percentage change in manufactured machine component of WPI

DMANU = Month-on-month/quarter-on-quarter percentage change in manufacturing component of WPI

DMET = Month-on-month/quarter-on-quarter percentage change in manufactured metal component of WPI

DMFOOD = Month-on-month/quarter-on-quarter percentage change in manufactured food component of WPI

DNFOOD = Month-on-month/quarter-on-quarter percentage change in primary non-food component of WPI

DPRI = Month-on-month/quarter-on-quarter percentage change in primary component of WPI

DTEX = Month-on-month/quarter-on-quarter percentage change in manufactured textile component of WPI

Exrate = Year-on-year percentage change in Indian rupee and US Dollar exchange rate.

Ex_rain = Deviation of actual rainfall from long period average.

FED = Federal fund rate

FOODG= Year-on-year percentage change in primary non-food component of WPI.

GFD_gap = Gross fiscal deficit (GFD) of central government measured as seasonally adjusted GFD less trend obtained through HP filter.

I = Policy rate

I^r = Real policy rate (policy rate minus year-on-year percentage change in aggregate WPI)

IDEX = Inflation Diffusion Index

INV_gap = investment gap measured as seasonally adjusted real investment less trend obtained through HP filter.

M_3G = Year on-year percentage change in broad money.

NEERG = Year-on-year percentage change in nominal effective exchange rate.

NFCG = Year-on-year percentage change in non-food credit.

REERG = Year-on-year percentage change in real effective exchange rate.

RNFCG = Year-on-year percentage change in non-food credit minus year-on-year percentage change in WPI.

OECD_G = Real growth in OECD GDP

OGAP = output gap measured as seasonally adjusted real GDP less trend obtained through HP filter.

OILG = Year-on-year percentage change in crude oil prices.

SD = Standard Devation

SK = Skewness

SD* SK= Standard deviation of year on year inflation times skewness of year on year inflation.

WPIG = Year-on-year percentage change in WPI.

Xrate = Annualized quarter-on-quarter percentage change in Indian rupee and US Dollar exchange rate.

π^e_GAP = Year-on-year change in aggregate WPI minus implicit inflation target of 5.0 per cent.

Annexure 2

TABLE 1. Key Macroeconomic Indicators

Year	*GDP growth (%)*	*M3 growth (%)*	*Reserve money growth (%)*	*Gross fiscal deficit-center (% to GDP)*	*Gross fiscal deficit – combined (% to GDP)*	*Current account deficit to GDP ratio (%)*	*Foreign investment to GDP ratio (%)*	*Global energy price growth (%) **	*Global non-energy price growth (%) **	*Global food prices growth (%) **	*INR/USD*
1980–81	7.2	18.1	17.4	5.7	7.4	−1.5	0.0	20.6	10.4	17.4	7.9
1981–82	5.6	12.5	7.9	5.1	6.2	−1.7	0.0	−0.5	−12.5	−8.3	9.0
1982–83	2.9	16.6	10.1	5.6	5.8	−1.7	0.0	−6.3	−15.8	−21.7	9.7
1983–84	7.9	18.2	25.5	5.9	7.2	−1.5	0.0	−10.6	9.7	9.7	10.3
1984–85	4.0	19.0	21.5	7.0	8.8	−1.2	0.0	−4.7	2.2	3.6	11.9
1985–86	4.2	16.0	8.4	7.8	7.9	−2.1	0.0	−3.9	−15.0	−19.2	12.2
1986–87	4.3	18.6	17.4	8.4	9.8	−1.9	0.1	−41.3	−5.7	−14.5	12.8
1987–88	3.5	16.0	19.4	7.6	9.1	−1.8	0.2	15.6	7.9	7.2	13.0
1988–89	10.2	17.8	17.7	7.3	8.5	−2.7	0.1	−14.0	24.5	29.6	14.5
1989–90	6.1	19.4	23.2	7.3	8.8	−2.3	0.1	17.0	−1.3	0.7	16.6
1990–91	5.3	15.1	13.1	7.8	9.4	−3.0	0.0	24.9	−6.3	−7.8	17.9
1991–92	1.4	19.3	13.4	5.5	7.0	−0.3	0.1	−12.5	−4.7	−1.5	24.5
1992–93	5.4	14.8	11.3	5.3	7.0	−1.7	0.2	−2.4	−1.9	0.3	30.6
1993–94	5.7	18.4	25.2	7.0	8.2	−0.4	1.5	−10.4	−0.2	0.3	31.4
1994–95	6.4	22.4	22.1	5.7	7.1	−1.0	1.5	−5.2	14.7	9.4	31.4
1995–96	7.3	13.6	14.9	5.1	6.5	−1.6	1.4	9.0	10.0	9.4	33.4
1996–97	8.0	16.2	2.8	4.8	6.3	−1.2	1.6	16.7	−2.1	7.4	35.5
1997–98	4.3	18.0	13.2	5.8	7.3	−1.4	1.3	−6.1	−2.8	−7.7	37.2
1998–99	6.7	19.4	14.5	6.5	9.0	−1.0	0.6	−28.7	−13.5	−8.4	42.1
1999–2000	7.6	14.6	8.2	5.4	9.5	−1.0	1.2	28.0	−11.7	−18.6	43.3
2000–01	4.3	16.8	8.1	5.7	9.5	−0.6	1.5	54.6	0.3	−3.4	45.7

(Table 1 Contd)

(Table 1 Contd)

2001–02	5.5	14.1	11.4	6.2	9.9	0.7	1.7	–10.6	–5.8	2.1	47.7
2002–03	4.0	14.7	9.2	5.9	9.6	1.2	1.2	–1.8	5.3	6.8	48.4
2003–04	8.1	16.7	18.3	4.5	8.5	2.3	2.6	17.9	9.8	8.4	46.0
2004–05	7.0	12.0	12.1	3.9	7.2	–0.4	2.2	31.2	16.5	12.6	44.9
2005–06	9.5	21.1	16.9	4.0	6.5	–1.2	2.6	38.3	9.1	–2.1	44.3
2006–07	9.6	21.7	23.9	3.3	5.4	–1.0	3.1	17.6	25.1	10.8	45.3
2007–08	9.3	21.4	31.0	2.5	4.1	–1.3	5.0	10.8	20.9	25.7	40.2
2008–09	6.7	19.3	6.4	6.0	8.5	–2.3	2.3	40.0	20.3	33.9	45.9
2009–10	8.6	16.9	17.0	6.5	9.4	–2.8	4.8	–37.3	–22.0	–16.5	47.4
2010–11	9.3	16.1	19.1	4.9	8.1	–2.7	3.4	26.5	22.5	8.9	45.6
2011–12	6.2	13.2	3.6	5.9	7.0	–4.2	2.7	30.1	20.7	23.9	47.9
2012–13	5.0	13.3	6.2	5.1				–0.4	–9.5	0.7	54.5

Source: Authors' estimates.

Note:* Growth over calendar years starting from 1980 onwards to 2012.

TABLE 2. Mean Inflation Rates and Weighted Contribution to Overall Inflation

Year	*WPI*	*Food items*	*Non-food articles*	*Fuel group and minerals*	*Non-food manufacturing*
1981–82	4.9	1.7	0.1	0.9	2.3
1982–83	7.6	3.6	1.1	0.5	2.4
1983–84	6.4	1.4	1.1	0.7	3.3
1984–85	4.5	0.6	–0.3	1.2	3.0
1985–86	5.8	2.9	1.1	0.7	1.2
1986–87	8.2	2.6	2.2	0.2	3.2
1987–88	7.5	2.4	–0.2	0.5	4.7
1988–89	7.4	1.4	0.4	0.5	5.1
1989–90	10.3	3.2	1.7	1.4	3.9
1990–91	13.7	5.2	1.9	1.5	5.1
1991–92	10.0	3.4	0.0	1.5	5.2
1992–93	8.3	2.0	0.9	2.0	3.4
1993–94	10.9	3.0	2.0	1.0	4.9
1994–95	12.6	3.6	1.5	1.3	6.2
1995–96	8.0	1.7	0.6	0.7	5.1
1996–97	4.6	2.6	–0.1	1.4	0.6
1997–98	4.4	1.4	0.2	1.9	0.9
1998–99	5.9	3.4	0.7	0.5	1.4
1999–2000	3.3	0.8	–0.4	1.4	1.5
2000–01	7.2	0.1	0.1	4.5	2.4
2001–02	3.6	0.5	0.3	1.7	1.1
2002–03	3.4	0.8	0.5	1.1	1.0
2003–04	5.5	1.2	0.8	1.3	2.3
2004–05	6.5	1.0	0.0	2.4	3.0
2005–06	4.4	0.9	–0.1	2.2	1.5
2006–07	6.6	1.9	0.2	1.4	3.1
2007–08	4.7	1.4	0.5	0.2	2.7
2008–09	8.1	2.2	0.5	2.2	3.1
2009–10	3.8	3.6	0.2	–0.1	0.1
2010–11	9.6	3.0	1.0	2.4	3.1
2011–12	8.9	2.0	0.5	2.9	3.6
2012–13	7.4	2.5	0.5	1.9	2.4

Source: Authors' estimates.

TABLE 3. Moments of WPI Distribution

Year	*Mean*	*Standard deviation*	*Skewness*	*Kurtosis*
1983–84	7.5	7.1	1.3	6.8
1984–85	6.5	7.7	3.3	21.9
1985–86	4.4	8.7	–0.9	3.9
1986–87	5.8	8.2	0.7	3.1
1987–88	8.1	8.7	1.6	6.0
1988–89	7.5	8.2	–0.7	3.8
1989–90	7.5	8.0	0.7	1.2
1990–91	10.3	7.3	0.9	2.9
1991–92	13.7	8.2	0.8	2.3
1992–93	10.1	11.6	5.0	38.7
1993–94	8.4	8.2	1.1	4.2
1994–95	10.9	7.7	2.6	14.6
1995–96	8.0	6.5	1.4	16.2
1996–97	4.6	8.4	–0.1	3.8
1997–98	4.4	7.7	0.8	5.7
1998–99	5.9	8.5	1.2	4.4
1999–2000	3.3	7.7	0.1	5.8
2000–01	7.2	11.4	1.6	6.5
2001–02	3.6	5.2	0.5	3.5
2002–03	3.4	7.6	1.8	10.2
2003–04	5.5	6.7	1.0	4.0
2004–05	6.5	11.7	8.4	114.8
2005–06	4.5	6.2	0.6	3.7
2006–07	6.6	5.8	2.5	14.4
2007–08	4.7	5.9	–0.1	4.9
2008–09	8.1	6.2	1.1	5.4
2009–10	3.8	10.4	2.2	10.2
2010–11	9.6	8.3	1.6	6.6
2011–12	8.9	6.3	1.5	11.2
2012–13	7.4	4.9	0.4	5.4

Source: Authors' estimates.

FIGURE 1. Kernel Density Function (KDF) of WPI Inflation

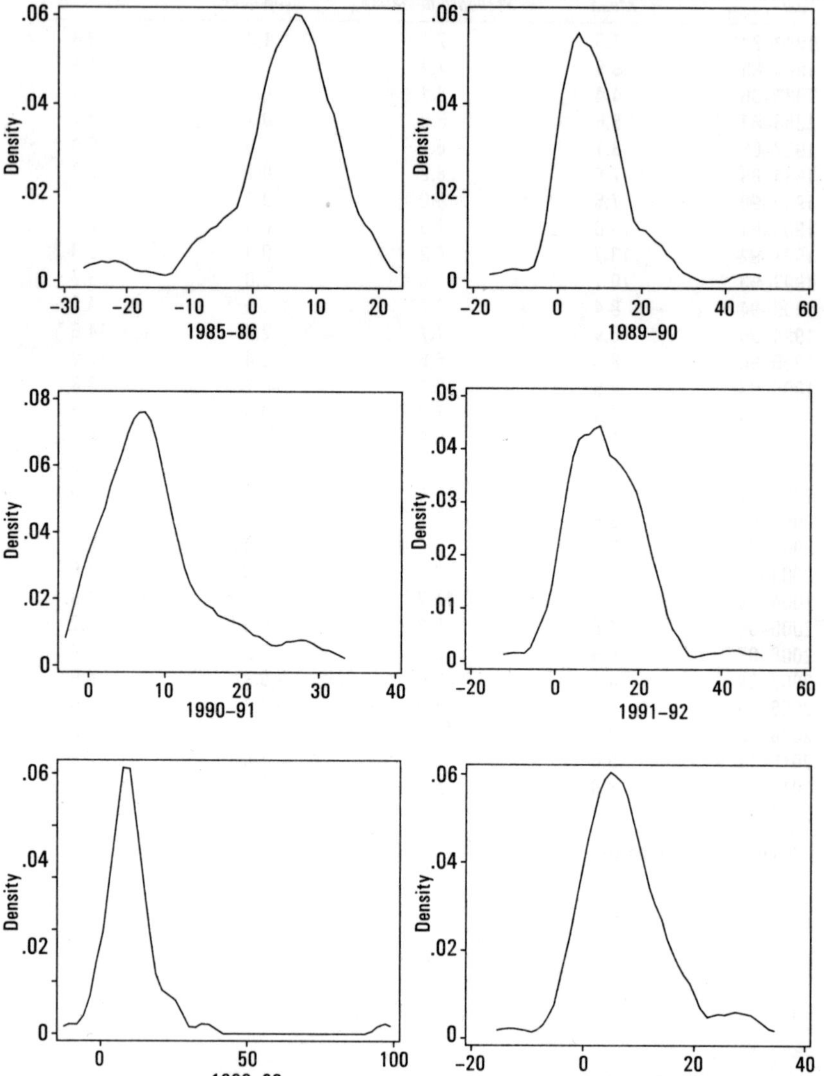

(Figure 1 Contd)

(Figure 1 Contd)

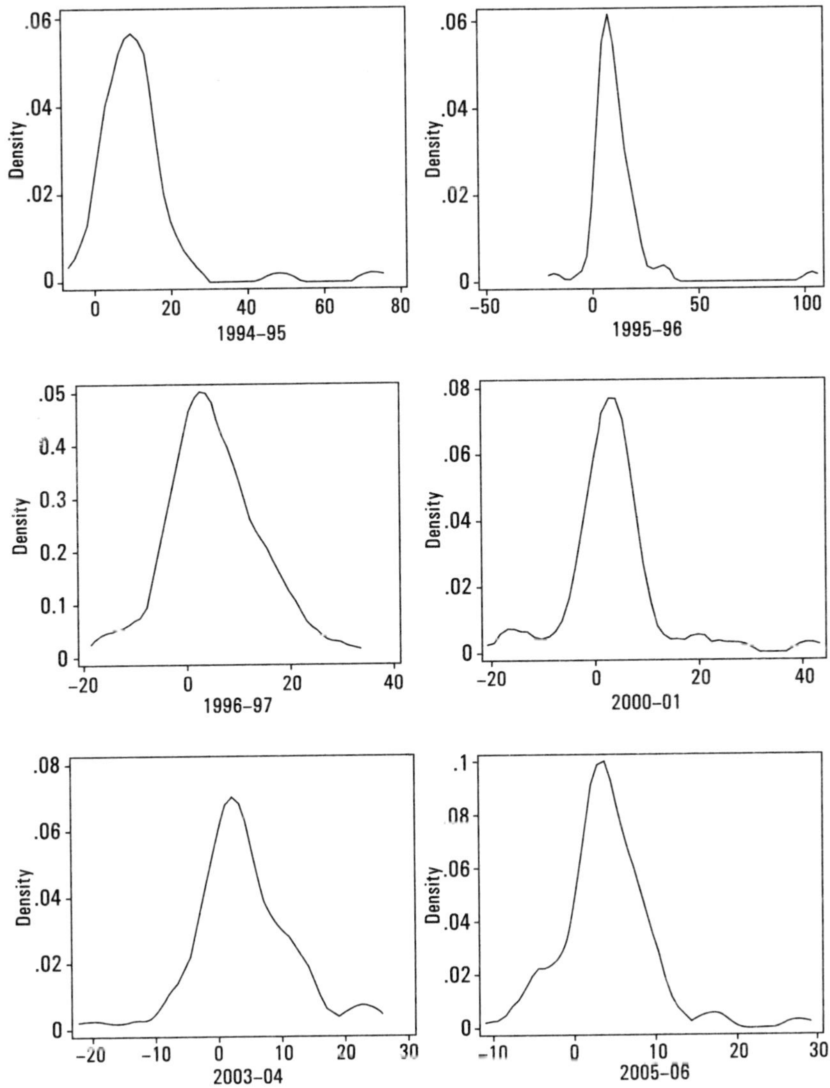

(Figure 1 Contd)

(Figure 1 Contd)

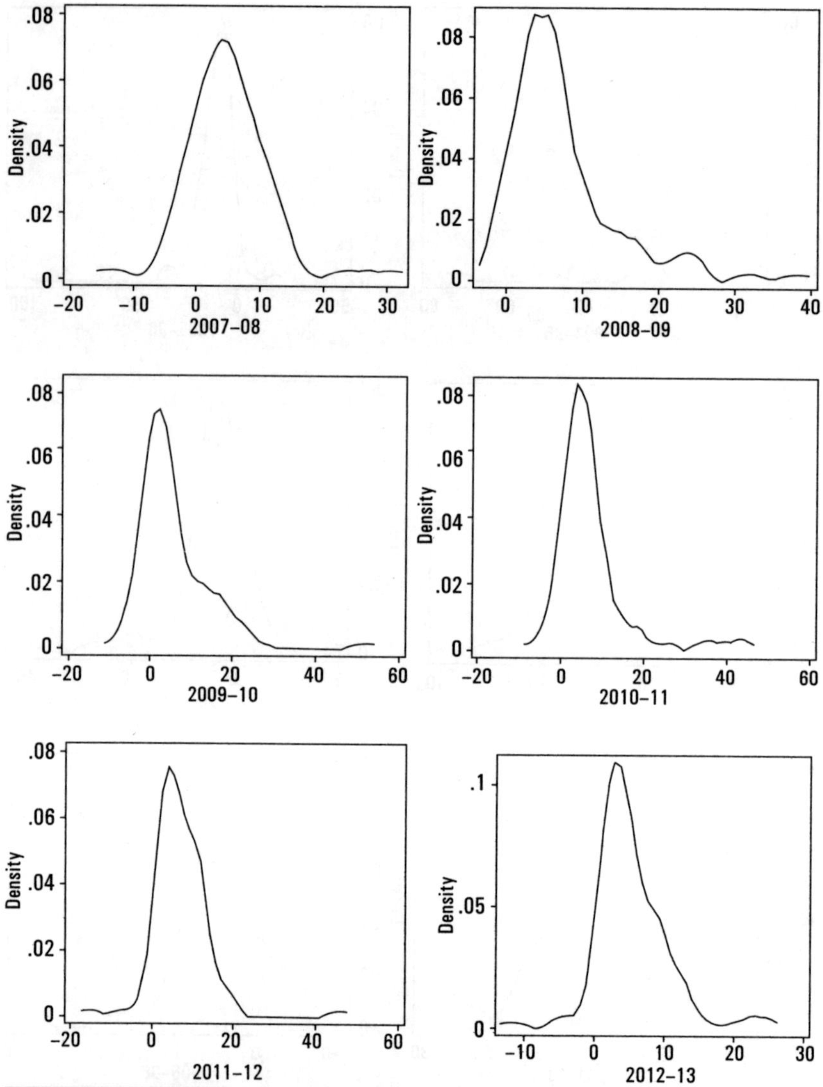

Source: Authors' estimates.

TABLE 4. Inflation Diffusion Index (IDEX) Values

Month	Non-weighted	Weighted	Month	Non-weighted	Weighted	Month	Non-weighted	Weighted
May 1982	54.3		Jul 1986	67.5		Sep 1990	62.7	
Jun 1982	59.6		Aug 1986	66.4		Oct 1990	74.5	
Jul 1982	60.8		Sep 1986	75.1		Nov 1990	70.7	
Aug 1982	65.6		Oct 1986	74.1		Dec 1990	71.2	
Sep 1982	67.3		Nov 1986	67.5		Jan 1991	69.3	
Oct 1982	62.4		Dec 1986	64.6		Feb 1991	65.4	
Nov 1982	69.7		Jan 1987	61.8		Mar 1991	60.3	
Dec 1982	67.0		Feb 1987	56.9		Apr 1991	59.1	
Jan 1983	62.3		Mar 1987	49.6		May 1991	67.8	
Feb 1983	65.3		Apr 1987	46.6		Jun 1991	70.1	
Mar 1983	56.1		May 1987	62.1		Jul 1991	72.3	
Apr 1983	58.5		Jun 1987	68.2		Aug 1991	72.2	
May 1983	65.1		Jul 1987	69.2		Sep 1991	65.9	
Jun 1983	62.1		Aug 1987	71.8		Oct 1991	61.3	
Jul 1983	61.1		Sep 1987	71.2		Nov 1991	66.7	
Aug 1983	71.1		Oct 1987	70.7		Dec 1991	68.5	
Sep 1983	74.8		Nov 1987	70.8		Jan 1992	65.1	
Oct 1983	69.3		Dec 1987	66.2		Feb 1992	65.2	
Nov 1983	72.7		Jan 1988	61.9		Mar 1992	66.3	
Dec 1983	73.1		Feb 1988	55.3		Apr 1992	58.9	
Jan 1984	66.0		Mar 1988	54.5		May 1992	65.1	
Feb 1984	61.9		Apr 1988	65.2		Jun 1992	59.2	
Mar 1984	48.9		May 1988	59.5		Jul 1992	54.8	
Apr 1984	48.8		Jun 1988	63.9		Aug 1992	53.7	
May 1984	58.4		Jul 1988	67.0		Sep 1992	59.4	
Jun 1984	69.4		Aug 1988	57.5		Oct 1992	61.4	

(Table 4 Contd)

(Table 4 Contd)

Month	Non-weighted	Weighted	Month	Non-weighted	Weighted	Month	Non-weighted	Weighted
Jul 1984	75.4		Sep 1988	67.8		Nov 1992	58.1	
Aug 1984	68.3		Oct 1988	73.4		Dec 1992	60.4	
Sep 1984	70.7		Nov 1988	62.5		Jan 1993	57.5	
Oct 1984	74.6		Dec 1988	58.6		Feb 1993	59.5	
Nov 1984	70.2		Jan 1989	61.9		Mar 1993	54.9	
Dec 1984	65.7		Feb 1989	60.6		Apr 1993	55.8	
Jan 1985	59.5		Mar 1989	59.4		May 1993	61.6	63.4
Feb 1985	58.1		Apr 1989	62.5		Jun 1993	59.4	66.2
Mar 1985	57.3		May 1989	68.0		Jul 1993	63.7	65.9
Apr 1985	71.4		Jun 1989	63.2		Aug 1993	64.6	62.7
May 1985	58.4		Jul 1989	67.4		Sep 1993	65.2	71.0
Jun 1985	61.0		Aug 1989	65.7		Oct 1993	66.1	70.7
Jul 1985	65.3		Sep 1989	71.2		Nov 1993	64.8	70.4
Aug 1985	64.9		Oct 1989	64.2		Dec 1993	69.7	74.3
Sep 1985	69.2		Nov 1989	58.9		Jan 1994	70.8	71.6
Oct 1985	69.7		Dec 1989	64.0		Feb 1994	67.0	68.7
Nov 1985	66.4		Jan 1990	55.7		Mar 1994	56.6	51.4
Dec 1985	66.5		Feb 1990	57.4		Apr 1994	65.4	64.5
Jan 1986	51.4		Mar 1990	61.2		May 1994	66.9	59.5
Feb 1986	58.2		Apr 1990	65.7		Jun 1994	59.2	56.6
Mar 1986	55.0		May 1990	67.5		Jul 1994	64.1	66.3
Apr 1986	48.9		Jun 1990	66.7		Aug 1994	59.0	54.5
May 1986	55.7		Jul 1990	66.0		Sep 1994	63.0	62.7
Jun 1986	63.3		Aug 1990	53.2		Oct 1994	65.4	67.5
Nov 1994	63.8	67.1	Mar 1999	57.8	64.2	Jul 2003	62.9	61.2
Dec 1994	61.9	69.3	Apr 1999	54.7	58.0	Aug 2003	61.6	59.8
Jan 1995	62.4	61.2	May 1999	56.8	61.6	Sep 2003	61.3	63.3
Feb 1995	60.3	55.0	Jun 1999	54.8	59.6	Oct 2003	56.3	51.4

(Table 4 Contd)

(Table 4 Contd)

Mar 1995	59.6	54.0	Jul 1999	56.2	59.8	Nov 2003	60.3	62.3
Apr 1995	62.2	55.7	Aug 1999	52.9	55.1	Dec 2003	61.6	62.3
May 1995	62.1	57.3	Sep 1999	54.6	60.5	Jan 2004	57.4	56.8
Jun 1995	59.5	63.7	Oct 1999	57.3	54.0	Feb 2004	55.0	55.8
Jul 1995	57.4	65.8	Nov 1999	60.0	55.9	Mar 2004	52.6	56.3
Aug 1995	60.4	67.5	Dec 1999	65.1	60.5	Apr 2004	55.8	56.8
Sep 1995	60.0	62.1	Jan 2000	57.4	55.8	May 2004	57.8	65.4
Oct 1995	60.8	61.0	Feb 2000	50.6	47.0	Jun 2004	61.5	61.5
Nov 1995	54.5	58.0	Mar 2000	57.7	58.7	Jul 2004	66.1	59.6
Dec 1995	60.6	70.0	Apr 2000	50.5	50.5	Aug 2004	71.6	74.3
Jan 1996	59.7	58.1	May 2000	51.5	52.3	Sep 2004	69.7	66.8
Feb 1996	58.6	64.0	Jun 2000	49.9	45.6	Oct 2004	70.7	60.4
Mar 1996	55.7	59.0	Jul 2000	49.0	51.1	Nov 2004	67.7	65.9
Apr 1996	58.7	66.5	Aug 2000	50.7	49.4	Dec 2004	63.3	65.1
May 1996	55.5	53.6	Sep 2000	50.0	53.9	Jan 2005	58.1	58.4
Jun 1996	49.1	53.1	Oct 2000	57.0	61.4	Feb 2005	61.5	60.4
Jul 1996	49.7	49.9	Nov 2000	54.2	57.9	Mar 2005	56.9	63.8
Aug 1996	51.6	54.9	Dec 2000	55.7	57.3	Apr 2005	58.0	60.1
Sep 1996	50.9	56.9	Jan 2001	52.3	49.0	May 2005	57.4	56.7
Oct 1996	52.4	55.6	Feb 2001	51.1	44.4	Jun 2005	60.9	60.1
Nov 1996	55.6	57.9	Mar 2001	50.1	57.0	Jul 2005	62.8	66.5
Dec 1996	57.8	66.7	Apr 2001	51.5	52.2	Aug 2005	64.0	54.4
Jan 1997	54.6	61.5	May 2001	53.3	58.9	Sep 2005	66.9	63.4
Feb 1997	54.5	51.7	Jun 2001	54.9	54.3	Oct 2005	71.0	61.0
Mar 1997	57.1	56.3	Jul 2001	55.6	57.4	Nov 2005	69.5	65.8
Apr 1997	59.2	61.0	Aug 2001	58.7	57.2	Dec 2005	61.7	61.9
May 1997	58.0	58.4	Sep 2001	59.5	63.4	Jan 2006	65.1	64.4
Jun 1997	58.0	65.2	Oct 2001	52.5	51.6	Feb 2006	67.2	68.2
Jul 1997	58.6	64.6	Nov 2001	60.6	62.0	Mar 2006	57.2	60.0

(Table 4 Contd)

(Table 4 Contd)

Month	*Non-weighted*	*Weighted*	*Month*	*Non-weighted*	*Weighted*	*Month*	*Non-weighted*	*Weighted*
Aug 1997	57.0	52.5	Dec 2001	61.1	64.6	Apr 2006	65.2	67.5
Sep 1997	53.7	56.4	Jan 2002	59.7	64.5	May 2006	67.5	71.0
Oct 1997	55.9	56.2	Feb 2002	61.2	61.9	Jun 2006	69.9	75.6
Nov 1997	53.2	60.1	Mar 2002	55.4	52.1	Jul 2006	67.5	60.2
Dec 1997	55.6	63.9	Apr 2002	53.2	52.4	Aug 2006	73.0	69.1
Jan 1998	53.9	61.4	May 2002	56.8	56.2	Sep 2006	76.2	76.4
Feb 1998	53.1	53.5	Jun 2002	51.8	55.7	Oct 2006	69.7	67.6
Mar 1998	53.7	49.3	Jul 2002	48.7	50.1	Nov 2006	66.3	63.6
Apr 1998	50.0	41.7	Aug 2002	50.8	51.0	Dec 2006	67.5	59.1
May 1998	54.9	60.2	Sep 2002	59.3	66.6	Jan 2007	61.5	61.3
Jun 1998	53.1	56.7	Oct 2002	61.3	63.5	Feb 2007	62.8	62.6
Jul 1998	49.1	53.0	Nov 2002	62.7	64.9	Mar 2007	59.5	56.5
Aug 1998	57.2	64.8	Dec 2002	63.0	71.6	Apr 2007	59.2	59.3
Sep 1998	54.7	62.6	Jan 2003	65.4	72.9	May 2007	55.4	54.8
Oct 1998	57.6	61.1	Feb 2003	59.4	68.8	Jun 2007	60.8	54.4
Nov 1998	54.6	57.3	Mar 2003	54.6	51.6	Jul 2007	63.9	60.0
Dec 1998	58.8	55.9	Apr 2003	54.7	49.0	Aug 2007	68.3	60.8
Jan 1999	57.2	55.6	May 2003	53.7	56.3	Sep 2007	65.2	63.4
Feb 1999	57.6	55.7	Jun 2003	57.8	67.1	Oct 2007	70.2	72.5
Nov 2007	67.5	72.1	Mar 2012	60.7	67.1			
Dec 2007	68.7	73.1	Apr 2012	59.3	66.8			
Jan 2008	62.1	67.5	May 2012	60.7	59.8			
Feb 2008	64.9	74.5	Jun 2012	68.9	69.4			
Mar 2008	62.7	69.8	Jul 2012	71.0	66.9			
Apr 2008	51.8	63.6	Aug 2012	69.4	68.4			
May 2008	62.7	61.7	Sep 2012	67.8	71.0			
Jun 2008	72.5	77.6	Oct 2012	66.5	67.8			

(Table 4 Contd)

(Table 4 Contd)

Jul 2008	73.9	69.6	Nov 2012	65.4	66.5
Aug 2008	66.9	66.2	Dec 2012	62.2	62.7
Sep 2008	66.8	59.7	Jan 2013	51.3	55.6
Oct 2008	60.9	61.4	Feb 2013	53.3	57.7
Nov 2008	51.9	52.0	Mar 2013	45.5	46.1
Dec 2008	43.8	44.9			
Jan 2009	51.2	50.8			
Feb 2009	47.5	45.1			
Mar 2009	45.3	51.0			
Apr 2009	44.6	46.2			
May 2009	58.8	63.7			
Jun 2009	57.4	55.0			
Jul 2009	61.6	61.9			
Aug 2009	65.8	69.4			
Sep 2009	66.6	69.7			
Oct 2009	65.0	71.6			
Nov 2009	67.3	80.0			
Dec 2009	66.3	74.6			
Jan 2010	56.3	66.9			
Feb 2010	56.1	59.0			
Mar 2010	57.3	55.5			
Apr 2010	55.8	61.4			
May 2010	54.1	60.5			
Jun 2010	58.1	55.9			
Jul 2010	59.2	60.2			
Aug 2010	63.1	65.6			
Sep 2010	64.6	64.2			
Oct 2010	69.5	76.0			
Nov 2010	67.2	74.9			

(Table 4 Contd)

(Table 4 Contd)

Month	*Non-weighted*	*Weighted*	*Month*	*Non-weighted*	*Weighted*	*Month*	*Non-weighted*	*Weighted*
Dec 2010	69.4	75.7						
Jan 2011	66.5	71.2						
Feb 2011	68.4	74.2						
Mar 2011	62.1	61.4						
Apr 2011	55.5	56.0						
May 2011	60.9	63.8						
Jun 2011	63.9	64.4						
Jul 2011	63.0	66.3						
Aug 2011	63.7	64.1						
Sep 2011	69.2	72.9						
Oct 2011	70.7	76.9						
Nov 2011	64.7	71.7						
Dec 2011	63.1	68.0						
Jan 2012	55.2	62.4						
Feb 2012	54.4	62.7						

Source: Authors' estimates.

TABLE 5. Comparison between CPIs and WPI

	CPI-IW	*CPI-combined*	*WPI*
Base year	*2001*	*2010*	*2004–05*
Population	Industrial Workers (78 Centers)	Rural villages (1,188 villages) + Urban Towns (310 towns, 1,114 quotations) in 35 States/UTs	Urban Towns (5,482 quotations)
Coverage—Commodity Group Weights (%)			
(i) Food Beverage and Tobacco	48.39	49.71	24.31
(ii) Fuel and Light	6.42	9.49	14.93^
(iii) Housing	15.29	9.77	-
(iv) Clothing, Bedding and Footwear	6.58	4.73	60.78#
(v) Miscellaneous *	23.32	26.31	
Total (i to v)	100	100	100
Basis for Weighting Diagram	Consumption pattern at selected centers during 1999–2000	61st round Consumer Expenditure Survey (2004–05)—NSSO	National Accounts Statistics (NAS), 2007

Sources: Central Statistics Office, Ministry of Statistics and Programme Implementation, Labour Bureau, Government of India; Office of the Economic Adviser to the Government of India, Ministry of Commerce and Industry and Authors' Estimates.

Notes: @ In CPIs the commodity groups are largely based on the Classification of Individual Consumption according to Purpose (CICOP) criterion. The commodity basket in CPIs is grouped Into (i) to (v) indicated in the table above. In WPI, the concept of wholesale price used for construction of the index comprises, as far as possible, all transactions at first point of bulk sale in the domestic market. The commodity basket is classified based on National Industrial Classification (NIC) which is comparable to International Standard Industrial Classification (ISIC) and the basket is grouped into Primary Articles (20.1%), Fuel and Power (14.9%) and Manufactured Products (65.0%).

* Miscellaneous group in CPIs consists primarily of price indices of medical-care, education, recreation and amusement, transport and communication, personal care items and household requisites among others.

^ Includes prices of domestic and industrial electricity, domestic and industrial fuel consumption.

In WPI classification non-food non-fuel items mainly includes WPI non-food manufactured products group (weight of 55% of the WPI basket). This group consists of a mix of consumer durables and non-durables as well as industrial basic, intermediate and capital goods. It also includes two sub-groups from primary article group, i.e., non-food primary articles (4.3% weight) and minerals (1.5% weight).

FIGURE 2. Inflation across Food and Non-Food Fuel Groups based on WPI and CPI

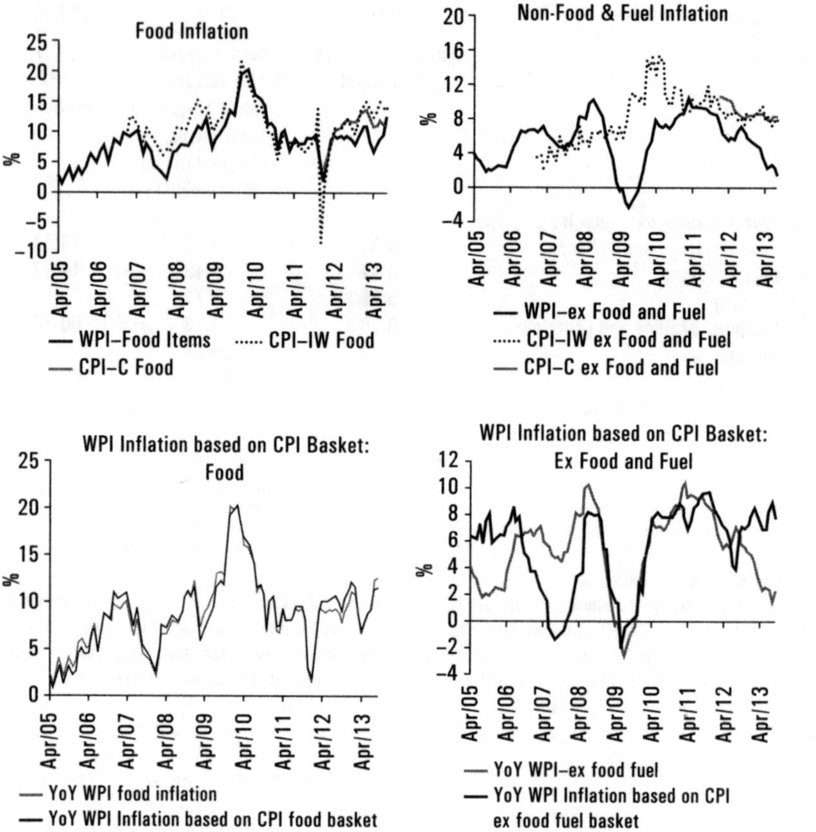

Sources: Central Statistics Office, Ministry of Statistics and Programme Implementation, Labour Bureau, Government of India; Office of the Economic Adviser to the Government of India, Ministry of Commerce and Industry and Authors' Estimates.

Annexure 3

TABLE 6. Break Estimates in Mean of Inflation—Monthly

			Lag length	
Variable	*Andrew–Quandt*	*Bai–Perron*	*SBC*	*AIC*
All Commodities	1995:5	1995:5	1	3
I. Primary	No Break	No Break	1	3
Food	No Break	No Break	2	2
Non-food	No Break	No Break	1	1
II. Fuel	No Break	No Break	1	1
III. Manufacturing	1995:7	1995:7	3	6
Food	No Break	No Break	1	1
Textile	1995:6	1995:6	3	3
Chemicals	1995:7	1995:7	1	3
Metals	No Break	No Break	3	3
Machinery	1992:10	1992:10	3	3

Source: Authors' estimates.

TABLE 7. Estimates of Persistence during Sub-Samples—Monthly (1982:4 to 2013:3)

	First sample	*Second sample*	*Full sample*	
Variable	*(Pre-break)*	*(Post-break)*	*No break*	*With break*
All Commodities	0.198**	0.339*	0.302*	0.269*
I. Primary	–	–	0.187*	–
Food	–	–	0.006	–
Non-food	–	–	0.298*	–
II. Fuel	–	–	0.194*	–
III. Manufacturing	0.318*	0.548*	0.565*	0.423
Food	–	–	0.112**	–
Textile	0.496*	0.548*	0.582*	0.523
Chemicals	0.230*	0.246*	0.260*	0.236
Metal	–	–	0.510*	–
Machinery	0.448*	0.390*	0.542*	0.418

Source: Authors' estimates.

Note: * and ** denote significance at 1% and 5% level, respectively.

FIGURE 3. Rolling Regressions of Sub-Components of WPI—Quarterly

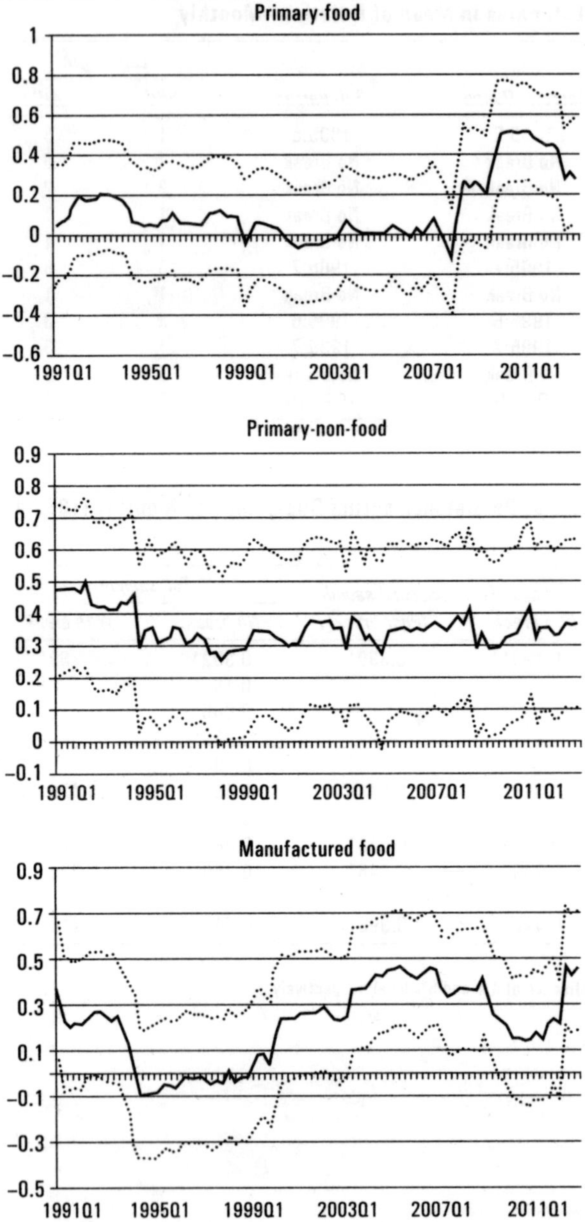

(Figure 3 Contd)

(Figure 3 Contd)

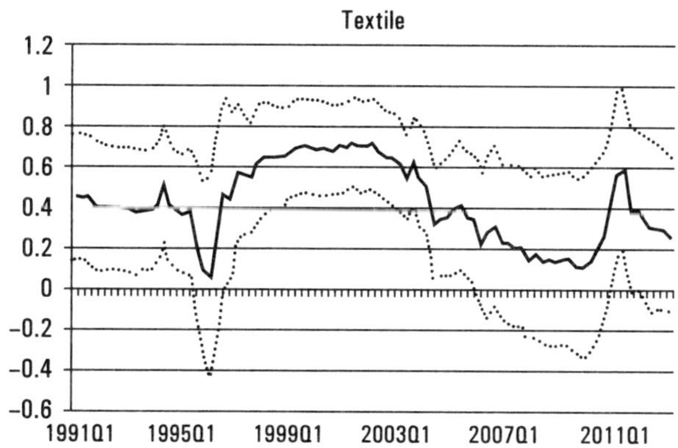

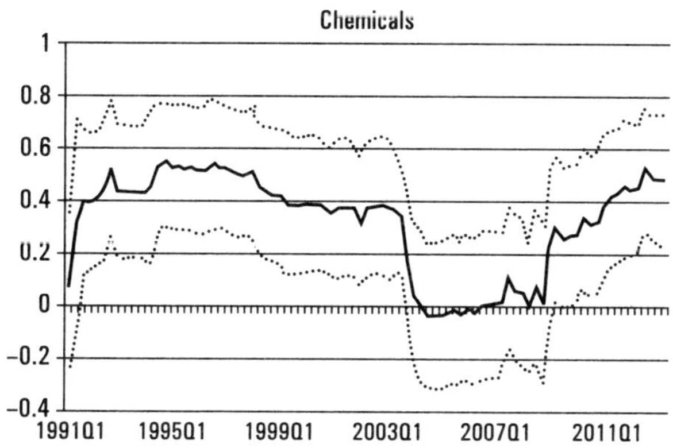

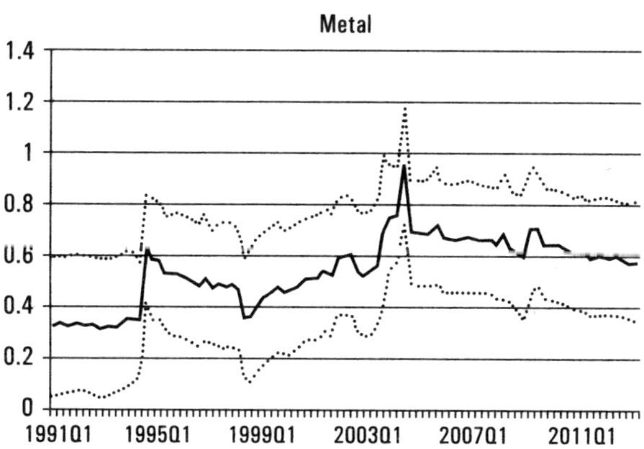

(Figure 3 Contd)

(Figure 3 Contd)

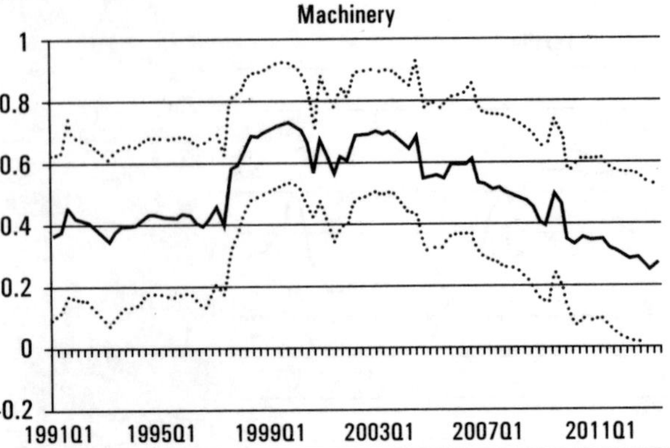

Source: Authors' estimates.

FIGURE 4. Rolling Regressions of Major Components—Monthly

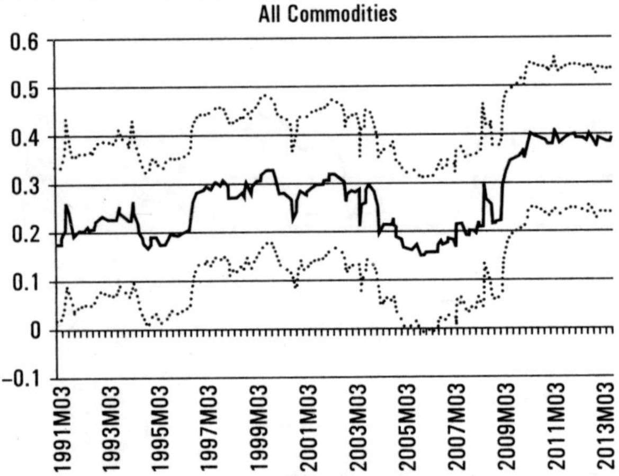

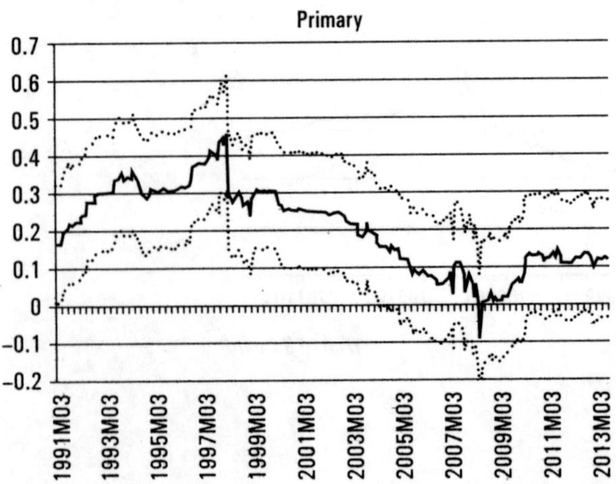

(Figure 4 Contd)

(Figure 4 Contd)

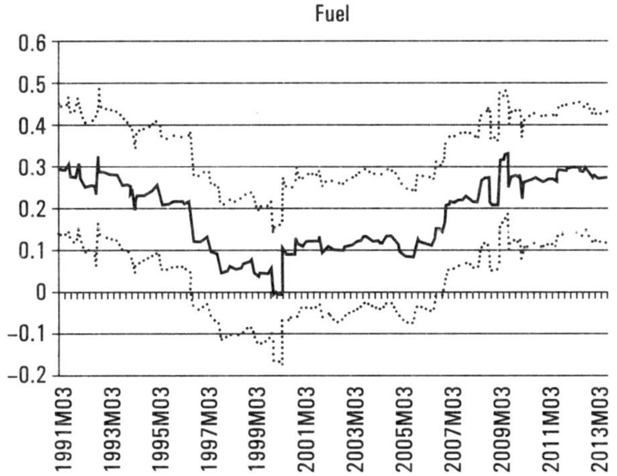

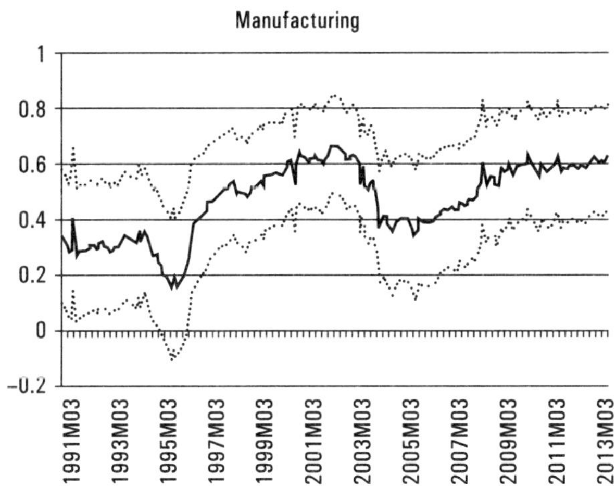

Source: Authors' estimates.

FIGURE 5. Rolling Regressions of Sub-Components—Monthly

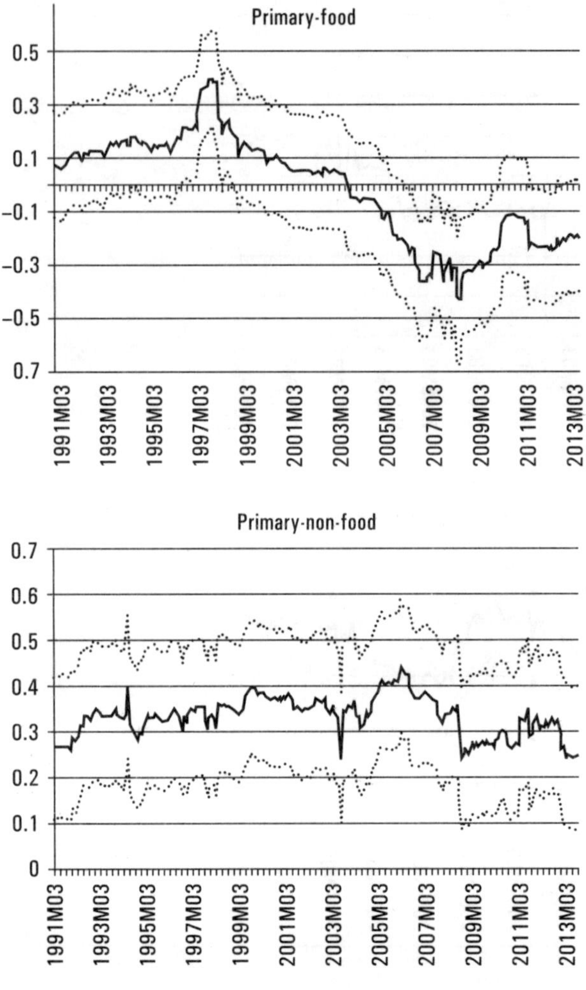

(Figure 5 Contd)

(Figure 5 Contd)

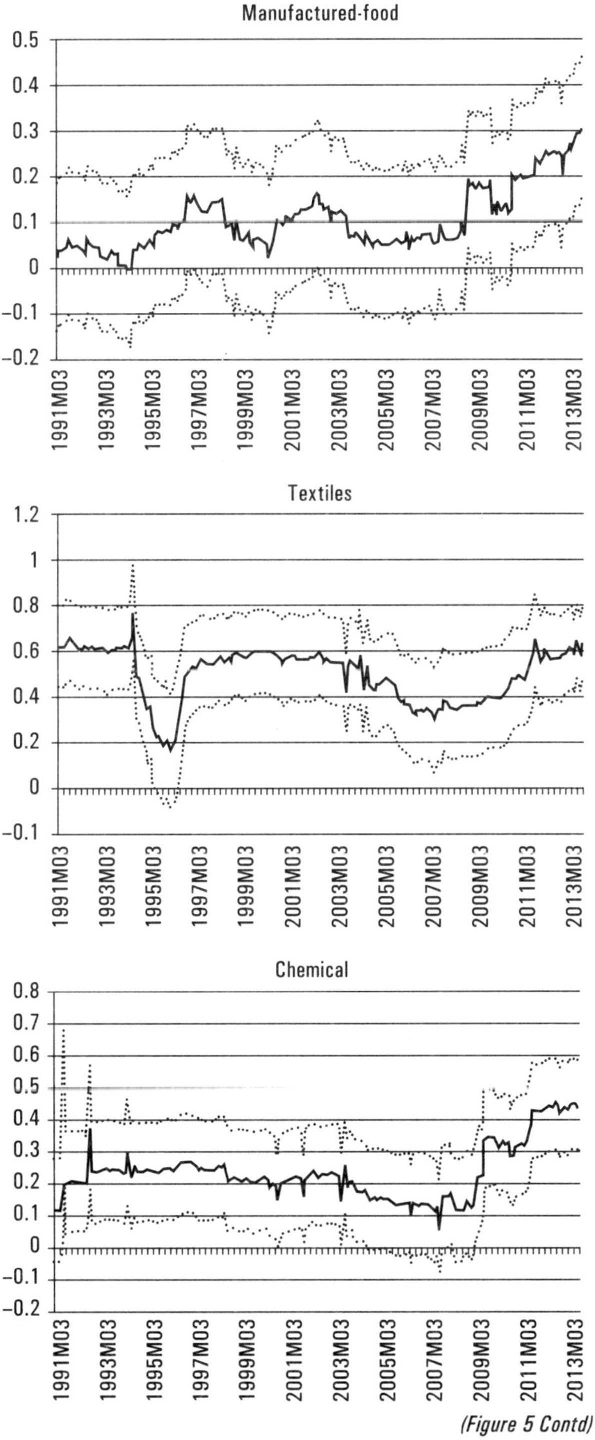

(Figure 5 Contd)

(Figure 5 Contd)

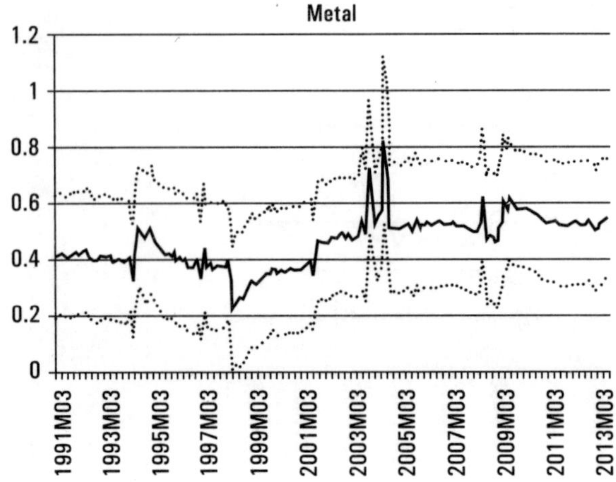

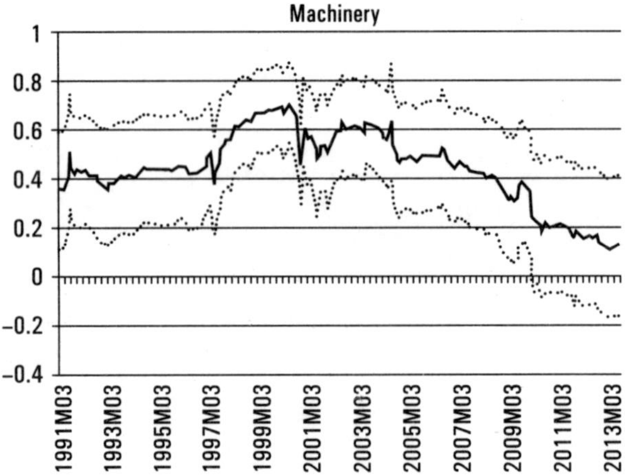

Source: Authors' estimates.

Annexure 4

TABLE 8. Inflation Targeting Countries—A Snapshot

Country	*Inflation targeting adoption date*	*Target set by*	*Current target (%)*	*Target type*	*Number on policy making committee*	*Meetings per year*	*Decision making process*	*Parliamentary hearings (per year)*	*Open letter*	*Frequency of inflation report (year)*
Armenia	2006	G,CB	4 ± 1.5	P + T	7	12	V	1	No	4
Australia	1993	G,CB	2–3	Range	9	11	C	2	No	4
Brazil	1999	G,CB	4.5 ± 2	P + T	8	8	V	6	Yes	4
Canada	1991	G,CB	2*	P + T	6	8	C	2	No	4
Chile	1999	CB	3 ± 1	P + T	5	12	V	4	No	4
Colombia	1999	CB	2–4	Range	7	12	V	2	No	4
Czech Republic	1997	CB	2 ± 1	P + T	7	8	V	Nil	No	4
Ghana	2007	G,CB	8.7 ± 2	P + T	7	6	C	Nil	No	4 to 6
Guatemala	2005	CB	4.5 ± 1	P + T	8	8	V	2	No	3
Hungary	2001	CB	3.0	Point	7	12	V	1	No	4
Iceland	2001	G,CB	2.5	Point	5	8	CV	2	Yes	4#
Indonesia	2005	G,CB	4.5 ± 1	P + T	7	12	C	Nil	No	4
Israel	1997	G,CB	1–3	Range	6	12	V	2	No	2
Mexico	2001	CB	3 ± 1	P + T	5	8	C	Y	No	4
New Zealand	1990	G,CB	1–3	Range	G	8	Gov	4	Other	4
Norway	2001	G	2.5	Point	7	6	C	Y	No	3
Peru	2002	CB	2 ± 1	P + T	7	12	V	1	No	4
Philippines	2002	G,CB	4.0 ± 1	P + T	7	8	V	Nil	Yes	4
Poland	1998	CB	2.5 ± 1	P + T	10	12	V	Nil	No	4

(Table 8 Contd)

(Table 8 Contd)

Country	Inflation targeting adoption date	Target set by	Current target (%)	Target type	Number on policy making committee	Meetings per year	Decision making process	Parliamentary hearings (per year)	Open letter	Frequency of inflation report (year)
Romania	2005	G,CB	3 ± 1	P+T	9	8	V	Nil	No	4
Serbia	2006	G,CB	4.0 ± 1.5	P+T	5	12	V	Nil	Yes	4
South Africa	2000	G	3–6	Range	7	6	C	3	No	2
South Korea	2001	CB , G	3 ± 1	P+T	7	12	V	Y	No	2
Sweden	1993	CB	2.0	Point	6	6	V	2	No	3^
Thailand	2000	G,CB	3.0 ± 1.5	P+T	7	8	V	Nil	Yes	4
Turkey	2006	G,CB	5.0 ± 2	P+T	7	12	V	2	Yes	4
United Kingdom	1992	G	2.0	Point	9	12	V	3	Yes	4

Source: Official central bank websites and "State of the Art of Inflation Targeting" by Gill Hammond, 2011, Centre for Central Banking Studies Handbook, No. 29, Bank of England.

Notes: C: Consensus, V: Vote, Gov: Governor, G: government, CB: Central Bank, Y: Yes.

P+T: point with tolerance band.

* mid-point of 1–3.

^3 inflation reports +3 others.

2 inflation reports

**Monetary council has 6 members.

Annexure 5

Data Sources

Data on OECD real GDP growth and oil prices are from the OECD and database on Primary Commodity Prices, respectively. Data on the US federal funds rate target are from the Fred database of the Federal Reserve Bank of St. Louis (http://research.stlouisfed.org/fred2/). Data pertaining to Indian economy are obtained from the RBI's Database on Indian Economy (http://dbie.rbi.org.in/DBIE/dbie.rbi?site=home), data put out on the website of the Central Statistics Office, Ministry of Statistics and Programme Implementation (http://mospi.nic.in/Mospi_New/Site/home.aspx), Labour Bureau, Government of India (http://www.labourbureau.gov.in/main2.html) and Office of the Economic Adviser to the Government of India, Ministry of Commerce and Industry (http://eaindustry.nic.in/). Data on the gross fiscal deficit of central government are obtained from the website of the Controller General of Accounts, Government of India (www.cga.nic.in).

Comments and Discussion

Kenneth M. Kletzer
University of California

After the disinflation of the 1990s, the rate of inflation for India gradually rose leading up to the global financial crisis. Despite the crisis, inflation did not abate after 2009 and continues to exceed the levels of inflation of advanced and other major emerging market economies. The return of inflation approaching 10% per annum and the depreciation of the rupee have become headline headaches for policy makers. As elsewhere, inflation is unpopular in India. The policy response to the financial crisis appropriately addressed the prospect that financial distress and recessions abroad would result in a domestic contraction. Stimulus under the circumstances of 2009 was a cautious policy. The subsequent decline in economic growth was modest but inflation was sustained.

This paper addresses three related topics associated with India's postcrisis inflation experience. The first concerns the statistics of inflation and the sources of its persistence. The second is how monetary policy may have contributed to this inflationary episode. Third, the paper considers the possibility of implementing flexible inflation targeting in India.

The empirical analysis of the paper uses the Wholesale Price Index (WPI) and its primary component series. The WPI is the most commonly cited price index for India and is used to communicate monetary policy to the public by the RBI. Its flaws as a measure of inflation and guide for monetary policy are widely acknowledged, although publication of the comprehensive All India CPI began only in February 2011. However, it is worth repeating that the WPI is not a producer price index (some prices are retail and others are wholesale) and that services are included in CPI. The paper addresses this by comparing the univariate analysis for the WPI and CPIs. Ideally, we would like to see a historical series constructed from the underlying survey data replicating a comprehensive CPI for studying the inflation process and consequences of monetary policy in India.

The moments of inflation for India are not surprising in that inflation displays typical skewness and kurtosis. The relationship between the dispersion of inflation rates across expenditure categories and mean or median inflation ought to tell us something about inflation dynamics. I am perplexed by the proposed index of diffusion (IDEX). As far as I can tell, it centers inflation about zero, and it uses an arbitrary band of five percentage points each side. I may be misreading, but the dispersion of inflation might be more meaningfully measured around an estimate of core inflation (for example, a moving average). The degree of diffusion could be measured by the frequency that individual category inflation exceeds various thresholds calculated for the data such as two standard deviations from the mean, median or a moving average.

The univariate analysis reveals a postcrisis increase in the persistence of nominal food price increases and that inflation in food products tends to lead inflation in the overall WPI over the entire data sample. The authors commendably resist the popular interpretation that food price rises cause inflation. It is worth recalling that food price increases are relative price changes and inflation is an overall rise in nominal prices. An empirical relationship between relative price increases and persistent nominal price rises reflects events in the money market—a change in either money demand or supply. Attributing inflation to food price shocks is uninformative about policy because the relationship is created by policy.

The results that food or fuel price increases lead to rising inflation may tell us something about the process of nominal price adjustment and monetary policy reactions to shifts in aggregate supply. For example, if the costs of resetting sticky nominal prices are lower for food products than for other manufacturing goods, then an increase in expected future inflation will lead to a transitory rise in relative food prices if price-setters are forward looking. Expected inflation depends on news about future monetary policy and its conditional response to aggregate supply and demand shocks. In this example, a rise in expected money growth would lead to a temporary increase in relative food prices and subsequent convergence of overall inflation to food price inflation: nominal food prices lead the price level but do not cause inflation.

How expectations are formed depends on how policy makers respond. Thus, if monetary policy accommodates aggregate supply shocks, price-setters ought to expect higher inflation to follow supply shocks. Because relative food price rises are found to lead to persistent increases in nominal food prices and overall inflation, price-setters will expect a monetary expansion to follow a relative food price shock. We ought to be concerned about how monetary policy responds to transitory and permanent commodity price shocks.

The analysis of persistence is appropriate and thrifty. The multivariate analysis begins with a new Keynesian Phillips curve that allows for backward and forward price-setting behavior. The main observation to highlight is that inflation continues to be comparatively sticky for India by international comparison (intrinsic persistence). The consequences of overall persistence of inflation verified by the univariate and multivariate regressions for policy are raised by the relatively large intrinsic and small expectational components. The resulting costs of disinflation and persistence of monetary accommodation of supply shocks create a challenge for central bank policy.

The important part of the empirical analysis is the estimation of the monetary policy rule. The specification is a generalized Taylor rule for which the lagged policy interest rate, inflation gap and output gap are significant. Reserve Bank policy displays sensitivity to both inflation and output as its stated policy goals, but it also shows a sluggish response to the inflation gap. Interest rate smoothing reflects policy adjustment. The lagged policy rate receives a coefficient estimate of 0.9, which is in line with other emerging markets. However, the coefficient estimate for the inflation gap is very small by comparison. Cumulatively, the policy rule is stable, but historically, policy rate adjusts are infrequent in the face of persisting inflation. In the preferred specification, a 1% rise in inflation leads to a 13 basis point quarterly rise in the policy (repo) rate followed by a 12 basis point rise the next quarter and so on. The predicted cumulative increase in the repo rate to a persistent one percentage point of inflation exceeding the inflation target over one year is 45 basis points. This falls short of a median emerging central bank response of roughly 150 basis points.

The authors do not highlight this result and its implication. They demonstrate empirically that the Reserve Bank has responded to persisting inflation either in small steps or with substantial lags. Eventually, the policy rate responds but it take a long time. When this equation is combined with the estimated new Keynesian Phillips curve at the end of Section III, we find that inflation indeed persists and a rule with a higher response to current inflation and less inertia could lead to shorter duration inflationary episodes.

Looking at the policy response after the Lehmann crisis in September 2008 in Figure 1, we can see that the Reserve Bank did respond aggressively to the crisis reducing the repo rate from 9.00% in October 2008 to 4.75% in April 2009. An accommodative policy response to the global financial crisis seems both prudent and a source of the ensuing inflation. As inflation returned, the repo rate was progressively raised in 0.25% steps from March 2010 until it reached its peak of 8.50% at the end of October 2011.

The cumulative 3.75 percentage increase over more than 18 months presumably was in response to WPI inflation of 10%, 5 percentage points over often stated target inflation. Assessing the appropriateness of the weights placed on economic growth (the output gap) and inflation since 2009 is beyond the scope of either the paper or a brief discussion. What we do learn from the multivariate analysis of Patra, Khundrakpam and George is that the interest rates have responded slowly to inflationary shocks for some time.

FIGURE 1. Repo Rate and Cash Reserve Ratios Postcrisis

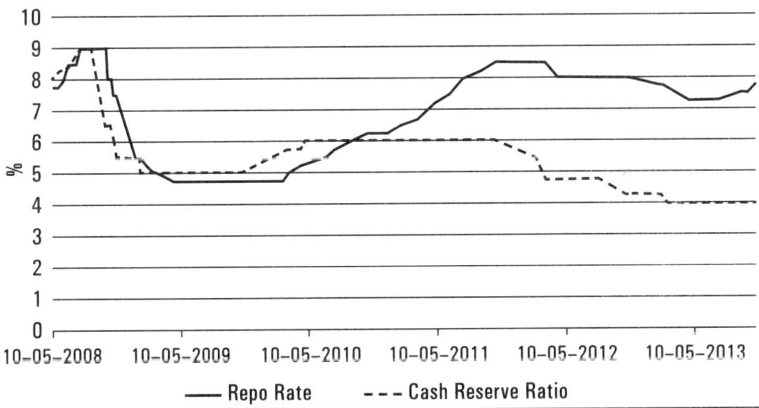

Source: RBI Database on the Indian Economy.

The remainder of the paper cautiously enters the debate over whether India should adopt an inflation targeting regime. The discussion is informative about the implications of a formal inflation targeting framework and the discussion so far. Of particular interest to the authors is the delegation of responsibility for setting goals for monetary policy and for implementing those goals. Two points made are worth stressing. The first is that India displays a de facto inflation target. Policymakers seem to agree that inflation should be around 5%, and the Reserve Bank sets its policy rate responsively to the inflation gap and the output gap, as under a flexible inflation target with multiple objectives.

The second point is that a framework with monetary policy goals set by the government and implementation determined by the central bank, following the model of the United Kingdom, is favored in the current discussion. As shown in Table 8 of Annex 4, several inflation targeting countries opted for joint goal setting by the government and the central bank. Given the history and current reality of fiscal dominance of monetary policy in

India, it is unlikely that the Reserve Bank could gain more independence than the clear assignment of responsibility for implementing a target which the government sets.

If India adopts an inflation targeting regime, then the Reserve Bank will face a challenge implementing an explicit target. The relationship between monetary policy actions and credit expansion or price-setting is not well understood. Indian finance is primarily intermediated by the commercial banks, and as we have learned, these do not extend new loans or increase credit to existing debtors very responsively to short-term interest rates or investment opportunities and returns. While understanding how markets and real activity respond to monetary policy instruments is a matter of ongoing research and practice, the data that are used to guide the formation of central bank policy need to make sense. The more realistic comprehensive CPI ought to be adopted over the WPI to measure inflation both internally at the Reserve Bank and externally for communicating with the public. The argument that credibility is served by sticking with a familiar but flawed price index is not convincing. Credibility should be easier to gain using a more meaningful measure of inflation.

The main results of the paper are the measurement of the persistence of inflation in India and of the short-run response of monetary policy to inflation increases. It appears that as supply shocks fade, inflation persists because the Reserve Bank raises its policy rate slowly in response to inflation as negative output gaps decline. This may well be a consequence of the lack of independence of the central bank. However, it does appear to be a source of inflation persistence in the empirical results presented here. The transition to a formal inflation targeting regime with instrument independence for the Reserve Bank should bring an opportunity for gaining greater credibility for generating lower inflation. The authors have thoughtfully summarized the parameters and issues for a reasoned consideration of monetary policy reform for India.

Surjit Bhalla
O[x]us Investment

I had made several points with regard to the Patra et al. paper at the time of the conference in July 2013. I have gone through the revised paper in some detail; unfortunately, I find that the authors have ignored the comments and suggestions for revision. This is their prerogative, but the least one would have expected is that the authors would dismiss, in an academic fashion, the suggestions made. My comments, therefore, remain as I had stated in July.

In today's post-global crisis scenario, India stands out as a singular exception to the prevailing disinflation scenario. Indeed, the six-year average CPI inflation ending in 2013 is within a whisker of 10%, and within spitting distance of the record six-year average of 10.1% observed in 1975. Recall that the 1975 average was caused by oil prices quadrupling in October 1973. No such easy explanation is available for the present Indian record. An analysis of the determinants of such inflation is what I was looking for in the Patra paper. Instead, what the paper delivers is a lot of elevator statistics (this went up and this down and at so much statistical significance) and precious little explanation as to why CPI inflation has raged on for the last six years at double-digit levels.

A pertinent inflation issue that was missed by the paper was the deep divergence between the WPI, which is used by the RBI, and the CPI. The excuse given by the RBI, time and again, is the fact that this CPI is a new index and is not comprehensive enough. However, the authors don't even mention, let alone discuss, the fact that a comprehensive rural (CPIAL) and urban (CPIIW) price index has existed for the last sixty years, and can be used to construct a synthetic all India index. If this had been done, then the authors would have found that there is no precedent to the deep divergence that exists today between the WPI and CPI. One of the simplest explanations behind this new phenomenon is the weighting diagram, i.e. the share of food in the index. The share of food in the CPI is an exorbitantly high 50%. On the other hand, its share in the WPI is at a much lower 22%. Therefore, an important explanation for high double-digit CPI inflation is inappropriate weights.

Incidentally, the Patra et al. paper makes no mention of the GDP or the implicit GDP deflator, which are extremely important to the study of inflation. To emphasize this point, the implicit GDP deflator accounts for all the goods and services in the economy and it would have been interesting point to focus on, especially given the deficiencies in the CPI and WPI. A reason behind this oversight could have been the case of "have data, will analyze" without focusing on the reasons behind the current situation. [In the revised paper, the authors have a sentence or two brushing aside the importance, or relevance, of the GDP deflator].

History of what is being analyzed—inflation: Between the broad range of years 1960 to 1993, inflation in India, irrespective of the chosen measure, not only averaged around 8% per annum but also had relatively low volatility. In the mid-1970s, there was a spike in inflation due to oil price rise. However, through the mid-1970s and even with the economic reforms in 1991, inflation stayed at this average level of 8%. It was during the period between 1996 to 2007 that inflation suddenly fell to an average of 4 to 5%, regardless of the inflation measure (whether it is GDP deflator, CPI or WPI). After 2007, the scenario completely changed and inflation went to double digits, in terms of both CPI and WPI. With this brief peek into history, the question arises as to what happened post-2008. The government and the RBI give a range of reasons behind the rise and fall of inflation—external factors, external shocks, oil prices. In these comments on the Patra et al. paper, an attempt is made to offer robust explanations as to what might have happened.

A favorite explanation for high inflation in India is "inflation expectations". Figure 2 depicts the inflation expectations measure as well as the actual WPI value. The inflation expectations measure is constructed using a survey conducted at the end of each quarter, in which people are posed questions on their expectations of inflation over a certain period of time—3 months, 6 months, etc. Note the close correspondence between the expectations of inflation and actual WPI inflation. The main point of the graph is the lack of any causal linkage between the inflation expectations measure and actual inflation. And therefore, the argument presented in the paper of inflation being affected by persisting expectations is without much empirical basis.

FIGURE 2. Inflation Expectations (Expectation and Actual year-on-year, in %)

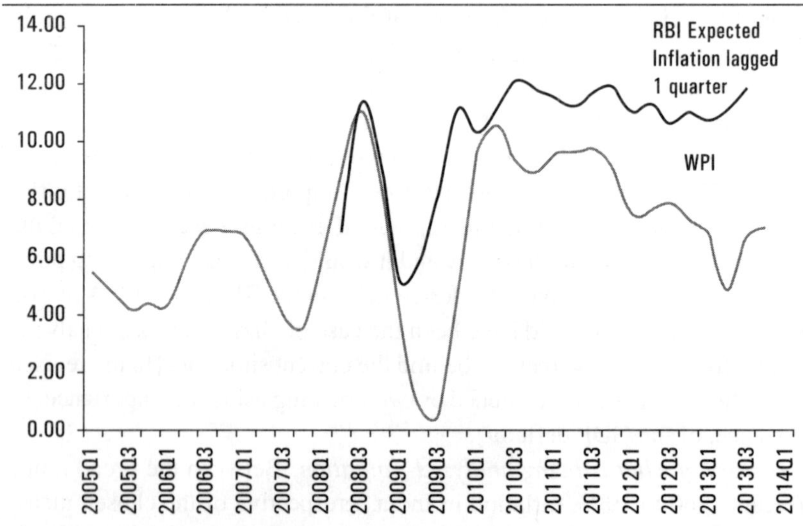

Sources: Reserve Bank of India, Data Handbook of the Indian Economy.

Imported Inflation: Figure 3 compares the inflation in India with other developing countries for the period of 1980–2012. The median inflation is used for developing countries and the CPI measure is used for India. The interesting fact to note, especially by government officials, is the existence of a close correlation between the two. The turning points of the curves are mostly captured, except for post-2008, which still need to be addressed. It is the answer to the post-2008 divergence that should have been the focus of the paper.

FIGURE 3. CPI Inflation in India and Developing Countries: 1980–2013; in %

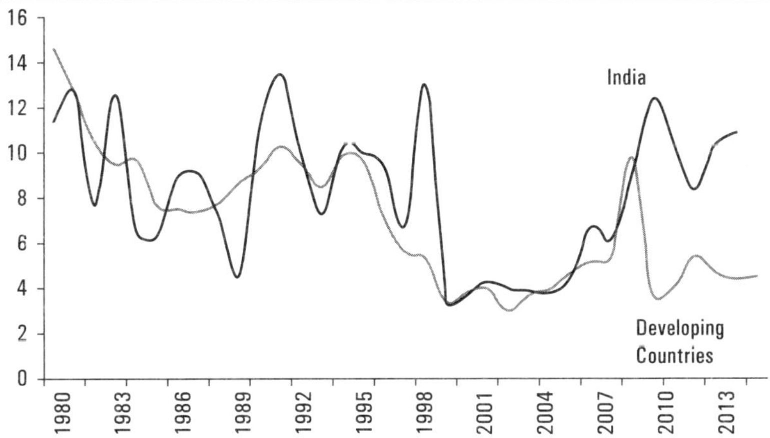

Source: World Bank, World Development Indicators.

Do supply shocks explain inflation? Supply shocks, especially food supply shocks, rainfall and droughts are often considered as important explanators of high inflation. With regard to agricultural supply shocks, it is noteworthy that the period of low inflation—1996 to 2007—was accompanied by very bad rainfall shocks. The period 1998 to 2003 (particularly 2002) was the third worst rainfall period in Indian history since 1871, which led to low agricultural growth as well. While there was a spike in onion inflation around this period, the aggregate inflation, surprisingly, still remained between 3 to 5% despite the food supply shocks.

Role of administered food prices in causing inflation: In Bhalla (2011a), I had offered an explanation for the high CPI inflation India was experiencing. In that paper I had contended that high procurement prices for foodgrains, sugar, cotton, etc., were causing the relative price of food to increase, and this increase in the relative price was a major cause of high inflation. For those unfamiliar with the operations of the Indian economy, prices of several crops—rice, wheat, sugar—are administered by the government. These prices are weighted by the share of these crops to create an index called the procurement price index.

The chain of causation is as follows. When the government raises the procurement price of agricultural output, then the price of the factors of production for that good—land, wages will rise. In the post-2008 period, wages, especially rural wages, rose at an unprecedented pace. But this had less to do with NREGA and more with the fast paced increases in the relative price of food.

To put this into perspective, between 1996 and 2004, the relative price of food stayed within a band ±5%, i.e., if the chosen index is 100, then the relative price of food was between 95 to 105. However, post-2005, the relative price of food exploded and shot up by 30%, simply in the span of four years (Figure 4).

FIGURE 4. Relative Prices (Indices, Base = 2004/05)

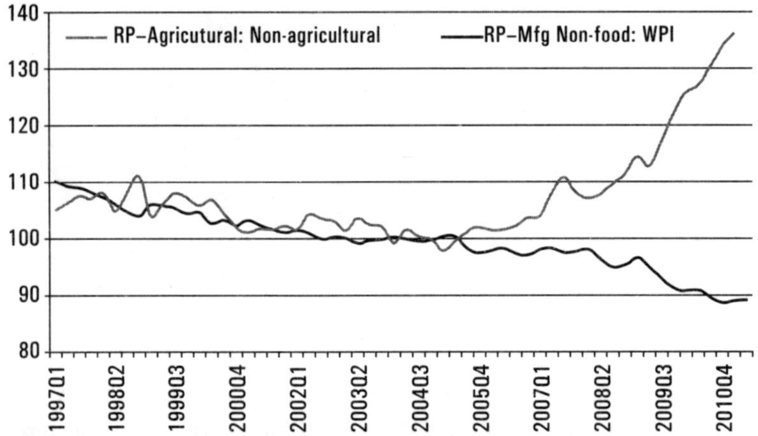

Source: Reserve Bank of India, Data Handbook of the Indian Economy.
Note: RP - Relative Price.

I ran a simple regression using percentage change in CPI inflation as the dependent variable and aggregate percentage change in the procurement price index (lagged 1 period) as the independent variable. The coefficient of the procurement price was 0.3, which implies that a 10 percentage point increase in procurements prices leads to a 3 percentage point increase in CPI. It is important to note that these results come with a simple one-variable regression. Dummy variables for three years have also been included, for 1983, 1991, and 1998 (procurement prices in India started in 1976).

Figure 5 depicts the CPI inflation, procurement prices and its values as predicted by the above regression. From 1978 to 2006 (the sample used for the regression), the predicted values are completely accurate. Moreover, it continues to predict accurately post the sample period as well. See Bhalla et al. (2011a) for details.

FIGURE 5. CPI vs. Procurement Prices (year-on-year % changes)

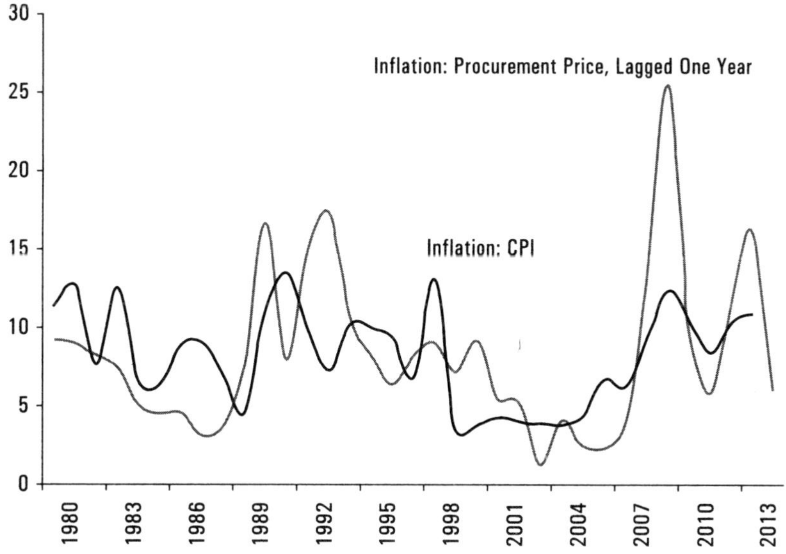

Source: Reserve Bank of India, Data Handbook of the Indian Economy.

"Taylor formulation": The authors estimate a Taylor formulation to explain the determination of short-term interest rates, the repo rate. A near identical exercise was conducted by Bhalla et al. (2011b) for 27 different countries. The results for India are very similar except for the role of exchange rate changes—Patra et al. do not find any statistical significance for exchange rate changes, while Bhalla et al. do. It would have been useful for the authors to explore this divergence in the results.

References

Bhalla, Surjit S., Ankur Choudhary, and Nikhil Mohan. 2011a. "Indian Inflation: Populism, Politics and Procurement Prices," *Developing Trends*, Oxus Research & Investments, 1 (2), July, 2011. Available at www.oxusinvestments.com.

Bhalla, Surjit, S., Ankur Choudhary, and Nikhil Mohan. 2011b. "Central Banks: The Good, the Bad and the Ugly," *Developing Trends*, Oxus Research & Investments, 1 (3 and 4), November, 2011. Available at www.oxusinvestments.com

General Discussion

Indira Rajaraman argued that RBI policy has been significantly handicapped by unreliable measures of the inflation rate. In particular, the CPI fully incorporates indirect taxes and the WPI includes some taxes. She believed that the shift to a value added tax after 2005 was a major factor contributing to the rise in inflation, and such changes should be excluded from an index used as an indicator for monetary policy. The monetary authorities should have a price index for policy purposes that excludes the direct effects of tax changes.

T.N. Srinivasan contended that the models and policy framework were basically those of high-income countries, such as the United States or the United Kingdom, and were insufficiently modified to reflect the specific circumstances of India. He also thought there was an inadequate explanation of the computation of potential output and questioned its usefulness. He pointed out that the paper also suggests that there is no coordination between monetary and fiscal policy: are the monetary authorities trying to correct for the actions of the fiscal authorities, or vice versa. Finally, he disapproved of a formulation of the policy objective that did not explicitly include the welfare of the Indian population as a goal.

Vijay Joshi pointed out that the paper suggested a worsening in recent year of the tradeoff between inflation and output growth. He attributed that to increased indexation of wages and suggested that the effort to reduce inflation would be more costly in terms of lost output than in the past. Second, he argued that adoption of a policy of inflation targeting was inconsistent with India's current practice of devoting considerable attention to managing the exchange rate. The monetary policy authorities cannot target two objectives and would be forced to choose. Finally, he noted that a regime of inflation targeting is also inconsistent with the notion of policy coordination, an issue raised by T.N. Srinivasan, unless the coordination is all on the side of the fiscal authorities. Advocates of inflation targeting explicitly reject the notion of policy coordination. He wondered how these issues could be resolved in the Indian context. Devesh Kapur added that the conflict was even greater because the monetary authorities were actually targeting three goals: minimizing inflation, maximizing output growth, and stabilizing the exchange rate.

Tom Richardson thought it strange that India still focuses on the WPI to guide its monetary policy instead of the CPI. He argued that the new All India CPI index closely follows the index for industrial workers during their period of overlap. Could not the industrial worker index be used to extrapolate the All India series back in time, enabling the new series to be adopted for analysis and policy guidance? T.N. Srinivasan thought the problems with the inflation measures went deeper than simply choosing between the CPI and WPI. The adjustments for quality change and new products were inadequate and the WPI should be eliminated in favor of a true producer price index.

MUNEESH KAPUR*
International Monetary Fund

RAKESH MOHAN†
International Monetary Fund

India's Recent Macroeconomic Performance: An Assessment and the Way Forward

ABSTRACT The sustained high growth in an environment of macroeconomic and financial stability—recorded by the Indian economy prior to the North Atlantic financial crisis (NAFC) has suffered a setback. While the macroeconomic policy response after the NAFC was admirably rapid, there was overshooting of the stimulus, and its withdrawal was gradual. The stimulus measures led to high growth, averaging 9%, during 2009–11, but also sowed the seeds for inflationary and balance of payments pressures, necessitating the subsequent moderation in domestic demand and growth. The domestic slowdown was then further exacerbated by domestic policy bottlenecks. Appropriate policies in regard to domestic oil prices and fiscal consolidation will make more resources available to the private sector and contribute to the recovery of private sector investment. Fiscal consolidation would also facilitate a reduction in inflation, which would then have a moderating impact on gold imports and a favorable impact on the real exchange rate, exports and current account deficit. Given the growth and inflation expectations, interest rates in India can be expected to remain above those in advanced economies, even when we move away from the present aberrations of near zero interest rates in the major advanced economies; therefore, a prudent approach with regard to the opening up of debt flows to foreign investors needs to be pursued.

Keywords: *Current Account, Capital Flows, Exchange Rate, Exports, Fiscal Policy, Gold, Growth, India, Monetary Policy, Oil Demand, Savings*

JEL Classification: *E52, E63, E63, F14, F40*

* *mkapur@imf.org*
† *rmohan@imf.org*

1. Introduction

The Indian economy recorded robust growth of 9% plus per annum during 2004–08, and the high growth phase was accompanied by the consolidation of key macroeconomic indicators. However, this process suffered a setback with the onset of the North Atlantic financial crisis (NAFC) in 2008. Growth rebounded initially in response to large monetary and fiscal stimuli but slowed down significantly subsequently; moreover, a substantial widening of the current account and fiscal deficits has occurred since 2008–09, along with inflation climbing to an elevated level. With the observed decline in domestic saving and investment (S–I) rates, there are concerns that India's potential growth rate has now fallen significantly (Mishra 2013c). Furthermore, given the large twin deficits, concerns have also been expressed about the possible emergence of a balance of payments crisis (for example, Acharya 2013; Mody and Walton 2013; Tarapore 2013b). These concerns came to the forefront during June–August 2013 following the mention of tapering of its unconventional monetary policy by the US Federal Reserve and the resulting volatility in the global and domestic financial markets. There is also a view that the high growth phase of 2004–09 was a debt-led cyclical boom, supported by unprecedented capital inflows, coinciding with an exceptional growth phase in the world economy (Nagaraj 2013).

Can India be placed on a sustained high growth path again so that it grows consistently over the next couple of decades and beyond? To what extent have domestic economic policies contributed to the slowdown that might have been expected in any case, as a result of the headwinds emanating from the NAFC?

Against this backdrop, this paper begins with an evaluation of India's recent growth experience in a cross-country perspective (Section 2). This is followed by an assessment of the role of domestic macroeconomic policies in the growth slowdown; this section also examines as to whether oil demand is responsive to price movements and as to how much of the recent growth slowdown can be explained through conventional determinants (Section 3). Section 4 then assesses the factors that have led to the widening of the current account deficit (CAD) and explores: (a) the role of income and price elasticities in external trade and (b) the determinants of demand for gold imports in order to understand the widening of the CAD. Section 5 focuses on some key issues in macroeconomic management going forward and concluding observations are in Section 6.

2. Recent Macroeconomic Trends: India in a Global Perspective

After the NAFC in 2008–09, India's real gross domestic product (GDP) growth rebounded sharply during 2009–11, but this rebound was short-lived and growth decelerated significantly in the following two years, as shown in Table 1. This deceleration in growth has been accompanied by a number of disconcerting macroeconomic developments since 2008–09. First, the noteworthy fiscal consolidation process witnessed during 2003–08 has suffered a setback and, despite some renewed correction, the fiscal deficit in 2012–13 was still more than double that of the pre-crisis year. Second, the CAD, which was relatively moderate and averaged around 1% of GDP during 1992–2008, widened significantly to just under 5% in 2012–13. Third, headline inflation, especially consumer inflation, has remained persistently high in the post-crisis period. Finally, private corporate investment has declined significantly.

TABLE 1. Key Macroeconomic Indicators: 2003–13

(%)

Year	*Real GDP growth (factor cost)*	*Real GDP growth (market prices)*	*GFD/ GDP (center)*	*CAB/ GDP*	*Non-oil CAB/ GDP*	*WPI inflation*	*CPI inflation*	*REER index@*	*Real policy rate#*
2003–04	8.1	7.9	4.3 (4.6)	2.3	5.0	5.5	3.9	96.8	–0.4
2004–05	7.0	7.8	3.9 (3.9)	–0.3	2.8	6.5	3.8	99.9	–0.6
2005–06	9.5	9.3	4.0 (4.7)	–1.2	2.7	4.4	4.4	102.7	1.7
2006–07	9.6	9.3	3.3 (4.3)		3.0	6.6	6.7	101.0	3.1
2007–08	9.3	9.8	2.5 (3.1)	–1.3	2.9	4.7	6.2	108.6	2.2
2008–09	6.7	3.9	6.0 (8.2)	–2.3	3.1	8.1	9.1	97.8	0.9
2009–10	8.6	8.5	6.5 (6.6)	–2.8	1.5	3.8	12.4	95.3	1.5
2010–11	9.3	10.5	4.8 (4.9)	–2.7	1.1	9.6	10.4	103.5	2.0
2011–12	6.2	6.3	5.7 (5.7)	–4.2	1.1	8.9	8.4	100.7	1.0
2012–13	5.0	3.3	4.9 (4.9)	–4.8	1.1	7.4	10.4	96.3	1.9

Source: Database on Indian Economy, Reserve Bank of India (http://dbie.rbi.org.in/DBIE/dbie.rbi?site=home); Economic Advisory Council to the Prime Minister.

Notes: @: 36-currency real effective exchange rate index (2004–5 = 100).

#: Nominal effective policy rate less 12-month moving average of non-food manufactured products WPI inflation.

Figures in parenthesis are GFD/GDP ratios including off-budget liabilities.

Part of the domestic slowdown is obviously the outcome of a sluggish global recovery. As Table 2 shows, global growth fell from an annual average of 4.8% during 2003–07 to an average of 2.9% during the subsequent five-year period (2008–12), and the slowdown is visible across all regions, including

TABLE 2. Key Macroeconomic Indicators: Variation Between 2008–12 (Average) and 2003–07 (Average)

(%)

	GDP growth	*CPI*	*CAB/GDP*	*Non-oil CAB/GDP*	*Variation in REER @*	*Revenues/ GDP*	*Expenditure/ GDP*	*Structural fiscal balance/ Potential GDP*
Argentina	–3.3	–0.4	–2.4	0.8	–13.5	7.3	7.7	–0.6
Australia	–1.0	0.1	2.2	1.3	17.1	–3.3	1.9	–5.1
Brazil	–0.8	–1.7	–3.1	–1.2	13.1	2.1	1.1	0.5
Canada	–1.4	–0.4	–4.1	–4.5	2.1	–2.2	2.5	–3.2
China	–2.4	0.7	–1.4	2.0	22.0	3.7	4.4	–0.8
France	–2.0	–0.1	–1.6	–2.1	–7.4	0.3	2.7	–0.7
Germany	–0.9	–0.0	1.3	4.6	–9.5	0.8	–0.2	1.5
India	–1.8	5.0	–3.0	–1.6	–5.9	–0.4	0.9	–1.9
Indonesia	0.4	–2.7	–2.0	–1.9	2.3	–1.3	–0.7	–0.8
Italy	–2.7	0.1	–1.4	–1.0	–4.8	1.9	2.4	1.5
Japan	–1.9	–0.2	–1.3	0.8	21.1	1.0	4.9	–2.6
Korea	–1.4	0.4	0.1	4.0	–22.9	0.9	0.7	0.4
Malaysia	–1.7	0.3	–1.7	1.2	1.4	0.6	1.7	–0.7
Mexico	–1.7	0.3	0.1	1.0	–11.1	2.5	4.5	–1.3
Russia	–5.6	–2.0	–4.1	–6.6	12.2	–2.0	4.5	–5.4
Saudi Arabia	0.3	2.5	–3.6	–2.6	14.5	–1.0	3.0	n.a.
South Africa	–2.5	2.2	–0.8	–1.7	0.6	0.9	4.8	–3.7
Thailand	–2.7	–0.3	1.3	4.0	1.6	–0.1	2.7	–2.7
Turkey	–3.7	–4.0	–1.4	–1.6	–4.3	1.5	0.7	1.1
UK	–3.6	1.4	0.3	1.2	–17.6	–0.3	5.1	–2.5
US	–2.1	–0.8	2.1	2.4	–7.5	–1.1	5.3	–3.7
Average	*–2.0*	*0.0*	*–1.2*	*–0.1*	*0.2*	*0.6*	*2.9*	*–1.5*
Median	*–1.9*	*–0.0*	*–1.4*	*0.8*	*0.6*	*0.6*	*2.7*	*–1.1*
World	–1.9	0.4	*n.a.*	*n.a.*	*n.a.*	*n.a.*	*n.a.*	*n.a.*
Advanced economies	–2.2	–0.2	0.6			–0.3	3.8	–2.3
Euro area	–2.4	–0.1	–0.1			0.3	2.7	–0.7
EDEs	–2.1	0.5	–1.4			*n.a.*	*n.a.*	*n.a.*

Source: World Economic Outlook Database (April 2013), IMF.

Note: @: REER is percentage change between 2012 and 2007.

emerging markets. Clearly, global demand has fallen as a result of the NAFC and there has been some rebalancing of current account balance/GDP ratios across G20 countries. The advanced economies—the United States, the United Kingdom, Germany—have recorded an improvement in their current account positions. These were mostly associated with real currency depreciations and weak domestic demand. Interestingly, since the NAFC, it is the advanced economies that have generally recorded real depreciation with the Emerging Market Economies (EMEs) recording real appreciation—the consequence of accommodative monetary policies in the advanced economies. Many EMEs have correspondingly recorded high CADs. Thus, the slowdown in global growth and demand had some adverse impact on demand and growth in India, along with other EMEs, while also contributing to the widening of CAD.

The slowdown in India's growth or widening of its CAD is thus not surprising in a cross-country perspective. However, what is of concern is the extent of the slowdown and the magnitude of key imbalances in India. In 2012, amongst the G-20 economies, India had the third largest CAD after Turkey and South Africa, and India's fiscal deficit was the second largest after Japan. Compared to India, fiscal deficits in Turkey and South Africa are more modest, while Japan has a surplus on its current account. Thus, the concern in the Indian context is the high level of twin deficits which, as the crisis literature shows, can be a source of future vulnerability. Advanced economies with debt/GDP ratios above 80% of GDP and persistent CADs are vulnerable to rapid fiscal deterioration: government borrowing costs increase much more quickly at higher debt levels, especially for countries also running CADs (Greenlaw et al. 2013). Debt thresholds are, however, typically lower for emerging economies (Reinhart and Rogoff 2009). External vulnerabilities (large CADs) and domestic credit booms explain the NAFC, like the previous crises in emerging markets (Lane and Milesi-Ferretti 2010). These vulnerabilities were again visible in the most recent turmoil during June–August 2013, when the countries with large CADs were hit the most.

There is also a view that global growth in the pre-NAFC period was well above potential and the post-NAFC slowdown is a return to the underlying potential growth path. The potential growth of developing countries was 6.3% during 2005–07, whereas the actual growth during this period averaged two percentage points higher at 8.3%; the output gap which was close to zero in 2005 reached 3.5% in 2007 (World Bank 2013). Going forward, the World Bank estimates that potential growth for developing countries will be lower at 5.5% for 2012–15. Thus, the ongoing slowdown in the Indian economy can also be viewed as a part of the worldwide phenomenon of slower potential growth in the post-crisis period.

While the growth slowdown, the widening of the CAD and the widening of the fiscal deficit in India are directionally in line with global trends, the domestic inflation outturn depicts a different picture. Inflation moderated or was largely unchanged in many economies on the back of weak demand in the post-2008 period. In India, however, it has been substantially higher in the 2008–12 period; see Table 2.

The brief global overview clearly shows deterioration in growth and current account positions for a number of EMEs. Thus, the Indian slowdown and high CAD are not an aberration from these global trends, *but what is striking is the extent of the slowdown and the deterioration.* This suggests that domestic factors have added to headwinds from the global economy.

We now turn to the role of domestic macroeconomic factors and policies. At the same time, it is worth noting that the domestic financial sector exhibited striking resilience to the NAFC, reflecting India's prudent approach to domestic and external financial liberalization (Mohan 2011a).

3. Domestic Macroeconomic Policies and Growth Slowdown

Part of the growth slowdown in the Indian context during 2011–13 vis-à-vis the immediate post-crisis years (2008–09 and 2009–10) could be attributed to the withdrawal of the large monetary and fiscal stimulus that was administered immediately after the crisis (Rajan 2013). Following the collapse of Lehman Brothers in October 2008 and the intensification of the NAFC, there were large capital outflows from India reflecting sales by foreign institutional investors in the domestic stock market. There was, however, no direct impact of the Lehman collapse on the Indian banking system due to its limited exposure to toxic assets, in turn reflecting the prudent regulatory framework in India with regard to the banks. The Indian financial markets also worked normally in the aftermath of the Lehman collapse, albeit with elevated volatility (Mohan 2011c). Notwithstanding these relatively positive domestic developments, there was a sharp slowdown in the domestic economy in the second half of 2008–09; there was a perception that the global developments would have a serious sustained adverse impact on the real economy, given the relatively high degree of openness of the Indian economy by that time. Moreover, a number of advanced economies had undertaken significant monetary and fiscal stimulus measures, although these were clearly in response to the sharp slowdown in their own growth and the severe disruptions to their financial markets. Here, it is relevant to note that the Reserve Bank of India was in a tightening mode as late as

July/August 2008 in response to the then prevailing domestic macroeconomic conditions. Nonetheless, given the sharp downturn in the global economy and the perceptions of these developments having a serious knock-on effect on the domestic economy, India, like many other EMEs, took both monetary and fiscal measures.

On the monetary side, the effective policy rate was cut sharply from 9.0% in September 2008 to 3.25% by April 2009; the cash reserve ratio was reduced from 9.0% to 5.0% over the same period. In addition, a number of other monetary and liquidity measures were instituted, which collectively had the potential to release liquidity of more than 10% of GDP (Mohan 2011c). On the fiscal side, the Government, inter alia, cut the CENVAT (the main Central indirect tax in the form of a VAT) rate from 14% to 8% between December 2008 and February 2009 and also increased plan expenditure. These measures were in addition to the stimulus already in the pipeline from implementation of the Pay Commission award and the agriculture debt waiver. Reflecting these actions as well as others, the Central government's headline gross fiscal deficit (GFD) increased from 2.5% of GDP in 2007–08 to 6.0% in 2008–09. Including bonds issued in lieu of cash subsidies with regard to oil, fertilizer and food sectors, the GFD/GDP ratio recorded an even sharper increase from 3.1% to an all-time high of 8.2%, which provides a better indicator of the boost to domestic demand from the fisc. Thus, both monetary policy and fiscal policy provided strong support—excessive with hindsight—to the domestic economy in 2008–09.

Monetary Policy

In contrast to the prevailing pessimistic outlook, real GDP growth in 2009–10 and 2010–11, however, turned out to be much stronger as shown in Table 3. Stronger growth started to be reflected in high inflation, initially in food inflation (by end 2009) and in underlying inflation by April 2010. Elevated international commodity prices and domestic structural imbalances in the availability of select domestic food items (pulses and other protein items) added to the inflationary pressures. Monetary accommodation was, however, continued until early 2010. The subsequent withdrawal was done in a phased and gradual manner during 2010–11 reflecting a number of factors: the high degree of uncertainty about the global as well as domestic outlook, the perception that the initial phase of high inflation was due to food prices, and the real-time data on domestic economic activity underestimating the strength of domestic demand at that time (Subbarao 2011). As inflationary pressures persisted and intensified, the pace of monetary tightening was

TABLE 3. Real GDP Growth: Forecast and Actual

(%)

Year and institution	Overall GDP		Industry		Services	
	Forecast/ projection	*Latest estimate*	*Forecast/ projection*	*Latest estimate*	*Forecast/ projection*	*Latest estimate*
2008–09						
Professional Forecasters @	8.1	6.7	8.1	4.1	9.7	9.4
PMEAC	8.5					
RBI	8.0–8.5					
2009–10						
Professional Forecasters @	5.7	8.6	4.1	10.2	7.5	10.0
PMEAC	7.0–7.5					
RBI	6.0					
2010–11						
Professional Forecasters @	8.2	9.3	9.0	8.7	9.0	9.8
PMEAC	8.2		8.7		8.8	
RBI	8.0					
2011–12						
Professional Forecasters @	8.2	6.2	8.2	2.7	9.6	7.9
PMEAC	9.0		9.2		10.3	
RBI	8.0					
2012–13						
Professional Forecasters @	7.2	5.0	6.0	2.0	8.8	6.5
PMEAC	7.6		7.0		9.1	
RBI	7.3					

Source: Macroeconomic and monetary developments (various issues), RBI; Economic review (various issues), PMEAC; central statistical organization.

Note: @: Forecast made in the last quarter of the preceding fiscal year (taken from the April/May issue of MMD) (for example, forecast made in the quarter ended March 2008 for the fiscal year 2008–09 and so on).

increased in 2011–12. This was in contrast to the rapid monetary and liquidity stimulus—the effective policy rate moved from 9.00% (repo rate) in September 2008 to 3.25% (reverse repo rate) in April 2009. Table 4 shows that the quantum and the pace of the monetary stimulus were more than those in most major emerging markets, despite the fact that no Indian financial institution had been substantially affected by the NAFC.

While inflationary pressures since 2010 are the outcome of factors noted above, one issue is: Did these also reflect the lagged impact of the high growth in monetary and credit aggregates in the pre-NAFC period? In the face of large and increasing capital flows—from 2.7% of GDP in 2003–04 to 8.6% in 2007–08—the Reserve Bank had deployed a range of instruments to manage these capital flows, including sterilized interventions.

TABLE 4. Policy Rates in Select Emerging Markets

(%)

Month	Brazil	Chile	China	India	Indonesia	Israel	Korea	Malaysia	Mexico	Russia	S.Africa	Thailand
Dec-2007	11.25	6.00	7.47	7.75	8.00	4.00	5.00	3.50		10.00	11.00	3.25
Jun-2008	12.25	6.75	7.47	8.50	8.50	3.50	5.00	3.50	7.75	10.75	12.00	3.25
Sep-2008	13.75	8.25	7.20	9.00	9.25	4.25	5.25	3.50	8.25	11.00	12.00	3.75
Dec-2008	13.75	8.25	5.31	5.00	9.25	2.50	3.00	3.25	8.25	13.00	11.50	2.75
Mar-2009	11.25	2.25	5.31	3.50	7.75	0.75	2.00	2.00	6.75	13.00	9.50	1.50
Jun-2009	9.25	0.75	5.31	3.25	7.00	0.50	2.00	2.00	4.75	11.50	7.50	1.25
Dec-2009	8.75	0.50	5.31	3.25	6.50	1.00	2.00	2.00	4.50	8.75	7.00	1.25
Jun-2010	10.25	1.00	5.31	3.75	6.50	1.50	2.00	2.50	4.50	7.75	6.50	1.25
Dec-2010	10.75	3.25	5.81	6.25	6.50	2.00	2.50	2.75	4.50	7.75	5.50	2.00
Jun-2011	12.25	5.25	6.31	7.50	6.75	3.25	3.25	3.00	4.50	8.25	5.50	3.00
Dec-2011	11.00	5.25	6.56	8.50	6.00	2.75	3.25	3.00	4.50	8.00	5.50	3.25
Jun-2012	8.50	5.00	6.31	8.00	5.75	2.50	3.25	3.00	4.50	8.00	5.50	3.00
Dec-2012	7.25	5.00	6.00	8.00	5.75	2.00	2.75	3.00	4.50	8.25	5.00	2.75
May-2013	8.00	5.00	6.00	7.25	5.75	1.50	2.50	3.00	4.00	8.25	5.00	2.50

Source: Haver Analytics.

Nonetheless, growth in broad money averaged more than 21% per annum during 2005–08, with growth in non-food credit averaging 28% and real GDP growth 9.5% during this three-year period. Actual growth in monetary and credit aggregates was also above the indicative projections set out by the Reserve Bank at the beginning of financial years. All these would suggest signs of overheating in the pre-NAFC period; indeed, inflation indicators did start increasing in 2007–08, but were compounded by the increasing oil prices at that time. Thus, the stimulus measures adopted after the NAFC added to the incipient inflationary pressures already emerging in the economy.

A related issue is: Is higher food inflation entirely the outcome of the minimum support price (MSP) policy and the Mahatma Gandhi National Rural Employment Guarantee Act (MGNREGA) (Bhalla 2013b)? Although a large increase in the MSP for the various crops has taken place during the recent years, especially since 2008–09, the causation is arguable. For example, there was a large increase in the actual prices (as measured by the wholesale price index (WPI)) of pulses during 2005–06 and 2006–07, but there was only a moderate increase in the MSP of these items. The MSP was then increased in 2007–08 and especially substantially in 2008–09, but even then the cumulative variation in the MSP between March 2005 and March 2010 was trailing the cumulative variation in actual prices for the three major pulses (*arhar*, *moong*, and *urad*) and also wheat, although the situation has reversed since then, as can be seen in Table 5. Why did the prices of pulses increase substantially beginning 2005–06? Strong growth in domestic food demand from 2003–04, accompanied by near plateauing of domestic production of pulses, is one plausible factor. Dietary patterns shifted in favor of protein-rich items on the back of higher incomes and this trend then seems to have got support from the MGNREGA scheme. The increases in MSP could then be viewed as an attempt by the government to incentivize farmers to increase domestic production of pulses to meet the rising demand.

Here, it is also relevant to note that the Reserve Bank of India had pointed to the possibility of overheating[1] as early as 2006, but there was a substantial

1. The RBI in its mid-term review in October 2006 had noted:

"Recent developments, in particular, the combination of high growth and consumer inflation coupled with escalating asset prices and tightening infrastructural bottlenecks underscore the need to reckon with dangers of overheating and the implications for the timing and direction of monetary policy setting. While there is no conclusive evidence of overheating in the Indian economy at the current juncture, the criticality of monitoring all available indications that point to excess aggregate demand is perhaps more relevant now than ever before." (RBI, 2006: 25).

TABLE 5. Minimum Support Prices and Wholesale Price Index

(March 2003 = 100)

Item		Mar-03	Mar-04	Mar-05	Mar-06	Mar-07	Mar-08	Mar-09	Mar-10	Mar-11	Mar-12	Mar-13
Rice	WPI	100.0	97.7	101.1	104.0	113.4	129.7	149.7	161.7	165.4	173.7	204.2
	MSP	100.0	103.8	105.7	107.5	109.4	121.7	169.8	188.7	188.7	203.8	235.8
	Gap	0.0	6.2	4.5	3.4	−3.5	−6.1	13.5	16.7	14.1	17.3	15.5
Wheat	WPI	100.0	104.8	104.1	120.5	132.8	144.4	155.6	178.4	178.7	177.7	212.0
	MSP	100.0	101.6	103.2	104.8	121.0	161.3	174.2	177.4	188.7	207.3	217.7
	Gap	0.0	−3.1	−0.8	−13.0	−8.9	11.7	12.0	−0.5	5.6	16.7	2.7
Gram	WPI	100.0	96.4	95.6	124.9	145.8	151.5	145.0	140.7	152.7	217.0	233.4
	MSP	100.0	114.8	116.8	117.6	118.4	131.1	141.8	144.3	172.[illegible]	229.5	245.9
	Gap	0.0	19.0	22.2	−5.8	−18.8	−13.5	−2.2	2.5	12.7	5.8	5.4
Arhar	WPI	100.0	106.9	98.9	107.8	129.0	152.2	174.8	246.0	222.8	197.2	231.0
	MSP	100.0	103.0	105.3	106.1	106.8	117.4	151.5	174.2	265.2	280.3	291.7
	Gap	0.0	−3.6	6.5	−1.6	−17.2	−22.8	−13.3	−29.2	19.0	42.1	26.3
Moong	WPI	100.0	89.3	91.2	128.2	143.7	117.6	140.3	266.5	222.8	211.0	247.0
	MSP	100.0	103.0	106.0	114.3	114.3	127.8	189.5	207.5	275.9	300.8	330.8
	Gap	0.0	15.4	16.2	−10.9	−20.5	8.7	35.0	−22.1	23.8	42.5	33.9
Urad	WPI	100.0	97.1	94.5	141.1	166.5	136.1	157.8	236.5	232.9	202.9	214.1
	MSP	100.0	103.0	106.0	114.3	114.3	127.8	189.5	189.5	255.6	285.7	323.3
	Gap	0.0	6.1	12.2	−19.0	−31.4	−6.1	20.0	−19.9	9.3	40.8	51.0

Source: Database on the Indian Economy, Reserve Bank of India.

Note: MSP = Minimum Support Prices; WPI = Wholesale Price Index. The row 'Gap' gives difference (percent) of MSP over WPI.

amount of skepticism about this assessment at that time. No doubt, there is a two-way feedback between actual prices and the MSP, but the previous analysis suggests that the higher order of initial increases in the MSP was necessitated by higher food demand on the back of high growth and rising incomes. The MSP story focuses on relative inflation. Similarly, the view that the MGNREGA has led to wage pressures stresses the cost-push view of inflation. But, high relative inflation cannot lead to persistent high overall inflation, unless it is generalized and accommodated. For example, non-food non-fuel consumer price index (CPI) inflation (rural and urban combined based on the new CPI series) has been around 8% since June 2012 (it was higher at around 10% during January–May 2012), which is suggestive of generalized pressures. In the face of persistently high food inflation, monetary policy can keep overall inflation within its comfort zone, but this would involve excessive tightening and large output costs for the other sectors of the economy. Thus, productivity gains in food production provide a more durable solution to increase food production in a non-inflationary manner.

Finally, the higher outlays on MGNREGA and the higher food subsidy bill are ultimately reflected in revenue deficits, which then add to domestic demand. If the revenue deficits had been contained through adjustments in other expenditures/higher revenues, then there might have been more merit in the cost-push argument—but only for explaining the short-term increase in inflation, not its persistence.

Real Interest Rates: Borrowers

The extent of monetary accommodation can be better gauged through movements in real interest rates, although these are beset with a number of conceptual issues in regard to the measurement of inflation expectations. The relevant measure of inflation and inflation expectations could differ for the various economic agents/groups in the country: while consumer inflation may be more relevant for households, manufactured products WPI inflation could be more appropriate for the industrial sector. Accordingly, in this paper, real lending rates are assessed both in terms of headline WPI inflation and non-food manufactured products (NFMP) WPI inflation. Real deposit rates are analyzed in relation to consumer inflation and also in relation to the inflation expectations of households. Apart from the issue of the appropriate inflation rate, a related issue is: Are inflation expectations better captured by the year-on-year (y-o-y) inflation rate or some sort of average inflation rate? If inflation expectations are relatively well-anchored, it is likely that the y-o-y inflation matters less and the more appropriate yardstick would be some sort of average inflation rate. Indeed, the empirical exercise carried out later on in the paper favors a real rate using a 12-month moving average of y-o-y inflation. Accordingly, the real interest rate is also presented using this indicator of inflation for the real policy rate.

While the nominal policy rate was being increased gradually during 2010 and 2011, the real policy rate was highly negative with respect to y-o-y headline WPI inflation and marginally negative with respect to y-o-y NFMP inflation. Thus, arguably, monetary policy was still in an accommodative mode over this phase, although most commentators characterized it as being too tight. Real policy rates moved from negative territory during 2010 and 2011 to positive territory in 2012, especially when the core inflation indicator is used as shown in Figure 1. The real interest rate trajectory is broadly similar in terms of the 12-month moving average of inflation, and, as can be expected, smoother. According to this measure, and using NFMP inflation, the real policy rate initially fell from an average of 2.2% in 2007–08 to 0.9% in 2008–09, but then edged up to 2.0% in 2010–11. It fell back to an average of 1.0% in 2011–12 (reflecting the more than expected increase in NFMP inflation), but again edged higher to 1.9% in 2012–13 (on the back of higher policy rate and some moderation in NFMP inflation). The real policy rate in terms of CPI inflation has been generally negative since mid-2008 (RBI 2014).

Bank lending rates and market rates broadly mirror the policy rates both in terms of nominal and real rates. Figure 2 shows that real commercial paper rates increased during the course of 2012 and were higher than those in the pre-crisis period, especially in terms of core inflation. In regard to commercial bank lending rates, the assessment is somewhat complicated by the move of the banking system from the benchmark prime lending rate system to the base rate system in July 2010, but the directional movement is broadly similar to that emanating from trends in the commercial paper rates; see Figure 3.

As shown in Figure 4, higher interest rates also had an adverse impact on corporate profitability and hence corporate savings and investment during this period. Corporate savings fell from 9.4% of GDP in 2007–08 to 7.2% in 2011–12, while corporate investment fell even more from 17.3% of GDP to 10.6%; see Table 6. What explains the larger decline in corporate investment vis-à-vis corporate savings since 2007–08? First, policy bottlenecks—such as obtaining environmental permissions, fuel linkages, or carrying out land acquisition—led to stalling of a number of large projects, which may in turn have discouraged new investment (Government of India 2013a). Second, the

FIGURE 1. Real Policy Rate

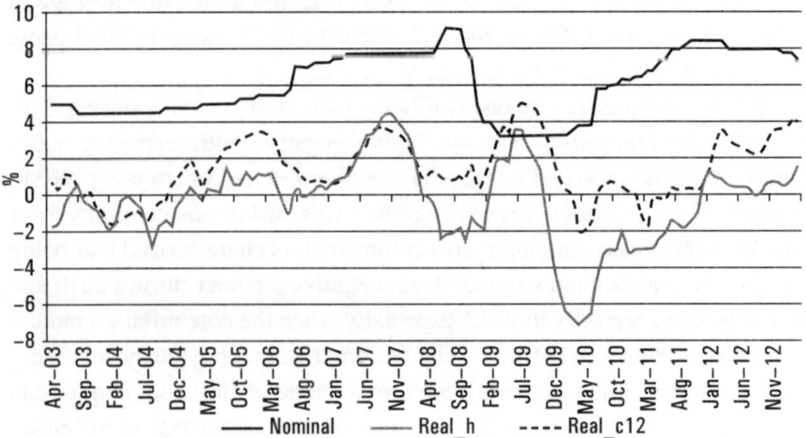

Source: Reserve Bank of India.

Note: Real_h and Real_c are real policy rates, defined as nominal policy rate adjusted for headline WPI inflation and non-food manufactured products WPI inflation, respectively.

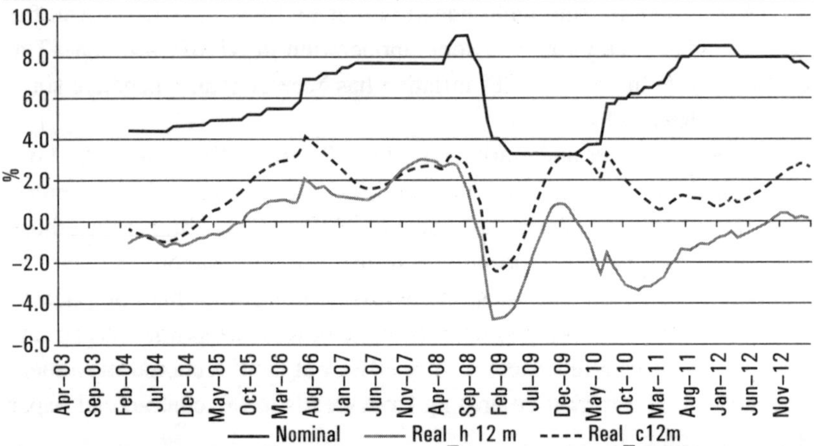

Source: Reserve Bank of India.

Note: Real_h12m and Real_c12m are real policy rates, defined as nominal policy rate adjusted for 12-month moving average of headline WPI inflation and non-food manufactured products WPI inflation, respectively.

large increase in fiscal deficit and the near trebling of government borrowing requirements appears to have led to some crowding out of the private sector. Third, there is a perception that the decline in domestic corporate investment since the NAFC is due to more outward foreign direct investment (FDI) on the back of domestic rigidities that impede domestic investment. This perception is, however, not borne out by data. Outward FDI by Indian corporates indeed increased substantially in the pre-NAFC phase from 0.3% of GDP in 2003–04 to 1.5% in 2007–08, but during this period domestic

FIGURE 2. Commercial Paper Rate

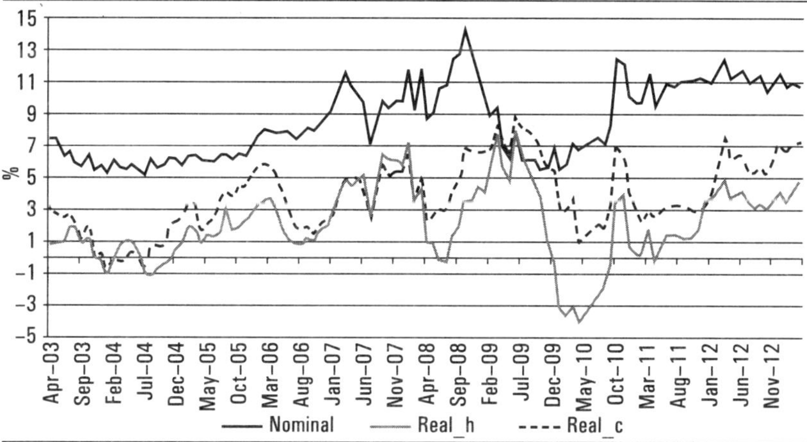

Source: Reserve Bank of India and Haver Analytics.

Note: Real_h and Real_c are real commercial paper rates, defined as nominal rate adjusted for headline WPI inflation and non-food manufactured products WPI inflation, respectively.

FIGURE 3. Base Rate

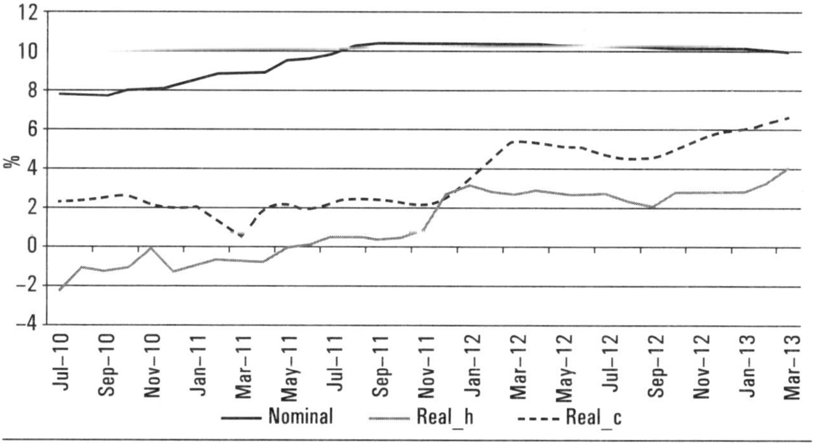

Source: Reserve Bank of India and Haver Analytics.

Note: Real_h and Real_c are real base rates , defined as nominal rate adjusted for headline WPI inflation and non-food manufactured products WPI inflation, respectively.

investment had also increased significantly. Since then, outward FDI has fallen to its 2003–04 levels (it was 0.4% of GDP in 2012–13) in tandem with the declining trend in domestic investment as can be seen in Table 9. The decline in domestic investment since 2007–08, therefore, cannot be attributed to more investment abroad.

Thus, as nominal as well as real lending rates tightened, especially beginning early 2012, the pace of investment activity and economic activity

FIGURE 4. Corporate Performance

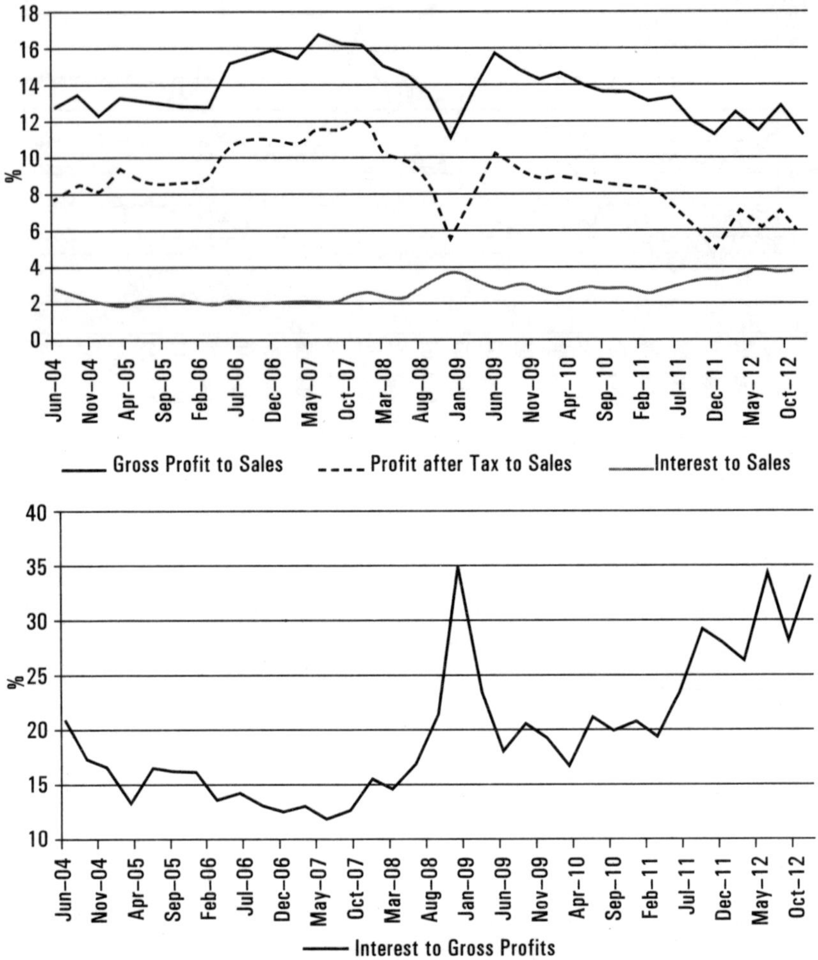

Source: CEIC.

slowed down as expected. While monetary policy supported growth during 2009–11, it contributed to the slowdown in the subsequent phase. Econometric evidence for India and elsewhere suggests that a 100 bps increase in the policy interest rate is associated, on average, with a growth slowdown of 25–50 bps, and the actual impact on growth during each monetary cycle of easing/tightening depends, inter alia, on the extent of transmission to market rates (Kapur and Behera 2012; RBI 2013c). The scale

TABLE 6. Savings and Investment

(% to GDP)

	Item	2003–04	2004–05	2005–06	2006–07	2007–08	2008–09	2009–10	2010–11	2011–12
1	Household sector	23.2	23.6	23.5	23.2	22.4	23.6	25.2	23.5	22.3
	a. Financial saving (i–ii)	11.0	10.1	11.9	11.3	11.6	10.1	12.0	10.4	8.0
	(i) Financial assets	13.7	13.8	15.8	17.8	15.5	12.9	15.3	12.7	10.8
	of which: Bank deposits	5.5	5.4	7.2	10.0	7.8	7.4	6.1	5.7	5.5
	(ii) Financial liabilities	2.5	3.7	5.0	6.6	3.8	2.9	3.1	3.6	3.1
	b. Saving in physical assets	12.1	13.4	11.7	11.9	10.8	13.5	13.2	13.1	14.3
2	Private corporate sector	4.6	6.6	7.5	7.9	9.4	7.4	8.4	7.9	7.2
3	Public sector	1.3	2.3	2.4	3.6	5.0	1.0	0.2	2.6	1.3
	of which: Government administration and quasi government bodies	–3.3	–2.3	–2.1	–1.0	0.5	–2.8	–3.1	–0.6	–2.0
4	Total domestic savings (1+2+3)	29.0	32.4	33.4	34.6	36.8	32.0	33.7	34.0	30.8
5	Gross capital formation	26.2	32.5	34.3	35.9	38.0	35.5	36.3	37.0	35.4
	a. Public sector	6.6	7.4	7.9	8.3	8.9	9.4	9.2	8.4	7.9
	b. Private corporate sector	6.6	10.3	13.6	14.5	17.3	11.3	12.1	13.4	10.6
	c. Household sector	12.1	13.4	11.7	11.9	10.8	13.5	13.2	13.1	14.3
	d. Valuables	0.9	1.3	1.1	1.2	1.1	1.3	1.8	2.1	2.7
6	Gross fixed capital formation	24.6	28.7	30.3	31.3	32.9	32.3	31.7	31.7	30.6
7	Change in stocks	0.7	2.5	2.8	3.4	4.0	1.9	2.8	3.1	2.1
8	Errors and omissions	0.7	0.4	0.4	0.2	0.1	–1.2	0.2	–0.1	–0.4
9	Total investment (5+8 = 6+7+ 8+5d)	26.9	32.8	34.7	35.7	38.1	34.3	36.5	36.8	35.0
	Memo:									
10	Saving-investment balance, net (4–9)	2.2	–0.4	–1.2	–1.1	–1.3	–2.3	–2.3	–2.8	–4.2
	a. Household financial savings, net	11.0	10.1	11.9	11.3	11.6	10.1	12.0	10.4	8.0
	b. Private corporate sector, net	–2.0	–3.8	–6.1	–6.6	–7.9	–3.9	–3.3	–5.4	–3.4
	c. Public sector, net	–5.3	–5.1	–5.5	–4.7	–3.9	–8.5	–9.0	–5.8	–6.6
11	Household financial savings (net) available for private corporate sector (10a+10c)	5.7	5.0	6.3	6.5	7.8	1.7	3.0	4.5	1.5

Source: Central Statistical Organization.

of the slowdown in the recent period has been much greater than suggested by these estimates and we will revisit this issue a little later.

On the extent of the slowdown, some caution is, however, warranted in reaching definitive conclusions, given the large revisions to GDP data in the recent past. There is divergence between industrial growth indicated by the data on the index of industrial production (IIP) and the Annual Survey of Industries (ASI), with IIP growth rates being significantly lower than the ASI growth rates in most of the years (Economic Advisory Council to the Prime Minister 2013). During 2003–12, IIP growth averaged almost four percentage points lower than the real growth of the gross value added from ASI data, with the difference being pronounced in 2011–12, the latest year for which the ASI data are available; see Table 7. Given that the IIP data are available at a high frequency (monthly) and provide a critical input for macroeconomic policy formulation, substantial revisions in IIP data can lead to incorrect policy inferences and actions. Accordingly, it is important to

TABLE 7. Industrial Growth

(%)

	Index of industrial production		*Annual survey of industries@*			*GDP at constant prices*	
Year	*Manu-facturing*	*General*	*Output*	*Net value added*	*Gross value added*	*Manu-facturing*	*Industry#*
2000–01	5.4	4.9	–0.1	–10.3	–8.4	7.3	6.0
2001–02	2.9	2.8	2.0	–1.3	0.9	2.3	2.6
2002–03	6.0	5.8	14.4	16.3	13.9	6.9	7.2
2003–04	7.4	7.0	7.8	11.5	9.5	6.3	7.3
2004–05	13.2	11.7	22.3	20.6	17.7	7.4	9.8
2005–06	10.3	8.6	11.4	17.2	15.0	10.1	9.7
2006–07	15.0	12.9	19.4	20.1	19.4	14.3	12.2
2007–08	18.4	15.5	10.0	16.1	14.6	10.3	9.7
2008–09	2.5	2.5	11.1	3.2	4.2	4.3	4.4
2009–10	4.8	5.3	11.6	9.7	11.5	11.3	9.2
2010–11	9.0	8.2	18.5	12.6	12.0	9.7	9.2
2011–12	3.0	2.9	15.3	10.7	10.4	2.7	3.5
2012–13	1.2	1.0	n.a	n.a	n.a	1.0	2.1
Averages							
1980s	7.4	7.6	8.1	7.3	7.9	6.2	5.8
1990s	6.5	6.3	7.3	6.8	6.9	5.8	5.7
2000s	8.6	7.7	11.0	10.3	9.8	8.0	7.8
2003–08	12.8	11.1	14.2	17.1	15.2	9.7	9.7
2008–11	4.8	4.7	14.1	9.1	9.5	7.0	6.6

Source: Central Statistical Organization.

Notes: @: Growth rates are based on ASI data deflated by WPI-Manufactured Products index.
#: including construction.

understand and reconcile the differences between the two sets of industrial data. Since it is the ASI data that determine the final GDP estimates, the problems in collecting IIP data should be corrected on a priority basis so that more accurate information is available for a short-term policymaking process.

Real Interest Rates: Depositors

Turning to deposit rates, the real rate in terms of consumer inflation has been broadly negative since 2008–09 reflecting the persistently elevated level of consumer inflation on the back of high food inflation. Thus, even as nominal deposit rates increased from the pre-2008 levels, real rates fell from an average of (+) 1.5% during 2003–08 to (–) 1.9% during 2008–13. Real deposit rates turn out to be more negative, if data on inflation expectations of households are used, which are available from 2006 onward. According to these data, during 2008–13, the real deposit rate averaged (–) 2.1% using households' "current" inflation expectations and (–) 3.3% using households' "one-year ahead" inflation expectations; see Figure 5. Administered interest rates on small savings have also been negative in real terms in the recent years and growth in small savings has been low or negative in this period.

Negative real deposit rates, along with the growth slowdown, seem to have contributed to the decline in household financial savings accompanied by a switch toward savings in physical assets (gold and property). Financial savings (gross) of households fell from 15.5% of GDP in 2007–08 to 10.8% in 2011–12, reflecting decline in all the major constituents—bank deposits, life insurance funds, and shares and debentures; see Table 6. The recent decline has taken gross financial savings in 2011–12 to below its 1997–98 levels (10.9% of GDP) and just close to its levels in the early 1990s (10.4% in 1992–93). Financial savings (net) of households declined by 3.6 percentage points of GDP between 2007–08 and 2011–12, while physical savings went up by almost a similar magnitude. Households' physical investments in gold increased from an average of 1.1% of GDP during 2003–08 to 2.7% by 2011–12. The overall household savings at 22.3% in 2011–12 were almost the same as in 2007–08 as shown in Table 6. The stability of the overall household savings rate is remarkable in the face of the significant deceleration in economic activity. Thus, rather than smoothing consumption, households appear to have focused on maintaining their overall savings propensities, perhaps a reflection of the elevated uncertainty in the economic environment. At the same time, the significant deterioration in public finances has not been countered by households through higher savings, which would indicate non-Ricardian behavior and also presents indirect evidence of some role for countercyclical fiscal policy.

FIGURE 5. Deposit Rate

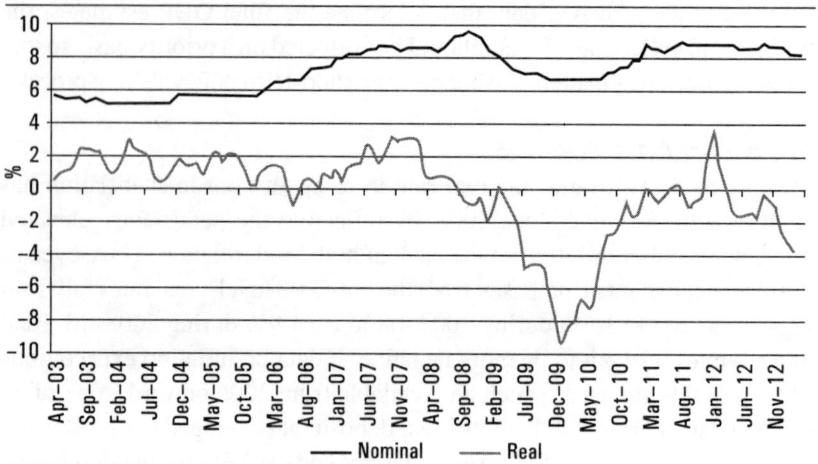

Source: Reserve Bank of India and Haver Analytics.

Note: Real interest rate is nominal deposit rate less y-o-y CPI (Industrial Workers) inflation.

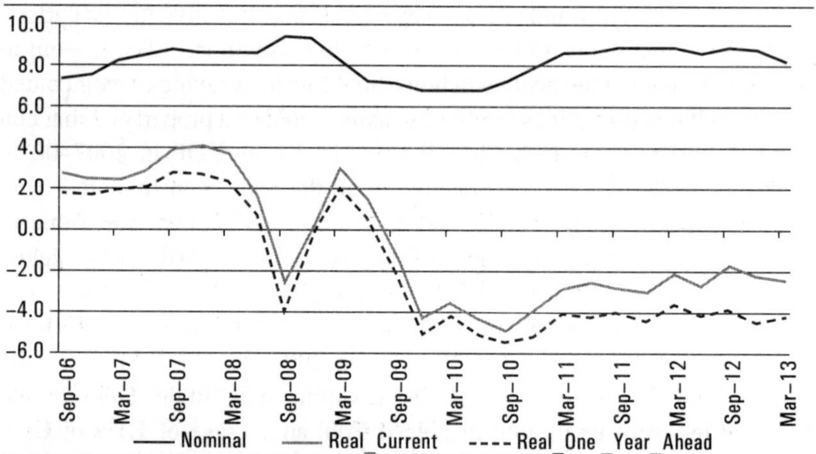

Source: Reserve Bank of India and Haver Analytics.

Note: Real_Current and Real_One_Year_Ahead are nominal deposit rate less "current" and "one year ahead" inflationary expectations, respectively, of households as per RBI's survey.

However, the significant decline in financial savings, if not reversed quickly, has adverse implications for medium-term growth prospects as well as external sustainability.

Does the relationship between real deposit rates and savings hold in other periods? Household savings, for example, increased between 1997–98 (18% of GDP) and 2003–04 (23%), even as deposit rates declined. Nominal deposit rates declined over this period and the decline was quite substantial (from around 11% to around 5–6%). But, this period was also marked by a significant fall in inflation. Real deposit interest rates during the early part of this period were almost unchanged and highly positive (4–5% until 2001–02, and 2–3% during 2002–03 and 2003–04; these were negative in one year only, 1998–99). Thus, the decline in nominal deposit rates tracked the inflation movements—or perhaps trailed the decline in inflation, given the fact that it takes some time for economic agents to revise their inflation expectations. The downward movement in banks' nominal deposit rates was also facilitated by the downward adjustment in the administered interest rates on small savings during this period. The available evidence, therefore, suggests that real deposit rates do matter for household savings.

Fiscal Policy

As noted, the fiscal stimulus measures in response to the NAFC included cuts in the CENVAT rate and higher plan expenditure, in addition to the already announced Pay Commission award and agricultural debt waiver. Reflecting these measures as well as the impact of growth slowdown on revenues, the Centre's headline fiscal deficit/GDP ratio jumped from 2.5% in 2007–08 to 6.0% in 2008–09 and further to 6.5% in 2009–10; see Table 8. The deficit, including the impact of bonds issued in lieu of cash subsidies for oil and others, as mentioned earlier, recorded an even higher order of increase from 3.1% of GDP in 2007–08 to 8.2% in 2008–09, but then moderated somewhat to 6.6% in 2009–10. In nominal terms, the Centre's fiscal deficit increased from ₹1,269 billion in 2007–08 to ₹3,370 billion in 2008–09 (vis-à-vis the budgeted amount of ₹1,333 billion) and ₹4,185 billion in 2009–10, an increase of 230% in just two years. Despite this substantial increase in its borrowing requirements, the borrowing costs declined—the weighted average yield on Central government's dated securities fell from 8.12% in 2007–08 to 7.23% in 2009–10—benefiting from the monetary policy stance and the large open-market operations of the Reserve Bank.

The fiscal stimulus began to be withdrawn in 2011–12 and 2012–13, and this could have had some impact on the immediate growth outcome. The quality of fiscal stimulus provided in the aftermath of the NAFC also seems to have exacerbated the slowdown in 2011–13. Revenue expenditure of the Central government increased from 11.9% of GDP in 2007–08 to 14.1% in 2008–09 (and maintained at this level in 2009–10). This increase was partly on account of subsidies, which increased from 1.4% of GDP during 2007–08 to 2.3% in 2008–09 and remained around these levels till 2012–13. Table 8 shows that the increase in subsidies was initially due to fertilizers and then due to the incomplete and delayed pass-through of high international crude oil prices to domestic prices. Oil subsidies increased from 0.1% of GDP during 2003–08 to 1.0% in 2012–13. However, these data represent only the

TABLE 8. Fiscal Position of the Center

(% to GDP)

	Item	*2003–04*	*2004–05*	*2005–06*	*2006–07*	*2007–08*	*2008–09*	*2009–10*	*2010–11*	*2011–12*	*2012–13*	*2013–14*
1	Gross fiscal deficit (GFD)	4.3	3.9	4.0	3.3	2.5	6.0	6.5	4.8	5.7	5.2	4.8
	Adjusted GFD *	[4.6]	[3.9]	[4.7]	[4.3]	[3.1]	[8.2]	[6.6]	[4.9]	[5.7]	[4.9]	[4.8]
2	Gross primary deficit	–0.0	–0.0	0.4	–0.2	–0.9	2.6	3.2	1.8	2.7	2.0	1.5
											(1.8)	
3	Revenue deficit	3.5	2.4	2.5	1.9	1.1	4.5	5.2	3.2	4.4	3.9	3.3
											(3.6)	
4	Revenue receipts	9.3	9.4	9.4	10.1	10.9	9.6	8.8	10.1	8.4	8.7	9.3
	a. Gross Tax	9.0	9.4	9.9	11.0	11.9	10.8	9.6	10.2	9.9	10.4	10.9
	(i) Corporation tax	2.2	2.6	2.7	3.4	3.9	3.8	3.8	3.8	3.6	3.6	3.7
	(ii) Income tax	1.5	1.5	1.6	1.7	2.1	1.9	1.9	1.8	1.8	2.0	2.1
	(iii) Customs duties	1.7	1.8	1.8	2.0	2.1	1.8	1.3	1.7	1.7	1.6	1.6
	(iv) Union excise	3.2	3.1	3.0	2.7	2.5	1.9	1.6	1.8	1.6	1.7	1.7
	(v) Service tax	0.3	0.4	0.6	0.9	1.0	1.1	0.9	0.9	1.1	1.3	1.6
	b. Non-tax revenue	2.7	2.5	2.1	1.9	2.1	1.7	1.8	2.8	1.4	1.3	1.5
5	Capital receipts	7.4	6.2	4.9	3.5	3.4	6.1	7.0	5.2	6.0	5.5	5.1
	a. Market borrowings (net)	3.1	1.6	2.9	2.7	2.6	4.4	6.1	4.2	5.4	4.9	4.3
	b. Disinvestment receipts	0.6	0.1	0.0	0.0	0.8	0.0	0.4	0.3	0.2	0.2	0.5
6	Total receipts	16.7	15.6	14.3	13.5	14.3	15.7	15.8	15.4	14.3	14.2	14.4
7	Revenue expenditure	12.8	11.9	11.9	12.0	11.9	14.1	14.1	13.4	12.8	12.6	12.6
	a. Interest payments	4.4	3.9	3.6	3.5	3.4	3.4	3.3	3.0	3.0	3.2	3.3
	b. Subsidies (I to iv)	1.6	1.4	1.3	1.3	1.4	2.3	2.2	2.2	2.4	2.6	2.0
	(i) Food	0.9	0.8	0.6	0.6	0.6	0.8	0.9	0.8	0.8	0.8	0.8
	(ii) Fertilizers	0.4	0.5	0.5	0.6	0.7	1.4	0.9	0.8	0.8	0.7	0.6
	(iii) Petroleum	0.2	0.1	0.1	0.1	0.1	0.1	0.2	0.5	0.8	1.0	0.6
	(iv) Others	0.0	0.0	0.1	0.1	0.1	0.1	0.1	0.1	0.1	0.1	0.1

(Table 8 Contd)

(Table 8 Contd)

8 Capital expenditure	3.8	3.5	1.8	1.6	2.4	1.6	1.7	2.0	1.8	1.7	2.0
a. Capital outlay	1.2	1.6	1.5	1.4	2.1	1.4	1.5	1.7	1.5	1.5	1.8
9 Total expenditure	16.6	15.4	13.7	13.6	14.3	15.7	15.8	15.4	14.5	14.3	14.6
Memo:											
Combined (Center and States) Finances											
10 Gross fiscal deficit	8.2	7.2	6.5	5.4	4.0	8.3	6.9	6.9	7.7	7.5	6.9
11 Gross primary deficit	2.0	1.3	1.0	0.0	−1.2	3.3	2.4	2.4	3.3	2.9	2.2
12 Revenue deficit	5.7	3.6	2.7	1.3	0.2	4.3	3.2	3.2	4.3	3.7	2.9

Source: Reserve Bank of India; Union Budget documents; and Economic Advisory Council to the Prime Minister.

Notes: Data for 2012–13 and 2013–14 pertain to revised and budget estimates, respectively. Figures in parenthesis are provisional estimates.

*: GFD including off-budget liabilities.

actual cash outgo on subsidies and exclude the expenditure covered through the issuance of bonds during 2005–09, especially in 2008–09.

The demand for oil is generally adjudged to be relatively price inelastic. In the Indian context, the problem has been compounded by the relatively sticky administered prices. However, estimates in this paper show that demand for oil does respond to prices in a significant manner. The estimated price elasticity of demand for petrol is (–) 0.66, for diesel is (–) 0.36 and for kerosene oil is (–) 0.54 as shown in Annex Table 1 (Annex 1). The price elasticity estimates for India in this paper are comparable to those of other countries: according to the four literature surveys covered in Hamilton (2008), the long-run price elasticity of demand for gasoline is (–) 0.6 to (–) 0.9. Given the estimated elasticities for India, and also the significant amount of under-recoveries, it is evident that had domestic prices reflected movements in international prices, there would have been some demand response, along with some expenditure switching leading to suppressed demand for other commodities. Furthermore, there would have been a beneficial impact on the fiscal balance, and lower crowding out of the private sector. Moreover, lower oil consumption demand would have led to lower oil imports and hence some containment of the CAD. We can use the estimated price elasticity to illustrate the likely impact on the CAD by focusing on diesel, which accounts for the bulk—almost 45%—of domestic petroleum consumption. During 2011–12 and 2012–13, the under-recoveries in the case of diesel are estimated to be around ₹11 per liter[2] (around 25% of the actual prevailing prices). If the diesel prices had been raised to eliminate the under-recoveries, then the estimated price elasticity of 0.36 suggests that diesel consumption would have been around 9% lower. This would have then lowered overall imports and the CAD by around 0.5% of GDP each in 2011–12 and 2012–13, a sizable impact.

In contrast to the upward trend in revenue expenditure, capital outlays of the Centre were broadly stagnant over this period at around 1.5% of GDP; see Table 8. Empirical evidence indicates that fiscal multipliers for government capital outlays exceed government consumption expenditure in India in the long run as in many other countries (Jain and Kumar 2013). According to Tapsoba (2013), the fiscal multiplier for government consumption is unity in the first year, but then turns negative and the long-run impact

2. Total domestic consumption of diesel was 65 million tonnes (MT) in 2011–12 and 69 MT in 2012–13, and the corresponding under-recoveries were ₹812 billion and ₹921 billion (Petroleum Planning and Analysis Cell, http://ppac.org.in/). Thus, the under-recovery was around ₹13 per kg or ₹11 per liter.

is also negative; in contrast, the first-year and the long-run multipliers for government investment are more than unity. These multiplier estimates, in conjunction with the actual stimulus nature, would suggest that higher revenue expenditures provided only short-lived boost to activity, while higher capital outlays would have had a more durable impact on economic activity. Thus, the quality of the fiscal stimulus in the aftermath of the NAFC imparted volatility of the growth path. Had ample fiscal buffers been there prior to the crisis, capital outlays could have been increased significantly, providing more durable support to the economy.

On the revenue side, gross tax collections have declined, as could be expected given the weakness in growth. Interestingly, the ratio of direct taxes—both income tax and corporate tax—to GDP has been broadly unchanged from 2007–08, but the pre-crisis upward trend has been halted. The decline in tax/GDP ratio is, therefore, on account of indirect taxes, especially excise collections, reflecting initially the drastic reduction in tax rates as part of stimulus measures, and later, the sharp slowdown of the manufacturing sector. While the CENVAT rate was increased to 10% in the Union Budget 2010–11 (February 2011) and further to 12% in the Union Budget 2011–12 (March 2012), it was still below the pre-NAFC level of 14%.

Given the actual growth outturn, it is apparent that stimulus measures were higher than necessary, and the need for the second and the third packages is debatable, as Finance Minister Chidambaram himself noted in April 2013.[3] Similarly, as the Economic Advisory Council to the Prime Minister (2013) observed, the recovery in growth was grossly underestimated initially, which had an adverse impact on adjustments in the monetary and fiscal stance in 2009–10 and 2010–11 and on inflation: "In retrospect, we could have tightened monetary conditions much earlier, and rolled back the tax incentives at least one full year earlier" (Economic Advisory Council to the Prime Minister 2013: 3). Moreover, the quality of the fiscal stimulus, with its focus on revenue expenditure/tax cuts and stagnant capital outlays, added to demand pressures. These demand pressures were mirrored in high inflation; and, negative real deposit rates, on the back of high inflation, contributed to higher gold imports and higher CAD. Similarly, the incomplete pass-through of high international crude prices to domestic petroleum prices dampened the expenditure adjustment effect, which could have reduced oil imports and hence reduced the pressure on the CAD—an issue which we discuss in Section 4.

3. Remarks at the Peterson Institute for International Economics in Washington, D.C., on April 19, 2013, available at http://www.iie.com/events/event_detail.cfm?EventID=275.

Saving–Investment Balance: Private Sector Crowding Out

The worsening of fiscal balances was mirrored in the deterioration in public savings from 5% of GDP in 2007–08 to 1.3% in 2011–12, largely on account of government administration. Thus, with the decline in both public and private corporate savings, the overall savings rate fell from 36.8% in 2007–08 to 30.8% in 2011–12, with the large chunk of decline occurring in 2011–12; see Table 6. On the investment side, public and private corporate investment fell by 7.7 percentage points between 2007–08 and 2011–12, but the strong increase in household investment (reflecting the increase in physical savings in gold and property) was effective in reducing the decline in the overall investment rate from 38.1% to 35.0%. The decline in the investment rate during 2008–12 at 3.1% of GDP was, thus, less than that of 6.0% in domestic savings, in turn mirrored in the significant widening of the CAD.

Since households are net savers, while the private corporate sector and the public sector are net users of financial savings, a more analytical way of looking at the S–I trends is to examine the trends in net balances of these three sectors. The household sector's net financial savings declined from 11.6% of GDP in 2007–08 to 8.0% in 2011–12; the public sector's net S–I deficit increased from (–) 3.9% to (–) 6.6% over this period. Thus, the net financial savings of the household sector that could become available to the private corporate sector (after taking into account the draft of the resources by the public sector) fell from an average of 6.3% of GDP during 2003–08 to just 2.7% during 2008–12; these numbers suggest significant crowding out of the private sector in the post-NAFC period, which then had an adverse impact on investment activity. Arguably, the higher fiscal stimulus directly did crowd out the private corporate sector. Furthermore, the stimulus added to inflationary pressures, which then led to negative real interest rates, greater demand for gold and lower household financial savings. If the fiscal stimulus had been moderate, then arguably interest rates for the corporate sector could have declined more than they did and that would have also provided an incentive for higher investment.

In this context, a valid counter-argument is that there was no crowding out: the higher public S–I gap since 2008–09 just reflects the fact that the government was responding to the collapse in the corporate sector investment. This counter-narrative would be true if the public S–I gap had increased on account of higher public investment. However, the public investment rate actually declined from its 2007–08 level as shown in Table 6. The increase in the public S–I gap, thus, is attributable to the decline in public savings and only a part of it is attributable to explicit stimulus measures (the reduction in excise duty). A large part of the decline in public savings owes to the increase in subsidies, especially oil; cash subsidies increased by one percentage point of GDP in 2008–09, but the increase was almost three percentage points once bonds issued in lieu of cash subsidies are also included. Higher government subsidies clearly were not a response to lower corporate investment.

But, why has corporate investment not picked up, even though the public S–I gap has narrowed since 2010–11? First, the public S–I gap is still higher than the pre-NAFC level. Second, and more importantly, the households' financial savings rate continues to decline. The policy bottlenecks alluded to earlier and monetary measures have also impacted corporate investment. The high CAD increased external vulnerability. Overall, the combined impact of the increase in the public S–I gap (given that it was driven by subsidies and lower revenues), and lower household financial savings reduced the availability of domestic resources to the corporate sector. The impact on corporate investment was also exacerbated by domestic policy bottlenecks, monetary measures and limited space for further external finance.

Quantifying the Growth Slowdown

The discussion above suggests that the accommodative monetary and fiscal policies put in place after the NAFC boosted growth during 2009–11, and then the phased reversal of these policies, partial so far in the case of fiscal policy, contributed to the growth slowdown during 2011–12 and 2012–13. Annex 2 empirically assesses the impact of monetary policy and global conditions on domestic growth. The results show that an increase of 100 bps in the real interest rate leads to a reduction of around 30 bps in GDP growth (non-agricultural non-community services GDP) with a lag of two quarters; see Annex Table 2. As regards global demand, a one percentage point reduction in global exports reduces domestic growth by almost 13 bps, while one percentage point reduction in global GDP growth reduces domestic growth by almost 50 bps. The estimated equations track actual growth relatively well for the 2003–08 period, but deviations are observed since then. The estimated equation under-predicts the actual outturn during 2009–10 by around 3.5 percentage points and overpredicts by around three percentage points on average during 2011–13; see Figure 6. Given that the model includes the monetary policy and the global demand impacts, one potential reason for the deviation since 2009 is the role of the fiscal policy, which has not been included in the explanatory variables.

FIGURE 6. Real GDP Growth

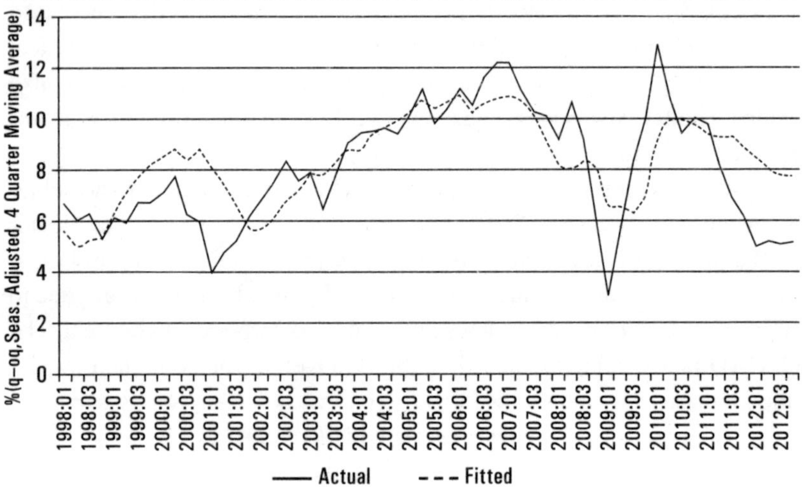

Source: Reserve Bank of India and the Authors' Estimates.

India's structural primary deficit increased by 4.0 percentage points of GDP in 2008–09 (IMF 2013a), reflecting both the stimulus measures in response to the fiscal crisis as well as other measures like the implementation of the Pay Commission award. The structural primary deficit subsequently fell, reflecting the fiscal consolidation measures, but the decline has been modest; the withdrawal of the stimulus was only 1.4 percentage points during the three-year period 2010–13 or an annual average of 0.35 percentage point of GDP. Assuming that the fiscal multiplier for India is similar (around 0.5) to that for other EMEs (Bi et al. 2013), the stimulus of 4% of GDP added almost two percentage points to the growth in 2009–10. In contrast to the large stimulus, the withdrawal of the stimulus was gradual and remains incomplete. The annual fiscal consolidation of 0.35% of GDP during 2010–11 to 2012–13, combined with the multiplier of 0.5, would suggest an adverse impact of less than 20 bps per annum on growth. Even if the fiscal multiplier is assumed to be higher at unity, the annual growth impact would be around 35 bps, abstracting from the lags. Thus, fiscal stimulus can largely explain the high growth in 2009–10, but the subsequent consolidation can explain only a very modest part of the slowdown. One view is that the growth gap during the 2011–13 period appears to be the outcome of the policy bottlenecks noted earlier—such as obtaining environmental permissions, fuel linkages, or carrying out land acquisition, which led to stalling of a number of large projects, and discouraged new investment (Bhalla 2013a). However, it is not clear as to whether these factors were more binding in the post-NAFC period vis-à-vis the pre-NAFC period and, if yes, to what extent.

4. The External Sector: Current Account

Large CADs in the 1980s, averaging around 2% of GDP, and their financing with debt flows was one of the factors contributing to the balance of payments crisis in the early 1990s. Since then and until the recent episode, India's CAD had remained modest, averaging 0.6% of GDP during 1991–92 to 2007–08. This was the result of consistent structural reforms throughout the period, including an overhaul of the external trade and payments regime, practice of a flexible but managed exchange rate, accompanied by judicious management of the capital account. Furthermore, the capital account was characterized by a healthy financing mix of non-debt flows and stable debt flows. Excess capital flows were absorbed by the Reserve Bank on its balance sheet leading to a large increase in foreign exchange reserves, as also improving the quality of its balance sheet with high-quality foreign assets. Foreign exchange interventions were appropriately sterilized through a mix of instruments (Mohan and Kapur 2011). The acquisition of foreign assets, apart from providing comfort to the external sector, was also important from the viewpoint of expansion of the Reserve Bank's balance sheet to meet the economy's monetary and credit needs (Mohan et al. 2013).

Against this backdrop of a healthy and vibrant external sector, widening of the CAD to 4.8% of GDP in 2012–13 has attracted a lot of concern (Subbarao 2013a). The widening reflects a variety of factors. First, sluggish global growth since 2009 has impacted India's export markets. As estimates reported later show, given India's income elasticities for exports and imports, the sharper decline in external demand vis-à-vis domestic demand could have contributed to the widening of the CAD. Second, despite sluggish global growth, international commodity prices have remained at relatively elevated levels, supported by ultra accommodative monetary policies of the advanced economies, abundant global liquidity, and near zero interest rates. India, being a net importer, especially of crude oil, has been hit hard. Net oil imports, already high at 4.1% of GDP in 2007–08, rose to 5.9% by 2012–13. Third, domestic supply and policy constraints led to increase in imports of coal—from around 0.5% of GDP during 2004–08 to 0.9% in 2011–12—notwithstanding large domestic stocks. Similarly, exports have suffered from the restrictions on iron ore mining activity since 2010–11.

Fourth, gold imports increased significantly from around 1.5% of GDP during 2004–08 to 3.0% in 2011–12 and 2012–13—high domestic inflation and negative real deposit rates on the one hand and sharp gains in international gold prices and expectations of further gains on the other hand seem to have made gold an attractive asset. Given the oil and gold trends, the non-oil non-gold current account balance (a surplus of around 4%) and the non-oil non-gold trade balance (a deficit of around 2%) have been broadly unchanged between 2007–08 and 2012–13; see Table 9. It is, however, important to note that the deterioration in overall trade balance as well as the non-oil non-gold trade balance had started well before the NAFC. The high growth phase of 2003–08 had led to a very significant increase in the trade deficit from 2.2% of GDP in 2003–04 to 7.4% in 2007–08 and further to 10.6% in 2012–13; the non-oil non-gold trade balance moved from a surplus of 1.6% in 2003–04 to a deficit of 1.9% in 2007–08 and, which as noted above, remained around these levels till 2012–13. The movements in the trade balance were mirrored in the current account balance over this period, although the impact was muted somewhat by the upward movement in net invisibles surplus (from 4.5% in 2003–04 to 6.1% in 2007–08). In the post-crisis period, the net invisibles surplus has been range-bound around its 2007–08 level and thus has not provided incremental support to the Balance of Payments (BoP).

Fifth, the real appreciation of the rupee might have also played a role. Here, the analysis is somewhat complicated by the divergences in alternative available measures of the real effective exchange rate (REER) as shown in Figure 7. For example, the RBI index exhibits a real depreciation of 4% between March 2008 and March 2010, while the BIS index exhibits a modest appreciation of 1%; in sharp contrast, the OECD and the IMF indices show a substantial real appreciation of 12–14% between March 2008 and March 2010. One reason for the difference is that the RBI index uses WPI inflation for India and CPI inflation for partner countries, whereas the OECD/IMF measures use CPI inflation for all countries. Since Indian CPI inflation has been higher than WPI inflation in the past few years, the OECD/IMF indices show a higher real appreciation. According to Bayoumi et al. (2011) and Chinn (2006), WPI- and unit-labor cost (ULC)-based REERs may be better indicators of price competitiveness than CPI-based measures. We discuss this issue further in Annex 3.

Sixth, the financing of the elevated CAD is also an issue. Inward FDI flows jumped significantly during 2006–09, but have since then more than halved from 3.4% of GDP in 2008–09 to 1.4% in 2012–13. Portfolio flows and debt flows financed almost two-thirds of the CAD in 2012–13.

TABLE 9. Balance of Payments

(% to GDP)

	Item	2003–04	2004–05	2005–06	2006–07	2007–08	2008–09	2009–10	2010–11	2011–12	2012–13
1	Merchandize exports	10.7	11.8	12.6	13.6	13.4	15.4	13.4	14.6	16.5	16.6
	a. Oil	0.6	1.0	1.4	2.0	2.3	2.2	2.1	2.4	3.0	3.3
2	Merchandize imports	13.0	16.5	18.8	20.1	20.8	25.2	22.0	22.3	26.7	27.3
	a. Oil	3.3	4.1	5.3	6.0	6.4	7.6	6.4	6.2	8.3	9.2
	b. Gold	1.1	1.5	1.3	1.5	1.3	1.7	2.1	2.4	3.0	2.9
	c. Non-oil non-gold	8.6	10.9	12.3	12.6	13.0	15.8	13.5	13.7	15.4	15.1
	d. Net oil imports	2.8	3.2	3.9	4.0	4.1	5.4	4.3	3.8	5.3	5.9
3	Trade balance	–2.2	–4.7	–6.2	–6.5	–7.4	–9.7	–8.7	–7.6	–10.1	–10.6
	a. Non-oil balance	0.5	–1.5	–2.3	–2.5	–3.2	–4.4	–4.3	–3.9	–4.8	–4.7
	b. Non-oil non-gold balance	1.6	–0.0	–1.0	–1.0	–1.9	–2.7	–2.2	–1.5	–1.8	–1.8
4	Invisibles, net	4.5	4.3	5.0	5.5	6.1	7.5	5.9	4.9	6.0	5.8
	a. Services, net	1.6	2.1	2.8	3.1	3.1	4.4	2.6	2.9	3.4	3.5
	b. Private transfers, net	3.5	2.8	2.9	3.1	3.4	3.6	3.8	3.1	3.4	3.5
	c. Investment income, net	–0.6	–0.6	–0.6	–0.7	–0.4	–0.5	–0.5	–1.0	–0.9	–1.2
5	Current account balance	2.3	–0.3	–1.2	–1.0	–1.3	–2.3	–2.8	–2.7	–4.2	–4.8
	a. non-oil balance	5.0	2.8	2.7	3.0	2.9	3.1	1.5	1.1	1.1	1.1
	b. Non-oil non-gold balance	6.1	4.3	4.0	4.6	4.2	4.8	3.6	3.5	4.1	4.1
6	Capital flows, net	2.7	3.9	3.1	4.8	8.6	0.6	3.8	3.6	3.6	4.8
	a. Capital inflows	12.3	13.7	17.3	24.6	35.4	25.8	25.3	29.2	25.6	25.6
	b. Capital outflows	9.6	9.8	14.3	19.8	26.8	25.2	21.5	25.6	21.9	20.7
7	Foreign investment, net	2.2	1.8	1.9	1.6	3.5	0.7	3.7	2.3	2.1	2.5
	a. FDI inward	0.7	0.8	1.1	2.4	2.8	3.4	2.4	1.5	1.8	1.5
	b. FDI outward	0.3	0.3	0.7	1.6	1.5	1.6	1.1	1.0	0.6	0.4
	c. Portfolio	1.8	1.3	1.5	0.7	2.2	–1.1	2.4	1.8	0.9	1.5

(Table 9 Contd)

(Table 9 Contd)

	Item	2003–04	2004–05	2005–06	2006–07	2007–08	2008–09	2009–10	2010–11	2011–12	2012–13
8	Debt flows, net	–0.1	1.4	1.3	3.1	3.3	1.0	1.2	1.8	1.6	1.7
	a. External assistance	–0.4	0.3	0.2	0.2	0.2	0.2	0.2	0.3	0.1	0.1
	b. External commercial borrowings	–0.5	0.8	0.3	1.7	1.8	0.5	0.2	0.7	0.5	0.5
	c. Short-term trade credits	0.2	0.5	0.4	0.7	1.3	–0.2	0.6	0.6	0.4	1.2
	d. Non-resident deposits	0.6	–0.1	0.3	0.5	0.0	0.3	0.2	0.2	0.6	0.8
9	Others	0.6	0.7	–0.1	0.1	1.8	–1.0	–1.1	–0.5	–0.1	–0.2
10	Overall balance	5.1	3.6	1.8	3.9	7.4	–1.6	1.0	0.8	–0.7	0.2
	Memo:										
	Current account balance (US $ billion)	14	–2	–10	–10	–16	–28	–38	–46	–78	–88
	Capital flows, net (US $ billion)	17	28	25	45	107	7	52	62	68	89
										End-March	
	External debt	17.2	18.1	16.8	17.5	18.0	20.3	18.2	17.5	19.7	21.2
	Short-term debt (residual maturity)	1.6	4.3	3.1	3.7	4.4	5.2	4.6	5.0	5.7	6.7
	Import cover of forex reserves—goods and services (months)	14.0	11.6	9.5	10.2	12.0	8.4	9.3	7.9	6.1	6.0
	Forex reserves/short-term debt by residual maturity (%)	1071	441	595	546	565	438	427	346	296	237
	Foreign exchange reserves (US $ billion)	113	142	152	199	310	252	279	305	294	293

Source: Reserve Bank of India; Ministry of Finance.

FIGURE 7. Real Effective Exchange Rate (REER) (2004–05=100)

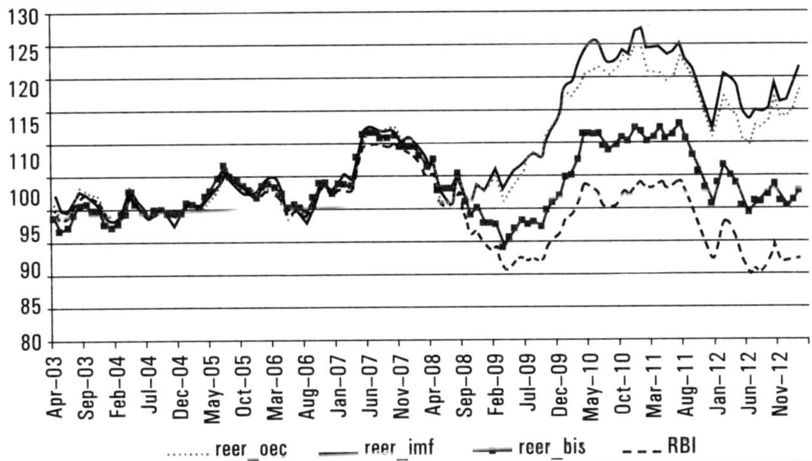

Source: Bank for International Settlements (BIS), International Monetary Fund (IMF), Organization for Economic Co-operation and Development (OECD), and Reserve Bank of India.

The stock of external commercial borrowings (including trade credits and non-residents investment in domestic securities) has increased multi-fold over the past decade from around US $30 billion (5–7% of GDP) during the four-year period 2000–04 to US $115 billion (9.2% of GDP) in 2007–08 and further to US $225 billion (12.2% of GDP) in 2012–13. While the jump between 2003–04 and 2007–08 could perhaps be largely attributed to the sustained high growth of the Indian economy, the increase since then has occurred in an environment of slowing domestic growth. The unconventional monetary policies in the advanced economies made such borrowings quite attractive compared to domestic sources. Moreover, there has been a phased liberalization of the policy regime on the ceilings in regard to external borrowings and investments by non-residents in domestic securities. Concomitantly, high external borrowings might have also been the outcome of the crowding out of the private sector in view of the fiscal stimulus and the high government borrowings since the NAFC.

Exports and Imports: Role of the Exchange Rate

The widening of the CAD over the past five years, as noted earlier, reflects a sluggish global economy, elevated international commodity prices, higher gold imports, plateauing of the invisibles surplus, and domestic supply constraints that have led to higher imports/lower exports. The role of the exchange rate has, however, attracted some debate. As the Economic Advisory Council to the Prime Minister (2013) notes, the conventional approach to an enlarged CAD would be to allow the currency to adjust downwards. This adjustment, they argued, might not lead to the expected changes in both imports and exports in view of: (a) large gold and oil imports and their relative insensitivity to exchange rate movements and (b) much of exports are exported as part of supply chains and in such situations large depreciation does not escape notice and is often neutralized by price re-negotiations. "It is therefore not surprising that the substantial depreciation of 20 per cent in the external value of the rupee (against the US dollar) did not boost exports," whereas "China was able to register 14 per cent growth in the dollar value of exports in December 2012 and as much as 25 and 22 per cent growth in January and February 2013. The Chinese yuan appreciated against the dollar over the past year by about 3 per cent" (Economic Advisory Council to the Prime Minister 2013: 33–34). A few comments on this issue are appropriate.

First, although the rupee depreciated by more than 20% in nominal terms between mid-2011 and end-2012, a large part of it offset the higher inflation differentials. Second, based on US dollar terms data, India's exports indeed performed poorly vis-à-vis China in 2012; however, in order to assess the exchange rate–export linkage, it is appropriate to take a medium-term perspective, given the lags with which exchange rate movements impact trade volumes. Table 10 shows that India's average export growth since the NAFC is comparable to that of China, whereas it was much lower in the pre-NAFC period. As regards the exchange rate, the Indian REER recorded an average annual depreciation of 1.0% during 2008–12, compared to an annual average appreciation of 4.1% in Chinese currency (both based on the BIS data). Given that the global economy is a common factor to both the economies, the REER movements favored India in the post-NAFC period and this appears to be reflected in the relative export performance.

Third, weak domestic supply response due to domestic rigidities, which are now well recognized, and which had an adverse impact on the domestic investment climate, could have offset the expected impact of depreciation. Estimates of single equation export demand functions implicitly assume elastic export supplies. Finally, the counterfactual—what would have been the path of exports had there been no real depreciation in 2012—might be the appropriate benchmark to judge the efficacy of exchange rate. Moreover, other policies such as taxation changes as well as government efforts toward product- and market-diversification also play an important role.

TABLE 10. Export Growth: China and India

(%)

	Volume of exports		*Value of exports (US $ terms)*					
	Total exports		*Total exports*		*Non-oil exports*		*Variation in REER*	
Year	*China*	*India*	*China*	*India*	*China*	*India*	*China*	*India*
2003	20.0	13.9	34.6	17.1	34.5	16.1	-7.1	-0.2
2004	18.2	14.7	35.4	30.0	35.9	26.7	-3.0	1.1
2005	24.5	12.3	28.4	30.0	28.0	20.4	-1.1	3.5
2006	24.2	10.5	27.2	22.3	27.5	17.7	1.3	-0.8
2007	19.3	16.4	25.6	23.1	25.8	18.2	3.7	6.5
2008	8.2	5.0	17.3	29.7	17.0	34.5	8.5	-4.8
2009	-10.7	3.3	-15.9	-15.2	-15.9	-17.9	4.4	-5.4
2010	28.4	15.4	31.3	37.3	31.4	37.5	-0.7	11.7
2011	9.4	13.8	20.3	33.8	20.3	31.0	2.5	-0.4
2012	5.7	1.2	7.9	-2.0	8.0	-8.3	6.0	-6.1
Averages								
2003–07	21.2	13.6	30.3	24.5	30.3	21.0	-1.2	2.0
2008–12	8.2	7.7	12.2	16.7	12.1	15.4	4.1	-1.0

Source: International Financial Statistics, IMF; World Economic Outlook, IMF; Bank for International Settlements.

Note: REER data are based on Bank for International Settlements (BIS) indices.

Value Added in Exports

As Rangarajan and Mishra (2013) and Economic Advisory Council to the Prime Minister (2013) note, the imported intermediate content of exports can dampen the competitive effects of depreciations. In this context, the joint OECD-WTO data on trade statistics on a value added basis are useful and relevant. These data, inter alia, provide the domestic value-added embodied in exports as a percentage of exports. This indicator provides a simple measure that illustrates how much value-added is generated throughout the economy for a given unit of exports. The lower the ratio, the higher the foreign content and so the higher the importance of imports to exports (OECD 2013).

For aggregate exports, the OECD-WTO data indicate that the value added ratio for India is higher than many Asian EMEs as can be seen in Table 11. The ratio averaged 82.5% for India during 1995–2009 (averaged over the five data points: 1995, 2000, 2005, 2008, and 2009). India's ratio was above that of European countries and the emerging Asian countries such as China (73.4%), Korea (64.3%), Malaysia (59.8%), Philippines (59.5%), and Thailand (64.9%). The major non-oil exporting countries with ratios above India during the sample included: Australia (87.0%), Japan (87.1%), United States (89.1%), Argentina (88.5%), Brazil (89.1%), and Indonesia (83.3%). Between 1995 and 2009, the value added ratio declined for India as

TABLE 11. Value Added Export Ratio: Total Domestic Value Added Share of Gross Exports (%)

Country	*1995*	*2000*	*2005*	*2008*	*2009*
Australia	88.2	86.5	87.0	86.1	87.5
Canada	76.5	69.2	74.9	78.7	80.5
France	82.2	75.5	75.2	72.8	75.3
Germany	81.3	75.6	74.4	72.2	73.4
Israel	71.4	66.2	62.1	65.1	69.4
Italy	78.1	74.7	72.9	77.2	79.9
Japan	93.2	90.1	86.3	80.7	85.2
Korea	76.3	67.1	62.3	56.6	59.4
Mexico	73.5	68.2	69.3	69.4	69.7
Netherlands	65.3	61.8	65.6	63.4	64.1
Spain	79.4	73.0	72.2	75.1	79.3
Switzerland	76.8	72.2	70.7	69.6	71.5
Turkey	88.8	84.7	79.2	73.7	78.2
United Kingdom	79.3	81.6	79.8	81.1	82.7
United States	91.6	91.1	88.9	85.4	88.7
Argentina	91.0	89.9	87.2	86.3	87.9
Brazil	90.3	88.5	87.0	88.5	91.0
China	88.1	81.2	63.6	66.7	67.4
Chinese Taipei	64.2	64.6	57.8	52.2	58.5
India	90.4	87.2	80.5	76.3	78.1
Indonesia	85.3	80.7	82.2	82.6	85.6
Malaysia	59.7	57.0	58.5	61.9	62.1
Philippines	69.1	54.1	54.4	58.3	61.6
Russian Federation	89.3	87.5	91.8	92.6	93.1
Saudi Arabia	98.0	98.2	97.0	97.1	97.0
South Africa	88.3	83.9	83.4	78.9	83.5
Thailand	70.2	65.2	61.5	62.2	65.5
EU27	90.5	87.4	86.5	84.9	86.4

Source: OECD (available at http://stats.oecd.org/Index.aspx?DataSetCode=TIVA_OECD_WTO).

for many other countries. The decline for India at 12.3 percentage points was less than that of China (20.8 percentage points) and Korea (16.9 percentage points), and was higher than other Asian EMEs.

The trends visible for aggregate exports carry through for most manufacturing industries, that is, the domestic value added ratio is higher for India for most manufacturing industries vis-à-vis other major economies. This is true for major industries such as food products, "textiles, leather and footwear," chemicals, metals, machinery and equipment, electrical equipment, transport equipment. The only category for which India lags the other economies in the manufacturing is the residual manufacturing group (manufacturing n.e.c.; recycling); this could perhaps be reflecting higher exports of oil products, on the back of the increase in domestic refining capacity, and the concomitant increase in crude oil imports. The ratio for this group declined from 85.7% in 1995 to 50.9% in 2008 and 2009. Interestingly, it is in the exports of services that the ratios for India are relatively lower than other economies (even though ratios for services' activities are higher than manufacturing activities).

These data would suggest that for India, given the relatively lower level of imported content of inputs in exports, the hypothesis that exchange rate depreciation can dampen the competitive effects of depreciation should not be strongly binding, at least in a cross-country perspective. Even as the value-added ratio has declined since the mid-1990s, the ratio for India is well ahead of many countries, especially the regional peers. Thus, if the exchange rate channel is effective in other countries, these data would suggest its efficacy in the Indian context as well.

Price and Income Elasticities: Cross-Country Empirical Evidence

As Table 12 shows, cross-country analysis broadly confirms that both prices and demand conditions have a significant impact on exports and imports. For a sample of developing and industrial countries, average long-run price and income elasticities are estimated at (–) 1.0 and 1.5, respectively, for both exports and imports (Senhadji 1998; Senhadji and Montenegro 1999). These findings are supported by studies, focusing on individual countries or for a more homogeneous group of countries; for example, Hooper et al. (2000) for G-7, Chinn (2013) for Japan, Bayoumi et al. (2011) for euro area, Thorbecke and Atsuyki (2012) for Germany, and Aziz and Li (2008) for China.

Elasticities based on aggregate trade flows could be biased as aggregate trade flows may have feedback effects on exchange rates (Auboin and Ruta 2013). Therefore, recent studies have focused on firm-wise behavior to estimate elasticities. For example, Berman et al. (2012) use a French firm-level data set and find that high-performance firms react to depreciation by increasing significantly more their markup and by increasing less their export volume and they find an average export elasticity of (–) 0.4 with respect to the exchange rate. Since aggregate exports are concentrated in high-productivity firms, heterogeneous pricing-to-market may partly explain the weak impact of exchange rate movements on aggregate exports. Using Chinese firm-level data, Tang and Zhang (2012) estimate an exchange rate elasticity of (–) 0.4 for exports (Table 12).

Currency undervaluation stimulates economic growth, particularly for developing countries (Rodrik 2008). Export surges in developing countries tend to be preceded by a large real depreciation, which is associated with significant reallocation of resources toward the export sector, especially into new products and markets (Freund and Pierola 2012). Real appreciation

TABLE 12. Income and Price Elasticities of Exports and Imports

Study	Period	Country coverage	Exports		Imports	
			Income elasticity	Price elasticity	Income elasticity	Price elasticity
1	2	3	4	5	6	7
Senhadji (1998)	1960–93	60 developing and industrial countries			Mean: 1.5 Min: 0.0 Max: 5.5	Mean: 1.1 Min: 0.0 Max: 6.7
Senhadji and Montenegro (1999)	1960–93	53 developing and industrial countries	Mean: 1.5 Min: 0.2 Max: 4.3	Mean: –1.0 Min: –0.0 Max: –4.7		
Hooper et al. (2000)	1956–94	Canada	1.1	–0.9	1.4	0.9
		France	1.5	–0.2	1.6	0.4
		Germany	1.4	–0.3	1.5	0.1
		Italy	1.6	–0.9	1.4	0.4
		Japan	1.1		0.9	0.3
		UK	1.1	–1.6	2.2	0.6
		US	0.8	–1.5	1.8	0.3
Aziz and Li (2008)	1995–2006	China	3.8	–1.6	1.3	0.9
Bayoumi et al. (2011)	1980–2009	Euro area	1.7–1.9	0.0 to –0.6		
		Extra-euro area	1.6–1.9	–0.1 to –0.3		
		Intra-euro area	1.4–1.5	+0.4 to –1.3		
Tang and Zhang (2012)	2000–06	China (firm-level data)		–0.4		
Thorbecke and Atsuyki (2012)	1980–2009	Germany	0.7–2.6	–0.6 to –1.0		
Berman et al. (2013)	1995–2005	France (firm-level data)		–0.4		
Chinn (2013)	1990–2012	Japan	1.0–4.0	–0.3 to –0.7	–2.9 to –6.7	0.2–1.0

Source: Respective studies.

leads to a deterioration in the current account balance, savings, and exports, and the impact is more pronounced in developing countries (Kappler et al. 2013). Export markets are characterized by the well-known hysteresis phenomenon (Baldwin and Krugman 1989): appreciation over some period of time could lead to loss of markets and this impact could persist even if the exchange rate returns to its neutral level after a period of appreciation. Both the United States and the United Kingdom experienced such effects in the 1980s and potentially such effects can be larger for countries like India with relatively greater share of low-tech exports.

Overall, as Auboin and Ruta (2013) conclude, currency undervaluation is generally found to have a positive short-term impact on exports, but the persistence of these effects appears to be limited to developing countries. Price elasticities of exports are statistically significant, but the magnitudes differ across countries and, as some studies show, are sensitive to the choice of variables. However, it also needs to be recognized that the exchange rate is just one of the factors that impact export performance. For example, sector-specific policies, effective industrial policy and fortuitous timing are more critical factors in the phenomenal growth in China's exports during 2000–07, although China's exchange rate policy also had a role (Berger and Martin 2013).

Recent Indian Evidence

Recent studies present mixed evidence on the efficacy of the exchange rate on exports in the Indian context (Rangarajan and Mishra 2013), although studies during the 1990s generally found high and statistically significant elasticities (for example, Joshi and Little 1994). Aziz and Chenoy (2012), using quarterly data for 1996–2008, find a positive and statistically significant impact of external demand (real GDP growth in partner countries) on exports; the estimated coefficient was 4.6. However, the coefficient on the REER at (–) 0.6, although with the correct sign, was statistically insignificant. None of the sub-sectors in manufacturing, including the low, value-added labor-intensive segments such as textiles, leather, and gems and jewellery were found to display any statistically significant sensitivity to the exchange rate. Rangarajan and Patra (unpublished), discussed in Rangarajan and Mishra (2013), find qualitatively similar results. IMF (2012), quoted in Rangarajan and Mishra (2013), finds negative and statistically significant impact of REER on exports—the long-run elasticity is estimated at (–) 0.1 for the full sample period (1982–2011) and somewhat higher at (–) 0.2 for the post-1990s period. The corresponding long-run elasticities on external demand were found to be 2.9 and 2.2 for the respective periods.

Although these studies suggest a much larger role played by external demand than exchange rates in determining exports, there are three possible explanations as to why existing studies fail to find strong export–exchange rate elasticities (Rangarajan and Mishra 2013). First, it is hard to estimate the elasticities using macrodata—exports and exchange rates are highly endogenous. Second, the imported intermediate content of exports can dampen the competitive effects of depreciations. Third, macroequations do not allow the export–exchange rate elasticity to vary depending on the position of the aggregate supply curve. Nonetheless, as they note, policy should be directed toward ensuring that the rupee does not appreciate in real terms and further worsen the trade balance, while also factoring in the potential impact of depreciation on capital flows and balance sheets of corporate and financial institutions.

Against this backdrop of cross-country evidence and the mixed evidence on the efficacy of the exchange rate on exports in the recent studies on India, we revisit the issue and estimate export and import demand equations (Annex 3). Empirical results show that both external demand (world real exports) and the REER have the expected impact on India's exports. Annual estimates using data for 1980–81 to 2007–08 show that an increase of 1% in world real exports is associated with an increase of 1.1–1.4% in India's exports in the long run. As regards the real exchange rate, estimates suggest that 10% real appreciation leads to a reduction of almost 2.1–6.5% in the volume of exports in the long run, see Annex Table 3.

Moving to estimates based on the post-reforms sample (1996–97 to 2007–08) and using quarterly data, the elasticity with respect to external demand is in a range of 1.6–1.9 (when world exports are used as an indicator of external demand) and 2.6–3.6 (world GDP as an indicator of external demand) across alternative estimates, somewhat higher than the annual estimates. Second, the absolute coefficient on the REER is substantially higher than the annual estimates: the coefficient is more than unity for RBI's REER and even higher for REERs of OECD and IMF, although the results are sensitive to inclusion of oil exports; see Annex Table 4 (Annex 3). Third, the results for overall exports broadly hold for exports of the major manufactured sub-groups (chemicals, manufactures, and machinery). Overall, these estimates show a stronger impact of global conditions—both demand and price factors—on India's exports and this seems consistent with the phased opening of the Indian economy to the global economy, and the process of domestic deregulation and liberalization result in a greater role for market forces. The quarterly results are, however, subject to the caveat of a shorter sample period, and the associated estimation uncertainties.

For imports, the long-run coefficients are also on the expected lines, that is, real appreciation and stronger domestic activity both contribute to higher imports. Income elasticity of imports with respect to domestic industrial GDP turns out to be around 1.55 in the long run in all the cases. Thus, the volume of imports changes more than proportionally in relation to variations in domestic demand. The coefficient on the REER ranges from 0.19 to 0.42 and, as in the case, of exports, is higher for the RBI-REER; therefore, 10% real appreciation increases imports by almost 2–4% across the various specifications; see Annex Table 6. Thus, our estimates suggest that the REER does affect India's trade performance in the expected direction.

Determinants of Gold Imports

Gold imports jumped from a monthly average of 62 tonnes during 2004–08 to 82 tonnes during 2009–13, while the increase in US dollar terms was much sharper from US$1.2 billion per month to US$4.1 billion over the same period, reflecting higher gold prices. High domestic inflation, low domestic deposit rates, bank loans for gold, the substantial increase in international gold prices, movements in the Indian rupee, and pent-up demand are potential contributors to the jump in the quantum of gold imports (Economic Advisory Council to the Prime Minister 2013; Rangarajan 2013; RBI 2013a; Vaidyanathan 1999). An econometric analysis of these potential determinants of gold demand is presented in Annex 4. The impact of gold prices on gold demand is not obvious a priori: on the one hand, as with any normal good, one would expect an increase in its price to reduce the quantity demanded, ceteris paribus; but on the other, recent price increases may increase interest in acquiring gold for the investment returns, if recent price increases are interpreted as signaling a likelihood of further increases in the future (Starr and Tran 2008). Gold is also a potential instrument for asset diversification by economic agents; therefore, movements in domestic stock prices are also included in the model. The real estate market is also a potential contributor to gold demand, and perhaps even more important than stock prices in the Indian context, but this variable is not included due to lack of time-series data.

The results indicate that higher gold prices—nominal as well as real—have a significant dampening impact on gold imports in the first few months, but have a lagged positive impact on demand for gold in the fourth/fifth month. As Annex Table 7 shows, the cumulative impact is negative, and statistically significant. Thus, both the channels discussed by Starr and Tran (2008) are seen in the Indian case, but the first impact predominates the second impact and hence gold prices have an overall negative impact on demand.

Higher domestic CPI inflation is also found to have a significant impact on gold imports, but no impact is found for WPI inflation. Estimates show that 1% increase in CPI inflation leads to an increase of 9% in gold imports in the long run. Higher domestic deposit rates, contrary to expectations, lead to more gold demand. This finding could perhaps be reflective of the fact that, over the last four years of the sample period, the real deposit rates were generally negative, notwithstanding some upward movement in nominal deposit rates. Thus, the increase in nominal deposit rates did not have the expected dampening impact on gold, as the real return on deposits was still negative; however, this hypothesis would need to be further examined. Stock market gains also lead to higher gold demand, with a lag, perhaps indicating a wealth diversification motive. Exchange rate depreciation reduces gold demand in all specifications and the effect is generally statistically significant; since the model also includes gold prices in rupee terms, which would capture the exchange rate impact indirectly, it is interesting that exchange rate depreciation has a direct additional negative impact on depreciation.

The model captures the various turning points well, although it has difficulty in explaining the increase in imports in 2010–11; (see Figure 8)—perhaps, the volatility and the uncertain economic environment in the aftermath of the NAFC could have induced more demand for gold. Overall, the results suggest that higher domestic CPI inflation and the continued negative real deposit rates could have contributed to higher gold imports, adding to

FIGURE 8. Gold Imports

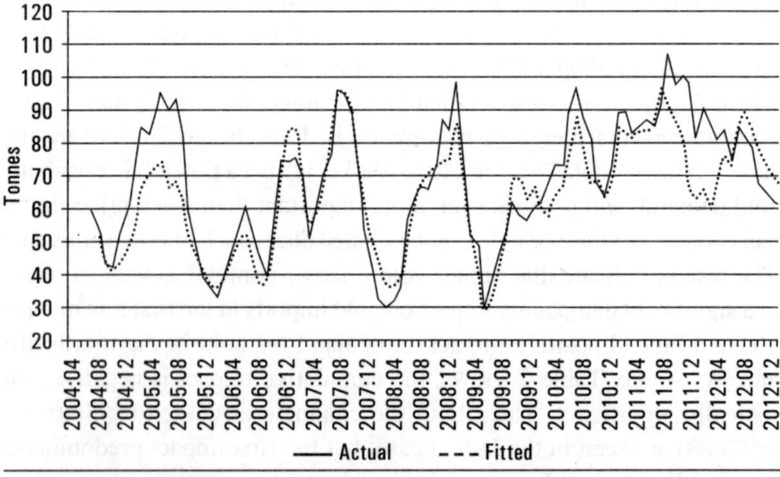

Source: Directorate General of Commercial Intelligence and Statistics (DGCI&S) and the Authors' Estimates.

the external vulnerability while also reducing domestic financial savings of households. While WPI inflation has come off from its recent highs in the past few months, CPI inflation—which is found to be related to gold imports—remains at persistently high levels. Success with inflation management and appropriate real returns on bank deposits should provide a durable solution to the surge in gold imports. As Tarapore (2013b) notes, curbing gold imports requires very attractive instruments which would be better than the return on gold—a 3% real rate plus the consumer price inflation of, say, 9% would yield a nominal return of 12% plus inflation adjustment for the capital and such an instrument would knock down the demand for gold. As the CAD and inflation come down, the cost of such an instrument would also come down.

5. Macroeconomic Management: Some Issues

External Sector

The levels of CAD during 2012–13 and the early part of 2013–14 were well above the estimates of a sustainable level, which is in the range of 2.3–2.5% of GDP (Rangarajan and Mishra 2013; RBI 2012). Estimates of sustainable CAD ought to be seen as an upper limit and not as desirable levels of CAD. Sustainable CAD estimates largely rely on the stabilization of external liabilities/GDP ratio and are better viewed as long-run solvency consistent levels. Sustainable levels can also be a challenge from the financing viewpoint, given the volatility of capital flows. Even the 2.3% estimate of the CAD requires net annual capital inflows of US$50–70 billion at present GDP levels (Rangarajan and Mishra 2013); the required magnitude of capital flows would be even higher than this estimate if the policy is to aim for some prudent build-up of foreign exchange reserves, especially in the context of no accretion to reserves since 2008.

Given the large oil and gold imports and also the large fluctuations in international oil and gold prices, the sustainable deficit needs to be reassessed. Since large fluctuations in prices of oil and gold impact the CAD significantly, it may be prudent to plan for a lower level of deficit so that in the event of large shocks to oil and gold prices, the vulnerability of the country to the widening of the CAD to large levels is contained. Against this backdrop, the proposal of Dr Y. V. Reddy to aim for an average current account balance of zero merits further consideration. Given large domestic savings, foreign savings play only a marginal role in investment and growth.

A zero average or low CAD does not mean—and is not—an argument for less current account openness. It is the openness of the economy to gross imports and exports of goods and services, and FDI inflows, rather than the volume of current account balance per se, that matters more for competition, productivity, investment, and growth. For example, China has persistently recorded high growth in the recent years, despite persistent surpluses.

Given the widening of the CAD, the policy regime with regard to debt capital flows has been liberalized to meet the external payment needs in the recent years. Some of the steps include: an increase in interest rate ceilings on foreign-currency non-resident deposits; removal of the interest rate ceiling on non-resident external rupee deposits and capping them at the same level as the domestic rupee deposits; and an increase in local-currency investment limits by non-residents; see Table 13. In the process, external sector sustainability indicators such as import cover and short-term debt to reserves recorded some deterioration (RBI 2013b). However, these and other external sector indicators still remain at comfortable levels, although their adequacy was questioned by the markets during the June–August 2013 episode.

The policy approach of opening the capital account to meet the persistently high CAD, however, potentially hinders adjustment—allowing more foreign capital might lead to real appreciation which would then itself lead

TABLE 13. Investment Limits for Foreign Institutional Investors (FIIs) in Debt Securities

	US $ billion			*% to GDP*		
End-March	*Government securities*	*Corporate debt securities*	*Total*	*Government securities*	*Corporate debt securities*	*Total*
1999	1.0	0.0	1.0	0.2	0.0	0.2
2005	1.8	0.5	2.3	0.2	0.1	0.3
2006	1.8	0.5	2.3	0.2	0.1	0.3
2007	2.6	1.5	4.1	0.3	0.2	0.4
2008	3.2	1.5	4.7	0.3	0.1	0.4
2009	5.0	15.0	20.0	0.4	1.2	1.6
2010	5.0	15.0	20.0	0.4	1.1	1.5
2011	10.0	40.0	50.0	0.6	2.3	2.9
2012	15.0	45.0	60.0	0.8	2.4	3.2
2013	25.0	50.0	75.0	1.4	2.7	4.1
Jun-13	30.0	50.0	80.0			
Memo:						
Actual investments						
2012	11.2	19.1	30.3	0.6	1.1	1.7
2013	15.2	19.7	35.0	0.8	1.1	1.9

Source: Reserve Bank of India and Securities Exchange Board of India.

to higher CAD and consequent enhanced external vulnerability (Panagariya 2013). For the euro area, the empirical evidence is supportive of this channel: abundant capital flows, high credit growth, and real appreciation largely determined current account balances in the euro area countries in the run up to the 2008 crisis (Atoyan et al. 2013). Offering more incentives to foreign capital in the current global uncertainty and the unprecedented external imbalance will make the country hostage to short-term, volatile capital (Nagaraj 2013; Subramanian 2013). Thus, the issue is that of causality: Whether higher CAD deficit necessitated more opening up of the capital account or it is the liberalized approach to capital flows which led to real appreciation and then higher CAD?

The empirical results presented in the paper indicate that exports and imports respond significantly to the domestic and foreign income variables as well as to the real exchange rate dynamics. In consonance with previous studies, income elasticities are greater than the price elasticities and, hence, growth dynamics at home and abroad are a key driving force beyond the trade and current account balance. Thus, during 2009–12, when external demand plummeted more than domestic demand, some worsening of the trade and current account balance was on the expected lines. At the same time, real exchange rate dynamics also have a significant impact on the external balance, even though price elasticities are lower than income elasticities. In this context, we may note that sustained higher domestic inflation over the past 4–5 years had a negative impact on external competitiveness through a higher REER. Thus, low and stable inflation would aid the maintenance of external competitiveness and reduce pressures for nominal depreciation, which then has adverse implications for domestic inflation, the government's fiscal position, and for corporate balance sheets.

Given the twin and elevated deficits, concerns were expressed during the first half of 2013 that India may face a 1990-like balance of payments crisis (Acharya 2013; Mody and Walton 2013; Tarapore 2013b). These concerns were evident during the June–August 2013 turmoil in the financial markets, notwithstanding a number of alleviating factors. The NAFC has clearly shown that all countries, even advanced countries with sophisticated financial markets, are susceptible to financial crisis. Therefore, prudent macroeconomic and financial policies play an important role in ensuring that a country does not face a crisis. In the Indian context, the range of macroeconomic and financial policies followed since the early 1990s had strengthened India's macroeconomic fundamentals before the NAFC and this helped India, as well as many other EMEs which had followed prudent policies, to see through the worst global financial crisis. These policies focused on pursuing a cautious approach to financial sector and capital market liberalization, management of the capital account, a flexible but managed exchange rate, improvement in the monetary–fiscal interface facilitated by fiscal consolidation, and continued structural reforms. These policies contributed to sustained high growth in an environment of macroeconomic and financial stability. It would be prudent to continue such policies, going forward.

Rapid financial sector and capital account liberalization often ends up in crisis. Opening the financial account appears to raise the frequency and severity of economic crises; financial openness is not a panacea and it could instead be poison. Benefits of financial openness are most likely to be realized when implemented in a phased manner, when external balances and reserve positions are strong, and when complementing a range of domestic policies and reforms to enhance stability and growth (Obstfeld 2009). Debt capital flows increase vulnerability to future crises, and this was clearly seen in the NAFC. Emerging and Developing Economies (EDEs) such as those in Central and Eastern Europe which saw large increases in debt flows and which also had large CADs did face crises in the aftermath of the NAFC. Given the structural growth, inflation, and interest differentials in favor of EDEs, a fully open capital account would inevitably lead to large flows in search of arbitrage—creating booms when they come in and busts once they leave. Thus, the management of debt flows assumes importance. Indeed, one factor that reduces India's external vulnerability, despite large twin deficits, is the fact the public debt is largely internally held.

It would be prudent to continue with this approach and further opening up of government securities market to non-resident investment needs to be carefully watched. Debt investments by non-residents in domestic securities are more volatile than in equities and can add to foreign exchange market pressures. More often, these flows react to monetary policy developments in advanced economies. For example, during June–September 2013, in response to Chairman Bernanke's comments on the likely time path for the roll-back of quantitative easing policies, foreign institutional investors sold both equities and debt securities in the Indian market, but the sell-off in debt securities (around US$10 billion) was five times that of equity investments (US$2 billion).[4] Open debt markets can lead to large destabilizing capital inflows and outflows in response to external developments and complicate

4. The stock of foreign portfolio equity at end-June 2013 was US$139 billion, while that of foreign portfolio debt was US$32 billion.

domestic macroeconomic management, particularly in the presence of perceived arbitrage opportunity resulting from high interest rate differentials.

There is a view that the traditional fears about foreign-currency borrowing by residents are not applicable to investments by non-residents in local-currency denominated bonds and hence the limits on the latter category of investments should be removed (Patnaik et al. 2013). Such a notion was clearly disproved during the June–August 2013 turmoil. High external borrowings denominated in foreign currencies add to the individual borrowing entity's vulnerability in the event of sharp currency movements, especially if such borrowings are not fully hedged. In the case of non-residents' investments in domestic rupee securities, although the domestic entities who have issued such paper do not bear the exchange rate risk, a sudden large sell-off by non-residents (for example, as witnessed during June–August 2013) puts sharp downward pressure on the currency, which then has adverse implications for the various sectors of the economy, including the corporate and the fisc, as well adding to inflationary pressures. Thus, large borrowings from foreign sources, whether these are denominated in foreign-currency or local-currency, add to the vulnerability of the domestic economy. The massive sell-off by non-residents in the local-currency bonds has an immediate impact on the currency and broader economy.

Price and Financial Stability: Institutional Issues

Inflation in India had seen a perceptible decline in the post-reform period. Alternative indicators of inflation had averaged 5–6% per annum between mid-1990s and the late 2000s, after averaging higher at 8–9% in the previous three decades. Inflation has now increased in the post-NAFC period, despite continued price stability globally at low levels. Both headline WPI and CPI inflation still remain well above comfort levels. Moreover, there is a substantial gap between the headline WPI inflation and the core WPI inflation on the one hand and between headline CPI and headline WPI inflation on the other. This poses challenges for monetary policy in its conduct, formulation, and communication, given that inflation expectations are likely to be influenced more by headline inflation, particularly headline CPI inflation. This also has implications for real interest rates facing the different economic agents—households, corporates, and government. Given the continued large weight of food in the various price indices, including the new consumer price indices, and the high volatility in food prices, it is apparent that an inflation targeting framework—with a focus on one inflation indicator as a target for monetary policy—is beset with a number of conceptual and practical challenges in the Indian context (Mohan 2011a). In the new CPI, food items have a weight of 59%, 37%, and 50% in the rural, urban, and all-India indices, respectively. The fuel group has a weight of 8–10%, taking the combined weight of food and fuel to 46–70% in the three indices. Given these large weights, the use of core measures of inflation in the conduct and formulation of monetary policy would lack credibility and thereby limit the use of an inflation targeting framework focused on a single inflation number. As a former chairman of the US Federal Reserve has recently noted, it is "neither necessary nor desirable to try to pin down the price stability objective by setting out a single highly specific target or target zone for a particular measure of prices" (Volcker 2013). While a conventional inflation targeting framework is problematic, price stability, with the objective of low and stable inflation, ought still to remain the key objective of monetary policy. In fact, against the backdrop of persistently high inflation and inflation expectations, the *Expert Committee to Revise and Strengthen the Monetary Policy Framework* has, inter alia, now recommended that headline CPI inflation should be the nominal anchor for the monetary policy framework. Low inflation should be the predominant objective of monetary policy in India, and this should be communicated without ambiguity to the public (RBI 2014).

Sustained price stability and financial stability are both essential for high growth. The NAFC has clearly shown that price stability per se does not guarantee financial stability. There is, therefore, now greater recognition that financial stability could be endangered if central banks were to be mandated with only price stability/inflation targeting objectives (Eichengreen et al. 2011). The United Kingdom, which had taken lead in separating financial regulation and supervision from the central bank in the 1990s, has again taken lead in reversing its earlier decision by returning responsibility for financial regulation and supervision back to the Bank of England. In a number of other countries too, the regulatory architecture is being revisited and central banks are being given responsibility for financial sector regulation and financial stability. A central bank's concern for stability must range beyond prices for goods and services to the stability and strength of financial markets and institutions generally (Volcker 2013).

A cross-country survey of regulatory and supervisory institutional arrangements with regard to the banking system and covering 136 countries shows the predominance of central-bank-led arrangements (Barth et al. 2013). In 89 countries, the central bank is the only such authority. In contrast, in 38 countries the central bank is not a supervisory authority at all. In the remaining nine countries, the central bank is one among multiple supervisors, with the United States being one of these countries. With regard to the broader financial system, the survey also provides information on whether a country has a single financial supervisory authority or multiple authorities. The results indicate that in 101 countries there are multiple authorities covering the financial sector, while in 25 countries there is a single authority covering the entire financial sector. "Most of the countries with a single authority are relatively small in terms of both population and GDP" (Barth et al. 2013: 11).

Issues relating to financial stability and the institutional arrangements thereof have attracted interest in the post-NAFC period. Advanced economies, particularly in Europe, are integrating prudential functions into the central bank (for example, Belgium, France, the United Kingdom, and the United States). Ireland has opted for a stronger form of integration where all supervision of markets and institutions is conducted by the central bank (Nier et al. 2011).

> It may often be desirable to identify a lead authority or policymaking committee and to vest it with the mandate and powers to conduct macroprudential policy. The central bank should play an important role, so as to harness its expertise in risk assessment and its incentives to mitigate systemic risk, as well as to ensure coordination with monetary policy. While participation of the treasury in the policy process is useful, a strong role can pose risks to the established autonomy of separate policy fields, such as monetary and microprudential policy, and lead to delay when policies are needed to constrain financial markets in good times. Separate arrangements for crisis prevention and crisis management will be useful in many cases" (Nier et al. 2011: 3).

In practice, these basic principles have led to the increasing prevalence of three models for macroprudential policymaking (IMF 2013b: 30):

- **Model 1:** The macroprudential mandate is assigned to the central bank, with macroprudential decisions ultimately made by its Board (as in Malaysia, and the Czech Republic). This setup is a natural choice in highly integrated arrangements where the central bank already concentrates the relevant regulatory and supervisory powers.
- **Model 2:** The macroprudential mandate is assigned to a dedicated committee within the central bank structure (as in the United Kingdom). This arrangement can help counter the risk of dual mandates for the central bank, by creating dedicated decision-making structures for monetary and macroprudential policy even as both functions are under the roof of the central bank. It also allows for the participation of separate supervisory agencies and external experts on the decision-making committee.

- **Model 3:** The macroprudential mandate is assigned to a committee outside the central bank, with the central bank participating on the macroprudential committee (as in Australia, France and the United States). This model can more easily accommodate a desire for a strong role of the Ministry of Finance (MoF). However, since a dominant role of the MoF risks delaying macroprudential action and can compromise the independence of participating agencies, including the central bank and separate supervisory agencies, some of these risks can be countered by assigning the central bank the chairmanship (as in Australia), a strong voice (as in Mexico), or a veto over policy decisions (as in Germany). They can also be countered by establishing only soft powers for the decision-making committee (IMF 2013b).

Against this backdrop, the proposals of the Financial Sector Legislative Reforms Commission (FSLRC) (Government of India 2013b) to restrict the Reserve Bank's role mainly to monetary policy and price stability need to be seriously debated (Tarapore 2013a). The FSLRC recommendation that the executive responsibility for safeguarding systemic risk should vest with the Financial Stability and Development Council (FSDC) Board runs counter to the post-crisis trend around the world of giving the collegial bodies responsibility only for coordination and for making recommendations: Should the responsibility of the FSDC Board be extended from being a coordination body to one having authority for executive decisions (Subbarao 2013b)? The proposed arrangement would compromise the synergy between monetary policy and policies for financial stability.

Globally, the mandates of the central banks have shifted over time in response to the evolving macroeconomic and financial conditions, but the outcomes have not been entirely satisfactory. For example, the US Federal Reserve was set up in 1913 with the objective of ensuring financial stability. Over time, the Fed succeeded in maintaining financial stability after the Great Depression, which policymakers and financial markets took for granted during the post-war era (Reinhart and Rogoff 2013). The consequence was that the objective of financial stability increasingly got de-emphasized, culminating in the 2008 financial crisis. Similar developments have taken place in other countries and the same logic seems to underlie the FSLRC's recommendations. Arguably, the success of the policymakers in India with maintaining financial stability over the past two decades, even as a number of emerging economies faced financial crises during the 1990s and the advanced economies in the 2008–2009 episode, has led to a situation where financial stability is being taken for granted. This might be a factor behind the recommendations designed to entrust the RBI with the narrow objectives of monetary policy/inflation targeting. Such an approach, as the international experience shows, runs the risk of financial instability down the road. Thus, the central bank needs to continue to be entrusted with multiple objectives. Multiple objectives need multiple instruments. As Reinhart and Rogoff (2013) note,

> Policies, such as changes in reserve and margin requirements and a variety of credit measures that have been discarded as antiquated, should be a part of the toolkit of the central bank in the United States and other advanced economies. These instruments have continued to play a central role in defining monetary policy in many emerging markets to the present day. [O]ver the past three decades both the academic literature and the policy practice have increasingly drifted to a world view where the short-term policy rate is a sufficient policy instrument. The theoretical underpinnings supporting that view usually assume complete markets, an assumption that is particularly at odds with a post-crisis environment riddled with a broad assortment of frictions arising from both market failures and a steady stream of complex regulatory changes set in motion by the crisis (pp. 49 and 53).

Fiscal Policy

Fiscal consolidation is necessary for sustained growth in an environment of macroeconomic and financial stability. As the NAFC has shown, high fiscal deficits and debt limit policy flexibility significantly, and contribute to the worsening of the overall economic situation. Weak public finances derail inflationary expectations, provide upward bias to the interest rate, impede investment activity and threaten sovereign credit ratings (Kelkar Committee 2012). The recent fiscal consolidation initiatives in India, including measures to rein in subsidies, are encouraging. In this context, it is relevant to note that fuel subsidies in India are found to be badly targeted, with the richest 10% of households receiving seven times more in benefits than the poorest 10% (Anand et al. 2013). Thus, there is scope for better targeting of fuel subsidies and fiscal consolidation, while protecting lower income households. Fiscal consolidation would allow government resources to enhance public investment and also to provide a durable way out of the ongoing slowdown. Historically, effective revival of the economy has been through a step up in public sector investment, which then triggered private sector investment and a revival of industrial growth (Tarapore 2013b).

While fiscal consolidation is clearly positive from a medium-term perspective, it could have a negative short-term impact on growth. However, this negative short-term impact on growth can be minimized, or even avoided, by calibrating the adjustment in expenditures. For example, according to estimates by Jain and Kumar (2013), the impact fiscal multiplier for non-defense capital outlays (2.1) is substantially higher than that of revenue expenditure (0.2) for the Central government. Thus, fiscal consolidation that directs expenditures away from revenue expenditure (subsidies) toward capital outlays could have a less negative, or even positive, impact on growth. Moreover, such a fiscal consolidation approach with relatively greater additions to the economy's productive capacity would provide monetary policy greater maneuverability and that could also be short-term growth positive.

A key lesson of the NAFC is that policymakers should have significant policy buffers, which can then be used in times of crises to stabilize the economy. In the Indian context, for example, the buffers were limited at the onset of the crisis and, in the face of the stimulus measures and the slowing economy, the combined deficits quickly reached high levels, exacerbated by high public debt levels, leaving India as an outlier among major emerging markets. Against this backdrop, a more ambitious medium-term fiscal consolidation plan beyond 2017–18 is critical. The earlier Fiscal Responsibility and Budget Management (FRBM) plan had targeted a 3% of GFD/GDP ratio for the Central government and the revised path also targets 3% deficit by 2017–18. Accordingly, it would be judicious to aim for balanced budget targets, say by the end of the decade. Stronger fiscal consolidation on these lines, along with the quality of its adjustment, would provide an environment conducive for higher domestic savings, lower domestic interest rates, and more flexibility to monetary policy in its operations.

6. Conclusion

The current growth slowdown has occurred after almost a decade of consistent high growth, including a sharp recovery from the 2008–09 crises. High growth during the pre-NAFC period, especially 2003–08, was underpinned by continuing fiscal correction, which then had a number of positive spillovers: increase in public savings, low inflation and anchored inflation expectations, low nominal and real interest rates, and sharp increase in corporate profitability and investments. The largely market-determined exchange rate system, in the context of a prudent approach to management and liberalization of the capital account and sterilized interventions, and in an environment of progressive deregulation and liberalization of the real economy, led to sustained increase in the exports of goods and services, which then kept the CAD at moderate levels.

The sustained growth process of the pre-NAFC period has suffered a setback in the past couple of years. This reflects a number of factors. First, while the macroeconomic policy response to the NAFC—both monetary and fiscal policy—was admirably rapid, there was, at least with hindsight, overshooting of the stimulus. The overshooting was reflected in very high growth—averaging 9%—during 2009–10 and 2010–11 but which sowed the seeds for inflation and current account pressures. Moreover, the quality of the fiscal stimulus, with its focus on tax cuts and increased revenue expenditure (particularly in subsidies) while keeping capital outlays stagnant, added to demand pressures, which were then reflected in high inflation. While the fiscal and monetary stimuli were large and rapid, their withdrawal was gradual and it remains incomplete in the case of fiscal measures. The incomplete and delayed pass-through of higher international oil prices to domestic prices added to fiscal pressures, while also impeding domestic expenditure adjustment in both oil and non-oil consumption that would have emanated from higher domestic oil prices. The adjustment in domestic oil consumption, had domestic prices been appropriately adjusted, would have also contributed to lower oil imports and lower CAD. The large monetary stimulus facilitated financing of the near trebling of the government borrowing needs at lower yields. The delayed and the incomplete withdrawal of the fiscal stimulus has also led to crowding out of the private sector, which in conjunction with other policy bottlenecks, has contributed to the massive decline in private corporate investment.

High inflation and negative real deposit rates have led to a switch away from financial savings toward savings in the form of gold, leading to higher gold imports and adding to CAD pressures. The current account was also hit by domestic policy bottlenecks, which, inter alia, have led to more coal imports and lower iron ore exports. The CAD was in any case expected to widen, given the two-speed global recovery since the NAFC, but domestic policies resulting in higher oil, gold and coal imports magnified the impact on the CAD. Unlike many other major EMEs, especially Asian EMEs, India had a deficit on its current account before the NAFC and the combination of domestic and global factors quickly took it up to 4.8% by 2012–13. The rapid policy response subsequent to the market turbulence of mid-2013 has reduced the CAD to an estimated 1.7% of GDP for 2013–14.

Overall, the above analysis suggests need for appropriate policies in regard to domestic oil prices which will help to contain fiscal subsidies as well as oil imports. In this context, the steps taken by the government in the past few months are welcome and would need to be continued with. Restoration of tax/GDP ratios, along with the proposed efforts toward the institution of the country-wide goods and services tax and the introduction of direct tax code bill and the recent measures to contain subsidies, should help to contain the fiscal deficit in the next couple of years. Taking into account the fiscal correction that is being programmed as also the fiscal consolidation record of 2002–07, the public sector savings should recover, and that would result in a recovery in the gross domestic savings rate by around 2–3% of GDP. A similar event occurred about 10 years ago when public sector savings had become negative (Mohan 2011b). The envisaged fiscal correction will make more resources available to the private sector and contribute to the recovery of private sector investment and private sector savings.

Fiscal consolidation would also provide the basis for a durable reduction in inflation and low and positive real interest rates for both depositors and borrowers and, in turn, a moderating impact on gold imports and the CAD. The analysis presented in this paper suggests that the ongoing slowdown has a large cyclical component, reflecting both domestic and global factors (see also, IMF 2013c). Growth has indeed slowed down since 2011–12, but this is not on account of any reversal in the reforms process, although the pace of new reforms may have been somewhat slower. India's "poor infrastructure, excessive regulation, small manufacturing sector, and a workforce that lacks adequate education and skills" cannot explain the current slowdown, as these deficiencies had existed when India was growing rapidly, although they must be addressed if India is to grow strongly and stably (Rajan 2013). The structural drivers of growth—the favorable demographics and the high savings and investment rates—are broadly intact. Based on these assumptions, even a conservative estimate would result in a sustained gross domestic savings rate of about 35%, which should facilitate growth of 8–8.5%, given the moderate incremental capital output ratios. This would also be contingent on the removal of the recent impediments to domestic investment activity and the recovery in the global economy. Finally, given the growth and inflation expectations, interest rates in India can be expected to remain above those in advanced economies, even when we move away from the present aberrations of near zero interest rates in the major advanced economies; therefore, a prudent approach with regard to opening up of debt flows to foreign investors needs to be pursued.

What then are the key policy priorities that can help to restore Indian growth to sustained rates in excess of 8%, which would be consistent with investment levels in the 35–40% range? For sustained growth, it is first essential to restore macroeconomic stability: of the highest importance is a reduction in medium-term inflation to levels achieved in the decade prior to the NAFC. This needs coordinated supply side and demand management measures: fiscal consolidation and appropriate monetary policy coupled with active measures to loosen supply constraints. Factor market reforms related to both labor and land are essential to make the economy more flexible in the face of burgeoning demand resulting from growing incomes. Among Asian EMEs, India is notable in the low share of its manufacturing sector in terms of both value-added and employment: this has also impeded the pace of rural–urban transformation. A realistic exchange rate policy combined with policies promoting labor flexibility and skill development need to be taken up consciously to promote growth in the manufacturing sector. The animal spirits released in Indian industry by the 1991 reforms seem to be dying down: they need to be revived in a focused manner. The revival of manufacturing competitiveness is essential to achieve 10% plus growth in this sector, without which it will not be feasible to achieve sustained growth rates in GDP of 8% plus.

It is well recognized by all that infrastructure investment is crucial to loosening supply side constraints and promoting manufacturing. Fiscal consolidation is also important here. Despite increasing private investment in infrastructure, it is necessary to enhance public investment in infrastructure on a sustained basis. For this to take place, the culture of economic user charges must be reinforced so that infrastructure investment is remunerative; second, with increasing incomes, expenditures on non-merit subsidies must be curtailed and directed toward infrastructure investments. The trend in recent fiscal consolidation efforts has been focused excessively on reduction in expenditures, more in capital expenditures, and less in revenue expenditures, such as subsidies. This needs to be reversed. Moreover, the Indian tax/GDP ratio has been relatively stagnant for a decade, despite high GDP growth and rising incomes. Revenue receipts/GDP ratio of the central government is now below the levels prevailing in the late 1980s. Public investment in both physical and social infrastructure will be difficult to achieve without revenue enhancement consistent with income growth.

It is apparent that reforms in key areas such as agriculture, and physical and social infrastructure, including urban infrastructure are needed on a continuing basis. The main organizing principle of most reforms carried out so far has been that of freeing the private sector from the myriad government controls that had existed for a long time. Whereas this process itself still has some distance to go, an issue is: Whether we have reached the limit of private sector-led acceleration in investment and output growth and will this now be increasingly constrained by the lack of public investment, both physical and social (Mohan 2011d)?

An underlying theme encompassing most constraints now is the lack of adequate delivery of public services in both quality and quantity. While the first generation of reforms empowered the private sector to perform to the best of its abilities, the second generation of economic reforms must focus on a similar empowerment of the public sector to deliver public goods and services for the benefit of all segments of the private sector, corporate entities, and the public alike. This proposition is not an argument for greater empowerment of the public sector to increase its control over the economy, as was the case in the past. The "public sector" needs to be seen in its widest definition, to encompass all levels of government from the local level to state and national levels, and their entities, which deliver public goods and services. Illustratively, four areas where we need to give focused attention and which can mainly be done by the public sector, even if some of it is to be delivered through public–private partnerships, are agricultural development, urban development, human resource development, and management of public services. What is common among these sectors is the lack of competence in public systems that govern these areas (Mohan 2011d). These issues assume added importance in view of governance issues that have come to the forefront in the recent period, and which call for significant improvement in the delivery of public services.

Annexes

Annex 1: Oil Consumption and Prices

In the context of the large increase in oil subsidies, an attempt is made to examine the determinants of demand for the key administered items (diesel, kerosene, and LPG) and also for petrol which has been controlled at times. Demand for the various oil products is postulated to depend upon income (real GDP) and the prices of the particular products relative to overall price movements (Asali 2011). Demand for total petroleum products is also modeled, and movements in the minerals oil index of the WPI are used as the relevant price variable. Thus, we estimate the following specification:

$$\text{Log}(C_t) = a1 + a2.\log(Y_t) + a3.\log(P_t/WPI_t) + e_t$$

where C is the consumption of the specific petroleum item or total petroleum products, Y is the real GDP, P is the price of the specific petroleum item (measured by the respective indices in the WPI basket), and WPI captures the general price level in the country. The empirical exercise covers the period from April 2001 to March 2013. Since the various variables are non-stationary, we employ a cointegration framework, and use the autoregressive distributed lag approach to cointegration.[5] Given the short sample period, the robustness of the results is tested and supported by the Johansen–Juselius approach.

The results indicate that the income elasticity is more than unity (around 1.2) for petrol and almost unity for diesel as shown in Annex Table 1. Income elasticity for LPG demand is below unity, perhaps indicative of supply constraints in meeting the demand. Income elasticity of demand for kerosene oil is negative, indicating its diminishing role; the share of kerosene in total petroleum products' consumption has halved from around 10% to 5% over the study period (2002–12). The elasticity of demand for overall petroleum products is estimated to be 0.5.

Turning to the price responsiveness, the price elasticities are found to be statistically significant for petrol, diesel and kerosene. The price elasticity is the highest for petrol (–0.66) followed by kerosene (–0.54) and diesel (–0.36). Thus, an increase of 10% in domestic prices is associated with a reduction of 3.6–6.6% for these three products. The price elasticities for LPG and overall petroleum consumption are negative, but not significant. The insignificant price elasticity of total petroleum consumption, even as the major components have significant and relatively high price elasticities, suggests merits of pursuing a disaggregated approach in order to assess the determinants of demand for oil.

Annex 2: Growth Slowdown

Accommodative monetary and fiscal policies boosted the growth during 2009–11 and the phased reversal of these policies, partial so far in the case of fiscal policy, contributed to the growth slowdown during 2011–12 and 2012–13. Anemic global growth over both these two periods has also been a factor. To assess the impact of monetary policy and global conditions on domestic growth—the two factors which are seen as the major contributors to the growth slowdown—we model growth on the lines of the IS curve framework in Kapur and Behera (2012). Given the monsoon induced volatility in agricultural output and the impact of government expenditures on "community, social and personal services," the empirical exercise focuses on GDP excluding these two components. Growth is postulated to depend on real domestic interest rates, external demand, real exchange rate, and

5. F-tests (not reported) confirm the presence of a cointegrating relationship among the variables.

ANNEX TABLE 1. Estimates of Oil Consumption in India

	Dependent variable				
	LHSDSA	*LPETROLSA*	*LSKOSA*	*LLPGSA*	*LPOLTOTSA*
1	*2*	*3*	*4*	*5*	*6*
LGDPRSA	0.96	1.18	–0.49	0.66	0.50
	(37.37)	(19.33)	(9.18)	(8.61)	(32.70)
LP_HSDSA	–0.36				
	(5.62)				
LP_PETROLSA		–0.66			
		(3.70)			
LP_SKOSA			–0.54		
			(4.78)		
LP_LPGSA				–0.35	
				(1.20)	
LMINOILSA					–0.06
					(1.48)
R-bar^2	0.996	0.997	0.940	0.986	0.984
Serial correlation	0.25	0.14	0.06	0.30	0.19
Normality	0.52	0.00	0.12	0.04	0.57
Short-run model					
ECM(–1)	–0.42	–0.18	–0.38	–0.29	–
	(6.10)	(3.23)	(3.73)	(2.69)	–
R-bar^2	0.48	0.53	0.27	0.21	–
ARDL model	1,0,0	2,0,1	1,0,3	1,0,0	0,3,3

Source: Authors' estimates.

Notes: Estimates are based on autoregressive distributed lag (ARDL) methodology, with model selection based on Schwarz Bayesian Information Criteria.

Estimates are based on quarterly data for the sample period 2001:2 to 2013:1.

Variables are defined as follows:

LHSDA, LPETROLSA, LSKOSA, LLPGSA and LPOLTOTSA are domestic consumption of diesel, petrol, kerosone, LPG and all POL products, respectively.

LP_HSDA, LP_PETROLSA, LP_SKOSA, LP_LPGSA and LP_MINOILSA are WPI indices of diesel, petrol, kersone, LPG and the sub-group "mineral oils" , respectively. All these indices are taken relative to overall WPI index.

LGDPRSA = Real gross domestic product.

All data are in log terms and seasonally adjusted.

Data for consumption of petroleum products are from Petroleum Planning and Analysis Cell.

Figures in parentheses are t-statistics.

real bank credit. Real interest rate is defined as an effective nominal policy rate less 4-quarter average of NFMP inflation. External demand is captured through real world exports or global GDP. For real exchange rate, RBI's 36-currency export-weighted REER index is used. The equation is estimated for the period of 1996–97 to 2007–08 using quarterly data and then used to make out of sample forecasts for the subsequent period. All the variables, except for the real interest rate, are in growth terms (quarter-on-quarter, based on seasonally adjusted data) and are found to be stationary.

The results show that an increase of 100 bps in the real interest rate leads to a reduction of 26–33 bps in GDP growth with a lag of two quarters; see Annex Table 2 (columns 2–5). Global demand impacts domestic economy in the same quarter and the estimated coefficients suggest that one percentage point reduction in global exports reduces domestic growth by almost 13 bps, while the impact of one percentage point reduction in global GDP growth is almost 40–56 bps. The coefficient on world exports is lower than that on world GDP, given the differences in the magnitudes of the two variables:

ANNEX TABLE 2. Determinants of Real GDP Growth (Non-Agricultural Non-Community Services GDP)

Explanatory variable	*Dependent variable: GDPRGQ* *Sample period: 1996:2 2008:1*			
1	*2*	*3*	*4*	*5*
Constant	6.38	6.45	5.62	5.15
	(5.91)	(6.10)	(4.78)	(4.10)
RIRQ(–2)	–0.32	–0.33	–0.26	–0.27
	(3.26)	(3.23)	(2.76)	(2.82)
WEXPRGQ	0.13	0.13		
	(2.40)	(2.43)		
GDPWORLDQ			0.40	0.56
			(1.99)	(2.42)
REERXQ				–0.09
				(1.74)
REERXQ(–3)		–0.08		
		(1.95)		
NFCRQ(–2)	0.14	0.14	0.14	0.14
	(3.21)	(3.15)	(3.26)	(3.10)
R-bar^2	0.30	0.32	0.29	0.31
DW	1.97	1.76	2.15	2.12
White test	0.43	0.62	0.69	0.90
JB test	0.91	0.89	0.91	0.69
LB-Q test	0.34	0.20	0.47	0.33

Source: Authors' estimates.

Notes: Dependent variable = GDPRGQ = growth (q-o-q) in real GDP excluding agriculture and community services.

RIRQ = real interest rate = nominal policy rate less 4-quarter average of q-o-q non-food manufactured products (NFMP) inflation.

WEXPRQ = growth (q-o-q) in world real exports.

GDPWORLDQ = growth (q-o-q) in world real GDP.

REERXQ = variation (q-o-q) in RBI's 36-currency real effective exchange rate.

NFCRQ = growth (q-o-q) in real non-food credit.

q-o-q growth rates are first-differences (annualized) of (log) seasonally adjusted data.

White test = significance level (p-value) for White test for the null of homoscedasticity of residuals.

JB test = significance level (p-value) for Jarque–Bera test for the null of normality of residuals;

LB-Q test = significance level (p-value) of Box-Pierce-Ljung Q-statistic for the null of no residual autocorrelation for four lags.

annual growth in real world exports averaged 7.7% vis-à-vis that of 3.8% in global GDP over the sample period (1997:3–2008:1). Real exchange rate movements have the expected impact: appreciation reduces the domestic output, while depreciation boosts the output. The estimated equations satisfy the regression diagnostics.

Annex 3: Determinants of Exports and Imports

Following Hooper et al. (2000) and Chinn (2013), export demand is postulated to depend on external demand and the real exchange rate and import demand on domestic activity and the real exchange rate. Since the variables of interest are non-stationary, we use cointegration and a vector error correction mechanism framework (Johansen–Juselius methodology) to assess the long-run and the short-run dynamics, as follows.

$$\Delta LEXPXt = a1 + a2.ECM(t-1) + \Sigma a3i.\Delta LEXPX(t-i) + \Sigma a4i.\Delta LREER(t-i) + a5.\Delta LWEXPR(t-i) + ut$$
$$\Delta LIMPQt = b1 + b2.ECM(t-1) + \Sigma b3i.\Delta LIMPQ(t-i) + \Sigma b4i.\Delta LREER(t-i) + b5.\Delta LY(t-i) + vt$$

Here Δ is the first-difference, L is logarithm, EXPQ and IMPQ are real volumes of exports and imports (measured by DGCIS' quantum index for exports and imports, respectively), WEXPR is world real exports (world exports in US $ terms divided by their unit value index) as an indicator for external demand, Y is an indicator of domestic activity (real GDP or real industrial GDP or real domestic demand), and REER is the REER. The ECM terms capture the deviations of exports and imports from their long-run equilibrium [(LEXPQ—c1—c2.LREER—c3.LWEXPR) and (LIMPQ—d1—d2.LREER—d3.LY), respectively]. The coefficients on the ECM terms measure the speed with which the deviation from the long-run equilibrium is corrected each period and are expected to be negative. World real exports are treated as weakly exogenous in the cointegrating Vector Autoregression (VAR) for exports, and domestic activity is found to be weakly exogenous in the imports VAR.

The baseline period for the study is 1980–81 to 2007–08 using annual data. In view of the NAFC and the severe disruptions in the global economy, we focus on the pre-NAFC period; as a robustness check, we also report results for the period up to 2011–12. The starting period of the study, 1980–81, coincides with the first phase of reforms that started in the early 1980s and hence the period is relatively homogeneous. The structural reforms introduced in the early 1990s and continued in the subsequent years with the objective of deregulation and liberalization provided a greater role for market forces and market prices. Thus, the role of price signals can be, a priori, expected to be more in the post-1990s period vis-à-vis the 1980s; for China, for example, Aziz and Li (2008) find evidence of increased responsiveness of exporters to market signals over time. Moreover, given the large intra-year volatility and two-way movements in exchange rates, econometric analysis based on annual data might not appropriately capture the impact of exchange rate changes on trade volumes. If so, the price elasticities using the annual data for 1980–2008 could be an underestimate of the actual elasticities. Therefore, as a robustness measure, we also present results for the post-reforms period using quarterly data on trade volumes for overall exports as well as major categories of manufactured products (for 1996–97 to 2007–08). The focus on the post-reforms period reduces the sample size substantially, and potentially limits the inferences drawn from cointegration analysis.

As regards the REER, as the earlier discussion showed, there is a substantial divergence in the movements indicated by the available REER indicators. Bayoumi et al. (2011) and Chinn (2006) report a similar divergence of alternative REER measures—ULC-based REER, CPI-based REER and WPI-based REER—in the context of the United States, the euro area, and other countries. For example, for Ireland, the CPI-based REER indicated an appreciation of 20% between 1995 and 2009, while the ULC- and WPI-based REER showed depreciation of 20–30%. And, based on their econometric analysis, Bayoumi et al. (2011) suggest that WPI- and ULC-based REERs are better indicators of price competitiveness than CPI-based measures. Accordingly, we present results for the three available REERs.

The share of oil exports in total exports has fluctuated substantially over the sample period, reflecting the movements in international crude oil prices as well as the quantum on the back of higher domestic crude production (mid-1980s) and the increase in domestic refining capacity (beginning early 2000s). Since these fluctuations in oil exports are unrelated to price and income variables, we also report results for an augmented specification with real oil exports (oil exports in US dollar terms divided by average crude oil prices) and also dummies for the outliers.

Exports: Annual Estimates

Beginning with exports, and using annual data for 1980–81 to 2007–08, the null hypothesis of at least one cointegrating vector cannot be rejected for both the basic and the augmented specifications for the REER-RBI measure and for the augmented specification for the REER-OECD and REER-IMF measures. Both external demand (world real exports) and the REER have the expected impact and these are statistically significant.[6] An increase of 1% in world real exports[7] is associated with an increase of 1.1–1.4% in India's exports in the long run; see Annex Table 3. The long-run coefficient on the REER is 0.21 to 0.65 across alternative specifications, and the coefficients are lower for the specifications using the OECD and the IMF measures of REER. In the short-run model, the coefficients on the ECM term for both the exports and REER equations are correctly signed and significant. Thus, deviations of exports from the long-run equilibrium get adjusted through adjustments in both exports and the REER. The short-run coefficients indicate significant contemporaneous impact of external demand on exports, although partly offset in the next year. The regression diagnostics for the short-run model are satisfactory. The results broadly carry through when the sample period is extended to 2011–12 and are more supportive.

ANNEX TABLE 3. Determinants of Exports (Annual Estimates)

	Results for REER-RBI				*Results for REER-OECD*		*Results for REER-IMF*	
L(EXPQ)	1.00		1.00		1.00		1.00	
L(REER)	0.37		0.65		0.27		0.21	
	(4.50)		(6.25)		(3.33)		(2.22)	
L(WEXPR)	−1.33		−1.10		−1.35		−1.42	
	(33.60)		(17.02)		(22.07)		(19.83)	
L(OILR)			0.06		0.04		0.02	
			(4.20)		(2.39)		(1.06)	
constant	3.93		1.02		4.50		5.26	
	(6.04)		(1.08)		(5.42)		(5.51)	
Short-run ECM model								
	DLEXPQ	*DLREER*	*DLEXPQ*	*DLREER*	*DLEXPQ*	*DLREER*	*DLEXPQ*	*DLREER*
ECM(−1)	−1.02	0.37	−0.45	0.69	−0.60	0.21	−0.47	0.09
	(5.39)	(1.98)	(3.07)	(2.74)	(7.70)	(2.00)	(6.98)	(0.72)
DLEXPQ(−1)	0.40	0.07	0.12	0.01	0.27	−0.03	0.20	0.22
	(2.55)	(0.47)	(1.02)	(0.03)	(2.50)	(0.22)	(1.78)	(1.03)

(Annex Table 3 Contd)

6. All estimations have been done using software WinRATS Pro 8.2 and CATS 2.0.

7. When real world GDP is used as indicator of external demand in lieu of real world exports, the null of no cointegration cannot be rejected for the 1980–2008 sample period. The null hypothesis is however rejected for the extended sample (1980–2012) as well as for the quarterly sample (1996:2–2008:1) .

(Annex Table 3 Contd)

Short-run ECM model

	DLEXPQ	*DLREER*	*DLEXPQ*	*DLREER*	*DLEXPQ*	*DLREER*	*DLEXPQ*	*DLREER*
DLREER(−1)	0.41	0.26	0.22	−0.10	0.24	0.61	0.12	0.58
	(1.86)	(1.19)	(1.42)	(0.38)	(2.04)	(3.89)	(1.04)	(2.77)
DLEXPQ(−2)	0.25	−0.26	−0.10	−0.58				
	(1.55)	(1.59)	(0.83)	(2.73)				
DLREER(−2)	0.72	−0.45	0.27	−1.22				
	(2.84)	(1.79)	(1.12)	(2.97)				
DLWEXPR	1.08	−0.14	0.76	−0.44	0.40	0.37	0.38	0.01
	(4.12)	(0.53)	(4.02)	(1.35)	(2.18)	(1.48)	(1.93)	(0.03)
DLOILR			0.03	0.00	0.02	0.00	0.02	0.00
			(3.51)	(0.14)	(3.55)	(0.01)	(2.50)	(0.09)
DLWEXPR(−1)	−0.86	−0.01	0.00	0.42	−0.52	0.00	−0.44	−0.18
	(2.80)	(0.02)	(0.00)	(1.19)	(2.98)	(0.00)	(2.55)	(0.56)
DLOILR(−1)			−0.02	0.02	−0.03	0.02	−0.02	0.00
			(2.17)	(1.31)	(3.42)	(1.62)	(2.81)	(0.25)
DLWEXPR(−2)	−0.31	0.44	0.37	0.67				
	(1.02)	(1.49)	(2.02)	(2.12)				
DLOIL(−2)			0.01	0.03				
			(1.38)	(1.74)				
dum85			−0.14	0.01	−0.11	−0.02	−0.12	0.00
			(4.48)	(0.22)	(3.98)	(0.51)	(4.14)	(0.04)
dum95			0.13	0.18	0.17	−0.03	0.18	−0.07
			(2.76)	(2.10)	(5.82)	(0.04)	(5.87)	(1.15)
dum97			−0.13	0.07	−0.11	0.05	−0.12	0.07
			(2.82)	(0.83)	(3.15)	(1.05)	(3.41)	(0.98)
Serial correlation @	0.41		0.26		0.07		0.69	
ARCH @	0.53	0.50	0.24	0.43	0.56	1.00	0.32	0.61
Normality @	0.83	0.19	0.74	0.40	0.99	0.22	0.91	0.05
R^2	0.58	0.27	0.90	0.40	0.88	0.66	0.87	0.40
VAR lags	3		3		2		2	
PV (r=0)	0.02		0.04		0.05		0.05	
PV (r=1)	0.21		0.89		0.47		0.41	

Source: Authors' estimates.

Notes: Sample period for the estimation is 1980–81 to 2007–08.

Variables are defined as follows: EXPQ = quantum index of India's exports; WEXPR = world real exports (nominal exports, deflated by unit export values); OILR = India's real oil exports (nominal oil exports divided by international crude oil prices); REER = real effective exchange rates compiled by RBI (36-currency export weighted), OECD and IMF, respectively.

dum85, dum95 and dum97 are dummies for 1985–86, 1995–96 and 1997–98, respectively.

PV (r=0) and PV (r=1) give p-values (Bartlett-corrected) for the null of no and one cointegrating vector, respectively.

@: p-values for the null hypotheses of no serial correlation, no conditional heteroscedasticity and normality of residuals.

Figures in parentheses are t-statistics.

Exports: Quarterly Estimates

Moving to the post-reforms sample (1996–97 to 2007–08) and using quarterly data,[8] we observe some differences. First, the elasticity with respect to external demand (proxied by world exports) is in a range of 1.6–1.9 across alternative estimates, somewhat higher than the annual estimates as shown in Annex Table 4. The elasticity with respect to world GDP, as an indicator of external demand, is as expected higher at 2.6–3.6. Second, the coefficient on REER is sensitive to the choice of the REER and inclusion of oil exports. With REER-RBI, the (absolute) coefficient is more than unity and significant when oil exports are included. With REER-OECD and IMF, the (absolute) coefficient is more than 1.6 and is statistically significant only when oil exports are excluded. Third, the results for overall exports are broadly true for exports of major categories of manufactured products (chemicals, manufactures, and machinery). The income elasticities range from 1.5 to 2.8 (with respect to world exports) and 2.9–5.1 (with respect to world GDP) for these three categories of exports. For the sub-group "manufactured goods classified chiefly material" (comprising exports of leather, textile yarn, textile fibers, made-up articles of textile yarn, non-metallic minerals, iron and steel, non-ferrous metals, and manufactures of metals), the elasticity of exports with respect to the REER is 1.6–3.8 across the various REER indicators. For exports of machinery and transport equipment, the price elasticities are 2.4–3.3 for the OECD and the IMF indicators, but are wrongly signed for the RBI's REER measure. Finally, for the "chemicals and related products" sub-group, the exchange rate elasticity is 1.7–2.9 for the OECD-IMF indicators, but is not significant (although correctly signed) for the RBI's REER measure. The regression diagnostics for the short-run model are satisfactory for most of the specifications, barring some issues with the normality of residuals for the "chemicals and related products" sub-group.

As a robustness check, given the small sample size, Annex Table 5 presents estimates for overall exports based on the Dynamic Ordinary Least Squares (DOLS) approach. Given the sensitivity of results to lags and the sample period, the table presents results for the baseline model (i.e., without including oil exports) for one and two leads and lags in the DOLS and also for rolling samples starting the second quarter of 1996 (the effective sample period begins the quarter ended December 1996 given the lags). The estimates based on the DOLS approach with one lead and lag are broadly in line with those from the Johansen–Juselius methodology.

8. These results are based on DGCI&S' quantum index of exports available for quarter-end months.

ANNEX TABLE 4. Determinants of Exports (Quarterly Estimates)

	Chemicals and related products			*Manufactured goods classified chiefly by material*			*Machinery and transport equipment*			*Total exports*					
Estimates using world exports															
LREER-RBI	0.87			3.26			−2.65			1.48	1.07				
	(0.63)			(1.86)			(2.04)			(1.23)	(1.75)				
LREER-OECD		2.18			2.50			3.33				2.35	0.81		
		(2.27)			(1.73)			(3.21)				(2.80)	(1.02)		
LREER-IMF			2.94			3.30			2.71					2.83	1.49
			(3.45)			(2.38)			(2.11)					(3.59)	(2.16)
LWEXPR	−2.41	−2.74	−2.75	−1.56	−1.55	−1.55	−1.94	−2.58	−2.41	−1.81	−1.65	−1.94	−1.77	−1.91	−1.81
	(13.58)	(14.97)	(19.85)	(9.42)	(5.61)	(6.84)	(11.60)	(12.99)	(11.48)	(12.63)	(12.62)	(12.14)	(10.04)	(14.86)	(12.05)
L(OILR)											−0.03		−0.01		−0.01
											1.85		0.75		0.64
Short-run ECM model															
ECM(−1)	−0.47	−0.63	−0.71	−0.64	−0.61	−0.65	−0.81	−0.90	−0.79	−0.40	−0.75	−0.54	−0.70	−0.58	−0.75
	(3.99)	(4.21)	(4.90)	(4.84)	(5.02)	(5.32)	(5.49)	(6.08)	(5.57)	(4.54)	(5.62)	(4.70)	(5.06)	(5.17)	(5.60)
Serial correlation @	0.96	0.92	0.58	0.58	0.34	0.39	0.37	0.94	0.90	0.50	0.87	0.88	0.60	0.88	0.85
ARCH @	0.67	0.86	0.93	0.84	0.44	0.41	0.08	0.19	0.11	0.96	0.79	0.50	0.76	0.42	0.99
Normality @	0.02	0.00	0.00	0.05	0.05	0.07	0.36	0.30	0.23	0.65	0.24	0.49	0.39	0.67	0.42
R^2	0.33	0.33	0.39	0.51	0.36	0.38	0.40	0.45	0.42	0.44	0.44	0.31	0.40	0.35	0.45
VAR lags	1	1	1	3	1	1	1	1	1	2	1	1	1	1	1
PV (r = 0)	0.09	0.06	0.01	0.02	0.01	0.00	0.00	0.00	0.00	0.03	0.01	0.02	0.03	0.01	0.01
Estimates using world GDP															
LREERX	1.16			3.75			−2.40			1.26	1.39				
	(0.83)			(2.70)			(2.11)			(1.22)	(2.43)				

(Annex Table 4 Contd)

(Annex Table 4 Contd)

	Chemicals and related products			*Manufactured goods classified chiefly by material*			*Machinery and transport equipment*			*Total exports*					
LREEROEC		1.73			1.56			2.88				1.63	0.82		
		(1.73)			(1.26)			(3.53)				(2.48)	(1.15)		
LREERIMF			2.48			2.37			2.37					2.10	1.37
			(2.60)			(1.94)			(2.31)					(3.41)	(2.21)
LWGDPR	−4.63	−5.05	−5.12	−3.24	−2.89	−2.96	−3.76	−4.87	−4.58	−3.44	−2.65	−3.61	−3.14	−3.60	−3.23
	(12.75)	(12.51)	(15.59)	(9.42)	(5.76)	(6.99)	(12.70)	(14.81)	(12.96)	(13.47)	(9.77)	(13.62)	(9.85)	(16.90)	(11.81)
L(OILR)											−0.06		−0.02		−0.02
											(3.91)		(1.56)		(1.52)
Short-run ECM model															
ECM(−1)	−0.47	−0.57	−0.62	−0.61	−0.66	−0.71	−0.89	−0.997	−0.88	−0.49	−0.94	−0.63	−0.76	−0.69	−0.82
	(4.10)	(4.12)	(4.61)	(5.77)	(4.87)	(5.13)	(6.12)	(6.85)	(6.24)	(4.42)	(4.64)	(4.55)	(4.97)	(5.05)	(5.47)
Serial correlation @	0.91	0.96	0.77	0.50	0.15	0.15	0.43	0.92	0.86	0.85	0.90	0.57	0.94	0.72	0.89
ARCH @	0.50	0.71	0.80	0.53	0.62	0.54	0.24	0.81	0.52	0.58	0.63	0.27	0.40	0.34	0.72
Normality @	0.01	0.00	0.00	0.22	0.04	0.06	0.42	0.06	0.05	0.51	0.78	0.65	0.56	0.80	0.65
R^2	0.32	0.30	0.34	0.57	0.33	0.36	0.46	0.52	0.48	0.41	0.52	0.31	0.42	0.36	0.46
VAR lags	1	1	1	2	1	1	1	1	1	2	2	1	1	1	1
PV (r=0)	0.07	0.07	0.02	0.00	0.01	0.01	0.00	0.00	0.00	0.04	0.07	0.03	0.03	0.01	0.01

Source: Authors' estimates.

Notes: Sample period for the estimation is 1996:2 to 2008:1.

Variables are defined as follows:

WEXPR = world real exports (nominal exports, deflated by unit export values); WGDPR = world real GDP; REER = real effective exchange rates compiled by RBI (36-currency export weighted), OECD and IMF, respectively.

OILR = India's real oil exports (nominal oil exports divided by international crude oil prices).

PV (r=0) gives p-values (Bartlett-corrected) for the null of no cointegrating vector.

@: p-values for the null hypotheses of no serial correlation, no conditional heteroskedasticity and normality of residuals.

Figures in parentheses are t-statistics.

ANNEX TABLE 5. Determinants of Exports—Quarterly DOLS Estimates (Using World Exports)

Sample starting from	Results using one lead and lag in DOLS						Results using two leads and lags in DOLS					
	REER		WEXPR				REER		WEXPR			
	Coefficient	*T-statistic*	*Coefficient*	*T-statistic*	*LB-Q(2)*	*LB-Q(4)*	*Coefficient*	*T-statistic*	*Coefficient*	*T-statistic*	*LB-Q(2)*	*LB-Q(4)*
Results using REER-RBI												
Dec-96	0.22	0.16	1.65	12.82	0.01	0.03						
Mar-97	–0.31	–0.23	1.72	13.09	0.02	0.05	–0.04	–0.02	1.74	11.17	0.02	0.06
Jun-97	–0.81	–0.62	1.78	13.37	0.04	0.14	–1.31	–0.70	1.85	11.59	0.05	0.19
Sep-97	–1.56	–1.12	1.87	12.61	0.07	0.22	–2.88	–1.46	1.99	11.61	0.04	0.09
Dec-97	–1.99	–1.31	1.93	11.39	0.09	0.28	–4.94	–2.12	2.19	10.30	0.02	0.03
Mar-98	–2.66	–1.44	2.01	9.45	0.13	0.36	–5.22	–2.02	2.22	9.13	0.08	0.09
Jun-98	–2.84	–1.43	2.04	8.60	0.02	0.08	–5.83	–2.05	2.30	8.19	0.00	0.00
Sep-98	–2.16	–1.01	1.94	7.49	0.03	0.09	–4.89	–1.43	2.20	6.36	0.01	0.01
Dec-98	–1.79	–0.73	1.90	6.40	0.02	0.10	–5.52	–1.28	2.26	5.21	0.00	0.00
Mar-99	–1.78	–0.70	1.91	6.20	0.02	0.08	–6.61	–1.30	2.37	4.63	0.00	0.00
Jun-99	–1.93	–0.71	1.90	5.76	0.02	0.09	–6.70	–1.31	2.35	4.56	0.00	0.00
Sep-99	–1.91	–0.75	1.90	6.29	0.02	0.08	–6.81	–1.44	2.35	5.03	0.00	0.00
Dec-99	–2.05	–1.03	1.84	7.79	0.11	0.31	–7.82	–1.93	2.38	5.98	0.01	0.00
Mar-00	–2.01	–1.08	1.75	7.80	0.40	0.43	–6.22	–1.47	2.16	5.03	0.04	0.00
Jun-00	–1.54	–0.8[illegible]	1.66	6.87	0.24	0.20	–4.54	–1.03	1.95	4.19	0.04	0.00
Sep-00	–1.40	–0.8[illegible]	1.61	7.07	0.26	0.29	–3.37	–0.78	1.79	3.76	0.09	0.00
Dec-00	–1.26	–0.78	1.54	7.02	0.32	0.49	–2.07	–0.50	1.57	3.31	0.19	0.23
Mar-01	–0.82	–0.48	1.46	6.14	0.53	0.85	–1.79	–0.41	1.49	2.96	0.26	0.53

(Annex Table 5 Contd)

(Annex Table 5 Contd)

Sample starting from	Results using one lead and lag in DOLS						Results using two leads and lags in DOLS					
	REER		WEXPR				REER		WEXPR			
	Coefficient	T-statistic	Coefficient	T-statistic	LB-Q(2)	LB-Q(4)	Coefficient	T-statistic	Coefficient	T-statistic	LB-Q(2)	LB-Q(4)
Results using REER-OEC												
Dec-96	–2.70	–2.92	1.99	14.21	0.12	0.30						
Mar-97	–2.36	–2.35	1.97	13.83	0.15	0.39	–3.01	–2.67	2.02	13.96	0.10	0.25
Jun-97	–2.18	–2.01	1.96	13.77	0.16	0.43	–2.86	–2.27	2.01	13.41	0.12	0.31
Sep-97	–1.94	–1.67	1.95	13.39	0.18	0.48	–2.51	–1.73	1.99	12.63	0.18	0.41
Dec-97	–2.01	–1.62	1.95	13.21	0.22	0.51	–2.36	–1.59	1.99	12.64	0.22	0.46
Mar-98	–2.03	–1.61	1.95	13.06	0.20	0.46	–2.70	–1.68	2.00	12.66	0.17	0.37
Jun-98	–2.24	–1.91	1.95	14.75	0.15	0.35	–2.84	–1.77	2.00	13.58	0.12	0.25
Sep-98	–2.62	–2.35	1.92	15.41	0.12	0.21	–4.03	–2.83	2.02	16.41	0.04	0.05
Dec-98	–2.56	–2.20	1.90	14.31	0.09	0.18	–4.85	–3.29	2.02	17.03	0.01	0.01
Mar-99	–2.50	–2.08	1.91	14.06	0.07	0.21	–4.82	–3.27	2.02	17.13	0.01	0.02
Jun-99	–2.55	–1.98	1.88	12.70	0.06	0.17	–5.16	–3.23	2.00	15.61	0.01	0.01
Sep-99	–2.56	–2.09	1.88	13.03	0.05	0.14	–5.32	–3.20	2.02	14.68	0.01	0.01
Dec-99	–2.43	–2.36	1.82	14.35	0.19	0.36	–4.60	–2.85	1.95	14.09	0.03	0.03
Mar-2000	–2.05	–2.04	1.72	13.09	0.57	0.38	–3.56	–1.98	1.82	11.00	0.18	0.04
Jun-2000	–1.79	–1.71	1.65	11.15	0.31	0.06	–2.78	–1.30	1.73	8.22	0.20	0.01
Sep-2000	–1.68	–1.66	1.62	10.40	0.33	0.08	–2.45	–1.06	1.68	6.58	0.23	0.01
Dec-2000	–1.55	–1.65	1.56	10.23	0.31	0.22	–1.39	–0.57	1.49	5.04	0.36	0.42
Mar-01	–1.38	–1.43	1.52	9.48	0.48	0.53	–1.37	–0.56	1.42	4.65	0.63	0.85

(Annex Table 5 Contd)

(Annex Table 5 Contd)

Results using REER-IMF												
Dec-96	−3.03	−3.69	1.94	18.65	0.36	0.27						
Mar-97	−2.74	−3.27	1.94	19.00	0.43	0.40	−3.53	−3.65	2.00	19.22	0.28	0.22
Jun-97	−2.60	−2.99	1.94	19.29	0.44	0.45	−3.39	−3.27	1.99	19.01	0.31	0.25
Sep-97	−2.42	−2.66	1.95	18.87	0.46	0.52	−3.14	−2.74	1.99	18.67	0.37	0.31
Dec-97	−2.43	−2.58	1.94	18.40	0.48	0.53	−3.01	−2.59	1.99	18.67	0.40	0.37
Mar-98	−2.43	−2.55	1.95	17.65	0.36	0.47	−3.15	−2.64	1.99	18.57	0.27	0.29
Jun-98	−2.48	−2.83	1.94	18.98	0.22	0.26	−3.22	−2.31	1.99	19.78	0.14	0.13
Sep-98	−2.60	−3.17	1.89	19.39	0.23	0.19	−3.79	−3.32	1.95	22.60	0.08	0.05
Dec-98	−2.52	−2.91	1.88	17.89	0.19	0.17	−4.04	−3.35	1.92	21.54	0.04	0.03
Mar-99	−2.48	−2.75	1.89	16.93	0.14	0.26	−4.12	−3.37	1.94	20.56	0.03	0.04
Jun-99	−2.45	−2.53	1.86	15.03	0.12	0.19	−4.09	−3.61	1.91	18.30	0.02	0.03
Sep-99	−2.50	−2.61	1.88	14.87	0.09	0.16	−4.37	−3.57	1.95	16.77	0.02	0.02
Dec-99	−2.36	−2.90	1.81	16.06	0.23	0.31	−3.86	−3.17	1.89	16.11	0.07	0.06
Mar-2000	−2.00	−2.45	1.72	14.22	0.60	0.26	−3.15	−2.34	1.79	12.72	0.27	0.06
Jun-2000	−1.74	−1.97	1.65	11.72	0.30	0.04	−2.68	−1.62	1.73	9.45	0.22	0.01
Sep-2000	−1.64	−1.83	1.63	10.35	0.32	0.03	−2.62	−1.31	1.72	6.97	0.21	0.01
Dec-2000	−1.44	−1.63	1.57	9.59	0.30	0.21	−1.50	−0.65	1.52	4.70	0.34	0.29
Mar-01	−1.24	−1.33	1.52	8.64	0.49	0.57	−1.11	−0.47	1.39	3.94	0.63	0.92

Source: Authors' estimates.

Notes: Sample period for the estimation ends in 2008:1 and starts from the quarter indicated in the first column.

Variables are defined as follows: WEXPR = world real exports (nominal exports, deflated by unit export values); REER = real effective exchange rates compiled by RBI (36-currency export weighted), OECD and IMF, respectively.

LB-Q(2) and LB-Q(4) = p-values of Box-Pierce-Ljung Q-statistic for the null of no residual autocorrelation for two and four lags, respectively.

IMPORTS

As regards the domestic activity variable, industrial GDP is found to be a better indicator vis-à-vis overall GDP, reflecting the tilt of the commodity composition of imports toward industrial raw materials. The null hypothesis of one cointegrating vector cannot be rejected. The long-run coefficients are on the expected lines and are statistically significant. Annex Table 6 shows that income elasticity of imports with respect to domestic industrial GDP turns out to be around 1.55 in all the cases. The coefficient on the REER ranges from 0.19 to 0.42 and, as in the case of exports, is higher for the RBI-REER. The short-run dynamics indicate that the ECM terms are correctly signed and, both the variables—imports and REER—adjust to the deviations from the equilibrium.

Annex 4: Determinants of Gold Imports

In view of the significant jump in gold imports, we empirically assess the role of the potential determinants—gold prices, domestic inflation, domestic interest rates, currency movements, and returns on other assets—highlighted in previous studies (RBI 2013a; Starr and Tran 2008; Vaidyanathan 1999). Using monthly data from April 2004 to December 2012—the period selection is governed by availability of monthly data on the value of gold imports—the following alternative specifications are estimated. The first uses nominal variables augmented by domestic price variables (equation 1) and the second uses the real variables (equation 2):

$$MG_t = a + trend + b.\ \Delta LPG_t + c.\Delta LP_t + d.RN_t + e.\ \Delta LBSE_t + f.\ \Delta E_t + u_t \ (1)$$

$$MG_t = a1 + trend + b1.\ \Delta LPGR_t + d1.RR_t + e1.\ \Delta LBSER_t + f1.\ \Delta ER_t + u_t \ (2)$$

Here ΔL is the first difference of log terms of the variables and the variables enter in the first difference as they turn out to be stationary.[9] MG is the volume of monthly gold imports, PG is the local-currency gold price, P is domestic prices (measured by WPI or CPI), RN is the nominal deposit interest rate, BSE is Bombay Stock Exchange (BSE Sensitive) index, E is the exchange rate (Rupees per US dollar), PGR is the local-currency gold price in real terms, RR is the real deposit interest rate, BSER is the real BSE index, and ER is the real exchange rate. The real variables are obtained by

9. Augmented Dickey–Fuller (ADF) tests indicate that the null of unit root cannot be rejected for the level series (other than monthly imports and WPI), but can be rejected at the 5% level of significance for their first-differences.

ANNEX TABLE 6. Determinants of Imports (Annual Estimates)

	Results for REER-RBI				*Results for REER-OECD*		*Results for REER-IMF*			
L(IMPQ)	1.00		1.00		1.00		1.00		1.00	
L(REER)	–0.39		–0.42		–0.32		–0.19		–0.21	
	(3.70)		(3.74)		(5.85)		(4.90)		(5.17)	
L(INDR)	–1.57		–1.57		–1.57		–1.55		–1.55	
	(32.33)		(32.04)		(45.04)		(59.84)		(60.60)	
CONSTANT	15.58		15.70		15.45		14.67		14.63	
	(15.12)		(14.86)		(23.26)		(29.34)		(29.68)	
Short-run ECM model										
ECM(–1)	–0.38	0.48	–0.33	0.48	–0.30	0.48	–0.93	0.54	–0.74	0.60
	(1.80)	(4.56)	(1.77)	(4.87)	(1.67)	(5.65)	(2.93)	(2.39)	(2.53)	(2.77)
DLIMPQ(–1)	0.17	–0.37	0.21	–0.37	0.04	–0.43	0.39	–0.12	0.34	–0.16
	(0.68)	(3.08)	(0.94)	(3.17)	(0.21)	(4.39)	(1.58)	(0.71)	(1.48)	(0.91)
DLREER(–1)	0.09	–0.17	0.17	–0.17	0.35	0.16	0.47	–0.03	0.50	–0.06
	(0.32)	(1.16)	(0.63)	(1.16)	(1.15)	(1.08)	(1.56)	(0.13)	(1.75)	(0.27)
DLIMPQ(–2)	0.30	–0.01	0.21	–0.04			0.38	0.23	0.27	0.17
	(1.42)	(0.09)	(1.10)	(0.40)			(1.99)	(1.66)	(1.47)	(1.26)
DLREER(–2)	0.32	–0.45	0.22	–0.48			0.53	–0.08	0.36	–0.13
	(1.10)	(3.06)	(0.83)	(3.35)			(1.84)	(0.37)	(1.30)	(0.65)
DLINDR	2.32	0.23	1.98	0.21	2.18	0.16	2.44	–0.37	2.10	–0.36
	(4.76)	(0.92)	(4.32)	(0.87)	(4.81)	(0.74)	(5.46)	(1.14)	(4.92)	(1.14)
DLINDR(–1)	–2.27	0.92	–1.84	1.03	–0.87	0.45	–2.17	–0.01	–1.70	0.12
	(3.17)	(2.55)	(2.74)	(2.89)	(1.98)	(2.19)	(3.40)	(0.01)	(2.71)	(0.25)
DLINDR(–2)	0.28	–0.38	0.32	–0.32			0.01	0.11	0.05	0.23
	(0.48)	(1.30)	(0.59)	(1.10)			(0.02)	(0.28)	(0.09)	(0.59)

(Annex Table 6 Contd)

(Annex Table 6 Contd)

		Results for REER-RBI			*Results for REER-OECD*			*Results for REER-IMF*		
dum84			−0.17		−0.22	0.02			−0.16	−0.03
			(2.48)		(2.87)	(0.41)			(2.40)	(0.63)
Serial correlation @	0.21		0.06		0.32		0.14		0.04	
ARCH @	0.15	0.78	0.23	0.89	0.59	0.16	0.43	0.78	0.37	0.61
Normality @	0.41	0.50	0.20	0.46	0.59	0.06	0.17	0.92	0.11	0.86
R^2	0.48	0.64	0.57	0.67	0.52	0.77	0.56	0.58	0.61	0.61
VAR lags	3		3		2		3		3	
PV (r=0)	0.01		0.02		0.01		0.03		0.03	
PV (r=1)	0.48		0.81		0.39		0.57		0.78	

Source: Authors' estimates.

Notes: Sample period for the estimation is 1980–81 to 2007–08.

Variables are defined as follows: IMPQ = quantum index of India's imports; INDR = India's real industrial GDP;

REER = real effective exchange rates compiled by RBI (36-currency trade weighted), OECD and IMF, respectively.

dum84 is dummy for 1984–85.

Rows PV (r=0) and PV (r=1) give p-values (Bartlett-corrected) for the null of no and one cointegrating vector, respectively.

@: p-values for the null hypotheses of no serial correlation, no conditional heteroskedasticity and normality of residuals.

Figures in parentheses are t-statistics.

deflating the nominal variables with either WPI or CPI in the respective specifications. The real interest rate is computed as the nominal deposit rate less y-o-y WPI (or CPI) inflation. Monthly dummies are included to capture seasonality. A trend term is also included, as a proxy for higher incomes over the time period, which could have a positive impact on demand (Vaidyanathan 1999); however, Starr and Tran (2008), in their panel study, find a negative relationship between recent income growth and gold demand, but a positive impact of income volatility on gold demand.

In all, four specifications are estimated as shown in Annex Table 7: columns 2 and 3 estimate equation (1) for CPI and WPI, respectively. Correspondingly, columns 4 and 5 estimate equation (2) for the real variables (nominal variables deflated by CPI and WPI, respectively).[10] All the specifications have relatively good explanatory power and the regressions diagnostics are satisfactory.

ANNEX TABLE 7. Determinants of Gold Demand

	Dependent variable: Monthly gold imports (LMG)			
	Sample Period			
Explanatory variable	*2004:4–2012:12*	*2004:4–2012:12*	*2004:4–2012:12*	*2004:4–2012:12*
1	*2*	*3*	*4*	*5*
Constant	1.77	1.73	1.79	1.76
	(5.14)	(4.98)	(4.77)	(4.83)
TREND	0.00	0.00	0.00	0.00
	(3.83)	(4.25)	(3.01)	(3.47)
LMG(−1)	0.25	0.24	0.34	0.31
	(3.86)	(3.67)	(5.18)	(4.54)
DLPG	−6.24	−6.43		
	(8.39)	(8.62)		
DLPG(−3)	−1.05	−0.99		
	(1.55)	(1.45)		
DLPG(−4)	1.23	0.91		
	(1.76)	(1.33)		
DLPG(−5)	1.56	1.61		
	(2.19)	(2.24)		
DLPG_R			−6.39	−6.77
			(8.42)	(8.99)
DLPG_R(−3)				−1.33
				(1.86)
DLPG_R(−5)			1.82	1.45
			(2.40)	(1.95)

(Annex Table 7 Contd)

10. The equations are estimated with six lags of each variable and the insignificant variables are excluded using the STWISE command in WinRATS.

(Annex Table 7 Contd)

Explanatory variable	Dependent variable: Monthly gold imports (LMG)			
	Sample Period			
	2004:4–2012:12	2004:4–2012:12	2004:4–2012:12	2004:4–2012:12
1	2	3	4	5
DLCPI{1}	6.84			
	(1.83)			
DDRATE{1}	0.26	0.20		
	(1.79)	(1.38)		
DDRATE{2}	0.43	0.46		
	(3.13)	(3.27)		
DDRATE_R{2}			0.08	
			(2.39)	
DLBSES{4}	0.58	0.77		
	(1.38)	(1.86)		
DLBSES_R{4}			0.74	
			(1.70)	
DLEXCH	–2.58	–1.92		
	(1.81)	(1.38)		
DLEXCH_R{1}				–1.94
				(1.39)
DLEXCH_R{5}			–3.21	–3.48
			(2.12)	(2.49)
DUM2006M6	–1.63	–1.65	–1.64	–1.63
	(5.62)	(5.61)	(4.95)	(5.05)
R-bar^2	0.68	0.67	0.62	0.63
DW	2.07	2.10	2.16	2.00
White test	0.52	0.53	0.34	0.65
JB test	0.47	0.46	0.68	0.58
LB-Q test	0.28	0.27	0.16	0.18

Source: Authors' estimates.

Notes: MG = monthly gold imports; PG = Price of gold in rupees;

CPI = Consumer price index; WPI = Wholesale price index.

PG_R = Price of gold in rupees deflated by CPI (column 4) and WPI (column 5).

BSES = Bombay Stock Exchange Index (BSE-30); EXCH = Exchange rate (Rupees per US dollar)

Prefix DL stands for log difference.

DDRATE = Variation in deposit rate; DDRATER = Variation in real (CPI-adjusted) deposit rate;

DLEXCH_R = exchange rate depreciation less CPI inflation (col. 4) and WPI inflation (col. 5)

Figures in parentheses are t-statistics.

White test = significance level (p-value) for White test for the null of homoskedasticity of residuals.

JB test = significance level (p-value) for Jarque-Bera test for the null of normality of residuals;

LB-Q test = significance level (p-value) of Box-Pierce-Ljung Q-statistic for the null of no residual autocorrelation for 6 lags.

Sample period for regression is April 2004–December 2012 and the regressions include monthly dummies.

References

Acharya, Shankar. 2013. "BoP: Zero Dark Thirteen?," *Business Standard*, March 13. Available at http://www.business-standard.com/article/opinion/bop-zero-dark-thirteen-113031300624_1.html

Anand, Rahul, David Coady, Adil Mohommad, Vimal Thakoor, and James P. Walsh. 2013. "The Fiscal and Welfare Impacts of Reforming Fuel Subsidies in India." Working Paper WP/13/128, International Monetary Fund.

Asali, Mehdi. 2011. "Income and Price Elasticities and Oil-saving Technological Changes in ARDL Models of Demand for Oil in G7 and BRIC," *OPEC Energy Review*, 35 (3): 189–219.

Atoyan, Ruben, Jonathan Manning, and Jesmin Rahman. 2013. "Rebalancing: Evidence from Current Account Adjustment in Europe." Working Paper WP/13/74, International Monetary Fund.

Auboin, Marc and Michele Ruta. 2013. "The Relationship Between Exchange Rates and International Trade: A Literature Review," *World Trade Review*, 12 (3): 577–605.

Aziz, Jahangir and Sajjid Chinoy. 2012. "India: More Open Than You Think," *Economic Research*, J. P. Morgan.

Aziz, Jahangir and Xiangming Li. 2008. "China's Changing Trade Elasticities," *China and World Economy*, 16 (3): 1–21.

Baldwin, Richard and Paul Krugman. 1989. "Persistent Trade Effects of Large Exchange Rate Shocks," *Quarterly Journal of Economics*, 104 (4): 635–54.

Bayoumi, Tamim, Richard Harmsen, and Jarkko Turunen. 2011. "Euro Area Export Performance and Competitiveness." Working Paper WP/11/140, International Monetary Fund.

Barth, James R., Gerard Caprio, Jr., and Ross Levine. 2013. "Bank Regulation and Supervision in 180 Countries from 1999 to 2011." Working Paper 18733, National Bureau of Economic Research.

Berger, Brett and Robert Martin. 2013. "The Chinese Export Boom: An Examination of the Detailed Trade Data," *China & World Economy*, 21 (1): 64–90.

Berman, Nicolas, Philippe Martin, and Thierry Mayer. 2012. "How Do Different Exporters React to Exchange Rate Changes?," *Quarterly Journal of Economics*, 127 (1): 437–92.

Bhalla, Surjit. 2013a. "India's Negative Growth Miracle," *Indian Express*, June 13.

———. 2013b. "What You Sow Is Not What You Reap," *Indian Express*, October 19.

Bi, Ran, Haonan Qu, and James Roaf. 2013. "Assessing the Impact and Phasing of Multi-Year Fiscal Adjustment: A General Framework." Working Paper WP/13/182, International Monetary Fund.

Chinn, Menzie. 2006. "A Primer on Real Effective Exchange Rates: Determinants, Overvaluation, Trade Flows and Competitive Devaluation," *Open Economies Review*, 17 (1 January): 115–43.

Chinn, Menzie. 2013. "Export and Import Elasticities for Japan: New Estimates." Working Paper 2013-004, Robert M. La Follette School of Public Affairs, University of Wisconsin-Madison.

Economic Advisory Council to the Prime Minister. 2013. "Review of the Economy 2012/13," April, Government of India, New Delhi.

Eichengreen, Barry et al. 2011. "Rethinking Central Banking," Committee on International Economic Policy and Reform. Available at http://www.brookings.edu/research/reports/2011/09/ciepr-central-banking

Freund, Caroline and Martha Denisse Pierola. 2012. "Export Surges," *Journal of Development Economics*, 97 (2): 387–95.

Government of India. 2013a. "Economic Survey 2013–14," February. Ministry of Finance, New Delhi.

———. 2013b. "Report of the Financial Sector Legislative Reforms Commission (Chairman: B. N. Srikrishna)," March. Ministry of Finance, New Delhi.

Greenlaw, David, James D. Hamilton, Peter Hooper, and Frederic S. Mishkin. 2013. "Crunch Time: Fiscal Crises and the Role of Monetary Policy," 2013 US Monetary Policy Forum. Available at http://research.chicagobooth.edu/igm/events/conferences/2013-usmonetaryforum.aspx

Gros, Daniel. 2013. "The Austerity Debate Is Beside the Point for Europe," *CEPS Commentary*, Centre for European Policy Studies, May 8.

Hamilton, James. 2008. "Understanding Crude Oil Prices." Working Paper 14492, National Bureau of Economic Research.

Hooper, Peter, Karen Johnson, and Marquez, Jaime. 2000. "Trade Elasticities for the G-7 Countries." Princeton Studies in International Economics No. 87, Princeton University, Princeton, NJ.

International Monetary Fund (IMF). 2013a. "India: Staff Report for the 2013 Article IV Consultation." International Monetary Fund, Washington, D.C.

———. 2013b. "Key Aspects of Macroprudential Policy." International Monetary Fund, Washington, D.C.

———. 2013c. "World Economic Outlook," October. International Monetary Fund, Washington, D.C.

Jain, Rajiv and Prabhat Kumar. 2013. "Size of Government Expenditure Multipliers in India: A Structural VAR Analysis." Working Paper 07/2013, Reserve Bank of India.

Joshi, Vijay and I. M. D. Little. 1994. *India: Macroeconomics and Political Economy, 1964–1991*. Washington, D.C.: World Bank Publications.

Kappler, Marcus, Helmut Reisen, Moritz Schularick, and Edouard Turkisch. 2013. "The Macroeconomic Effects of Large Exchange Rate Appreciations," *Open Economies Review*, 24 (3): 471–94.

Kapur, Muneesh and Harendra Behera. 2012. "Monetary Transmission Mechanism in India: A Quarterly Model.'' Working Paper 09/2012, Reserve Bank of India.

Lane, Philip and Gian Maria Milesi-Ferretti. 2010. "The Cross-Country Incidence of the Global Crisis." Working Paper WP/10/171, International Monetary Fund.

Mishra, Prachi. 2013. "Has India's Growth Story Withered?," *Economic and Political Weekly*, 48 (15): 51–59. April 13.

Mody, Ashoka and Michael Walton. 2013. "What Type of Crisis for India?," *Business Standard*, May 6.

Mohan, Rakesh. 2009. "Transforming Indian Banking: In Search of a Better Tomorrow." *Monetary Policy in a Globalised Economy*. New Delhi: Oxford University Press.

———. 2011a. *Growth with Financial Stability*. New Delhi: Oxford University Press.

———. 2011b. "The Growth Record of the Indian Economy: A Story of Sustained Savings and Investment," in Rakesh Mohan 2011a.

———. 2011c. "The Global Financial Crisis: Causes, Impact, Policy Responses, and Lessons," in Rakesh Mohan. 2011a.

———. 2011d. "Economic Reforms in India: Where Are We and Where Do We Go?," in Rakesh Mohan 2011a.

Mohan, Rakesh, Michael Debabrata Patra, and Muneesh Kapur. 2013. "Currency Internationalization and Reforms in the Architecture of the International Monetary System: Managing the Impossible Trinity." Working Paper WP/13/224, International Monetary Fund.

Mohan, Rakesh and Muneesh Kapur. 2011. "Managing the Impossible Trinity: Volatile Capital Flows and Indian Monetary Policy," in Rakesh Mohan 2011a.

Nagaraj, R. 2013. "India's Dream Run, 2003–08: Understanding the Boom and Its Aftermath," *Economic and Political Weekly*, 48 (20): 39–51, May 18.

Nier, Erlend, Jacek Osiński, Luis Jácome, and Pamela Madrid. 2011. "Institutional Models for Macroprudential Policy," Staff Discussion Note 11/18, International Monetary Fund.

Obstfeld, Maurice. 2009. "International Finance and Growth in Developing Countries: What Have We Learned?," *IMF Staff Papers*, 56 (1): 63–111.

Organization for Economic Cooperation and Development (OECD). 2013. OECD-WTO Trade in Value Added (TiVA). Available at http://stats.oecd.org/Index.aspx?DataSetCode=TIVA_OECD_WTO

Panagariya, Arvind. 2013. "The Tyranny of the Balance-of-Payments," *Times of India*, March 9. Available at http://articles.timesofindia.indiatimes.com/2013-03-09/edit-page/37580432_1_current-account-deficit-cad-capital-inflows

Patnaik, Ila, Sarat Malik, Radhika Pandey, and Prateek. 2013. "Foreign Investment in the Indian Government Bond Market," SEBI DRG Study No. 1, Securities and Exchange Board of India.

Rajan, Raghuram. 2013. "The Case for India," Project Syndicate, September 11. Available at http://www.project-syndicate.org/print/how-to-fix-india-s-economy-in-the-short-term-by-raghuram-rajan

Rangarajan, C. and Prachi Mishra. 2013. "India's External Sector: Do We Need to Worry?," *Economic and Political Weekly*, 48 (7): 52–59, February 16.

Rangarajan, C. 2013. "Containing the Demand for Gold," Speech at the 6th International Gold Summit, May 15. Available at http://eac.gov.in/aboutus/ch_speech.htm

Reinhart, Carmen and Kenneth Rogoff. 2009. *This Time is Different: Eight Centuries of Financial Folly*. Princeton: Princeton University Press.

———. 2013. "Shifting Mandates: The Federal Reserve's First Centennial," *American Economic Review: Papers & Proceedings*, 103 (3): 48–54.

Kelkar Committee. 2012. Report of the Committee on Roadmap for Fiscal Consolidation (Chairman: Vijay Kelkar). Ministry of Finance, Delhi.

Reserve Bank of India (RBI). 2006. "Mid-Term Review of Annual Policy Statement for the Year 2006–07." Reserve Bank of India, Mumbai.

———. 2012. "Macroeconomic and Monetary Developments: First Quarter Review 2012–13." Reserve Bank of India, Mumbai.

———. 2013a. Report of the Working Group to Study the Issues Related to Gold and Gold Loans NBFCs in India (Chairman: Mr. K. U. B. Rao), February. Reserve Bank of India, Mumbai.

———. 2013b. "Macroeconomic and Monetary Developments in 2012–13," May. Reserve Bank of India, Mumbai.

———. 2013c. "Real Interest Rate Impact on Investment and Growth: What the Empirical Evidence for India Suggests?," August. Reserve Bank of India, Mumbai.

———. 2014. Report of the Expert Committee to Revise and Strengthen the Monetary Policy Framework (Chairman: Urjit R. Patel), January. Reserve Bank of India, Mumbai.

Rodrik, Dani. 2008. "The Real Exchange Rate and Economic Growth," Brookings Paper on Economic Activity, 39 (Fall): pp. 365–439.

Senhadji, Abdelhak. 1998. "Time Series Estimation of Structural Import Demand Equations: A Cross-Country Analysis," *IMF Staff Papers*, 45 (2): 236–68.

Senhadji, Abdelhak and Claudio Montenegro. 1999. "Time Series Analysis of Export Demand Equations: A Cross-Country Analysis," *IMF Staff Papers*, 46 (3): 259–73.

Subbarao, Duvvuri. 2011. "Monetary Policy Dilemmas: Some RBI Perspectives," *Reserve Bank of India Bulletin*, October, 45 (10): 1655–62.

———. 2013a. "India's Macroeconomic Challenges: Some Reserve Bank Perspectives," *Reserve Bank of India Bulletin*, April, 47 (4): 29–40.

———. 2013b. "The Global Financial Crisis and the Indian Financial Sector: What Have We Learnt and How Have We Responded?" *Reserve Bank of India Bulletin*, July, 47 (7): 1–10.

Subramanian, Arvind. 2013. "Setting Some Conditions," *Business Standard*, July 24.

Starr, Martha and Ky Tran. 2008. "Determinants of the Physical Demand for Gold: Evidence from Panel Data," *The World Economy*, 31 (3): 416–36.

Tang, Heiwai and Yifan Zhang. 2012. "Exchange Rates and the Margins of Trade: Evidence from Chinese Exporters," *CESifo Economic Studies*, 58 (4): 671–702.

Tapsoba, Sampawende J. A. 2013. "Options and Strategies for Fiscal Consolidation in India." Working Paper WP/13/127, International Monetary Fund.

Tarapore, S. S. 2013a. "A Plot to Destroy RBI," *Business Line*, May 2.

———. 2013b. "Let the Rupee Slide, and Fast," *Business Line*, June 13.

Thorbecke, Willem and Kato Atsuyki. 2012. "The Effect of Exchange Rate Changes on Germany's Exports." Discussion Paper 12-E-081, Research Institute of Economy, Trade and Industry.

Vaidyanathan, A. 1999. "Consumption of Gold in India: Trends and Determinants," *Economic and Political Weekly*, 34 (8): 471–76, February 20.

Volcker, Paul. 2013. "Central Banking at a Crossroad," Remarks at the Economic Club of New York, May 29.

World Bank. 2013. "Global Economic Prospects," vol. 7, June. Washington, D.C.: World Bank.

Comments and Discussion

Shankar Acharya
ICRIER

The paper by Kapur and Mohan (henceforth KM) provides an informative and thoughtful review of the deterioration in India's macroeconomic performance since the global financial crisis of 2008–09 (which KM dub the North Atlantic Financial Crisis) and up to the summer of 2013. It adds the welcome dimension of placing India's performance in the context of overall macro performance of other major developing countries. However, for a paper presented in mid-July 2013, it is surprisingly muted, almost soothing, on the evolution of the serious *crisis* in the Indian economy that had clearly unfolded by then.[11] How else would one describe a situation where economic growth had collapsed, industrial output had stagnated for two years, jobs were being shed, consumer inflation was close to 10% for the fifth consecutive year, the current account deficit (CAD) in the balance of payments was nearly 5% of GDP by 2012–13, investment was fleeing abroad, external debt maturing in fiscal 2013–14 exceeded US$170 billion, and the rupee was depreciating rapidly, touching new lows (or highs against the US$!) each week?

The paper is also somewhat reticent in drawing pointed attention to the major policy errors of the United Progressive Alliance (UPA) government, which had been mainly responsible for engendering this sorry state of India's economic affairs. In this brief comment I will outline five key policy errors (out of a long list), which not only helped precipitate the crisis but also made it difficult to bring about any swift recovery.

Before doing this, I must point out one conspicuous dimension which is missing from KM's macroeconomic review, namely, employment. This is a particularly striking omission when one recalls that the father of modern macroeconomics, John Maynard Keynes, was motivated in his seminal work principally by the high and persisting unemployment in the 1930s in the United Kingdom and other industrial nations. Admittedly, there are big problems with India's employment data. But it would still have been

11. For more critical reviews of macroeconomic developments, see Acharya (2012a, 2012b).

useful to use the available information to outline trends, especially given that India's much touted demographic dividend is in serious danger of turning into a major unemployment/underemployment disaster. Let me now turn to the government's major policy errors.

Fiscal Blowout of 2008–09

In the six years to 2007–08 the combined (Centre and states) fiscal deficit had been brought down from nearly 10% of GDP to 4%. This remarkable fiscal consolidation was squandered in the single, pre-election year of 2008–09 when the combined deficit (inclusive of off-budget items) leapt to over 10% of GDP. The Central government budget deficit target of 2.5% of GDP, presented by the Finance Minister, Mr P. Chidambaran, in February 2008, was massively overshot in the course of the year to yield an outcome of 8.2% of GDP (including off-budget items), easily the biggest overshooting in India's history. Although later it was rationalized as "fiscal stimulus" to counteract the global crisis, in fact, the great bulk of the overshooting occurred before the Lehman crisis of September 2008, mainly in the form of pay increases, subsidy hikes, and MGNREGA rollout.

This unprecedented splurge of fiscal profligacy may indeed have cushioned the fall-out from the global crisis for a year or two. But the composition of the huge expenditure hikes (mainly government pay, subsidies and entitlement programs) made subsequent retraction politically difficult. As a result, the persisting high fiscal deficits since 2008 have fuelled the long bout of inflation, kept interest rates high, reduced public savings, and fed the rising CAD.

Exchange Rate Mismanagement since 2009

Although senior government spokesmen tended, in 2013, to project India's external deficit pressures as a recent problem, in fact, the CAD had been consistently above the Prime Minister's "safe benchmark" of 2.5% of GDP since 2009–10, and rising to 4% of GDP in 2011–12 and 2012–13. This meant that by summer 2013 that we were in the fifth year of a dangerously high CAD. A significant contributory factor had been the authorities' (government plus RBI) shift, since the Spring of 2009, to a relatively "hands-off" policy toward the rupee's exchange rate. So when capital inflows recovered after 2009, the rupee was allowed to appreciate strongly in 2009 and 2010, despite a sharply rising CAD. This is borne out by most indices of real effective exchange rates, as KM point out. The authorities would have done better to have followed the well-tested, pre-2008 policy of limiting appreciation and building reserves through dollar purchases by the RBI, accompanied by calibrated sterilization policies. The failure to do this led to an overvalued rupee, which weakened India's international competiveness and helped fuel the pattern of rising external deficits that culminated in extreme external liquidity pressures and steep depreciation of the rupee in summer 2013.

The Supply Shocks of 2010–12

These were multiple, all reflecting policy and governance weaknesses. They include the sudden and damaging tightening of environmental regulations in 2010; the eruption of serious scams in 2G telecom spectrum allocation, coal block allocations, and various land scams (all with roots in earlier years), and their debilitating aftermaths in the impacted sectors; the sweeping judicial restraints on iron ore mining in Karnataka and Goa; the fiasco of missing coal and gas supply for many thousand megawatts of freshly completed power projects; the anti-investment, retrospective tax measures of the 2012 budget; and the generalized "policy paralysis" in regard to activation, completion and clearances of major projects. All these supply problems reduced production, investment and growth and some also directly hurt the external balance, as in the case of coal and iron ore.

While each of these supply-side problems had distinct characteristics and policy histories, together they constituted a major (and persisting) supply shock to the Indian economy and seriously undermined the business climate.

The Neglect of Manufacturing

In a more medium-term framework, and in marked contrast to the great majority of emerging nations, the share of manufacturing in GDP has stagnated at around 15–17% for decades in India. While the problem is long-standing, the failure to enhance the share during the past decade was a significant contributory factor in the current economic crisis. During the high growth period, from 2003 to 2011, services (including construction) accounted for well over 70% of all growth, while industry (essentially manufacturing and mining) accounted for less than 20%. This lopsided pattern could not sustain high growth for long, and has not done so once services expansion started to flag. The major policy impediments to industrial growth have been unreformed rigidities in the labor market, growing impediments to land acquisition (now enshrined in the cumbersome new Land Acquisition Act), and the continuing weaknesses in infrastructure, especially power, roads, railways, and ports. Slow industrial growth has led to limited growth of jobs for low-skilled labor and a steady widening of the merchandize trade deficit, which, in turn, widened the CAD.

More generally, the prolonged drought in economic reforms since 2004 probably has had a cumulatively negative impact on overall productivity growth in all major sectors of the economy.

Food Grain Procurement and Distribution Policies

Five consecutive years of double-digit consumer price inflation has been a new and unwelcome development in India. Aside from the persistence of high fiscal deficits, major supply shocks and, perhaps, an overly accommodative monetary policy, the last few years have seen a strong pattern of rising government minimum support prices for food grains (wheat and rice) combined with high levels of government procurement, highly subsidized food entitlement distribution through an inefficient public distribution system and a reluctance to undertake open market sales of very high excess food stocks. The result has been that the government has, in effect, become the largest hoarder of food grains, thus contributing to the rise in food prices and, possibly, rural and urban wage inflation.

Outlook

In their concluding section, KM seem to be fairly optimistic on reviving growth and restoring macroeconomic stability. They say "the structural drivers of growth—the favorable demographics and the high savings and investment rates—are broadly intact." As I have pointed out, where labor demand is not buoyant, it is hard to reap a demographic dividend from burgeoning labor supply. As for high investment and savings rates, these are already trending down in a context where the returns, in the form of growth, are not happening. Much of the high investment reflects a huge backlog of unfinished or stalled projects; thus fresh investments may be less forthcoming, especially in a difficult business climate. Moreover the simultaneous existence of low growth and high investment is also due to the worsening of economic policies in recent years, some of which may not be easy to reverse. Restoring fiscal balance will also be challenging, given low buoyancy in revenues, the enduring legacy of expanded entitlement programs (and associated subsidies), and the rising claims for capital infusions from highly stressed public sector banks. With existing infrastructure companies highly leveraged, it is difficult to see how the extant infrastructure bottlenecks will be swiftly resolved.

In sum, a recovery in growth, lower inflation, and better macro balances are likely to be slower in coming and harder to achieve than KM suggest. The damage from bad economic policies of the last few years will take time to reverse.

Vijay Joshi

University of Oxford

The purpose of the Kapur–Mohan paper is to (a) explain the main features of India's recent adverse macroeconomic experience (marked slowdown in growth, large CADs, inflation well above the target), (b) assess the extent to which macroeconomic policy was responsible for these unsatisfactory outcomes, and (c) suggest how macroeconomic policy should be managed in future.

Growth Slowdown

My argument in this section is based on Tables 1 and 6 in the paper.

Unsurprisingly, in 2008/09, the year in which the global credit crisis exploded, India's growth rate fell to 6.7%, that is, two percentage points below the annual average of the previous five years. It then rebounded to almost 9% a year in the following two years (2009/10 and 2010/11) but fell back sharply to around 5.5% in the following three years (2011/12–2013/14).[12]

The authors have two explanations for the slowdown from 2011/12 onward. First, they argue that it was the result of the withdrawal of accommodative monetary and fiscal policies, which were implemented during the 2008/09 crisis and kept in place for the following two years. But this, as they recognize in their section on "Quantifying the Growth Slowdown," cannot explain much because real monetary tightening from 2011/12 was quite mild, and fiscal consolidation was also very modest. The main explanation for the slowdown is clearly the large fall in corporate investment in 2011/12 and its failure to revive thereafter.[13] (National accounts figures for corporate investment are not yet available after 2011/12 but all informal indicators point to such non-revival.) How is this fall to be explained? Let us adopt the term "gap" to denote the difference between investment and saving. The

12. GDP is expected to grow in 2013/14 by around 5%.

13. Note that corporate investment collapsed in 2008/09 but recovered during the high-growth years of 2009/10 and 2010/11.

authors' second explanation for the slowdown is that corporate investment in 2011/12 was "crowded out" by a rise in the public sector "gap." As it happens, the rise in the public sector "gap" in 2011/12 is too small to explain the magnitude of the fall in corporate investment.[14] The authors appear to have a slightly different hypothesis in mind. In their view, the fall in corporate investment in 2011/12 was a delayed effect of the rise in the public sector gap in earlier years. (These earlier years must refer to 2008/09 and 2009/10, since the public sector "gap" fell in 2010/11.)[15]

This "lagged crowding out" hypothesis faces a serious problem. There is no explanation of the underlying theory or lag structure. Moreover, there is an obvious competing explanation of the slowdown that the authors make no attempt to evaluate. This more plausible causal story would start with an autonomous fall in corporate investment and in the corporate "gap" in 2011/12. To cushion the resulting slowdown, fiscal consolidation was put on hold, so the public "gap" rose. Since there was accompanying high inflation, household financial savings fell and the household gap increased. The sum of the rise in the public and household "gaps" outweighed the fall in the corporate "gap," so the foreign "gap," that is, the CAD, rose. I find this story much more plausible.

This alternative story needs an explanation of the "autonomous" decline in corporate investment. In my view, two factors were important. One of these the authors completely ignore, the other they underplay. The factor they ignore altogether is that corporate investment was hobbled by an overhang of debt. This arose from heavy borrowing (financed by debt, not equity) by corporates in the go–go years of 2003/04–2007/08. When the boom burst in 2008/09, companies continued borrowing to complete their unfinished projects but they became progressively more weighed down with debt. Eventually, the need to deleverage prompted the cancellation or postponement of new investment.[16] There is a second explanation for the drop in corporate investment in 2011/12 and thereafter. The authors do mention it briefly, in passing, but it is far more important than they make out. This is the souring of the investment climate that occurred because of various

14. Moreover, the causality could be quite different. The identity public gap + corporate gap + household gap = foreign gap (i.e. the current account deficit) is just that, an identity. It is compatible with a different causal story in which the leading factor is the fall in corporate investment, and public sector investment and saving play a passive role, as explained in the main text later.

15. Readers will notice that I have tried to tell the authors' story with more attention to the precise timing than they do themselves.

16. See Reserve Bank of India (2012) and Nagaraj (2013).

significant governance failures. From 2010, the government got mired in various scams, such as those in telecom and mining. The exposure of these was a good thing for the future of Indian democracy but the short-term economic effects were unhelpful. Output of critical materials was adversely affected (for example mine closures ordered by the Supreme Court led to a huge fall in the output of iron ore). The government entered a period of policy paralysis, ministers and civil servants became excessively cautious and unwilling to make decisions, and many projects, which required government clearances, came to a standstill. The spate of scandals heightened public sensitivities over land acquisition and environmental impacts. But the government was not able to put in place speedy and fair systems to deal with these issues, so investments were held up. On top of all this, the government shot itself in the foot by various silly initiatives like retrospective taxation of some foreign companies. The net effect of all this was that the risk premium on investment went up sharply.[17]

Which is the more plausible story: One that accords prime place to crowding out by the public sector or one that accords prime place to the effects of a debt overhang and an adverse change in the expected rate of profit on new investment (Keynes would have called it "a fall in the marginal efficiency of capital")? The authors advance the "crowding out" story; I much prefer the alternative story. The main point is that the authors make no attempt to discriminate between these two explanations.

As regards restoring rapid growth, the authors have little to say apart from advocating fiscal consolidation. While the latter is indeed a crucial medium-run requirement, it is far from sufficient as a recipe for re-igniting growth in the short run, if the above analysis is correct.

Widening of External Imbalance

I have no quarrel with the list of usual suspects identified in the paper to explain the pronounced widening of the CAD in 2011/12 and 2012/13: sluggish global demand, high world commodity prices, domestic supply constraints, shift toward gold in household savings, and appreciation of the real exchange rate in earlier years. How do they rank in relative importance? In my view, the authors underplay the importance of the real exchange rate.

Their views are in part guided by econometric exercises that estimate income and price elasticities of demand for exports. As one would expect,

17. The investment climate was also adversely affected by macroeconomic concerns such as the continuing high inflation and the worsening current account deficit.

they find an income elasticity of demand for exports greater than 1. But they come up with price elasticities of demand that are less than 1, not only in the short run but also in the long run, in the model with annual data (albeit somewhat higher in a quarterly disaggregated model over a shorter time-period.) Like many such estimates, theirs are unconvincing. This is because they are based on single-equation models, which mix up demand and supply. Robust elasticity estimates can only come out of a structural model in which export demand and export supply equations are estimated in a simultaneous equation framework. In my book on India's macroeconomics with Ian Little, we estimated such a model for the period 1960–90.[18] Across a wide range of specifications, we found the short-run price elasticity of demand to be greater than 1, and the long-run elasticity to be around 3, with more than 80% of the long-run effect coming through within two years. (But these estimates are now quite old and need to be updated.)

The importance of this point for recent Indian experience is that, in my judgment, the RBI made absolutely the wrong call on exchange rate policy for two years from August 2009 to August 2011. During this period, capital inflows were strong but the RBI abandoned its traditional policy of managing the exchange rate, and allowed the rupee to find its level in the foreign exchange market without any intervention. The rupee rose and the real effective exchange rate appreciated by around 10% (regardless of which index is chosen: RBI, BIS, IMF), and remained at that level for two years. Thereafter, the exchange rate fell but by then the damage had been done. The "strong rupee" played a major role in the export slowdown and import surge of 2011/12 and 2012/13, and the consequent widening of the CAD to well above 4% of GDP.

Inflation

The authors' discussion of inflation is curiously narrow and restricted to monetary policy. I agree with their argument that in contrast to much popular commentary, monetary policy was highly accommodative in the face of rapid inflation until well into 2011/12. (At first, the real policy rate of interest fell; then it rose but only in the sense of becoming somewhat less negative.) It is only in 2012 that monetary policy became moderately restrictive, so it is not surprising that inflation proved to be so stubborn. This is correct, but there is more to the persistence of inflation than the timing of monetary policy. Two factors deserve special mention. First, government intervention in the

18. See Joshi and Little (1994) for more details.

food market has been inept. Procurement prices for cereals were raised an astonishing 75% from 2007 to 2011. At the same time, the government showed marked reluctance to unload its huge food stocks to moderate food prices. Second, indexation mechanisms are stronger than they used to be due to the indexation of wages in the NREGA program. (This scheme is important way beyond the number of workers employed under its aegis, because it sets a rising floor to rural money wages.) In turn, this makes it easier for inflationary expectations to get entrenched. It is notable that rural farm money wages grew 17% a year from 2008 to 2012.

Stronger formal and informal indexation mechanisms (large revisions of procurement prices, indexation of NREGA wages, more generous pay commission awards, in addition to dearness allowance revisions of wages in organized industry) have important implications for future policy. They imply that (a) the traditional policy of avoiding contractionary monetary policies during droughts, and simply waiting for a better harvest, is much less likely to work in future and (b) the output cost of bringing inflation down may be greater in the future than it was in the past. In other words, India will probably face a much sharper short-run trade-off between inflation and growth than hitherto.

The new inflation environment has brought into focus the question "Should India adopt inflation targeting?" The authors' discussion of this critical issue is cursory and rather superficial.

Fiscal Policy

I have no quarrel with the authors' view that the fiscal stimulus was withdrawn too late after 2008/09 and that its composition was defective. But fiscal consolidation, as pointed out earlier, is not enough to revive growth.

I also agree with the authors that, in the medium run, fiscal consolidation is imperative. But the challenge is bigger than the authors make out. Since 2008, the ratio of government debt to GDP has fallen somewhat, because of high inflation. Past experience shows that nominal interest rates on government debt are quite sticky. When inflation is brought under control, the real government borrowing rate will rise. That will make it harder to reduce the debt ratio. A connected point is that the interest rate on government borrowing is artificially low due to statutory state capture of bank lending (i.e., "financial repression"). This practice needs to be unwound because it keeps deposit rates too low for savers and the cost of borrowing too high for companies. But when it is unwound, the government borrowing rate will rise. So, the true debt position today is worse than it appears. To reduce it to safe levels, medium-term fiscal adjustment will have to be sharper than generally recognized.

The Boom of 2003–08

Another shortcoming of the paper is that the authors follow the general tendency of regarding the period of 2003/04–2007/08 as a model of good policy. This is not quite right. The good outcomes during this phase were, to a significant degree, due to favorable conditions such as a strong tail-wind from the world economy and the absence of food or oil shocks. Policy was not as good as it is often cracked up to be. Several points are noteworthy: (a) During this period, there were large annual net capital inflows of up to 10% of GDP. These were taken into foreign exchange reserves, with only modest exchange rate appreciation. As a result, broad money and bank credit expanded at a very rapid rate, and the resulting monetary overhang contributed to inflation later on. More aggressive sterilization of the inflows would have helped. (b) Apparently, fiscal consolidation made large strides: the overall (i.e., Center + States) fiscal deficit fell from 9% to 4% of GDP over the period. But the improvement in the cyclically adjusted deficit was surely far less. Fiscal adjustment should have been sharper during what was a period of above-trend growth. (c) Companies borrowed like there is no tomorrow, with dire results later on. This suggests that monetary and credit policies should have been tougher. (d) The period was characterized by little, if any, genuine supply-side reform. This paved the way for a reduction in the potential rate of growth in due course.

General Discussion

Surjit Bhalla liked the approach used in the paper to distinguish between domestic and external influences on the economy and he agreed with the conclusion that India's recent economic problems are very much of its own creation. However, he thought that evidence of a relationship between the fiscal deficit and inflation was lacking. Similarly, he could find little evidence of a link between interest rates and either public or private saving.

T. N. Srinivasan argued that it was difficult to evaluate the policies without a model in which a counterfactual could be developed. Without one, the authors were essentially waving their hands. He wanted the paper to be more explicit about the structure of the underlying macroeconomic model. Furthermore, he believed that the growth slowdown predated the global financial crisis in the fall of 2008, and that it was due to long-standing problems such as the CAD and a long list of governance failures. During the global crisis, the primary shock was the drop in exports, and he did not believe that monetary easing was an appropriate offset in those circumstances.

Prema-chandra Athukorala argued that the export slowdown could be traced to demand factors. India's share in exports from developing countries is declining, and India's export slowdown is more pronounced than that of China and other East Asian countries. He believed that the primary problem was that the policy reforms had not made India an attractive location as a production node within the regional production network that has developed in East Asia. In particular, India's policy reforms have not attracted export-oriented FDI. Thus, among the supply-side issues is the question of why investors have not come to India.

Govinda Rao applauded the timeliness of the paper's focus on macroeconomic issues but he thought that they were dominated by the fiscal challenge and that within the fiscal area the problems were concentrated in the growth of subsidies and transfers. Devesh Kapur added that the elections of 2008 had to be part of the story because of the additional fiscal spending that they induce. The same problem has been predicted to rise in 2014. He also argued that there was a fundamental lack of public trust in the governance system as reflected in Indian households investing in gold and Indian corporations expanding their investments outside India. Anupam Khanna was concerned about an excessive government focus on attracting foreign capital. Much of the capital inflow has been short term in nature and could easily be reversed in the future. He thought there were similar time bombs associated with domestic capital investments that could also generate pressures for investors to exit.

Mihir Desai agreed with Vijay Joshi's emphasis on developments in the corporate sector to account for the slowdown in industrial production and investment. In addition, he thought that it was possible to see the period of 2003–08 could be seen as being anomalous, instead of as a benchmark for sustainable growth. It occurred against the backdrop of a debt-ridden global economy, and large capital inflows into India that spurred domestic investment. Thus, the baseline for expected future growth should be scaled down to a rate well below that of 2003–08. Surjit Bhalla disagreed and thought that the experience during those years was very much in line with that of countries that experience sustained growth expansions.

Renu Kohli pointed out that interest rates were abnormally low in 2010 and 2011, and the low borrowing costs encouraged the rise in government spending. Shankar Acharya thought that both fiscal and monetary stimulus were appropriate responses to the global crisis, but that the composition of the fiscal stimulus was wrong and it proved difficult to reverse. He also disagreed with allowing the exchange rate to appreciate during the period.

References

Acharya, Shankar. 2012a. *India after the Global Crisis*. New Delhi: Orient BlackSwan.

———. 2012b. "India and the Global Crisis," in C. Fred Bergsten and C. Randall Henning (eds), *Global Economics in Extraordinary Times*. Washington, D.C.: Peterson Institute for International Economics.

Joshi, Vijay and I. M. D. Little. 1994. *India—Macroeconomics and Political Economy*, Washington, D.C./New Delhi: World Bank Publications/Oxford University Press.

Nagaraj, R. 2013. "India's Dream Run: Understanding the Boom and Its Aftermath," *Economic and Political Weekly*, 48 (20): 39–51.

RBI. 2012. *Financial Stability Report*, December, Department of Communication, Mumbai.

FARZANA AFRIDI*
Indian Statistical Institute, New Delhi

VEGARD IVERSEN†
University of Manchester, UK

Social Audits and MGNREGA Delivery: Lessons from Andhra Pradesh

ABSTRACT Using unique panel data assembled from official reports, we study the impact of social audits on Mahatma Gandhi National Rural Employment Guarantee Act delivery in Andhra Pradesh. Within a dynamic framework where beneficiaries, auditors, and transgressors interact and learn, we find a positive but insignificant impact of audits on employment generation and a modest decline in the leakage amount per labor-related irregularity: outcomes with high beneficiary stakes. This occurs alongside an increase in material-related irregularities with lower beneficiary stakes. Although we find evidence suggestive of beneficiary "learning" and of audit effectiveness in detecting irregularities, repeated audits did not deter irregularities. This highlights the need for a time-bound process where transgressors are punished and responsibilities for follow-up of social audit findings laid out and credibly enforced.

Keywords: *MGNREGA, NREGS, NREGA, Social Audits, Corruption*

JEL Classification: *H1, I3*

* *fafridi@isid.ac.in*
† *vegard.iversen@manchester.ac.uk*

The authors would like to thank the Government of Andhra Pradesh, particularly R. Subrahmanyam and Sowmya Kidambi for fruitful discussions and for facilitating access to the social audit reports. We are indebted to Devesh Kapur, Dilip Mookherjee, and to other IPF participants for incisive comments and Yamini Aiyar, Neelakshi Mann, Tom Newton-Lewis, and Jyotsna Puri for thoughtful remarks. This paper has also benefitted from comments by participants at 3ie's Delhi seminar, IGC South Asia conference (Lahore), and an NREGA conference at IGIDR, Mumbai. Swati Sharma provided excellent research assistance. The authors acknowledge financial support from the International Growth Centre (IGC, LSE-Oxford), No-POOR (European Union), and the Planning and Policy Research Unit (PPRU) at the ISI, Delhi. The usual disclaimers apply.

1. Introduction

In spite of mixed experiences (e.g., Adato et al. 2005; Mansuri and Rao 2013), people's participation and social accountability (e.g., Joshi and Houtzager 2012) as mechanisms to foster transparency and improve public program delivery in developing countries are, once more, in vogue. In the public work projects implemented under India's largest program to date, the Mahatma Gandhi National Rural Employment Guarantee Act (MGNREGA; Government of India 2005), "social" audits have been made mandatory. The responsibility for audit implementation is vested with *gram sabhas* (p. 9, Section 17, I and II of the Act), which are plenary meetings of adult residents of *gram panchayats* (GPs) (village councils). The Act thus empowers intended beneficiaries to scrutinize program expenditures and to monitor and keep track of program delivery.[1]

Without sufficient institutional support, however, the expectation that beneficiary-led audits should spontaneously arise is unsustainable. Inspired by the civil rights movement spearheaded by the Mazdoor Kisan Shakti Sangathan (MKSS)[2] in Rajasthan and other similar initiatives, the state government of Andhra Pradesh (AP) responded swiftly to this weakness in the Act (Aiyar et al. 2013). The early establishment of a pilot audit scheme was followed by the first steps toward a full institutionalization of the social audit process in the state (ibid.). By November 2007, social audits had been implemented in 400 of AP's 650 MGNREGA Phase-I sub-districts, a record no other Indian state can match (Aakella and Kidambi 2007).[3]

The AP social audit model is perceived as successful both within and beyond India's borders (Subbarao et al. 2013). The scaling up of this model to other Indian states makes it pertinent to distil lessons about what these affordable audits have been able to achieve so far.[4] To the best of our knowledge, this is the first attempt to rigorously assess the impacts of a

1. In a study of Food for Work Programs in three districts of AP, predating MGNREGA, Deshingkhar and Johnson (2003) highlight the democratic deficiencies of gram sabhas.

2. Translated into English, MKSS is short for the Association for the Empowerment of Workers and Peasants.

3. This first phase implementation of MGNREGA started in February 2006 and targeted the 200 poorest districts in the country.

4. The cost of social audit implementation in AP has been low, absorbing between 0.5 and 1% of annual MGNREGA expenditure. The Ministry of Rural Development, Government of India, issued a circular to all state governments in 2012 earmarking up to 1% of annual MGNREGA expenditure for social audits.

large-scale community monitoring initiative in India. By highlighting the strengths and shortfalls of AP's unique social audit experience, our aim is to improve effectiveness of community monitoring in AP and elsewhere.

The ideal design for identifying the causal effect of social audits on program delivery would be to randomize social audit implementation. Since the social audits in AP were not rolled out randomly, districts where social audits were conducted early may have had more (or fewer) program failures than districts audited later on. Comparing MGNREGA outcomes between early and late social audit recipients could therefore distort estimates of audit impacts.

In this paper we adopt the next best strategy by resorting to a panel data set assembled through meticulous extraction and translation of information from original social audit reports. The panel covers the years 2006–10 and comprises official data from up to three rounds of social audits from an initial sample of 300 GPs in eight districts of AP. Our analysis focuses on whether program performance measured by irregularities in program implementation—the immediate concern of social audits as well as employment and program expenditures—is affected by additional audits within the same sub-district over time.

Among these performance indicators, we prioritize outcomes that relate directly to malpractices and irregularities that speak to widespread concerns about leakages and corruption in large public programs in India.[5] In addition, data on the local bureaucracy and elected panchayats enable us to assess the interaction between local government characteristics and program leakages which is crucial for improving public program delivery. We control trends that could potentially impact the quality of program delivery and corruption: *mandal*-level (subdistrict-level) attributes and secular and district-level time trends to account for and filter out the potential rise in households' awareness about program entitlements, the growing sophistication of audit teams, and the general rise in program activity.

Once we address these potential confounders, for our study period, we detect a positive but insignificant effect of social audits on employment generation and find no effect on the aggregate number of MGNREGA irregularities detected by the audit process. We find a marginally significant decline in the complaint amount per labor-related irregularity. This is accompanied by an increase in more sophisticated and harder-to-detect

5. Other likely effects and potential benefits from social audit participation are discussed later.

material-related irregularities.[6] These main results are robust to sensitivity checks that account for reporting biases and the potential endogeneity of audit intensity. We conclude that while audits may be effective in *detecting* irregularities, their impact, if any, on *deterring* malpractice is modest. This highlights the need for a time-bound process where transgressors are punished and responsibilities for follow up of social audit findings are laid out and credibly enforced.

The remainder of our paper is organized as follows: Section 2 presents a brief review of experiences with participation and bottom-up monitoring of public service delivery. We focus, selectively, on monitoring processes that quite closely resemble AP's social audits. Section 3 narrates the development of the social audit model of AP. Section 4 describes the data and presents descriptive statistics while Section 5 explains our conceptual framework. The estimation methodology is presented in Section 6. Results are discussed in Section 7 while Section 8 concludes and spells out the policy implications.

2. Literature Review

Our theoretical entry point is the question of whether a particular form of monitoring or auditing affects the quality of public service delivery. This is tangential to the broader theme of community-based development, and to questions of social accountability and whether "participation" works (e.g., Joshi and Houtzager 2012; Mansuri and Rao 2013).[7] As noted by Aiyar et al. (2013: p. 251), the vision of the MKSS is embedded in a discourse on rights-based democratic action, where social audits not only represent an anti-corruption tool but "a platform on which citizens can be empowered to directly exercise their democratic rights." Social audits thus ensure bottom-up involvement and opportunities for stakeholders to learn by doing through the repeated interaction with audit teams and as the process of MGNREGA delivery unfolds.[8]

6. In our conceptual framework, we link this to learning among beneficiaries, auditors, and transgressors and attempt to decipher the underlying logic of this shift.

7. Mansuri and Rao (2013) distinguish, conceptually, between "organic" and "induced" participation. The AP social audit model is an example of induced participation.

8. Conceptually this resembles Joshi and Houtzager's (2012: p.146) definition of social accountability as "citizen-led action for demanding accountability from providers" which privileges the "short" and direct route to service providers (Ringold et al. 2012). This is in contrast to the "long" and indirect route—via the electoral process—to improve service delivery (ibid.).

In a particularly relevant study, Adato et al. (2005) seek to identify the impacts of "participation" on the quality of public work programs in South Africa. Evidence from 101 South African public work programs suggests that participation—conceptualized and measured as varying in degree, e.g., where the community is either the sole decision-maker, a joint decision-maker or taking on an advisory role—is reported to strongly affect scheme performance as measured by the project budget share spent on labor, log number of days of work created, and the log number of training days on offer.

The suggestion, thus, is that local stakeholder involvement affects delivery along dimensions that the same stakeholders or beneficiaries can be expected to care deeply about. Even if such effects on the quality of delivery were not immediately discernible, for instance because learning operates with a time-lag, exposure to and participation in a social audit is likely to bolster awareness about MGNREGA entitlements and rules.[9]

Thus, a plausible conjecture is that participatory audits are more likely to be effective when addressing program outcomes with high beneficiary stakes. High stakes may not, however, be sufficient since beneficiaries also need the knowledge or capacity to act on their interests (as represented by their stakes).[10] This begs the question of how best to strengthen beneficiary capacity. In MGNREGA, beneficiary learning appears to take place mainly "by doing" which may limit the effectiveness of participatory audits for outcomes that are less transparent and irregularities that are hard to detect. The capacity to detect is, in general, likely to depend on the complexity of relevant public program outcomes, as suggested by Khemani (2008). We return to this discussion later.

A few studies have touched upon the effectiveness of community-based monitoring. Bjorkman and Svensson (2009) (BS from now on) report the findings of experimentally induced community monitoring of health care provision in Uganda. Their intervention comprised of a two afternoon community meetings where a variety of participatory methods were introduced to "encourage community members to develop a shared view on how to improve service delivery and to monitor the provider" (ibid.). Information on patient rights and entitlements was disseminated while focus group discussions were organized to reach out to and absorb the views of marginalized groups. Local suggestions for improvements, and how to obtain these

9. Some such findings are reported in Aiyar et al. (2013) and, in addition to the above, include changes in the perceptions of government officials and greater confidence to approach such officials.

10. Ringold et al. (2012) highlight the importance of capacity.

without injecting additional resources, were synthesized in an action plan. Simple as this may sound, it is not very different from what a well organized social audit would set out to achieve.[11]

The next step in the intervention closely resembles the public hearing in the AP social audit model: a one afternoon event at the health facility where all staff is present followed by a meeting between community members and health staff. The final and mandatory outcome of this process is a "contract," a shared and agreed plan of action that sets out what needs to be done, how, by whom, and by when.

The simplicity is an appealing aspect of the BS design and in spite of the limited duration, the reported impacts are remarkable. Apart from affecting process monitoring, service delivery improvements are reported for a series of relevant outcomes. There are ultimately impacts on health, including a radical decline in under-5 mortality.

In another community mobilization attempt, this time to improve the quality of public education provision in Uttar Pradesh (UP), Banerjee et al. (2010) shared information about the quality of schools, report cards showing children's reading ability and possible routes for improvement (e.g., via Village Education Committees) in community meetings where teachers, local government representatives, and village residents were all present. In contrast to BS, this particular evaluation found no impact of such village-wide meetings on community participation, teacher effort, or learning outcomes.[12]

If, as in the Uganda example, transformative effects can be achieved through such simple interventions, optimism on behalf of the AP social audit model seems justified given the many parallels between the BS intervention and the AP model. But what about the lessons from UP? A comparison between the UP and the Uganda interventions may, as Khemani (2008) suggests, throws up a fundamental contrast between the experience of or observability of substandard teaching and the quality of health services which local users may possibly have a better eye for and comprehension of. Put differently, community mobilization to improve education provision

11. There is a notable tension between the short-term and snapshot interventions BS (2009) and Banerjee et al. (2010) report on and the longer term engagements advocated and deemed necessary in the social accountability literature (Joshi and Houtzager 2012).

12. BS's and Banerjee et al.'s (2010) identification of impacts were made easier by randomized interventions: the attribution of desirable change to social audits, on the other hand, is made harder both by the absence of a credible source of exogenous variation in the quality of social audits and by the likelihood that problem areas are more likely to attract audits.

may involve tougher pedagogical challenges. While stakes are expected to be high for both health and education, initial capacity constraints may be more binding for educational outcomes. A similar argument may apply to the distinction between labor and material-related irregularities in MGNREGA projects.

Another missing ingredient, both in the AP model and the UP intervention, is the "contractual outlay" to address grievances and how, by whom, and by what time these grievances should be addressed. This underscores the importance of effective grievance redressal in community-based monitoring efforts: hence, even if the AP social audit process is found to be effective in *detecting* irregularities, this would be a necessary but not sufficient condition to *deter* irregularities. What difference would it have made to BS's result if the final contract had been omitted? We return to this issue in our discussion of policy implications.

3. The History of Public Works and the Genesis of the AP Social Audit Model

Prior to MGNREGA, and like other Indian states, AP's performance in the implementation of public works was often dismal (Aiyar et al. 2013) and regularly undermined by the capture of vested interests, in particular through collusion between private contractors and local politicians (e.g., Deshingkhar and Johnson 2003).[13]

The social audit process was initiated in AP by setting up the Strategy and Performance Innovation Unit (SPIU) under the state's Rural Development Department in 2006. SPIU was mandated with conducting the social audits of MGNREGA projects and headed by a director, a state civil servant, and assisted by a consultant, formerly with the MKSS. Eventually, the responsibility for conducting regular and systematic audits of MGNREGA projects was transferred to a new and autonomous arm of the Department of Rural Development (the Society for Social Audits, Accountability and Transparency (SSAAT)) in May 2009. As of today, the SSAAT director is an independent consultant and not part of the state government.

This initiative makes AP unique and distinct from other Indian states where audits have either not been conducted or been implemented in an

13. As part of our retrospective household survey in 2011, we asked 1,500 beneficiary households in AP about their satisfaction with the scheme. While indicative, we found a strong stakeholder endorsement and satisfaction with MGNREGA in AP.

ad hoc and unsystematic manner.[14] AP's record on social audit implementation is similarly unique. Systematic and standardized audits have been carried out in all 23 districts of AP with an average of over two rounds of audits completed per GP between 2006 and 2010.

3.1. The Social Audit Process in AP[15]

The first step in conducting the social audit is a notification to the relevant sub-district or mandal office with reference to Right to Information (RTI) obligations and requesting unrestricted access to muster-rolls and other relevant MGNREGA project documents (ibid.). A team comprising state and district auditors will, upon their arrival in the mandal headquarter, first recruit and then, in a two-day workshop, intensively train village social auditors about MGNREGA rights and regulations, how to conduct the social audits, and how to obtain information under RTI legislation (ibid.). The village social auditors are MGNREGA beneficiaries and residents of the mandal.

The social audit teams will then, over a period of about a week, organize social audits in all GPs of the mandal. In each GP, official labor expenses are verified by visiting laborers listed in the worksite logs ("muster-rolls"). Complaints by individuals or groups of beneficiaries and the audit team are recorded and attested using a standardized audit report template.[16] For verification of material expenditure, the audit team is mandated to undertake worksite inspections. Except for the more obvious and easy-to-detect (ETD) irregularities such as "ghost" or non-existent projects, the verification of material expenditure is typically perceived to be more complex and demanding. Thus, the social audit process in AP uniquely combines a top-down approach (i.e., timing and conduct of audits controlled by the SSAAT) with grassroots participation (i.e., village social auditors and local stakeholders).

Once the audits of all GPs have been completed, a mandal-level public hearing with mandatory attendance for all implementing officials is organized to discuss the audit findings. Those present, typically include "wage seekers from the villages in the mandal, the social audit team, branch postmaster, key implementing officials, members of the vigilance cell, elected representatives, and a district-level ombudsman" (Aiyar et al. 2013: p. 261).

14. Even though some states have recently responded to the Act by conducting "regular" social audits, the exercise has been largely superficial with claims of no irregularities in program implementation.

15. In narrating the content of the AP social audit model, we draw extensively on Aiyar et al. (2013).

16. The auditors are expected to verify labor records for all beneficiaries. This may not be true in practice.

Complaints will be read out, testimonies verified, and accused officials given an opportunity to defend themselves.

After the public hearing a decision taken report (DTR) is created by the officer presiding over the hearing. In this report the responsibility for each confirmed malfeasance is pinned on a program functionary or, as the case may be, on multiple functionaries.[17] Until 2010, the mechanism for redressing issues raised by the social audit and mentioned in DTRs was weak.[18] However, in 2010, the state set up a vigilance cell within the Department of Rural Development (Aiyar et al. 2013). Under this mechanism, copies of the DTRs are sent to key program functionaries for follow-up action within days of the public hearing, including the district vigilance officer. The vigilance office then issues an action taken report (ATR) which lists the action taken against errant officials in the DTR (ibid.).

4. Data

Our panel data were extracted and codified from the official and original Telugu social audit reports for 100 randomly sampled mandals across eight districts of AP.[19] In each randomly chosen mandal, three GPs were selected based on the following criteria: the GP which was the administrative headquarter of the mandal, one GP randomly selected from all GPs reserved for a female sarpanch, and one randomly selected from GPs not reserved for a female sarpanch in that mandal in 2006. Our initial sample, thus, comprises 300 GPs from 100 mandals.

The GP-audit reports have two components: a standard audit report card which records the date of the audit along with the demographic characteristics of the GP, and more importantly, audit team impressions about process performance since the last audit including a financial misappropriations estimate. These impressions and estimates are based largely on the second component of the audit report—the list of complaints filed by individuals, groups, or by audit team members. The complaints are recorded during the

17. The SSAAT has introduced checks and balances to prevent local program functionaries who are being audited from corrupting audit team members.

18. In the above parlance, the social audit process lacked procedural tightness.

19. These eight districts were Mahbubnagar, Medak, Nizamabad, Warangal, and Khammam (north or the Telangana region), Anantpur and Kurnool (south or the Rayalseema region), and Guntur (west or the coastal region). MGNREGA was implemented in February 2006 in all these districts, except Kurnool and Guntur, which implemented the program from April, 2007 onward.

door-to-door verification of labor expenditures and during project site inspections to verify material expenditures by technical members of the audit team. Each complaint is supported by affidavits and brought up during the public hearing. As noted earlier, during the public hearing the responsibility for each complaint is pinned on one or multiple MGNREGA functionary(-ies). We use data on all verified complaints, following the public hearing.

These data are available from the first round of audits that began in 2006 and until 2010.[20] We construct a panel of audit reports for each GP with an average of over two reports per GP for the period 2006–10. We supplement the official audit data with data from interviews with the mandal parishad development officer (MPDO) and the GP sarpanch elected in 2006 for a five year term. These retrospective surveys were conducted during April–June, 2011. Data from the Census (2001) provide village-level characteristics such as infrastructure and access to public services.

In addition to the audit data, we also obtained information on program performance from the Department of Rural Development's (AP) web site for the financial years 2006–07 to 2010–11.[21] These data on program expenditures and employment were cumulated across financial years prior to the financial year in which the audit occurred and then linked to each GP by the audit date. The data, therefore, inform us about program expenditures and person days of work covered in each audit. We also linked program expenditures and person days of work generated post audit (and before the next audit) to each GP to assess the effect of an audit on subsequent program performance.

4.1. Descriptive Statistics

The social audit data facilitate comparisons by audit round and complaint type. Table 1 presents a breakdown of the average number of complaints by type across all rounds. We categorize complaints into three types—labor related, those related to materials used in MGNREGA projects, and the provision of work-site facilities mandated by the Act—labeled "other complaints". Labor complaints account for 87% of all complaints. This is not surprising since the problems that trigger labor complaints more directly affect beneficiary households. At the same time, the average real amount per

20. Original audit reports that were missing were supplemented with abridged versions of the audit reports available from the SSAAT web site: http://125.17.121.162/SocialAudit/ Web site

21. The following link was accessed between July–August, 2013 to obtain information on program expenditures and employment: http://nrega.ap.gov.in/Nregs/FrontServlet?requestType=NewReportsRH&actionVal=Display&page=Newreportcenter_ajax_eng

TABLE 1. Summary Statistics Across All *gram panchayats*

Variable	*Number of audits*	*Mean*	*Std. dev.*	*Min.*	*Max.*
All complaints	711	5.822	5.298	0	43
Labor complaints	711	5.061	4.594	0	30
Material complaints	711	0.683	1.519	0	18
Other complaints	711	0.077	0.306	0	3

Source: Authors' calculations from data extracted from official social audit reports.

material-related irregularity (₹28,786) was more than twice the real amount per labor-related irregularity (₹10,289) over the three audit rounds.

Table 2 shows trends by complaint type. If we restrict attention to audit rounds 1–3, there is a discernible rise in the total number of complaints between rounds 1 and 3 (Row 1), driven mainly by a disproportionate increase in the number of material complaints (173%) relative to the increase in the number of labor complaints (13%).[22]

TABLE 2. Number of Complaints by Audit Round

	Audit 1	*Audit 2*	*Audit 3*
Variable	*N=284*	*N=261*	*N=166*
All complaints	5.123	6.249	6.349
	(4.306)	(5.375)	(6.487)
Labor complaints	4.602	5.475	5.199
	(4.067)	(4.995)	(4.739)
Material complaints	0.415	0.689	1.132
	(0.740)	(1.186)	(2.541)
Other complaints	0.105	0.084	0.018
	(0.370)	(0.304)	(0.133)

Source: Authors' calculations from data extracted from official social audit reports.
Note: Standard errors in parentheses.

Table 3 disaggregates the type of complaint by audit round and captures broad trends: the rise in labor complaints appears to be mainly driven by administrative inefficiencies, specifically, a sharp rise in complaints for

22. There are notable differences in trends in irregularities across districts as shown in Table A1 in the Appendix. The district-wise trends in the number of complaints suggest that the five Telangana districts feature among the seven worst districts, with Anantapur and Kurnool only marginally worse than the *best* Telangana district (Medak). For material complaints, the Telangana districts are the five worst districts. This is suggestive of a different political economy of MGNREGA irregularities in Telangana. It is also evident that the average number of complaints is increasing, and dramatically in four of the five Telangana districts, with Khammam as the only and very notable exception. For Anantapur and Kurnool, audit 3 numbers are lower than everywhere else, but we have few third round audits in these districts.

TABLE 3. Proportion of Type of Complaint by Audit Round

Variable	*Audit 1*	*Audit 2*	*Audit 3*
Labor related	*N=262*	*N=236*	*N=151*
Non-payment/delay in wages	28.385	34.778	47.802
	(29.469)	(32.982)	(33.870)
Non-provision of work	15.012	10.001	7.697
	(23.794)	(20.238)	(18.048)
Impersonations/*benami* wage payments	19.301	26.023	16.901
	(27.418)	(30.511)	(25.996)
Excess wage payments/bribes	19.883	15.850	14.376
	(26.958)	(23.399)	(20.559)
Wage records missing	6.6034	6.023	6.711
	(14.371)	(14.807)	(15.634)
Material related	*N=86*	*N=96*	*N=65*
Non-existent work	14.438	28.675	25.146
	(32.070)	(39.484)	(37.783)
Poor quality of materials	44.864	18.663	6.239
	(47.489)	(34.787)	(24.206)
Excess payments/bribes	15.310	30.092	50.727
	(35.073)	(40.253)	(43.325)
Expenditure records missing	4.360	4.513	8.183
	(19.247)	(18.961)	(23.125)

Source: Authors' calculations from data extracted from official social audit reports.

Note: Standard errors in parentheses. Statistics conditional on a labor/material complaint being filed in an audit in a GP. Missing category of "other" in both labor and material-related complaint.

delayed payment or non-payment of wages over the three audit rounds. In contrast, we register a steep decline in complaints related to non-provision of work. Impersonations/*benami* wage payments and excess wage payments/bribes also decline, but marginally, between audits 1 and 3. There is no significant change in the audit teams' access to wage records as shown in the row "wage records missing." For the material component, grievances related to "non-existent work" and "excess payments/bribes" rose significantly alongside a sharp drop in irregularities related to "poor quality of materials." We also observe an increase in missing materials expenditure records.[23]

Finally, Table 4 summarizes program outcomes audited in each round. Real program expenditures more than doubled in the period after the first audit. Water conservation projects had the highest share of total program expenditure in audit 1 but this share along with that of drought and flood control fell in subsequent audits. There was a marginal increase in the share

23. Note that if expenditure records (viz. receipts of materials purchased) are not available to the audit team and those expenditures have been officially incurred, the auditors interpret this as leakage of program funds.

TABLE 4. Program Performance by Audit Round

Variable	*Audit 1* *N=282*	*Audit 2* *N=255*	*Audit 3* *N=161*
Total expenditure (in 2006 rupees, lakhs)	8.906	22.488	23.117
	(14.1)	(22.944)	(24.725)
Proportion of water conservation works	0.441	0.287	0.190
	(0.305)	(0.243)	(0.189)
Proportion of drought and flood control	0.086	0.027	0.012
	(0.160)	(0.081)	(0.072)
Proportion of rural connectivity works	0.023	0.086	0.089
	(0.081)	(0.153)	(0.138)
Total employment generated in person days	11615.71	31314.55	33104.46
	(18626.6)	(36375.54)	(36721.22)
Proportion of SC person days generated	0.298	0.275	0.253
	(0.264)	(0.221)	(0.179)
Proportion of ST person days generated	0.122	0.136	0.156
	(0.249)	(0.268)	(0.276)

Source: Authors' calculations from data extracted from official social audit reports.

Note: Standard errors in parentheses. Expenditure deflated using the consumer price index for rural labor (http://labourbureau.nic.in/indtab.pdf), with base year as 2006. Rows (2)–(4) are calculated as proportions of row (1). Rows (6)–(7) are calculated as a proportion of row (5).

of program expenditures on rural connectivity works from audit 1 to 3. On employment generation, total person days increased almost threefold during this period but there were no significant changes in the share of SC (marginal decline) or ST (marginal increase) person days. Thus, overall, we observe a sharp rise in program activity during the study period.

While the summary statistics are suggestive of the trends in program performance, our main challenge is to obtain convincing clues about the impacts of social audits on corruption and on the quality of program delivery. We introduce our conceptual framework before addressing the methodological challenges.

5. Conceptual Framework: Linking Stakes, Capacity, and Learning

Except for Joshi and Houtzager's (2012: p. 155) emphasis on the need "to examine social accountability actions as one part of a broader and longer process of engagement between collective actors and the state", the existing literature tends to bypass the repeated behavioral interactions between and learning by beneficiaries, social audit teams, and public officials (transgressors) that repeated social audits may give rise to.

This section outlines some basic assumptions we make about the behavioral response of all actors in the audit process that aid the interpretation of our empirical results. We first assume that the state commits to conducting regular social audits. However, the first round of the social audit, given low state credibility, takes public officials (or transgressors) by surprise. Further, the cost of effort for basic program delivery transgressions is low. Second, local MGNREGA beneficiaries have high stakes in employment availability and in timely and due pay. There is, moreover, sufficient capacity on the part of audit teams and local beneficiaries to detect transgressions in basic program delivery.

As a result, we expect more ETD irregularities in the initial audit round. In subsequent audit rounds, beneficiaries may become more effective participants while auditors become more adept. We should, thus, observe a decline in ETD irregularities. At the same time, transgressors expect audits in the future and benefit from staying one step ahead of the auditors.

We thus anticipate an evolving dynamic process with improved auditing and signs of more effective local participation through learning. The drawback is that transgressions may also become more sophisticated. The introduction of monitoring may thus result in substitutions of one type of irregularity for another as transgressors learn to manipulate the new system while discovering other avenues for rent extraction (Olken and Pande 2011). Hence, if we assume that auditors' learning is unable to catch up with learning by those who are audited, then we would observe more harder-to-detect irregularities.[24] Figure 1 links, in a simplified manner, our discussion of beneficiary capacity and stakes to this evolving process of learning and response.

Our assumptions are borne out by the data. While AP had conducted multiple audits in all mandals by 2010–11, state commitment to monitoring had no precedent. Further, in the first audit round, 80% of all labor-related complaints were filed by local beneficiaries. Roughly half of these were in the "hard-to-detect (HTD)" category. Among beneficiaries, therefore, stakes appear to trump complexity from the start. In contrast, social audit teams submitted 80% of the material complaints in the first audit round. By audit round 2, there was already a greater diversity in beneficiary complaints, with a higher share of material complaints, spread across ETD and HTD.

24. However, even if audits become more effective in detecting irregularities, deterrence may remain weak. In order to change transgressor behavior, we thus need to assume either that being caught is sufficiently "costly" even in the absence of formal punishment or that beliefs about strong, future punishment are widespread.

FIGURE 1. Beneficiary Stakes and Capacity of Participatory Social Audits

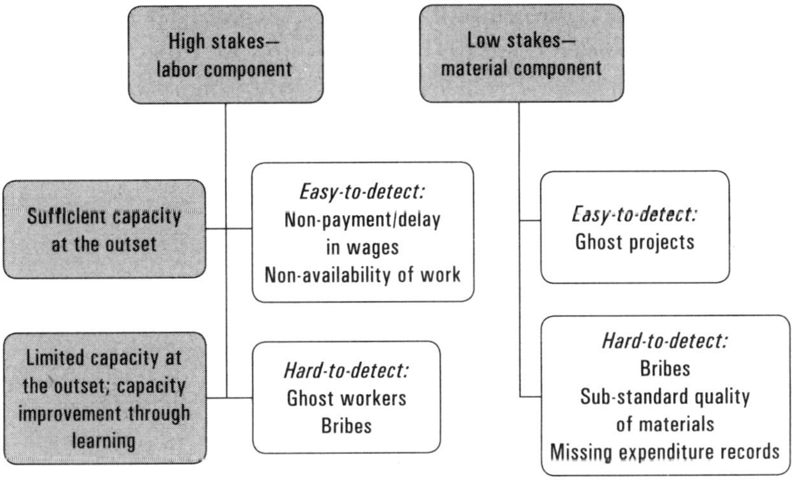

Source: Authors' calculations from data extracted from official social audit reports.

Note: ETD labor-related irregularities comprise of non- and delayed wage payment and non-availability of work. HTD labor-related irregularities comprise of *benami* and bribes. ETD material-related irregularities relates to "ghost" or non-existent project. HTD material-related irregularities comprise material bribes, substandard material quality, and missing material records.

By audit round 3, the latter accounted for 60% of the material complaints filed by beneficiaries.

Contrast this with the complaints filed by the social audit team which divide, more sharply, between ETD and HTD irregularities, for labor and materials and change little over time: the share of HTD irregularities in all labor complaints submitted by the audit team is never below 88%. For material complaints, the corresponding audit team figure is 76%. The share of HTD irregularities filed by the audit team for both labor and material complaints, however, increases by about 10 percentage points from audit round 1 to 3. These observations suggest that the social audit process imparts substantive learning on local beneficiaries. At the same time, and given that the large majority of social audit team complaints involve HTD irregularities, beneficiary learning is not sufficient to ensure that the participatory part of the process can fully handle the more complex labor and material irregularities. The top-down part—represented by the social audit team—and the participatory process, thus, appear to perform vital complementary roles.[25]

25. Olken (2009) finds that top–down audits may be more effective in curtailing corruption in public programs as opposed to a bottoms–up approach envisaged by community monitoring.

To summarize, if audits effectively detect malfeasance *and* the threat of punishment for malfeasance is credible, we expect ETD irregularities to decline with repeated audits. At the same time, we expect more HTD irregularities in later audit rounds due to the increasing sophistication of transgressors even as auditors and beneficiaries learn.[26]

6. Methodology

As noted, we take advantage of the panel structure of the data to assess whether program implementation improves with repeated social audits within the same mandal, over time, while controlling other trends that could potentially impact corruption and the quality of program delivery.

Our main specification is given by:

$$Outcome_{njklt} = a_0 + \sum a_n Audit_n + a_4 \mathbf{X}_{jkl} + a_5 D_k + \sum \eta_t Year_t + \sum \gamma_{lt} (D_l * Year_t) + \mu_{njklt} \quad (1)$$

The analysis is conducted at the GP-audit level. The findings of social audit n in GP j in mandal k in district l in year t is denoted by $Outcome_{njklt}$. Our outcomes comprise the different complaint variables described in section 4. The main coefficient of interest is the round of the social audit, or $Audit_n$, n taking values 2 and 3 with the first audit as the reference year. The coefficient on $Audit_n$ will tell us whether, relative to the first audit, irregularities in program implementation are higher or lower. X_{jkl} is a vector of time-invariant GP-level characteristics that includes attributes of the sarpanch elected in 2006 (for a five year term) such as gender, caste, education and age, the GP's access to health and education facilities, and the distance from the nearest town. It also includes a dummy variable for whether the GP is the mandal headquarter.

A few factors may confound the interpretation of a_n. First, recall that the audit is conducted at the level of the mandal. All GPs within a mandal are audited by a single audit team within a period of about one week. Some

Villagers' perception of corruption in a village road construction program in Indonesia rose by only 0.8% when actual corruption in the program rose by 10%.

26. In an ideal scenario, one would use independent measures of corruption or malfeasance in the program. Unfortunately, data are available only for malfeasance reported in the social audits. This is likely to be an underestimate of the true level of corruption or the true number of irregularities since some beneficiaries may not register their complaints, e.g., due to threats or intimidation.

mandals may be systematically better or worse at administering the program since the mandal-level bureaucracy plays a critical role in MGNREGA implementation. We therefore use mandal-level dummies, $D_{k.}$, to control this unobserved variation in the timing of the audit and in mandal-level implementation capability.

Second, the social audit findings, reported as the complaint types discussed earlier, might be influenced by (a) changes in awareness about program entitlements or beneficiary confidence in the integrity of the audit process because of repeated exposure and (b) by improvements in audit quality as audit team members become more adept at detecting discrepancies. For the former, with constant implementation quality, we would observe an increase in the number of beneficiary complaints over time.

To capture (a) we account for linear time trends by including dummies ($Year_t$) for the year in which the particular audit was conducted (dummy for each year between 2006 and 2010). The assumption here is that aver age awareness among beneficiaries would be higher in say, 2008 relative to 2006, due to repeated program exposure and irrespective of the number of audits conducted. A similar argument holds for (b).

Third, as pointed out earlier, some districts are more likely to be more (less) effective MGNREGA implementers. For instance, biometric beneficiary identification was introduced in some districts before others. Such district-level variations in technological advances, in program activity (i.e., number of MGNREGA projects or program expenditures) or in bureaucratic capacity, could influence the quality of program delivery and reported irregularities directly. Thus, to account for differences in program implementation trends across districts, we interact the dummy variable for each district with the dummy for each audit year (D_l*Year_t) and include these as additional controls.

In our second line of inquiry, we study the effect of audits on real program expenditures and employment generation. Specifically, we estimate the following model:

$$NREGA_{jkl,(t+1)} = \beta_0 + \sum\beta_n Audit_{n,t} + \beta_3 X_{jkl} + \beta_4 D_k + \sum\theta_t Year_t + \sum\delta_{lt}(D_l*Year_t) + \varepsilon_{njklt} \quad (2)$$

$NREGA_{jkl,(t+1)}$ is employment and expenditure under the program in GP j in mandal k in district l at time $t+1$. $Audit_{n,t}$ is a dummy variable for the nth audit in period t. The other variables are as described for our first specification. Note that our data pertain to audits 1 to 3. Since the outcome variable relates to the years between successive audits, the audit dummy variables included in the specification are for audits 1 and 2 for the years in our study. The corresponding MGNREGA data are for the cumulated outcome after the nth audit and before the $(n+1)$ audit. Thus β_n is an indicator of the impact of an audit on subsequent expenditures and employment generated under the program.

A remaining challenge is to decipher the interpretational possibilities that social audit data, in their present form, give rise to. Put differently, even if the social audits were implemented as RCTs with "impacts" amenable to robust identification, beneficiary complaints data could suffer from reporting biases that our (or an RCT-based) methodology is unable to fully account for. For instance, a decline in complaints may be due to intimidation by transgressors of beneficiaries who complained in previous audit rounds. Thus, fewer program irregularities may not reflect a genuine decline in malfeasance. In a similar manner, local politics may affect complainant behavior with a rise in complaints reflecting political maneuvering to harm, e.g., an incumbent.

To address this concern we undertake a robustness check of our main results by restricting the analysis to complaints filed by the audit team alone. We thus assume that the members of the audit team are unlikely to be intimidated or threatened and less likely to be swayed by local political biases.

7. Results

We first discuss results for the number of reported irregularities followed by program performance outcomes. Table 5 presents results on variation in the reported total, labor-related and material-related irregularities across audits, controlling for elected sarpanch and GP attributes, overall time trends (which, as noted, pick up changes in audit quality and awareness levels), district-specific trends, and mandal fixed effects. The specification, thus, assumes that unobservable differences in mandal characteristics and district specific trends may influence program quality. In column 1, the dependent variable is the total number of complaints filed in a social audit, while in columns 2 and 3 the outcomes of interest are the total numbers of labor and material complaints, respectively.[27]

27. When we account for whether the district belongs to the most disadvantaged and politically sensitive area of Telangana (north-west AP) or not, the results suggest that while the total number of complaints decreased by audit 3 in non-Telangana districts, Telangana experienced increases in complaints in both audits 2 and 3. Non-Telangana districts showed a decline in labor complaints filed in audit 3 relative to audit 1. Material-related complaints

TABLE 5. Effect of Social Audits on Total Irregularities

	All irregularities	*Labor-related irregularities*	*Material-related irregularities*
	(1)	*(2)*	*(3)*
(1) Audit 2	2.528*	1.740	0.818**
	(1.430)	(1.158)	(0.407)
(2) Audit 3	2.695	1.409	1.345**
	(1.973)	(1.680)	(0.553)
(3) Constant	9.457	11.73**	−2.788
	(6.375)	(5.565)	(1.694)
(4) Audit 3 – Audit 2	0.166	−0.330	0.526*
	(1.028)	(0.963)	(0.275)
R-square	0.420	0.448	0.282
Number of audits	685	685	685
Year fixed effects	Y	Y	Y
Mandal fixed effects	Y	Y	Y
District-specific trends	Y	Y	Y

Source: Authors' calculations from data extracted from official social audit reports.

Notes: All specifications include controls for sarpanch's age, sex, caste, education, prior political experience; availability of bank, communication, medical facility, and middle school in the GP; proportion of cultivated area which is irrigated, distance to town, population density, and whether the GP is the mandal headquarter. Standard errors clustered at the GP level reported in parentheses. ***significant at 1%, ** 5%, and *10%.

In column 1, the coefficient on audit 2 is positive and significant while the audit 3 coefficient is insignificant. Thus, overall, aggregate irregularities were higher in audit 2 than in audit 1 while there is no significant difference between audits 2 and 3 (row 4). Next, column 2 shows that labor complaints were not higher in rounds 2 and 3 relative to round 1. However, in column 3 we find more material complaints in audit rounds 2 and 3: a 197% and 324% increase, respectively, relative to round 1. There were also more such complaints in audit 3 than in audit 2 (row 4). Thus, there appears to have been a secular rise in irregularities related to material expenditure. Hence the increase in total complaints, albeit insignificant in audit 3, was likely driven by the rise in material complaints.

In Table 6, we classify labor- and material-related irregularities into "ETD" and "HTD" as discussed in the conceptual framework section earlier. Hence, within the labor component of the program—non-payment or delays in wage payments and non-provision of work are ETD while *benami* and bribe-related irregularities are classified as HTD. The results suggest that any increase in the number of labor-related irregularities was due to more

were significantly higher in Telangana districts in audit 3. It is possible that the effect of social audits in non-Telangana regions is insignificant because the levels of corruption or program mismanagement are very low in those areas, to begin with.

TABLE 6. Effect of Social Audits on Type of Irregularities

	Labor-related irregularities				*Material-related irregularities*			
	Easy to detect		*Hard to detect*		*Easy to detect*	*Hard to detect*		
	(1)	*(2)*	*(3)*	*(4)*	*(5)*	*(6)*	*(7)*	*(8)*
	Non-payment/ delay in wage payment	*Non-provision of work*	*Benami/ impersonations*	*Bribes*	*Non-existent projects*	*Poor quality of materials*	*Bribes*	*Missing records*
(1) Audit 2	1.262*	–0.513***	0.730	0.280	0.356**	0.204	0.077	0.097***
	(0.690)	(0.197)	(0.582)	(0.397)	(0.149)	(0.158)	(0.213)	(0.0354)
(2) Audit 3	1.279	–0.460	–0.079	0.278	0.350	0.131	0.317	0.330***
	(0.924)	(0.285)	(0.768)	(0.650)	(0.226)	(0.189)	(0.284)	(0.101)
(3) Constant	8.740***	1.754**	0.723	1.021	–1.902**	0.344	–2.054*	–0.040
	(2.386)	(0.752)	(3.745)	(1.529)	(0.907)	(0.406)	(1.153)	(0.227)
(4) Audit 3 – Audit 2	0.016	0.053	–0.809*	–0.001	–0.006	–0.073	0.239*	0.233***
	(0.417)	(0.149)	(0.461)	(0.400)	(0.128)	(0.094)	(0.139)	(0.078)
R-square	0.498	0.335	0.332	0.286	0.234	0.221	0.239	0.246
N	685	685	685	685	685	685	685	685

Source: Authors' calculations from data extracted from official social audit reports.

Note: Results reported for the specification in Table 5, including all controls. Standard errors clustered at the GP level reported in parentheses. ***significant at 1%, **5%, and *10%.

complaints about non-payment or delay in wage payments in audit 2 relative to audit 1 (column 1). These were, however, not significantly higher in audit 3 relative to audit 1 or between audits 2 and 3 (column 1, row 4). We thus conclude that there was an insignificant increase in the number of complaints related to non-payment or delay in wage payments over the three audit rounds. Interestingly, the number of complaints related to non-provision of MGNREGA work declined in both rounds 2 and 3, albeit insignificantly in the latter as shown in column 2. As a result, there was no significant decline in irregularities related to the non-provision of work over successive audits (column 2, row 4). Further, there was an insignificant effect of audits 2 and 3 on irregularities due to corrupt practices (i.e., *benami* wages, bribes, etc. in columns 3 and 4) relative to round 1. However, the negative coefficient in row 4, column 3, suggests that irregularities related to ghost workers may have declined between audits 2 and 3.

Columns 5–8 show that the increase in material-related complaints in audit 2 was driven by the rise in ETD ghost or non-existent projects (column 5, row 1), and the harder-to-detect irregularities due to missing official records on material expenditure (column 8, row 1). However, by audit 3, the number of non-existent projects was not higher than in audit 1 (column 5, row 2). Overall, the secular increase in material-related complaints over the three audit rounds seems to have been driven by the significant increase in bribes and missing expenditure records (columns 7 and 8, row 4).

In Table 7, we present results for the effect of audits on direct measures of program performance, as in equation (2). Our sample is restricted to GPs with three audits between 2006 and 2010. Relative to program performance post audit 1, there was an insignificant increase in real program expenditures post audit 2 as shown by the coefficient on audit 2 in column 1. Interestingly, there was a marginal decline in the proportion of program expenditures on rural roads projects where the avenues for corruption may be higher as shown in column 2 (World Bank 2011). Total MGNREGA employment generated increased insignificantly (column 3) while there was no change in the proportion of SC and ST person days in total MGNREGA employment (columns 4 and 5). These findings line up with those in Tables 5 and 6—suggesting that the impacts of audits on program outcomes were, at best, marginal.

To summarize, we observe insignificant changes in the ETD complaints, but a substantive rise in HTD, material complaints. These patterns are consistent with the earlier discussion of stakes and evidence on beneficiary learning. In spite of such learning and the greater capacity of the participatory part of the audit process to detect irregularities, illustrated by the

TABLE 7. Effect of Social Audits on Program Performance

	Expenditure		*Employment*		
	(1)	*(2)*	*(3)*	*(4)*	*(5)*
	Total real expenditure (in lakh ₹)	*Proportion of rural connectivity works*	*Total employment generated in person days*	*Proportion of SC person days generated*	*Proportion of ST person days generated*
(1) Audit 2	18.73	−0.128*	24581.8	0.016	−0.007
	(12.12)	(0.075)	(15079.0)	(0.048)	(0.042)
(2) Constant	17.27	0.098	39999.9	−0.150	0.929***
	(27.05)	(0.170)	(37536.4)	(0.235)	(0.278)
R-square	0.666	0.491	0.649	0.616	0.733
N	391	390	391	390	390

Source: Authors' calculations from data extracted from official social audit reports.

Notes: Results reported for equation 2 in the text. Controls as described in Table 5. Columns (2) and (4)–(5) are calculated as proportions of columns (1) and (3), respectively. Standard errors clustered at the GP level reported in parentheses. ***significant at 1%, ** 5%, and *10%.

increasingly advanced complaints submitted by beneficiaries, the social audits were ineffective in systematically reducing the ETD irregularities. We interpret the observed rise in material-related malfeasance, without an accompanying reduction in the ETD irregularities, as an underlying change in the anatomy of corruption and a failure of the social audit process to deter malpractice: it appears that transgressors adapted to the new monitoring regime by looking for additional avenues of rent extraction as suggested by Olken and Pande (2011).[28] Given that the average real amount per material-related irregularity was significantly greater than for irregularities related to labor (mentioned earlier), the structural shift in program leakages suggests that the benefits from rent extraction were sufficiently higher than the cost of effort and any expected punishment following detection of material-related theft.

28. Quoting Aiyar et al. (2013):

> With the help of an information technology company—Tata Consultancy Services—the government of Andhra Pradesh developed an end-to-end management information system (MIS) through which job cards, work estimates, and payment orders are issued. The data are collected and input (*entered electronically*) at the mandal level, and consolidated at the state level. Information on each job card holder, including number of days worked and total wages received, is accessible through the MIS. All data are public and available for scrutiny. To streamline payment processes, wages are paid directly through workers' post office or bank accounts. (Authors' emphasis)

7.1. Robustness Checks

The results on leakages, so far, are from a sample with variation in the number of audits across mandals. It is possible that mandals which were audited more frequently during 2006–10 report higher incidence of MGNREGA irregularities because they were relatively more corrupt. As a result, the coefficient on audit 3 would, for instance, be biased upwards. To account for this possibility, we report the results in Table 8 for the data restricted to GPs where three audits were conducted during 2006–10. Our results are largely unchanged from those for the unrestricted sample. While the number of irregularities related to non-payment and delays in wage payment (column 1, rows 1 and 2) and bribes (column 4, row 1) increased, complaints related to non-provision of MGNREGA work (column 4, row 1) declined relative to audit 1. The secular rise in material complaints was driven by an increase in material-related bribes (column 7, row 4) and missing expenditure records (column 8, row 4).

So far, we have analyzed the data for complaints filed by individuals, groups of beneficiaries as well as discrepancies unearthed by the audit team itself. Even though our specification attempts to address the challenges posed by beneficiary learning, other beneficiary biases and threats to or intimidation of beneficiaries, may influence the reporting of irregularities. This in turn would influence our interpretation of outcomes of interest and get reflected in changes in the number of irregularities over time. To address this possibility, we restrict attention to the irregularities registered by the audit team which should be immune from such biases. As before, improvement in audit quality is accounted for by the time trends. Table 9 shows these results for the same outcomes reported earlier. Crucially, our conclusions are unchanged when we observe the coefficients reported in row 4 across all columns. In Table 10, we include an additional control for the real expenditures under the program in each GP in the financial year(s) prior to the date of the audit (or for the period audited) to account for the possibility that the number of irregularities would rise if the intensity of the program increases (even after controlling secular trends). Once more, our results are consistent with those in previous tables.

A final interpretational concern is from a welfare perspective: it may be more relevant to study whether the rupee value (in real terms) per complaint has changed with more audits rather than the number of complaints. Hence, while the number of complaints has risen, the rupee amount of these irregularities may have declined when compared to the early days of the program. Table 11 shows the results for the same specifications as earlier but with

TABLE 8. Effect of Social Audits on Type of Irregularities (Restricted Sample)

	Labor-related irregularities				*Material-related irregularities*			
	Easy to detect		*Hard to detect*		*Easy to detect*		*Hard to detect*	
	(1)	*(2)*	*(3)*	*(4)*	*(5)*	*(6)*	*(7)*	*(8)*
	Non-payment/ delay in wage payment	*Non-provision of work*	*Benami/ impersonations*	*Bribes*	*Non-existent projects*	*Poor quality of materials*	*Bribes*	*Missing records*
(1) Audit 2	2.118*	–0.533*	0.913	1.104*	0.445*	0.160	–0.106	0.0446
	(1.179)	(0.298)	(0.740)	(0.561)	(0.260)	(0.167)	(0.316)	(0.0446)
(2) Audit 3	2.370*	–0.272	0.541	1.079	0.496	0.0231	0.130	0.245**
	(1.228)	(0.341)	(0.927)	(0.824)	(0.314)	(0.200)	(0.342)	(0.105)
(3) Constant	7.327**	0.888	–10.63***	–1.809	–3.147**	0.686	–2.631	0.372
	(3.109)	(1.059)	(3.894)	(1.983)	(1.265)	(0.885)	(1.769)	(0.393)
(4) Audit 3 – Audit 2	.252	.261	–.372	–.025	.050	–.136	.236*	.200**
	(.381)	(.159)	(.562)	(.610)	(.177)	(.108)	(.134)	(.098)
R-square	0.541	0.316	0.260	0.280	0.234	0.226	0.260	0.281
N	444	444	444	444	444	444	444	444

Source: Authors' calculations from data extracted from official social audit reports.

Note: Results reported for the specification in Table 5, including all controls. Sample restricted to those GPs which conducted 3 audits. Standard errors clustered at the GP level reported in parentheses. ***significant at 1%, ** 5%, and *10%.

TABLE 9. Effect of Social Audits on Type of Irregularities Filed by Auditors

		Labor-related irregularities				*Material-related irregularities*			
		Easy to detect		*Hard to detect*		*Easy to detect*		*Hard to detect*	
		(1)	*(2)*	*(3)*	*(4)*	*(5)*	*(6)*	*(7)*	*(8)*
		Non-payment/ delay in wage payment	*Non-provision of work*	*Benami/ impersonations*	*Bribes*	*Non-existent projects*	*Poor quality of materials*	*Bribes*	*Missing records*
(1)	Audit 2	0.062	0.012	0.043	0.328	0.000	0.218	0.0456	0.098***
		(0.075)	(0.016)	(0.104)	(0.207)	(0.085)	(0.158)	(0.157)	(0.0350)
(2)	Audit 3	0.061	0.019	0.151	0.639**	–0.050	0.137	0.078	0.335***
		(0.082)	(0.022)	(0.144)	(0.282)	(0.157)	(0.190)	(0.205)	(0.102)
(3)	Constant	0.432	0.242	–0.199	–0.643	0.084	0.251	–1.356	–0.077
		(0.327)	(0.156)	(0.509)	(0.573)	(0.561)	(0.417)	(1.024)	(0.170)
(4)	Audit 3 – Audit 2	–0.001	0.006	0.107	0.310**	–0.050	–0.080	0.033	0.236***
		(0.027)	(0.012)	(0.067)	(0.136)	(0.101)	(0.094)	(0.088)	(0.079)
	R-square	0.221	0.197	0.212	0.218	0.208	0.222	0.235	0.265
	N	685	685	685	685	685	685	685	685

Source: Authors' calculations from data extracted from official social audit reports.

Note: Results reported for the specification in Table 5, including all controls. ***significant at 1%, ** 5%, and *10%.

TABLE 10. Effect of Social Audits on Type of Irregularities with Program Expenditure Controls

	Labor-related irregularities				*Material-related irregularities*			
	Easy to detect		*Hard to detect*		*Easy to detect*		*Hard to detect*	
	(1)	*(2)*	*(3)*	*(4)*	*(5)*	*(6)*	*(7)*	*(8)*
	Non-payment/ delay in wage payment	*Non-provision of work*	*Benami/ impersonations*	*Bribes*	*Non-existent projects*	*Poor quality of materials*	*Bribes*	*Missing records*
(1) Audit 2	1.118*	–0.495**	0.496	0.235	0.303**	0.198	0.002	0.095***
	(0.669)	(0.197)	(0.597)	(0.386)	(0.148)	(0.157)	(0.236)	(0.0355)
(2) Audit 3	1.236	–0.461	–0.045	0.304	0.333	0.136	0.333	0.330***
	(0.913)	(0.286)	(0.809)	(0.650)	(0.224)	(0.190)	(0.282)	(0.102)
(3) Constant	6.126**	0.977	–2.944	–1.140	–2.453***	0.552	–3.088**	–0.229
	(2.424)	(0.788)	(3.620)	(1.470)	(0.901)	(0.457)	(1.376)	(0.251)
(4) Audit 3 – Audit 2	0.117	0.034	–0.541	0.069	0.030	–0.061	0.330**	0.234***
	(0.423)	(0.150)	(0.479)	(0.408)	(0.127)	(0.094)	(0.149)	(0.080)
R-square	0.504	0.331	0.373	0.297	0.244	0.224	0.274	0.247
N	672	672	672	672	672	672	672	672

Source: Authors' calculations from data extracted from official social audit reports.

Note: Results reported for the specification in Table 5, including all controls plus real program expenditure in each audit round. Standard errors clustered at the GP level reported in parentheses. ***significant at 1%, ** 5%, and *10%.

TABLE 11. Effect of Social Audits on (Real) Rupee Amount Per Irregularity

	(1) Amount per irregularity	(2) Amount per labor irregularity	(3) Amount per material irregularity	(4) Amount per irregularity	(5) Amount per labor irregularity	(6) Amount per material irregularity
(1) Audit 2	−3458.7	−8291.1	−45926.9	−2050.8	−6633.1	−27132.7
	(9947.4)	(10113.8)	(262742.1)	(8358.7)	(8085.1)	(79573.9)
(2) Audit 3	−59368.2	−73238.9*	−71959.0	−53398.4	−60754.6*	−40963.9
	(42187.7)	(41618.7)	(275962.3)	(37596.0)	(34555.5)	(101915.1)
(3) Constant	36466.7	32094.5	456951.0***	41108.1	29407.2	361792.9
	(27818.7)	(40237.1)	(131314.5)	(30225.2)	(33101.2)	(290588.1)
(4) Audit 3 – Audit 2	−55909.47*	−64947.78*	−26032.11	−51347.53*	−54121.51*	−13831.16
	(33727.33)	(33481.35)	(38229.92)	(30456.29)	(27972.14)	(30603.26)
R-square	0.380	0.443	0.711	0.349	0.420	0.611
N	560	536	162	645	627	239

Source: Authors' calculations from data extracted from official social audit reports.

Note: In columns 1–3, the sample is restricted to audits in which a complaint amount was filed. In columns 4–6, the sample includes all audits in which a complaint/type of complaint was filed. Results reported for the specification in Table 5, including all controls. Standard errors clustered at the GP level reported in parentheses. ***significant at 1%, ** 5%, and *10%.

the dependent variable now representing the rupee amount per complaint (in 2006 rupees). The first three columns are restricted to audits where a complaint amount was mentioned while the next three columns are restricted to audits where any complaint was filed. If no amount was mentioned in the complaint, the amount per complaint is coded as zero. Missing amounts are more likely for complaints related to non-provision of work or wage payment delays. Across both definitions of the dependent variable, we find that the amount per complaint declined between the second and third audits for total complaints and labor complaints (row 4—columns 1, 2 and 4, 5) while there is no difference in the material complaint amounts (row 4—columns 3 and 6). This again suggests that the social audits may have had only a marginal impact on labor-related irregularities but have made little difference on the material front.[29]

7.2. Heterogeneity

In this section, we discuss whether and how the quality of MGNREGA implementation is associated with mandal-level characteristics. In the mandal survey, we interviewed current MPDOs. However, in several mandals MPDOs were transferred frequently. Frequent transfers of MPDOs could indicate political interference—either in response to irregularities in program implementation or, alternatively, be the cause of such irregularities. Note that we do not find a correlation between the number of irregularities in an audit for which the MPDO has been held responsible and the number of MPDOs posted in that mandal since 2006. We next split the sample by those mandals with less than median MPDO transfers (in our sample of 100 mandals the median number of MPDOs in each mandal since 2006 was 2, excluding the current MPDO) and those with higher than median transfers. The results are reported in Table 12.

The top panel in Table 12 reports the results for less than median transfers of MPDOs. We find a significant decline in non-provision of MGNREGA work (column 4) in both audits 2 and 3 relative to audit 1. Overall, there was a marginal increase in missing material expenditure records between audits 2 and 3 (column 11) but no overall change in the number of labor- or material-related irregularities between audits 2 and 3 (columns 2 and 7, respectively).

In contrast, the bottom panel regressions for higher than median MPDO transfers suggest a significant and monotonic increase in the number of

29. A caveat to the results reported in Table 11 is potential selection bias: data on amounts are available only if an amount was mentioned in the complaint.

TABLE 12. Effect of Social Audits on Total and Type of Irregularity by Bureaucratic Transfers

	All	*Labor-related irregularities*						*Material-related irregularities*			
			Easy to detect		*Hard to detect*			*Easy to detect*		*Hard to detect*	
	(1)	*(2)*	*(3)*	*(4)*	*(5)*	*(6)*	*(7)*	*(8)*	*(9)*	*(10)*	*(11)*
		Total	*Non-payment/delay in wage payment*	*Non-provision of work*	*Benami/ impersonations*	*Bribes*	*Total*	*Non-existent projects*	*Poor quality of materials*	*Bribes*	*Missing records*
					Panel I. Less than median number of MPDO transfers						
Audit 2	0.372	0.428	1.186	−0.878***	0.0120	0.633	−0.153	0.0614	−0.197	0.0732	0.0268
	(2.303)	(1.881)	(1.300)	(0.262)	(0.920)	(0.586)	(0.567)	(0.161)	(0.189)	(0.382)	(0.0353)
Audit 3	−0.725	−1.189	−0.0464	−1.152**	−0.835	0.973	0.289	−0.0836	−0.161	0.376	0.222
	(3.366)	(3.044)	(1.769)	(0.476)	(1.276)	(0.840)	(0.682)	(0.218)	(0.239)	(0.461)	(0.137)
Constant	7.548	7.545	4.061	0.498	4.222	0.138	−1.007	−0.310	−0.0479	−0.425	−0.0237
	(5.809)	(5.521)	(2.529)	(0.872)	(3.512)	(1.903)	(0.364)	(0.404)	(0.994)	(0.146)	(1.267)
Audit 3– Audit 2	−1.097	−1.616	−1.232	−.273	−.846	.340	.442	−.145	.035	.302	.195*
	(1.946)	(1.887)	(.843)	(.336)	(.669)	(.448)	(.357)	(.122)	(.092)	(.233)	(.109)
R-square	0.519	0.530	0.578	0.337	0.350	0.378	0.345	0.303	0.243	0.277	0.325
N	366	366	366	366	366	366	366	366	366	366	366
					Panel II. More than median number of MPDO transfers						
Audit 2	0.574	−0.332	0.540	−0.498	−0.669	−1.190	1.721***	0.114	0.780*	0.404**	0.408***
	(2.932)	(2.675)	(0.764)	(0.306)	(1.618)	(1.140)	(0.581)	(0.270)	(0.437)	(0.197)	(0.155)
Audit 3	0.826	−1.180	0.971	−0.401	−1.549	−1.580	2.454**	0.172	0.661	0.647*	0.755***
	(3.683)	(3.276)	(1.100)	(0.399)	(1.866)	(1.701)	(0.960)	(0.461)	(0.485)	(0.334)	(0.276)
Constant	−14.38**		−1.179	0.538	−6.514***	1.067	−5.312***	−2.854**	−1.464***	−0.422	−0.469
	(6.387)	(5.296)	(2.937)	(0.747)	(2.336)	(1.177)	(2.021)	(1.317)	(0.510)	(0.982)	(0.327)
Audit 3– Audit 2	.252	−.348	.431	.096	−.879	−.389	.732	.057	−.119	.242	.346**
	(1.370)	(1.207)	(.468)	(.143)	(.701)	(.748)	(.467)	(.233)	(.124)	(.168)	(.140)
R-square	0.389	0.433	0.461	0.495	0.371	0.254	0.282	0.256	0.301	0.273	0.292
N	310	310	310	310	310	310	310	310	310	310	310

Source: Authors' calculations from data extracted from official social audit reports.

Note: Results reported for the specification in Table 5, including all controls. Standard errors clustered at the GP level reported in parentheses. ***significant at 1%, ** 5%, and *10%.

material-related irregularities relative to audit 1 (column 7). This was driven by an increase in material-related bribes (column 10) and missing expenditure records (column 11) in audits 2 and 3 relative to audit 1. Thus, it is apparent that the results on material expenditures presented earlier for the entire sample are driven by mandals with frequent MPDO transfers. If transfers were in response to irregularities, then there should have been a declining trend in the number of irregularities in these mandals. On the contrary, the number of material-related irregularities rose consistently within these mandals. This suggests that transfers of bureaucrats could be an instrument used by the political class to influence the delivery of MGNREGA at the local level.

8. Policy Implications and Concluding Remarks

The AP social audit model is being scaled up and adopted by other Indian states and other public programs. In the introduction, we briefly reviewed what evidence tells us about the potential of participatory monitoring of the type the AP model has been developed around. Our first observation, which simply borrows Mansuri and Rao's (2013) conclusion, is that effective induced participation is difficult to achieve. At the same time, carefully crafted participatory interventions may (dramatically) improve (health) service delivery (BS 2009). Given the many similarities between BS's (2009) intervention and AP's social audits, there are thus grounds for optimism on behalf of the AP model. The zero impact of community mobilization and information sharing on teaching quality and learning outcomes in UP, reported by Banerjee et al. (2010), offers an important and sobering caveat. As our empirical results demonstrate, in relying on participation and social accountability, it is necessary to tread carefully and recognize potential pitfalls.

Detection of audit "impacts" is made harder both by the fact that social audits were not implemented randomly and by the type of information (complaints) recorded by the social audit team. We, therefore, analyze the marginal impact of *repeated* audits within the same GPs during 2006–10. Controlling mandal-level attributes, overall and district-level time trends to address the confounders discussed earlier, we observe a marginal reduction in the real amount per labor complaint but an insignificant effect of the repeated social audit process on reducing the aggregate number of complaints. This is accompanied by an overall increase in the aggregate number of harder-to-detect material-related irregularities over successive audit rounds with no change in the number of ETD irregularities.

Based on our behavioral assumptions, we expected a decline in the ETD irregularities in which beneficiaries have high stakes and audit teams, as well as beneficiaries, have sufficient detection capacity. Although there is some indication of an overall decline in the amount of theft in labor-related irregularities, we do not observe a decline in any ETD labor- or material-related irregularities with successive audit rounds.[30] Given our results, we can claim that while the top-down and participatory elements of the audit process have been effective in *detecting* irregularities, the audits are not an effective deterrent and have thus been unable to *reduce* irregularities.

Any marginal decline in the amount per labor-related administrative irregularity is, moreover, outweighed by the accompanying increase in the number of material-related complaints. We have seen that the complaints submitted by beneficiaries become increasingly sophisticated while the audit team complaints remain mostly confined to HTD irregularities. Given that we control time trends, we interpret the observed shift in the pattern of irregularities as reflective of transgressors responding to a new monitoring regime and the need to stay one step ahead of this monitoring regime. The threat of punishment may not have been credible for higher level program functionaries who are likely to be responsible (as much as, if not more than, lower level functionaries) for HTD, material-related malfeasance.

Note that the majority of labor-related irregularities were pinned on a GP-level, contractual functionary—the field assistant—who is typically a GP resident. The "naming and shaming" element of the public hearings might have been an effective deterrent for this particular functionary. However, social sanctions are unlikely to have a significant impact on curtailing malpractice among higher level program functionaries who are typically non-residents of the GP, such as the MPDO.

These results take us back to BS (2009) and to the social contract that their participatory process culminates in. We refer to this as the *tightness* of the social audit process. In spite of the promising prospects for community-based monitoring of work provision and of labor-related expenditures, for the years that we have studied (2006–10), the follow up and enforcement of social audit findings in AP were weak: this may contribute to explain the limited success of the social audit process in deterring malfeasance. As shown in Table 13, while this weakness may have been mitigated by the

30. During the period of our study the state introduced significant technological innovations in the monitoring and processing of labor payments. A centralized computer system where muster-rolls are verified and payments made on a weekly basis through computer generated pay orders at the mandal level may, alongside the audits, have helped to mitigate leakages in labor payments.

TABLE 13. Disciplinary Action and Recoveries by District (2006–13)

District	Total number of irregularities	Number of irregularities for which person(s) held responsible	Type of disciplinary action (%)			Irregularity amount		
			Minor	*Medium*	*Major*	*Total amount involved (₹)*	*Amount recovered (%)*	*Amount to be recovered (%)*
Mahbubnagar	9,698	9,698	25.717	0.711	0.227	12,131,7391	9.6	90.4
Medak	16,814	16,814	13.173	0.708	0.095	139,046,861	35.11	64.89
Warangal	11,977	11,977	11.106	2.230	0.159	81,227,702	3.13	96.87
Anantapur	10,006	10,006	45.336	1.550	0.870	9,028,2892	3.74	96.26
Kurnool	11,013	11,013	19.653	1.308	0.200	60,401,875	7.23	92.77
Guntur	17,833	17,833	10.307	2.739	3.381	88,547,954	7.13	92.87
Nizamabad	12,278	12,278	7.058	9.742	1.844	88,436,603	9.76	90.24
Khammam	17,768	17,768	2.113	0.873	0.242	52,563,447	12.18	87.82
Total	107,387	107,387	14.738	2.414	0.965	721824725	12.758	87.242

Source: Authors' calculations from data extracted from official social audit reports.

Note: Data for the entire district summarized from http://119.226.159.35/ATR/reportshome.do (accessed on 7th October, 2013). Disciplinary action is a percentage of the number of irregularities for which person(s) was held responsible. The remaining category is "Other actions" (referred to "as per rules" or "close of action" in the official data).

Minor disciplinary actions: censure, fine, stoppage of increments, recovery of irregularity amount, and hearing.

Medium disciplinary actions: suspension, show-cause notice, ineligible for contractual work, charge-memo, enquiry committee instituted.

Major disciplinary actions: termination/dismissal/removal, criminal action (FIR/charge-sheet/detention/conviction).

establishment of the vigilance cells in AP in 2010, less than 1% of irregularities for which one or multiple program functionaries were held responsible ended in termination/dismissal/removal from service or criminal action for the period under study (and until 2013). Furthermore, 87% of the missing amounts were yet to be recovered. The effectiveness of social audits in deterring theft and other malpractice, in spite of all their other inherent merits, may thus be undermined by a single design weakness, or slip-up. A key lesson for AP and for states emulating the AP model would thus be to ensure that social audits culminate in the type of enforceable and credible "contract" that allocates responsibilities, defines timelines, and ensures that those who have been found guilty of irregularities are promptly punished. The credibility of the social audit process rests ultimately on the ability and willingness of the state government to take effective remedial action and punish offenders.

In principle, the modest impact of social audits could also reflect a problem of capacity on the part of social audit teams. In our discussions earlier, we assume that as the social audit process is repeated, core social audit personnel learn and amass new knowledge and understanding. This should make audits increasingly effective and auditors more able to detect more sophisticated irregularities. This conjecture is only plausible if core personnel stays put or learning is effectively transferred to new staff.[31]

Apart from the results outlined earlier, our work here underlines the need for incorporating rigorous program evaluation in the roll out of audits. Furthermore, greater vigilance in the documentation of social audit evidence, which could be critical for assessing the impact of these audits, is essential. For instance, all social audit reports include questions on the total rupee amount of irregularities, the total amount of MGNREGA expenditures subjected to audit, etc., to be filled in by the audit team. But these data are not entered in the vast majority of social audit reports for the period and sample under study. Careful documentation of audit findings would, again, require improvements in the training of auditors and greater emphasis on the importance of more complete documentation in the training modules.

The AP experience has uniquely benefitted from the top level and strong political commitment to the social audit process. The state has also demonstrated a strong willingness to experiment with the use of technology and

31. Experience-based skill accumulation may become obsolete if the portfolio of MGNREGA projects undergoes significant change. This is an issue other adopting states need to pay attention to. Intensification of scrutiny may shift priorities toward projects with more material expenditure and harder to detect irregularities.

other mechanisms to strengthen monitoring and the quality of MGNREGA delivery (Murali 2013). These favorable initial conditions have, no doubt, critically aided and bolstered the potential of the social audit process in AP. A key question is whether similar preconditions are likely to be present in the other states that are now seeking to replicate the AP model. Our study underlines the advantages of a top-down component in designing social audits to leverage grassroots participation.

Following the transition from the work fare programs prior to the rights-based MGNREGA, between 2004–05 and 2008–09 there has been a three-fold increase in Central government funds allocated to rural work projects (Afridi 2008). In 2011–12, the Act had provided employment to almost 40 million households at an annual expenditure of almost ₹40,000 crores across the country while the cost of conducting these audits is merely 1% of this expenditure. The potential benefits of the program are large but the cost of making certain that they are realized is low. In moving forward, we reiterate the high stakes in ensuring the success of the social audit mechanism.

Appendix

TABLE A1. Number of Irregularities Per District Per Audit

Audit#	*Mahbub-nagar*	*Medak*	*Warangal*	*Ananta-pur*	*Kurnool*	*Guntur*	*Nizama-bad*	*Khammam*
	[N=36]	[N=37]	[N=41]	[N=36]	[N=33]	[N=33]	[N=36]	[N=32]
Audit1	4.972	3.297	4.317	6.111	5.121	2.090	4.972	10.625
	(3.714)	(2.259)	(2.240)	(3.970)	(3.621)	(2.517)	(3.009)	(6.791)
	[N=36]	[N=33]	[N=39]	[N=36]	[N=33]	[N=12]	[N=36]	[N=36]
Audit2	7.333	5.181	6.949	4.389	5.848	2.833	5.167	9.833
	(4.296)	(3.486)	(5.370)	(3.728)	(6.251)	(1.850)	(4.532)	(7.588)
	[N=6]	[N=36]	[N=42]	[N=14]	[N=9]		[N=32]	[N=27]
Audit3	6.667	5.611	8.405	2.214	3.444		7.75	5.518
	(3.502)	(7.184)	(7.960)	(2.326)	(2.297)		(6.289)	(4.577)

Source: Authors' calculations from data extracted from official social audit reports.
Note: Number of observations in square brackets. Standard errors in parentheses.

References

Aakella, K. V. and S. Kidambi. 2007. "Social Audits in Andhra Pradesh: A Process in Evolution," *Economic and Political Weekly*, 42 (47): 18–19.

Adato, M., J. Hoddinott, and L. Haddad. 2005. "Power, Politics and Performance: Participation in South African Public Work Programs," Research Report 143, International Food Policy Research Institute, Washington, D.C.

Afridi, F. 2008. "Can Community Monitoring Improve the Accountability of Public Officials?" *Economic and Political Weekly*, Mumbai, 43 (42): 35–40.

Aiyar, Y., S. K. Mehta, and S. Samji. 2013. "India: Implementing Social Audits," in K. Subbarao et al. 2013. Chapter 11, pp. 249–68.

Banerjee, A. V., R. Banerji, E. Duflo, R. Glennester, and S. Khemani. 2010. "Pitfalls of Participatory Programs: Evidence from a Randomized Evaluation in Education in India," *American Economic Journal: Economic Policy*, 2(1): 1–30.

Bjorkman, M. and J. Svensson. 2009. "Power to the People: Evidence from a Randomized Experiment on Community Based Monitoring in Uganda," *Quarterly Journal of Economics*, 124 (2): 735–69.

Deshingkhar, P. and C. Johnson. 2003. State Transfers to the Poor and Back: The Case of the Food for Work Programme in Andhra Pradesh. *Working Paper 222*, Overseas Development Institute, London.

Government of India. 2005. *Mahatma Gandhi National Rural Employment Guarantee Act*. Available at http://www.rural.nic.in/sites/programmes-schemes-MGNREGA.asp (accessed on May 20, 2014).

Joshi, A. and P. Houtzager. 2012. "Widgets or Watchdogs? Conceptual Explorations in Social Accountability," *Public Management Review*, 14 (2): 145–62.

Khemani, S. 2008. "Does Community Monitoring Improve Public Services? Based on Evidence from Uganda and India the answer is 'Yes' and 'No'," World Bank Research Brief, September.

Mansuri, G and V. Rao. 2013. *Localizing Development – Does Participation Work?* Washington, D.C.: The World Bank.

Murali, A. 2013. *India: Technological Innovation for Effective Management Information Systems*, in K. Subbarao et al. 2013. Chapter 10, pp. 233–48.

Olken, Ben. 2009. "Corruption Perceptions vs. Corruption Reality," *Journal of Public Economics*, 93 (7–8): 950–964.

Olken, Ben and Rohini Pande. 2011. "Corruption in Developing Countries," NBER Working Paper No. 17398.

Ringold, D., A. Holla, M. Koziol, and S. Srinivasan. 2012. *Citizens and Service Delivery—Assessing the Use of Social Accountability Approaches in Human Development*. Washington, D.C.: The World Bank.

Subbarao, K., C. del Ninno, C. Andrews, and C. Rodriguez-Alas. 2013. *Public Works as a Safety Net: Design, Evidence and Implementation*. Washington, D.C.: The World Bank.

World Bank. 2011. *Curbing Fraud, Corruption and Collusion in the Roads Sector*. Washington, D.C.: The World Bank.

Comments and Discussion

Devesh Kapur
University of Pennsylvania

The Mahatma Gandhi National Rural Employment Guarantee Act (MGNREGA) notified in 2005, guaranteed 100 days of wage employment annually to every rural household whose adult members volunteered to do unskilled manual work. In addition, it has two other goals: create durable assets and rural infrastructure for the local community and strengthen rural local elected bodies (GPs).

Given the high degree of leakage and corruption in India's poverty programs, the Act carefully detailed transparency and accountability procedures, laying out the role of the state and different public authorities, but its distinguishing feature has been the central role of "social audits." These were embedded, as the authors' state, "in a discourse on rights-based democratic action," where they were meant to not only serve as an anti-corruption tool "but a platform on which citizens can be empowered to directly exercise their democratic rights." How have social audits affected the performance of MGNREGA? The paper examines this important question, using data from AP, the state which has been the poster-child of social audits.

Since Dilip's comments focus on the empirics, my comments speak to some of the broader issues that this paper raises. One, the role of social audits; two, how do we measure success; and three, what policy implications can we draw from the AP study.

If the goal of social audits is to improve the performance of public programs, then one must ask why no East Asian country used social audits and yet their performance on poverty programs has been much better? After all if we think about countries such as Taiwan or South Korea, there were no social audits and their programs were reasonably effective. The reason of course is that they had a functioning public administration. Social audits are a sign that basic public administration is dysfunctional. The Indian state has been characterized in many ways, as a soft state, a *mai-baap* (mother-father) state, a flailing state, even in some parts, a mafia state, but increasingly its multiple weaknesses have resulted in it becoming a "bypass state". Policy makers and civil society have struggled to find ways to bypass a dysfunctional public administration and social audits are one such mechanism. It is an open question whether these bypass mechanisms complement or substitute for an inherent weak public administration and whether these processes will actually strengthen public administration or further prolong the weaknesses of public administration in India.

The paper's core result is that social audits result in "a significant decline in complaints related to the non-provision of MGNREGA work and in the complaint amount per labor-related irregularity", but "accompanied by an increase in more sophisticated and harder to detect material-related irregularities." In other words, while audits may be effective in *detecting* irregularities, they appear to have little *deterrent* effect. The paper makes a convincing case that the better outcomes on labor-related irregularities (compared to material related) are because participatory audits are more likely to be effective when addressing program outcomes with high beneficiary stakes and beneficiary capacity relative to the issue being audited. The stakes are higher for individual specific goods (wages) relative to collective goods (public works where materials are used). And a poor uneducated person can easily tell when s/he has not been paid (or paid less) but will find it much harder to inspect the quality and quantity of construction material. Moreover, since beneficiary learning in MGNREGS is mainly due to "learning by doing" processes, the capacity to detect is likely to decline as the complexity of program outcomes increases.

However, if the effectiveness of local participation appears to have improved through dynamic processes of learning better auditing, transgressors also learn, as evident in the increasing sophistication of the transgressions. The inter-linkages between three variables—beneficiary capacity, the stakes, and the relative difficulties in detecting irregularities—mean that the introduction of monitoring may result in the substitution of one type of irregularity by another as transgressors "learn" and shift to other avenues for rent extraction. The evidence presented in the paper makes a compelling case for what social audits can achieve—and what they cannot. The participatory part of the process is insufficient to handle the more complex labor and material irregularities and, hence, external audit processes are an important complement to the participatory processes of social audits.

The most troubling finding of the paper is the gulf between detection of irregularities and its low deterrence effect. The paper finds that during the period under study, less than "1% of irregularities for which one or multiple program functionaries were held responsible ended in termination/dismissal/removal from service or criminal action. Furthermore, 87% of the theft amounts have yet to be recovered." The reasons for this dismal state of affairs are not clear, but it appears to point to a larger issue. Large public programs do not exist in a vacuum. However clever the design, sooner or later they will run into the headwinds stemming from other parts of the system—in this case, the chronic weaknesses of India's justice system.

The authors point out that in 2010 AP introduced vigilance cells but are unable to comment on its effects since the period of their analysis ends in 2010. But it is possible to speculate on the likely consequences by drawing a parallel between the growth of vigilance officers and corruption in the Indian public sector. In 1980 there were very few vigilance officers in government departments and Public Sector Undertakings (PSUs). Since then (and we don't have precise data), they have increased manifold and one could argue that corruption in government departments has also increased commensurately! Audit without swift and rigorous follow up, seldom has significant deterrent effects.

Overall, how should one evaluate the relative success of the social audit program? The evidence in the paper is that labor-related problems went down but material-related problems went up. One could ask whether this trade-off was worthwhile. However, "success" might be measured in a different way, namely the counterfactual that things would have been worse in the absence of these audits. The paper does point this out, but is unable to examine this hypothesis because the absence of a base line stemming from the way the programs were rolled out. Additionally, the paper mentions that there were significant technological innovations in the monitoring and processing of labor payments, the use of IT technologies to verify muster-rolls and payments made on a weekly basis, and the introduction of biometric identification of beneficiaries. The independent role of technology to limit malfeasance relative to other factors would have been interesting to tease out.

The yardstick of success could be different, namely success with regard to the overall goals of the MGNREGA program. Conceptually, MGNREGA is basically a conditional cash transfer program where the cash transfer is conditional on the beneficiary doing some work. The evidence in the paper suggests that the cash transfer part has been reasonably effective and labor is getting wages. These may be less than the ideal, but it is occurring to a substantial degree (at least in AP). However, MGNREGA has two additional goals. The wages are for work that is supposed to create tangible assets for the community, a sort of joint product, and that is where the materials come in. But the evidence on rural assets—what was created and its quality—is weaker.

But let us assume that not very much is created, in which case we have to ask why do we need MGNREGA successful with all these bells and whistles and audits, etc., instead of simply having direct cash transfer? Why not simply use *Adhaar* to make direct cash transfer payments, if the key goal is to improve the incomes of the rural poor? One objection might be that the link to public works results in self-selection—only those in real need will come forward to perform manual labor—resulting in better targeting.

Recently, the Minister of Rural Development (the nodal Ministry for MGNREGA) argued that the scheme has three goals: one, to provide wage employment; two, to create durable community assets; and, three, to empower GPs. Even in states where the scheme had been successful, "only two out of the three objectives have been fulfilled. In no states, all three objectives have been fulfilled" (*The Hindu*, December 15, 2013). The Minister said that in AP, the pace setter for MGNREGA, has provided wage employment and durable assets, while simply bypassing the locally elected GPs. In Madhya Pradesh and Rajasthan, GPs have been empowered and wage employment has been created but few community assets have been created.

Most programs have externalities and inadvertent consequences. The social audits appear to have larger social learning-by-doing effects, as the poor get a sense of what their rights are, learn how to negotiate with local functionaries, and the lessons that they learn from this program can be carried over to other programs. But success could also be defined in a different way. As others have pointed out, the direct wage effects of MGNREGA on beneficiaries underestimate its benefits. The indirect wage effects might be larger in the sense that MGNREGA might create a floor wage in rural India and hence raise wages for all rural labor. But that might also have inflationary consequences that might undermine the purchasing power of urban poor.

Finally, there might be longer term institutional effects. If the success of MGNREGA has resulted in bypassing and thereby undermining GPs (as in AP), that is likely to have negative consequences for a range of issues. Additionally, and perhaps even more troubling is a much larger institutional effect that we need to think about. It is interesting to note that during the period that AP was a poster-child of MGNREGA (2006–10), it was also perhaps one of the most egregious states with regard to "grand corruption" in India at that time. It is a model with a distinguished past. Mrs Gandhi did exactly that in the 1970s—even as she weakened institutions, she unveiled a whole slew of pro-poor programs. Is it possible that even a well run pro-poor program such as MGNREGA in AP might be a case of a healthy tree in a decaying forest? And if so, are we then focusing on the critical question?

Dilip Mookherjee
University of Boston

This paper studies a vitally important issue in governance and leakages in delivery of public programs: the extent to which social audits involving the local community are effective in limiting leakages and promoting accountability of local governments. To this end, they study the experience of AP, which has implemented social audits of the MGNREGA employment generation program since 2009. They assemble a detailed set of data on complaints filed with the audit teams at the village level over successive years, covering three rounds of audits. A regression analysis studies the statistical association between conduct of successive audit rounds and the number of complaints of different kinds filed, and on scale of programs implemented, while controlling secular time trends and a large range of village-specific factors.

Despite the impressive data collected, the authors describe a number of factors that make it difficult to make any clear inferences regarding the effectiveness of the audits. Some of the problems concern the nature of the audit program itself: the rollout and the timing of the audits in each location were not random, and little is known about how these were decided. Not every village was audited the same number of times, and the audits were held at different times. Were areas with higher levels of perceived corruption more likely to be audited, and audited sooner? Without knowing the source of variation in frequency and timing of audits, it is difficult to provide causal interpretations of correlations between successive audit rounds and complaints filed. It is also hard to know whether residents that came forward to complain were subject to intimidation by concerned officials and party workers, and whether this might have prevented many complaints from being filed. If this were the case, the number of filed complaints might be negatively correlated with the actual extent of corruption.

Even if the preceding problems could be controlled in some way, there are additional problems of a conceptual nature in drawing inferences regarding effectiveness of audits from data concerning complaints filed. Any audit procedure that is effective raises the probability of detection of corrupt acts (the *detection* effect), and at the same time reduces the number of corrupt acts (the *deterrence* effect). The number of corrupt acts reported is the confluence of the two effects which pull in different directions. For a given level of deterrence, the detection effect would cause more complaints. On the other hand, for a given level of detection, the deterrence would cause fewer complaints. The net effect on observed complaints could go either way.

Hence it is very difficult to identify the effectiveness of audits by the numbers of complaints filed.

Further problems arise in the interpretation of data concerning changes in the number and types of complaints following successive audit rounds. These owe to learning effects for both auditors and officials being investigated. While auditors may become more adept at detecting irregularities, officials may move on to other harder-to-detect irregularities.

The authors make a distinction between ETD and HTD acts, and between those kinds of complaints in which local residents have high personal stakes (i.e., labor irregularities) and where they have lower stakes (material irregularities). They hypothesize that auditing will be more effective for areas where residents have a higher personal stake, and that mutual learning will result in a shift in the pattern of observed irregularities from ETD to HTD. Accordingly, they test the predictions that (a) labor irregularities will decline over successive audit rounds, relative to material irregularities, and (b) the pattern of irregularities will shift from ETD to HTD types of complaints.

Their empirical results turn out to provide only mixed support for these predictions. My reading of their results leads me to believe that they overstate the extent of support. Part of the reason is that they rely on the significance of effects only in a statistical sense. Table 5 shows that the increase from the first round to both audit rounds 2 and 3 in the number of labor irregularities exceeded that for material irregularities, but was less precisely estimated.

The results are equally ambiguous concerning differential patterns for ETD and HTD irregularities. Table 6 shows that a large quantitative increase in delays/non-payment of worker dues (which are ETD) exceeds that of every other kind of complaint by at least 50%. Missing records and ghost projects, two ETD material irregularities, rise significantly in both quantitative and statistical sense (columns 8 and 5), while the two HTD material irregularities (poor quality of materials and bribes in columns 6 and 7) rise by smaller magnitudes and fail to be statistically significant for either round 2 or 3. At the same time, non-provision of work (column 2) which is also ETD, shows a significant fall.

I agree, however, that the evidence fails to provide comfort on any dimension. Maybe citizens were becoming more aware of their entitlements as a result of the audits, thus causing complaints regarding non-provision of work to fall? Maybe this also caused the threefold rise in program expenditures and employment generated? The disaggregated evidence (Table 7) however shows no association between successive audit rounds and program expenditures or employment, after controlling for time trends and village characteristics.

Particularly chilling is the evidence concerning lack of adequate follow-through of detected irregularities with suitable disciplinary action. Table 13 shows that only 13% of amounts of irregularity had been recovered by 2013; less than 1% saw major disciplinary actions and less than 18% saw any kind of disciplinary action whatsoever. The absence of legal or administrative penalties leaves one wondering whether there were any political repercussions to the officials in question: will there be any impacts on their re-election (as has been witnessed in Brazil following disclosure of results of irregularities discovered by federal audits six months prior to elections (Ferraz and Finan 2008)? We will have to wait and see.

General Discussion

Rohini Somanathan (Chair) kicked off the session by congratulating NCAER for choosing a topic that was crying out for attention given how much faith the government and nongovernmental organization (NGO) activists have placed in social audits to improve service delivery to the poor and overall governance.

Pranab Bardhan agreed that this was a topic well worth pursuing. Of course, increasing complaints need not mean that malfeasance is increasing; quite often it can be the success of the program that increases the number of complaints. Different incentives are also likely to be at play regarding labor and materials irregularities. Benjamin Olken's work on Indonesia suggests that beneficiaries in social audits care much more about labor irregularities because of the direct impact on their incomes, and materials problems are often seen as somebody else's concern. On Devesh Kapur's concern about deterrence, the lack of follow-through and penalties is a general problem in India at all levels. Social audits are not needed in China because there are incentives and punishments at all levels that kick in, conditioning behavior. Bardhan felt that this general problem in India should not take away from the importance of carrying out social audits, both for checking fraud as well as raising awareness among beneficiaries.

Jeff Hammer noted that complaints are a joint probability of something bad happening, its detection, and someone speaking up. Since the data for this paper were limited to villages with at least three audits, what the authors are really identifying is the speed at which any of these three things changed over time. For example, it may take longer for people to figure out that materials are being stolen as opposed to labor irregularities. So it's not that one shouldn't use social audits for material irregularities, but one may just have to wait longer before people catch on: more patience may be required. Hammer also suggested that if the authors are planning more work they might try to find out if under MGNREGA the government was building the things that the Gram Sabha wanted them to build. He noted that in his own work on decentralization in Karnataka, state government officials had paid little heed to the GPs and had built what they thought fit, and this too could be related to what was likely to be more lucrative.

Karthik Muralidharan wanted to know if there had been any discussion about the trade-offs between top-down and bottom-up audits. That seemed to be the really important question. Were bottom-up audits considered more cost effective, for example, by being able to cover more villages than top-down audits? He also asked if the authors' data had any information on asset quality going beyond materials pilferage. He noted new panel data that he and his associates had collected building on the original 2002 teacher absence data for 1,200 villages in India. The data suggested that the only thing that seemed to make a difference in primary education was top-down monitoring. They could not find any significant impact of PTA activity. So, the larger point may not be so much whether communities could be effective or not, but whether they had any powers to do anything based on what they found, and therefore, condition service delivery behavior.

Karthik noted that the Afridi–Iversen results were consistent also with just the time trend of the awareness of the program: poor people don't quite know what their entitlements are, and over time they become aware of their wage-related entitlements, and so the margin of corruption shifts toward materials. This is in a way a bit sad, because it is the physical assets being created that are the real public goods that one would hope the social audit could help monitor, as opposed to just reducing labor irregularities in the wage transfer, a private good. So in that sense, it is not obvious that one needs the social audit since over time workers will learn more about their entitlements. Finally, though the cost of social audits was only 1% of the total MGNREGA expenditures of ₹40,000 crores, this was still a very large sum of money, and it is not obvious that social audits were the best available form of evaluation. Brazil had essentially done top-down independent audits using random representative samples, audits that were public and highly credible, and where the findings were backed up with actions.

Surjit Bhalla emphasized that however one audits MGNERGA, top-down or bottom-up, the fact remains that National Sample Survey (NSS) data clearly show that this is not a program for the rural poor, but mainly benefits the rural non-poor. NSS added a module with detailed questions on whether respondents participated in MGNREGA or not in 2011–12.

This data suggested that in AP there were 7.5 million people who worked on MGNREGA, out of which 1.1 million were poor and 6.4 million were non-poor. The poor who worked in MGNREGA were in the bottom 15%, and the non-poor were in the 55th percentile. The notion that some of these non-poor were the transitory poor is not supported by asset ownership data from NSS. The poor in MGNREGA spent ₹19 per year on jewellery and those who were not poor spent ₹884, so 0.2% of total expenditures for the poor and 5% for the non-poor. These NSS incidence data suggest that since 60% of the money on MGNREGA goes in wages, only some 14% of the money meant for the poor actually reaches the poor.

Shekhar Shah mentioned that in its latest form, MGNREGA also allows the creation of assets on private land under certain conditions, such as for Scheduled Castes (SCs)/Scheduled Tribes (STs). In some states this meant that entire villages were enrolled in MGNREGA and signed worker cards for MGNREGA work on each other's land, with the actual physical work of digging tube wells or building ponds all done by contractors who were in collusion with almost everyone in the village. In that situation, what could social audits do?

Anupam Khanna noted that experiences with social audits can vary tremendously. His work in Indonesia on village road projects suggested that social audits there worked better on detecting fraud on materials and construction and what was difficult was the labor part, for example, identifying ghost workers. The question that may need to be answered is whether social audits work only for very specific types of projects. On the dynamics of corruption, Khanna also noted that in his experience, and recent episodes in India also support that, it seemed to be the case that the culprits were learning faster than the victims.

Farzana Afridi agreed with Muralidharan's comment that social audits need to be complemented with top-down audits, particularly for auditing materials and assets created under MGNREGA. She mentioned that they were planning to collect further data on the type of assets being created under MGNREGA; so for example, one could ask whether roads or irrigation projects were bring created in AP's Telangana region, which has scarce rainfall and many droughts. Certainly in their field work, villagers often complained that officials preferred to build roads more than anything else, presumably because it was easier to pilfer from road projects. With such data, one of the things that they could look at would be the kind of assets that were being created and whether these were changing over time. It is harder to get information on the quality of the assets. Afridi agreed that collecting and analyzing the data over a longer period of time would shed more light on the impact of social audits on the scheme.

Afridi noted that she herself completely agreed that cash transfers would be more efficient than MGNERGA, with or without social audits. AP, however, has used social audits, and other states are following suit, so their paper is trying to look whether it can be effective or not. She recommended that everyone attend the IPF Policy Roundtable the next day since it would deal with cash transfers. She agreed with Shekhar Shah's point about private assets but noted that during the period they were looking at, from 2006 to 2010, MGNREGA only allowed public works, and the new rule on building private assets under some conditions came somewhat later.

Vegard Iversen pointed out that the remit of social audits in AP did not extend to material expenditures because these were audited in a more standard, top-down fashion, and this may not have been clear in their presentation. This is not to say that the top-down audits did not suffer from problems. If the participatory process had bite, then it should have had an impact on complaints, given other controls for labor-related irregularities. So, though there are signs that the participatory process is doing something, it is not doing enough for the reasons that they point out, namely that before 2010 the deterrent effects of the social audit process was simply not strong enough.

Iversen responded to the question on the dynamics of corruption and agreed that corruption is changing over time as their paper observes. On the observation that in Indonesia material related irregularities were easier to detect than those relating to labor, it was important to note that the AP social audits were built on the inspiration and learning from earlier audits in Rajasthan and in other parts of India, and these earlier audits had focused awareness and knowledge on detecting irregularities in labor records.

References

Ferraz, Claudio and Frederico S. Finan. 2008. "Exposing Corrupt Politicians: The Effects of Brazil's Publicly Released Audits on Electoral Outcomes," *Quarterly Journal of Economics*, 123 (2): 703–45.

The Hindu. 2013. "NREGA Needs Flexibility, Objectives Not Met in States: Ramesh," *The Hindu*, December 15. Available online at http://www.thehindu.com/news/national/nrega-needs-flexibility-objectives-not-met-in-states-ramesh/article5462983.ece.

